Italian Neorealism
and
GLOBAL CINEMA

Italian Neorealism
and
GLOBAL CINEMA

Edited by Laura E. Ruberto & Kristi M. Wilson

WAYNE STATE UNIVERSITY PRESS   DETROIT

Library of Congress Cataloging-in-Publication Data

Italian neorealism and global cinema /
edited by Laura E. Ruberto and Kristi M. Wilson.
p. cm. — (Contemporary approaches to film and television series)
Includes bibliographical references and index.
ISBN-13: 978-0-8143-3324-2 (pbk. : alk. paper)
ISBN-10: 0-8143-3324-9 (pbk. : alk. paper)
1. Motion pictures—Italy. 2. Realism in motion pictures.
3. Motion pictures, Italian—Foreign countries—Influence.
I. Ruberto, Laura E. II. Wilson, Kristi M.
PN1993.5.I88I76 2007
791.43'612—dc22
2006033483

∞ The paper used in this publication meets the minimum requirements
of the American National Standard for Information Sciences—
Permanence of Paper for Printed Library Materials, ANSI Z39.48-1984.

Designed and typeset by Maya Rhodes
Composed in Caslon Open Face, Triplex Cond, and Adobe Caslon Pro

For FÉLIX and DANTE

Contents

Acknowledgments

We would first like to thank our contributors, scholars who recognized the potential to place different film traditions in dialogue with one another and in relation to Italian neorealism. It has been a pleasure to work with academics working in different national traditions. We have benefited greatly from creating a global intellectual discussion on cinema.

We would like to extend our sincerest gratitude to everyone at Wayne State University Press for seeing this project through, particularly Jane Hoehner, our first editor at the press, and Annie Martin, with whom we completed the volume. Colleagues at various universities where we have worked were also extremely helpful to us along the way: Orrin Robinson, of Stanford University, offered advice about publishing an anthology and put us in contact with a contributor; Brenda Schildgen, of the University of California–Davis, recommended Wayne State University Press to us; and Dina Fachin, a doctoral candidate at the University of California–Davis, edited our filmography. We thank Mark A. Smith and Peter Freund of Berkeley City College for their technical expertise. We are also grateful to Stephanie Jed and Lisa Lowe, both of the University of California–San Diego.

We first developed the idea for this volume while working as graduate students in the Literature Department at the University of California–San Diego, where we had the opportunity to teach in the department's Film and Fiction Series. In particular, Pasquale Verdicchio's Children of Neorealism and Cynthia Walk's Images of Nazi Germany classes were inspirational. Similarly, classes we have each taught—in particular, Laura's course on neorealism and global cinema at San Francisco State University and Kristi's course on neorealism and Latin American cinema at the University of California–San Diego—further formed the volume's final shape.

We worked on this project over the course of a number of years and from sometimes distant locations—as editors we went from living a few miles apart to, at times, continents apart. Our work on this volume sometimes intersected with our individual academic projects, our teaching obligations, and our families. We thank Tomás F. Crowder-Taraborrelli and Matthew Mulligan Goldstein for their intellectual support, technical advice, and editorial work on the project. Moreover, we thank them for their style, unwavering encouragement, companionship, and consistent supply of strong coffee.

LAURA E. RUBERTO AND KRISTI M. WILSON

literary adaptations like Erich Von Stroheim's *Greed* (1924), and dramas based on real events like Sergei Eisenstein's *Battleship Potemkin* (1925). During and after World War I newsreels and documentaries brought to theaters worldwide unprecedented images of human devastation and carnage. Film had a way of making the global seem local, and the effect of movement and, later, sound created an immediacy that still photos and written narratives could not approach. Even in noncombatant countries like Argentina, moviegoers (many of whom had migrated from Spain and Italy) routinely watched newsreel footage before a feature Hollywood film to get information about the fate of their hometowns and relatives. Thus audiences' earliest experiences of viewing feature films were intricately linked to the documented reality of global social issues, just as the experiences of real-life tragedy and entertainment were interconnected. Even in countries that appeared to be on the margins of the European theater of war, spectators grew accustomed to viewing these two different types of filmmaking in one sitting. The experience of this juxtaposition created a fascination with the idea of a strong narrative meshed with an equally strong depiction of social strife. In the decades after World War II, Roberto Rossellini saw this process of fusing the global and local (or personal) as pushing the limits of documentary. In a 1959 *Cahiers du Cinéma* interview with Fereydoun Hoveyda and Jacques Rivette, Rossellini defended his return to neorealist technique as an improvement over his documentary approach in the film *India Seen by Rossellini* (1957–58).

> What mattered to me was the man. I have tried to express the soul, the light that is inside these men, their reality in its absolute intimacy and uniqueness, attached to an individual with all the meaning of the things that are around him. For the things that are around him have a meaning, since there is someone who looks at them, or at least this meaning becomes unique by virtue of someone looking at them: the hero of each episode who is also the narrator. If I had to make a strict documentary I would have had to forsake what went on inside, in the hearts of these men. And besides, to push documentary to its limits, I think it was also necessary to look at the hearts of these men. (in Hillier 182)

Of course, attempts to document contemporary social issues in a narrative fashion, as described above, were not initially limited to the art

2

Introduction

Laura E. Ruberto and Kristi M. Wilson

Neorealism in the Age of Globalization

Neorealism is generally associated with a set of films produced by the Italian film industry during the post–World War II years. Well before a language developed to give neorealism its theoretical identity, however, filmmakers all over the world had been preoccupied with an issue that would become a primary concern of neorealism—how to reflect social reality. In fact, since the birth of cinema, the question of how best to represent reality on celluloid was crucial to the sometimes divergent ways in which national film industries developed.[1] In the interwar years, the tumultuous period that saw the development of national film industries, global capitalism was being theorized in both political and cultural circles as a cause of social unrest and a call to disrupt class hierarchies. Producers and directors found themselves pulled between two central poles of interest: profit and social responsibility. Thus the issue of representing reality often became central to considerations about how to entertain, educate, and promote a sense of national identity. That said, this volume by definition foregrounds the multifaceted nature of the term "national cinema." We recognize, among other things, Andrew Higson's assertion that the concept of national cinema is almost rendered moot by potentially competing factors, such as formal qualities, economic conditions, political pressures, and cultural dynamics.

In the first decades of the twentieth century, moving pictures gave audiences vivid images of realities they had never experienced firsthand with such historical films as D. W. Griffith's *The Birth of a Nation* (1915),

1

of filmmaking. Neorealism, for one, grew out of Western literary styles, such as naturalism, realism, and, most importantly, Italian verismo, which strove to illustrate the stark realities of the peasant and working class with a detached, "scientific" mode of narration.

The essays collected herein consider the effects of Italian neorealist films on global cinema. More specifically, they elicit an understanding of the influence of Italian neorealism on directors and broadly defined national film traditions beyond 1945–52, the period conventionally associated with the neorealist "genre" in Italy.[2] That said, we concur with Michael Martin's assertion that "any discussion of national cinema must of necessity consider the ambiguous categories of 'culture' and 'identity,' and the socio-historical factors that determine a national cinema's development" (22). On the one hand national cinema can be seen as an insidious and isolationist concept, one that collapses many forms of identity into a hegemonic vision of culture. As Higson points out, it has "almost invariably been mobilized as a strategy of cultural (and economic) resistance; a means of asserting national autonomy in the face of (usually) Hollywood's international domination" (37). This collection underscores the possibility of a cinema of resistance in many different national contexts.

Each essay in the collection—ranging from Millicent Marcus's piece on contemporary Italian films about anti-Mafia crusaders and the memorialist legacy of neorealism to Natalia Sui-hung Chan's essay on neorealism and Hong Kong cinema—examines the ways in which the characteristics of Italian neorealism interact with and inform other national-cultural identities and the film traditions attributed to them. Neorealism proves to be a loosely and, as we shall see, somewhat controversially defined set of didactic political films that address social issues. Further, the neorealist format tends to provide ideological and aesthetic alternatives to mainstream Hollywood film narratives.

Upon first seeing Rossellini's *Rome, Open City* (1945) and Vittorio De Sica's *Bicycle Thief* (1948), many aspiring and established directors from countries all over the world were immediately fascinated by a refreshing postwar aesthetic that successfully brought engaging narrative technique to bear upon social issues. These films seemed to show filmmakers how a national identity could be shaped and/or redefined by cinema (an idea akin to what Antonio Gramsci called a national popular culture, which we take up in the latter half of this introduction). Considered at the time a response to twenty years of Fascist rule and a call to action for national Italian postwar reconstruction, these films suggested uncharted possibilities for cinema. For filmmakers wary of the power and influence of material coming out of Hollywood, the first neorealist films also pointed toward other cinematic styles and themes, aesthetic alternatives to an ever-growing supply of American imports.[3] Satyajit Ray, for one, describes his first encounter with Italian neorealism as a life-changing experience.

> I was to work for six months in London in my agency's head of-
> fice. Doubtless the management hoped that I would come back
> a full-fledged advertising man wholly dedicated to the purpose
> of selling tea and biscuits. What the trip did in fact was to set
> the seal of mortal doom on my advertising career. Within three
> days of arriving in London I saw *Bicycle Thieves* [*sic*]. I knew
> immediately that if I ever made *Pather Panchali*—and the idea
> had been at the back of my mind for some time—I would make
> it in the same way, using natural locations and unknown actors.
> All through my stay in London, the lessons of *Bicycle Thieves*
> [*sic*] and neorealist cinema stayed with me. On the way back I
> drafted out my first treatment of *Pather Panchali*. (9–10)

As Moinak Biswas suggests in his essay in this volume, with respect to Indian filmmakers, the crucial encounter between postcolonial societies, hegemony, and neorealism (which can be dated to a 1952 film festival in Bombay) has yet to be properly theorized.[4] Biswas's example of an Indian national film tradition that is immediately connected to Italian neorealism is not meant to suggest that directors outside Italy simply imported neorealist techniques into their own sociohistorical contexts. Indeed, neorealism—in combination with local cinematic, political, and intellectual traditions—produced and continues to produce innovative styles of filmmaking that at times appear irreconcilable with Italian neorealism. For example, as Tomás F. Crowder-Taraborrelli argues, Gabriel García Márquez's studies with Cesare Zavattini at the Centro Sperimentale di Cinematografia (CSC) in Rome produced an entirely new strain of literary and filmic technique in Latin America.

Some contemporary film scholars acknowledge Italian neorealism's influence on Latin American Third Cinema but argue that neorealism did not go far enough in using film as a tool for social commentary. John Hess, for one, suggests that for Latin American filmmakers of the 1950s, Italian neorealism was not active enough in its social critique to satisfy many Latin American directors' efforts to reject the Hollywood

Bicycle Thief
(Vittorio De Sica,
1948)

entertainment monopoly, apply their techniques to the revolutionary movements of the 1960s, and challenge issues of national underdevelopment. As García Márquez's use of the genre of Italian neorealism in his short story "La Santa" suggests, even within a film style that emphasizes histories from below, a Europe/Latin America hierarchy exists, against which Latin American artists will always have to struggle for self-representation. As a counterpoint to critiques like Hess's, Kristi M. Wilson's and Antonio Traverso's essays in the present collection demonstrate in different ways the ongoing relevance of neorealism's collaborative, low-budget technique and Zavattinian theory for late twentieth-century Latin American cinema.

A Contested Identity

At a spring 2000 showing of Fritz Lang's *Fury* (1936) at the San Diego Museum of Photographic Arts, film curator Scott Marks, while introducing the movie in connection with several different film genres, insisted that Italian neorealism was a *style*, not a *genre*. While this collection of essays does not set out to prove beyond the shadow of a doubt that neorealism is either at the exclusion of the other, the question of neorealism's contested identity seems related, in perhaps contradictory ways, to its tendency to be claimed and recontextualized by different national film movements in various time periods.

Perhaps neorealism can be least controversially defined as a select group of Italian films made between 1945 and 1952 that, though never forming a self-conscious movement (like the French nouvelle vague), shared some loosely accepted conventions. With the release of De Sica's *Umberto D* in 1952 and the infamous letter against the film written by Undersecretary of Public Entertainment Giulio Andreotti, neorealism continued in Italy, albeit much more quietly and sporadically.[5]

For years film scholars discussed neorealism as a new form of realism, something utterly different from anything produced during or before Fascism. Such a position ushered in a celebration of the potential of the Resistance to shed any and all memories of the Ventennio, the two decades of Fascist rule. Simultaneously, scholars and critics often saw Italian directors at the end of World War II—at times by choice and at times by necessity—as working against a dominant Hollywood studio film paradigm that had reached the continent well before the war, and had, in particular, already penetrated the Italian movie houses. Eventually, however, neorealist directors were criticized on their own soil: either for selling out to American-style cinema (see films such as Giuseppe De Santis's *Bitter Rice* [1949] and De Sica's *Miracle in Milan* [1951]) or for not taking the social issues they seem to be examining seriously enough, laying out the problems but offering little in the way of answers (see films such as De Sica's *Bicycle Thief* and *Umberto D*).[6]

Today film historians recognize that earlier appraisals of neorealism as a post-Fascist, isolated movement failed to take into consideration, among other things, the history of cinematic inventions and novelties, what Mikhail Bakhtin might call the heteroglossia inherent in the medium of film production. For example, Giuliana Bruno argues in *Streetwalking on a Ruined Map* that the films of Elvira Notari and other Neapolitan silent-era filmmakers were precursors to neorealism, and that this relationship has been "forgotten or minimized" by movements that read neorealism as an almost natural outcome of Fascism (30). Indeed, today it is no longer shocking to say that the "neo" in neorealism was not actually anything new, but rather marked a continuation and an evolution of the Italian motion picture industry. As the writer and filmmaker Pier Paolo Pasolini once explained, "It is useless to delude oneself about it: neorealism was not a regeneration; it was only a vital crisis, however excessively optimistic and enthusiastic at the beginning" (in Sitney 1).[7]

Neorealism, from the time of its unofficial inception in Italy with Rossellini's *Rome, Open City*, seems to have come with a built-in mandate concerning flexibility that resembles, in Nietzschean terms, an "art of dissimulation"—there may be rules, but they will be broken. Today, films considered neorealist break these unwritten rules in one way or another, yet, for reasons that remain obscure, still present themselves as neorealist. In *Italian Film in the Light of Neorealism*, Millicent Marcus summarizes some of these unwritten "rules governing neorealism," filmmaking imperatives that include "location shooting, lengthy takes, unobtrusive editing, natural lighting, a predominance of medium and long shots, respect for the continuity of time and space, use of contemporary, true-to-life subjects, an uncontrived, open-ended plot, working-class protagonists, a nonprofessional cast, dialogue in the vernacular, active viewer involvement, and implied social criticism" (22). The purpose of these "rules" is, as Zavattini, the widely proclaimed theorist of neorealism, describes, to oblige the viewer to reflect on reality. In "A Thesis on Neorealism," Zavattini clarifies his position.

(margin annotation: defining characteristics of neorealism)

> [W]e are now aware that reality is extremely rich. We simply had to learn how to look at it. The task of the artist—the neorealist artist at least—does not consist in bringing the audience to tears and indignation by means of transference, but, on the contrary, it consists in bringing them to reflect (and then, if you will, to stir up emotions and indignation) upon what they are doing and upon what others are doing; that is, to think about reality precisely as it is. (in Overbey 67–68)

Although neorealism is often defined in terms of technical characteristics, most neorealist films do not make consistent use of the same prescribed techniques. As Zavattini suggests, what leads critics to group stylistically different films under the rubric of neorealism has to do with their insistence on a similar mood, a similar desire to "stir up emotions and indignation." Thus Marcus concludes, "Indeed, for many critics, neorealism is first and foremost a moral statement, 'una nuova poesia morale' [new moral poetry] whose purpose was to promote a true objectivity—one that would force viewers to abandon the limitations of a strictly personal perspective and to embrace the reality of the 'others,' be they persons or things, with all the ethical responsibility that such a vision entails" (23). Her description resonates with Rossellini's own understanding of neorealism, laid out in *Cahiers du Cinéma*: "Per me il neorealismo è sopratutto una posizione morale. Divine poi posizione estetica, ma in partenza è morale. . . . L'importante non sono le immagini, ma le idée" (For me, neorealism is above all a moral position. It

then became an aesthetic position, but at the beginning it was moral.
. . . Ideas, not images, are important) (in Verdone 43). Preston Sturges's
1941 comedy *Sullivan's Travels* presents an anecdote about the prospect
of the type of visionary filmmaking in Hollywood outlined above. In the
opening scene, a young, idealistic filmmaker, Sullivan, debates the merits
of making a movie about social issues with Hollywood studio heads.
After viewing the finale of Sullivan's new film, in which two men representing "capital" and "labor" battle and eventually destroy each other
from atop a moving train, the following debate ensues:

> Sullivan: You see? You see the symbolism of it? Capital and la-
> bor destroy each other. It teaches a lesson, a moral lesson. It has
> social significance. . . . I want this picture to be a commentary on
> modern conditions, stark realism, the problems that confront
> the average man.
>
> Studio executive: Who wants to see that kind of stuff? It gives
> me the creeps. . . . How about a nice musical? (*Sullivan's Travels,*
> Paramount Studios)

After spending some time with the less fortunate, Sullivan changes his
mind and adopts the studio executive's point of view that Hollywood-
style comedy, by diverting the attention of the poor away from their
troubled existence, can function as a profitable, if temporary, cure-all
for the spirits of the economically depressed masses. One of the goals
of this collection is to show the diverse ways in which neorealism has
helped film directors escape the aesthetic and political limitations of
Sullivan's Hollywood dilemma. The fact remains that few directors from
the United States seem to have been able to escape such a dilemma.
Herbert Biberman (*Salt of the Earth,* 1954) and David Riker (*La ciudad,*
1998) are exceptions, as are certain black independent filmmakers of the
1970s and 1980s.[8] In 1962, Satyajit Ray commented on what he saw
as the artistically bankrupt nature of the Hollywood studio system in a
book titled *Our Films, Their Films.*

> Once in a long while we've had a *Grapes of Wrath,* a *Marty,* an
> *Ace in the Hole,* a *Sierra Madre,* a *Little Foxes,* and we've been
> grateful for them. Even today, the average standard of Ameri-
> can films—for reasons of sheer technical polish—is probably
> higher than anywhere else in the world. But the great film, the
> truly personal film, the film that is shaped and coloured by one

8

man's vision and feeling and sympathies, is rare, if not altogether extinct. And there is little hope of an immediate revolution. Twenty years ago, in Hollywood, a young man named Orson Welles had a couple of bold flings at unconventional film making. . . . Yet Welles failed to survive as an artist. *Citizen Kane* and *The Magnificent Ambersons* had both had an oblique influence on future film makers, but Welles himself had to go into exile in Europe. (140)

In the end, neorealism's importance in film history and influence on directors around the world—in effect, neorealism's staying power—is much more relevant than the question of whether neorealism was originally a style or a genre.

Since neorealism was never an organized school, this "new moral poetry" might best be understood by looking at some of the films widely recognized as neorealist. Rossellini's 1945 *Rome, Open City*, which chronicles the underground Resistance movement in Rome, is generally considered the first such film and, as such, has often been used as a reference point in defining the genre. When we look at films by the three directors most often associated with neorealism—Rossellini, De Sica, and Luchino Visconti (filmmakers whom Peter Bondanella calls the "masters of neorealism" or "auteurs")—we can find evidence of neorealism's flexibility—that is, that no one film follows all of the rules.[9] For example, Rossellini used professional actors in *Rome, Open City*—Anna Magnani and Aldo Fabrizi—and the film was heavily scripted, with little improvisation. On the other hand, this film initiated what, through the relationship between the partisan Francesco and his quasi-stepson, would become a rarely talked about connection in neorealist films: the narration of the problems facing Italy's poor through the symbolic relationship of two men.[10] In fact, Laura E. Ruberto's essay in this collection demonstrates this tendency to depict male-male bonds and suggests ways in which contemporary European films reconfigure the relationship across gender and cultural lines. Moreover, much of what later became known as characteristic of neorealist films—natural lighting, for instance—occurred in *Rome, Open City* by default because the film was made with little money and few supplies since Rome had only recently been liberated. In De Sica's *Ladri di biciclette* (*Bicycle Thief*), we find that although the film almost religiously follows the "continuity of time and space" rule, uses some nonprofessional actors and colloquial speech, and reflects particular historical conditions, it also relies on an intricate and contrived plot, was made with a huge, Hollywood-style budget, and avails itself of all manner of movie-making artifice.[11] One noteworthy exception to this list is Visconti's 1948 *La terra trema* (*The Earth Trembles*), a film that "fits many of the traditional definitions of Italian neorealism better than any other work of the period" (Bondanella, *Italian Cinema* 68). Visconti shot on location, used real fishermen, did away with his script of Giovanni Verga's *I Malavoglia* in order to let the fishermen improvise, and, most radical for the time, kept the villagers' real, undubbed voices in the final cut. Opting against the more common practice of post-synchronization, which often lent a flawless quality to a film (the director could have an Italian actor play a German character and dub in the German later), Visconti made use of the fishermen's Sicilian dialect, a language most film audiences did not understand, so that a voice-over and a written prologue in standard Italian were later added.

When all is said and done, it is each film's capacity to "stir up emotions or indignation" that perhaps best points to why these films (and not others that may share stylistic similarities) have continued to jostle and shift the boundaries of what can be expressed on film. Ultimately, the essays in this collection suggest that neorealism may be a genre or style that is in part defined by its influence, by its ability to inspire politicized, ideological, and aesthetic alternatives to Hollywood narrative tendencies, while simultaneously accomplishing the task of entertaining.

Mussolini and Italian Film

> Fascist Italy spreads in an increasingly faster world the light of Roman civilization.
> Inscription on publicity poster used for the inauguration of Cinecittà,
> 1937 (in Hay 201)

One of the more uncomfortable facts that critics and historians of neorealism have had to contend with is Italian cinema's deep roots in Fascism. The pages of *Cinema*, a pre–World War II Italian film industry journal, support the controversial claim that neorealism was not an altogether new movement in cinema, but rather a continuation of prewar ideas. Marcia Landy argues that "in their zeal to regenerate Italian cultural practices, the neorealists created their own myths. The most blatant myth was the myth of 'newness,' of 'beginning.' Although the neorealists sought to examine the nature of Fascism, they obscured their own beginnings in the Fascist era" (*Italian Film* 4).[12] Many young Italian men (and a few women) involved in the burgeoning Italian film scene wrote for *Cinema,* and under the editorial guidance of Vittorio Mussolini, the duce's son, it became a critical stopping point for the cognoscenti of the Italian film industry.[13] De Santis, a filmmaker whose own position within neorealism has always been debated, began writing for *Cinema* in the 1930s, becoming one of a group of *Cinema* critics who encouraged more realism in film. These men formed a group, unofficially known as the Verga Group, named after the nineteenth-century Italian realist writer. They promoted a return to the kind of realism and narrative truth-seeking that could be found in the work of the nineteenth-century *veristi.*

In his work for *Cinema,* De Santis called for a revitalization in Italian film. As Antonio Vitti explains, "De Santis's criticisms always attempt to stimulate the search for a cinema more representative of social and cultural realities" (*Giuseppe De Santis* 13). He hoped to produce what Antonio Gramsci calls a "national popular culture" through the artistic medium of film. Although little is known of De Santis's awareness of Gramsci during Fascism, De Santis's membership in the Italian Communist Party (PCI), his self-identification as a Marxist, and his work with the Resistance can easily lead us to connect the two thinkers.[14] Gramsci, Italy's leading Communist intellectual, promoted the production of culture that came from the experiences of the working and rural classes; such "national popular culture" would stand against so-called high culture. He recognized the absence of a national popular culture in Italy: "E perché non esiste in Italia una letteratura 'nazionale'?" (Why is there no "national" literature in Italy?) he asks (*Letteratura* 123; *Selected* 366). This lack of national popular culture was caused and perpetuated, Gramsci suggests, by the lack of organic intellectuals who could produce such culture. Instead, traditional intellectuals dominated Italian culture by either ignoring the life of the populace or patronizing them. Gramsci explains the distance between intellectuals and the people in his notebooks.

> Perché manca una identità di concezione del mondo tra "scrittori" e "popolo," cioè i sentimenti popolari non sono vissuti come propri dagli scrittori . . . cioè [gli scrittori] non si sono posti e non si pongono il problema di elaborare i sentimenti popolari dopo averli rivissuti e fatti propri. (*Letteratura* 122)

"Writers" and "people" do not have the same conception of the world. In other words the feelings of the people are not lived by the writers as their own . . . they [the writers] have not and do not set themselves the problem of elaborating popular feelings after having relived them and made them their own. (*Selected* 365)

As Vitti suggests, De Santis, a native of Ciociaria, acted as an organic intellectual and undertook to develop forms of national popular culture in all of his work (*Giuseppe De Santis* 86, 109).

Jumping ahead to the 1960s, we can see a similar rhetoric around notions of cinema, indigenous culture, and entertainment in the form of the Third Cinema movement. In 1969 the Argentine filmmakers and theorists Fernando Solanas and Octavio Getino wrote a manifesto for filmmaking outside the first-world studio system titled "Tercer Cine" ("Towards a Third Cinema"). They proposed a "cinema of subversion": "Every image that documents, bears witness to, refutes, or deepens the truth of a situation is something more than a film image or purely artistic fact; it becomes something which the system finds indigestible" (in Armes, *Third World Filmmaking* 100). Through a new way of making and viewing cinema, they hoped to produce a "decolonization of cinema," a removal of the outside influences on indigenous cultures of the world dominated by Western imperialism and colonialism. Their Third Cinema would not only document events but "attempt to intervene in the situation as an element providing thrust or rectification" (in Armes, *Third World Filmmaking* 100). They challenged Hollywood productions, dubbed "first cinema," as well as the alternatives to Hollywood, such as nouvelle vague, which they called "second cinema." Instead, Solanas and Getino, echoing some of the Verga Group's ideas, saw the thrust of this cinematic revolution in the documentary genre, which could lead to the "construction of a throbbing, living reality which captures truth in any of its expressions" (in Armes, *Third World Filmmaking* 99). In effect, Solanas and Getino were calling for a Gramscian-style national popular culture of cinema. It seems, in fact, that in many nations (Italy included) neorealist-like film traditions developed during periods of flux, or what we might call national identity crises. Neorealism—undogmatic and malleable—offered a pattern for constructing a unique culture of a nation. A similar pattern was put to work, as our contributors argue, in such diverse places and spaces as postindependence India, cold war Czechoslovakia, and 1950s English immigrant filmmaking communities.[15]

In the postwar Italian context, the practical way to achieve such a national popular cultural production was to combine various cinematic techniques (this is where De Santis's ideas diverge from those of Solanas and Getino, as well as from those of some of his contemporary Italian filmmakers). He supported and encouraged a kind of film that was part documentary, illustrating the everyday realities on the Italian landscape, and part drama. He believed that film could not be revolutionary if no one wanted to watch it. From Hollywood he learned the power of drama and thought it could ultimately be used to achieve socialist goals. De Santis explains at least one way filmmakers, by studying Hollywood films, could learn to speak to and for the Italian people: in a discussion of "popular fiction and folk heroes in the Western genre," he says that "by drawing on the popular narrative mode and on indigenous tales [cinema] could . . . speak the language of the masses and stir their sentiments" (in Vitti, *Giuseppe De Santis* 38). Such an understanding of drama is in line with Gramsci's view that melodrama has roots in folklore.[16] Lastly, De Santis (taking cues from Sergei Eisenstein) believed that filmmaking was an art form and that attention to the technical aspects of cinema and lessons in editing were important parts of proper drama and documentary. Only by combining all of these characteristics could a national popular cinema be produced.

One of De Santis's most influential pieces was cowritten with Mario Alicata and published in *Cinema* in 1941, "Verità e poesia." Alicata and De Santis further the notion of a national popular culture, and they set the stage for postwar cinema, namely, neorealism. They proclaim the value of realistic cinema and understand realism as "the true and eternal measure of every narrative significance—realism intended not as the passive homage to an objective, static truth, but as the imaginative and creative power to fashion a story composed of real characters and events" (in Overbey 131). They trace this style of cinematic realism back to nineteenth-century European literary realists like Flaubert, Chekhov, Maupassant, and Verga, and comment on how German, French, and U.S. directors have made use of these writers. What they are most interested in, however, is critiquing contemporary Italian film, which they find either "trapped amongst the rhetoric of D'Annunzio" or full of "sentimental comedies" (in Overbey 134). They are, in fact, searching for a national popular culture. They find the key to such cultural productions in Verga's version of Italian verismo. Verga's writing

> could give inspiration to the imagination of our cinema which looks at things in the space-time of reality to redeem itself from the easy suggestions of a moribund bourgeois state. For those

who ask for artificiality, rhetoric, and badly-coined medals and awards, for those who seek to follow the examples of other cinematic productions whose technical perfection provides no salvation from their miserable humanity and poverty for reason, Giovanni Verga's works will perhaps mean nothing, for his works indicate the only historically valid direction: a revolutionary art inspired by, and acting, in turn, as inspiration to a humanity which hopes and suffers. (in Overbey 135)

The kind of cinema that Alicata, De Santis, and others promoted in their writing in the 1930s, though visible in the Italian cinema of the period (and earlier), would not fully develop into neorealism until the postwar reconstruction period.

Yet the Verga Group was not the only place in Italy where cinematic realism was being exalted. In fact, Mussolini had his own brand of realism in mind, one he hoped could be used to strengthen Italy's Fascist identity.[17] Mussolini rose to power in 1922, and three years later funded the production institute LUCE (L'Unione Cinematografica Educativa [Union for Cinematic Education]). It was not until the 1930s, however, that he fully realized the power of media: he started a film school, the Centro Sperimentale di Cinematografia (CSC), the Center of Experimental Cinematography, in 1935, and Italy's answer to Hollywood, Cinecittà (literally, "the city of cinema"), in 1937. Many directors, scriptwriters, and producers who would one day be connected to neorealism began under Mussolini's rule at the above-mentioned institutions. Rossellini is perhaps the most famous of these men. His war trilogy (1941–43) and many other films made at Cinecittà were funded by the Fascist government, and many were propaganda pieces (see Bondanella, *Italian Cinema* 1–31). Rossellini's early work, as well as his post-neorealist films, combined the use of sets with on-location shooting, often used "real" footage (of, for instance, naval ships), and focused on the telling of a plausible narrative. Critics like Bondanella even use the term "documentary" to describe Rossellini's wartime productions. In any case, Mussolini, perhaps following Hitler's success with Riefensthal-style propaganda films, called for documentary-style realism in film. He seemed especially pleased with films that showed the strength and virility of his regime, though not all Fascist-funded cinema fit this ideal. Historical films under Mussolini that recalled the power of the Roman Empire and pseudo-documentaries that demonstrated the force of his army were caught up in the formation of what Barbara Spackman calls the Fascist "rhetoric of virility." Paradoxically, many of Mussolini's filmmakers later became part of the Resistance movement, and many were also part of the Verga Group.[18]

Before Mussolini, the Italian film industry had an initially strong start (with such silent wonders as *Cabiria* [1914] and *The Last Days of Pompeii* [1913]) but suffered under the weight of French and U.S. imports. In his efforts to recapture and modernize the iconography of the Roman Empire to his political advantage (linking the idea of Rome's future under Fascism to its "purer," ancient Roman predecessor), Mussolini turned to cinema, recognizing its powerful potential as a tool that could convey political and ideological content to the masses.

About This Anthology

While we initially attempted to organize the essays into distinct categories (geographical region, subgenre, and so forth), our efforts were undermined by the way in which the essays themselves seemed to resist such organization. For example, several of our essays address the theme of the child as adapted from Italian neorealism; however, they do so from drastically different locations and time periods. Likewise, several of the essays address the development of a politicized national film tradition that counters a monolithic Western aesthetic. However, this shared concern traverses such a wide range of locations and historical periods that rendering such a connection is tenuous at best. Thus, we concluded that a rough chronological approach to presenting the essays would best showcase neorealism's intricate web of influence.

Our first essay, "On the Ruins of Masculinity: The Figure of the Child in Italian Neorealism and the German Rubble-Film," by Jaimey Fisher, looks critically at the way in which scholars since the 1940s have compared German rubble-films (films shot between 1945 and 1951, often in scenes of postwar devastation) to Italian neorealist films. Fisher's analysis moves beyond an understanding of rubble-films as falling short of the overt political content of neorealist films to a more nuanced comparative exploration of the tendency of both neorealist and rubble-films to work against the conventional portrayal of heroic masculinity in mainstream feature films. Fisher looks in particular at such Italian films as *Rome, Open City, Bicycle Thief,* and *Paisan* (1946), and such German films as *Somewhere in Berlin* (Gerhard Lamprecht, 1946), *And Someday We Will See Each Other Again* (Hans Müller, 1947), and *In Front of Us, There Is Life* (Gerhard Rittau, 1948). His work attempts to open both styles of filmmaking up to a different type of gendered politics by examining the role of the male child as a solution of sorts to problems posed by the postwar defeat of the heroic male protagonist.

Lubica Učník's essay, "Aesthetics or Ethics? Italian Neorealism and the Czechoslovak New Wave Cinema," bypasses a discussion of neorealist aesthetic properties, or the techniques said to define the genre, in favor of a definition of neorealism as a method of ethical-political engagement with the everyday. Accordingly, Učník explores a series of parallel trends between Italian neorealist and Czechoslovakian filmmakers and offers a rare glimpse—in the English-speaking world, at least—of the rich history of Czech filmmaking, emphasizing the first evidence of a style akin to Italian neorealism (Otakar Vávra's 1943 film *Farewell*), Soviet-inspired socialist realism, and the entrance of Italian neorealism and French New Wave film into the Czech Film Academy of Music and Arts curriculum. She ends with a discussion of the ongoing relevance of Italian neorealism to contemporary Czech cinema.

Likewise Moinak Biswas's "In the Mirror of an Alternative Globalism: The Neorealist Encounter in India" explores India's first experience with Italian neorealism (the 1952 International Film Festival). Biswas analyzes a tendency in film criticism to associate a radical break with tradition in Indian film with the advent of this festival and the subsequent first Satyajit Ray film, *Pather Panchali* (1955). Many film critics argue that as a result of the neorealist films shown at the 1952 festival, modern, realist film techniques were ushered into India, thus freeing Indian cinema from a more traditional style of filmmaking that stressed such things as nonsecular narrative structure and spectacle over narrative. Biswas adds his voice to those of a number of cultural critics who argue that the binary opposition between tradition and modernity is a product of contemporary criticism and suggests that Indian film history be reread against the discourse of the influence of Italian neorealism as a harbinger of modernity. More specifically, he suggests that *Pather Panchali*, through its realist style of narration, did not usher in the modern age of Indian cinema. Rather, Ray's film refined an already existent (if "incompletely operative") realist textual principle in Indian cinema. Biswas's essay demonstrates the ways in which the impulse to understand Ray's realism as the genesis of modern Indian film is ideologically implicated in a modern nationalist project.

David Anshen's "*Alphaville:* A Neorealist, Science Fiction Fable about Hollywood" explores connections between neorealist film techniques and Jean-Luc Godard's 1965 sci-fi thriller in which an unreal, fictional world becomes the real world of postmodern, late capitalism. Anshen demonstrates that neorealist form and content can be found in the campy, comic-book world of Godard's technological dystopia. He suggests that Godard remained bound by the ideals of his mentor, André Bazin, who championed neorealism for its commitment to real physical space. In *Alphaville,* however, integrity of space creates distorting results that turn familiar locations (for example, a hotel room) into surreal settings. Anshen suggests that the film is an engagement with and comment on the connection between realism and fiction, and as such, shares many of Italian neorealism's central features. *Alphaville* is primarily concerned with representing the historical reality of late capitalism. As the film unfolds, the dialectic between the familiar and the strange becomes a critique of contemporary life. Anshen's essay complicates the familiar notion of a clear-cut boundary between French New Wave cinema and Italian neorealism.

During the 1950s and 1960s various films made in Italy, England, and the United States were strikingly similar in their insistence on a documentary style reminiscent of neorealism. While working on this collection, we were approached by the Italian film scholar Paolo Speranza, who introduced us to a wealth of material from postwar Italy. A particular issue of *Cinemasud: A Journal of Cinematic Culture* caught our eye. We reprint in our collection an essay by Antonio Napolitano from the 1966 edition of *Cinemasud* titled "Neorealism in Anglo-Saxon Cinema." Napolitano argues, perhaps contrary to popular assessment, for neorealist trends in select Hollywood and British films from the Rank Corporation. In particular, he observes similarities between the English Free Cinema movement and certain independent trends in the 1950s in the United States. This essay gives us a fascinating glimpse at lesser-known Hollywood and British films, and at the same time offers evidence for earlier attempts than ours within Italy to explore connections between global cinema and Italian neorealism.

Tomás F. Crowder-Taraborrelli's "A Stonecutter's Passion: Latin American Reality and Cinematic Faith" looks at the philosophical problems of defining "reality" in non-European cinematic contexts, the issue of Latin American self-representation in film and literature, and Colombian author Gabriel García Márquez's relationship to Italian neorealism. Crowder-Taraborrelli examines García Márquez's underexplored history as an aspiring filmmaker who traveled to Rome to study scriptwriting with Zavattini. He argues that cinematic discourse, especially the heated debates about how to represent reality, commonly associated with Italian neorealism, greatly influenced García Márquez's narrative style. Focusing on his film *Miracle in Rome* (1988) and a subsequent short story revision of the film, "The Saint," Crowder-Taraborrelli discusses García Márquez's style, often know as "magical realism," as a Latin American form of narrative self-representation that is simultaneously indebted to and critical of Zavattini and De Sica's brand of neorealism.

Kristi M. Wilson's "From Pensioner to Teenager: Everyday Violence in De Sica's *Umberto D* and Gaviria's *Rodrigo D: No Future*" responds to critics like John Hess who have questioned the continued relevance of Italian neorealism to Latin American film. While acknowledging the influence of Italian neorealism on Latin American directors who studied at the CSC in Rome, Hess claims that neorealism did not go far enough politically in its attempts to change society and suggests that neorealist filmmakers lacked the type of revolutionary vision that might have prompted them to interrogate their country's Fascist past. Wilson argues that De Sica (in collaboration with scriptwriter Zavattini) did not avoid the issue of what he regarded as ongoing Fascism but took what he saw as the residue of Mussolini's legacy in postwar Italy as one of the central themes of his work. In *Umberto D* (1952), for example, Umberto and his dog, Flick, fall victim to a type of brutal everyday Fascism that has settled into Italy's bureaucratic institutions. Wilson compares *Umberto D* to *Rodrigo D: No Future* (1990), Colombian poet and filmmaker Victor Gaviria's 1989 film about a group of teenagers in Medellin. She argues that the latter, a radically experimental film, is more than just an homage in title to *Umberto D; Rodrigo D* is traditionally neorealist in form, fusing fiction and social reality, and is best understood in dialogue with De Sica and Zavattini's film.

Italian neorealism has likewise been associated with Brazilian cinema in the broad context of the 1960s Third Cinema (Tercer Cine) movement in Latin America. Antonio Traverso's "Migrations of Cinema: Italian Neorealism and Brazilian Cinema" reflects on the legacy of Glauber Rocha, the father of the Cinema Nõvo movement, whose films include *Black God, White Devil* (1964), *Anguished Land* (1967), and *O dragão da malade contra o santo guerreiro* (1969). Traverso considers the influence of Rocha, Cinema Nõvo, and Italian neorealism on three relatively recent political films that greatly affected Brazilian and international audiences: *Pixote: A lei do mais fraco* (Hector Babenco, 1981), *Central Station* (Walter Salles, 1998), and *City of God* (Fernando Meirelles and Kátia Lund, 2002).

The next essay in the collection likewise stretches in time from World War II to more recent times, but links Italian neorealism with filmmaking in Latin America through a triangular relationship with African cinema. Rachel Gabara's "'A Poetics of Refusals': Neorealism from Italy to Africa" interrogates the scholarly tendency to write about African cinema as an art form that exists in a continual state of isolation from European cinematic traditions (both colonial and neocolonial), perpetually reacting against or rejecting the conventions therein. By contrast, Gabara reads the work of the Senegalese filmmaker Ousmane Sembène and the work of earlier African directors through the lens of Italian neorealism as it made its way to Africa via the New Latin American Cinema movement (in the work of such directors as Fernando Birri, Nelson Pereira dos Santos, Tomás Gutiérrez Alea, and Julio García Espinosa, among others). Gabara argues that the Italian neorealist, the New Latin American Cinema, and the sub-Saharan African cinema movements share radically new techniques of filmmaking that reject the trends set by the American films that flooded their markets. Gabara suggests that although they were united by a type of realism that rejected Hollywood style, each movement used realist techniques to serve different ends.

More emphatically echoing a contemporary cinematic moment, Natalia Sui-hung Chan's essay, "Cinematic Neorealism: Hong Kong Cinema and Fruit Chan's *1997 Trilogy*," examines the impact of Italian neorealism on Hong Kong cinema through the theoretical work of the film theorist Lam Lin-tong, who argues that neorealism's appeal for third-world filmmakers (often themselves enmeshed in decolonization and independence movements) lay in its qualities of political resistance. More specifically, Chan explores the connections between neorealist technique, the films of the independent filmmaker Fruit Chan (*Hong Kong 1997 Trilogy*), and the social crisis that followed the country's 1997 "Hand-over" to China. Her essay does not simply suggest that Chan borrowed from Italian neorealist filmmakers; rather, she argues for a complex transmission of neorealist style through Hong Kong New Wave cinema of the 1970s, in particular the work of Western-trained filmmakers such as Tsui Hark, Ann Hui, Allen Fong, and Patrick Tam.

Thomas Stubblefield's "Re-creating the Witness: *Elephant*, Postmodernism, and the Neorealist Inheritance" explores U.S. independent cinema through Gilles Deleuze's theory that Italian neorealism marked the advent of what he calls the "pure optical image" in cinema. Accordingly, the action presented in neorealist films is more observed by than participated in by on-screen performers. While coming to full fruition in films such as *L'Avventura* (1960) and *Rear Window* (1954), the inchoate stage of such a relationship is found in Rossellini's *Rome, Open City*, in particular in the film's recurring narrative device of the witness.

19

Stubblefield argues that in Gus Van Sant's recent film *Elephant* (2003), we see a similar form of spectatorship structuring the dominant narrative. He suggests that such an appropriation serves as a postmodern pastiche of the neorealist enterprise. Accordingly, *Elephant* enters into dialogue with its predecessor neorealist films and is implicitly set against its sister mediums of television, the Internet, and even video games, all of which loom large in the film characters' lives. While the film's central theme is the Columbine school shootings, ultimately, its revamping of the "pure optical image" fails to uncover discernable cause or culpability in the event, giving rise to larger questions regarding the plausibility of postmodernist aesthetics in the representation of the tragedies of its age.

Looking at European "immigration films" from the 1990s, Laura E. Ruberto argues in "Neorealism and Contemporary European Immigration" that these films are sympathetic to the immigrants' plight at a time when Europe is undergoing major political and cultural changes. Moreover, many of the films use a neorealist approach to communicating ideas about the status of the immigrant in late twentieth-century European culture. Her essay focuses on two films: Gianni Amelio's *Lamerica* (1994), an Italian/Albanian production, and the Belgian *La promesse* (1996), directed by Luc and Jean-Pierre Dardenne. In Amelio's work, neorealism's influence is direct and explicit, whereas in the Dardenne brothers' film, the link is more ambiguous. In both cases, Ruberto argues, a neorealist sensibility, retooled for the late twentieth century, creates films that encourage audiences to evaluate more seriously the cultural effects of globalization.

In "'O Cuorp' 'e Napule: Naples and the Cinematographic Body of Culture," Pasquale Verdicchio looks at the city of Naples as it has been represented by many well-known filmmakers over the years. He argues that, traditionally, Naples has been orientalized on the screen, depicted as an exotic location within Italy and collectively dismissed, along with Africa and the Orient, as a primitive, uncivilized space. Walter Benjamin and Asja Lacis described Naples as a "porous" city whose inhabitants were imbued with a passion for improvisation. Without accepting it uncritically, Verdicchio reinterprets Benjamin and Lacis's use of the term "porous" to indicate the "preservation of space and opportunity" where Neapolitan spatial politics are concerned in the work of late 1990s Italian filmmakers Mario Martone, Antonio Capuano, and Pappi Corsicato. In particular, Verdicchio explores a collective film project titled *I Vesuviani* (1997), in which the three directors participate with their films, *La salita*, *Sofialoren*, and *La stirpe de iana*, respectively. Verdicchio argues that each director reactivates some of the conventions of neorealist cinema in an effort to de-exoticize Naples and to reassert the city to its rightful place as a site of social activism and as the original center of the realist mode of representation in Italian cinema, a tradition that dates back to the films of director Elvira Notari.

Our final essay, "In Memoriam: The Neorealist Legacy in the Contemporary Sicilian Anti-Mafia Film," by Millicent Marcus examines three contemporary Italian films: Marco Tullio Giordana's *I cento passi* (2000), Pasquale Scimeca's *Placido Rizzotto* (2000), and Alessandro di Robilant's *Il giudice ragazzino* (1994). Marcus suggests that these films form a mini-genre of political cinema that is heavily indebted to the politically engaged cinema of Rossellini, De Sica, and Visconti. Marcus's analysis brings to light a previously undiscussed tendency in neorealism toward what she calls a "memorialist impulse," or a propensity to eulogize martyrs of the Resistance who might otherwise disappear, unnoticed by the annals of history. The memorialist impulse can also be found in contemporary political cinema that takes as its central theme anti-Mafia crusaders. Marcus argues that in both Italian neorealism and contemporary anti-Mafia films, the memorialist impulse always works in the service of current political issues. Her analysis links both contemporary anti-Mafia films and Italian neorealism to an earlier literary practice of memorializing heroic history that can be traced back to Ugo Foscolo's 1807 *Dei Sepulchri*.

Each of the essays in this collection takes on neorealism's complex relationship to a different national film tradition, style, or historical period. What results is a critical and novel examination of a short period in Italian cultural history that has had and continues to have wide-ranging international influence, an approach that we hope frames future studies. The global impact of neorealism continues to compound the complex relationship between ideas of nation, national cinema, and national identity. While the idea of a national cinema clearly has limitations, it has at times proved to be a useful cinematic mode of identification connected to popular resistance and political transformation—a strategy put to use by many filmmakers discussed in this volume. This collection imagines neorealism's radical potential to question longstanding ideological structures related to the production and distribution of film within national and global contexts.

Notes

1. The history of photography was itself prefigured by nature-themed dioramas. Similarly, in the first two decades of the motion picture industry, "even the most advanced story films retained much of the method of animated lantern slides"; it was only in the years prior to the first talkie that filmmakers began to see the storytelling potential of a series of pictures in motion (Robinson 120). Alternately, as film critic Amédée Ayfre points out in a 1952 piece in *Cahiers du Cinéma*, Louis and Auguste Lumiere never conceptualized their invention of the *cinématographe* as anything other than a tool to reproduce reality (see Hillier).

2. We put the term "genre" in quotation marks here to underscore the way in which the term "neorealism" will be problematized in this introduction and in the collection as a whole.

3. War and postwar films from the United States that had international distribution include *Gone with the Wind* (1939), *Gilda* (1946), *Casablanca* (1942), *Modern Times* (1936), and *Citizen Kane* (1941). De Sica comments on the colonizing effects of Hollywood film distribution in *Bicycle Thief* in his depiction of postwar destitution. His lead character, Antonio Ricci, competes with hundreds of men for the job of hanging movie posters that advertise *Gilda* around the city. Hollywood film thus serves as a starting point for Antonio's tragic downfall.

4. The convergence of international politics and filmmaking can be seen in U.S. involvement in this Indian film festival. In January 1952 the Italian-born Hollywood director Frank Capra traveled to India for the International Film Festival, having been asked to attend the event by the U.S. State Department. According to Capra's autobiography, Chester Bowles, U.S. ambassador to India, was concerned that the film festival was a front for an international Communist meeting. At the time Capra was a member (along with many others in print journalism, radio, television, and movies) of the President's Advisory Committee, a committee that advised "the State Department on how to best present the image of America on the 'Voice of America' radio, and other information media" (427). Thus the request that he fly to the subcontinent should not have been surprising. However, in the same month that he was asked to represent the United States, he was under scrutiny by the House Un-American Activities Committee. Capra had, in fact, been blacklisted under suspicion of being a Communist or Communist sympathizer. The International Film Festival in India (which is still held annually) was noncompetitive, and after two weeks in Bombay, the screenings moved to Calcutta, Madras, and Delhi. The

1952 festival is remembered as the first time contemporary Italian films were screened in India.

5. Andreotti wrote a public letter disparaging the film and De Sica for, among other things, "washing Italy's dirty laundry in public" (in Sitney 107). See also Wilson's essay in this volume.

6. See Bondanella, *Italian Cinema;* Brunetta; Sorlin, *Italian National Cinema.*

7. For discussions of the various precursors of neorealism, see Bondanella, *Italian Cinema;* Brunetta; Bruno; Marcus; Sitney.

8. Chris Norton considers this topic in his analysis of Michael Roemer's *Nothing but a Man* (1964), Billy Woodberry's *Bless Their Little Hearts* (1984), and Charles Burnett's *Killer of Sheep* (1977), films he describes as the result of a "digestion" of Italian neorealist techniques. See Antonio Napolitano's 1966 translated essay in this collection for more insight into the connection between U.S. and British film and neorealism.

9. For Bondanella's discussion of the "masters of neorealism," see, in particular, pages 31–73, and page 74 (*Italian Cinema*) for his explanation of why they are "auteurs." There were, in fact, many other Italian filmmakers during the postwar years who made films designated as neorealist, figures such as Luigi Zampa, Pietro Germi, Renato Castellani, Giuseppe De Santis, and Aldo Vergano.

10. See the essays by Jaimey Fisher and Antonio Traverso in this volume for an expanded discussion of the image of the child in neorealism.

11. For instance, De Sica paid the Roman Fire Department to fake a thunderstorm (Bondanella, *Italian Cinema* 57).

12. Fascist-era films were remarkably diverse in content and style. There were realist movies such as Mario Camerini's 1932 *Gli uomini, che mascalzoni!* (*Men, What Rascals!*); documentary-like films such as *Camicia nera* (*Black Shirt;* 1933); films that glorified ancient Rome, such as Carmine Gallone's 1937 classic *Lo scipione africano* (*Scipio the African*); and finally films that depicted Italy's colonial goals in Africa, such as Augusto Genia's 1936 *Lo squadrone bianco* (*The White Squadron*). In addition to Landy's *Fascism in Film,* see Reich and Garofalo's *Re-viewing Fascism: Italian Cinema, 1922–1943* for an extended study of Fascism and film.

13. According to Vitti, the *Cinema* "circle included Michelangelo Antonioni; Domenico Purificato; Dario Gianni and Massimo Puccini; Carlo Lizzani; Pietro Ingrao; Francesco Pasinetti; Antonio Pietrangeli; Giuseppe De Santis; Mario Alicata," and Luchino Visconti (*Giuseppe De Santis* 7).

14. Gramsci founded the PCI in 1921 and its newspaper, *L'Unità*, in 1924. He was imprisoned by Mussolini in 1926 until his death in 1937. While today all of his writings are available in Italian, his *Prison Notebooks* (*Quaderni del carcere*) were not published until 1952. By 1948, when De Santis made *Bitter Rice*, only Gramsci's letters from prison had been published. Lizzani, in his story on the making of *Bitter Rice*, attests to De Santis's and his film crew's knowledge of Gramsci's letters from prison: "Di Gramsci si conoscevano soltanto le 'Lettere,' appena pubblicate. I suoi scritti sulla letteratura, sugli intellettuali e sul Risorgimento ci erano ancora ignoti" (We only knew about Gramsci's 'Letters,' which had just been published. We still did not know anything about his writings on intellectuals and on the Risorgimento) (25). For further discussion of Gramsci and cinema, see Ruberto; Verdicchio.

15. Our reference to England is specifically to the Free Cinema movement and to the fact that most of its directors were postwar immigrants. See Napolitano's essay in this collection.

16. Marcia Landy, in a study of the British film *They Were Sisters* (1945), demonstrates this connection when she quotes Gramsci's quip that "The language of melodrama is folklore." She continues, listing the main characteristics of folklore that overlap with melodrama: a "reliance on anachronism, provincialism, and excessive affect" (*Italian Film* 109).

17. For an excellent critical history of Italian cinema under Fascism, see Hay. Dispelling any myths about the all-encompassing power of Fascism and film, Hay concentrates on popular films of the 1920s and 1930s, and traces a Fascist period national popular culture.

18. For detailed discussions about the contradiction in having Fascist Party filmmakers who were also staunch anti-Fascists, see Bondanella, *Italian Cinema;* Brunetta; Marcus.

Chapter 1

On the Ruins of Masculinity: The Figure of the Child
in Italian Neorealism and the German Rubble-Film

Jaimey Fisher

Italian and German Cinema after World War II

In a 1947 article titled "Quo Vadis Italia" in the German film journal *Neue Filmwelt,* K. H. Bergmann praises postwar Italian cinema's turn to "realism" and concludes that the "Italian film has reached its leading position in today's cinema by boldly breaking the bridges to the past and daring to venture to a cinematic new world.—They have dared to do it and won, and we—we should learn from them."[1] Though Bergmann's claim of a complete cinematic break is dubious—it is now well established that many of neorealism's "radical" innovations had been evolving throughout the Fascist period[2]—the comment is noteworthy for its desire to link early postwar cinema in Italy to that of Germany. Although critics worldwide had praised the Italian films, such a direct call to adopt neorealist approaches had a special resonance in Germany, where the film industry faced, like the rest of the country, widespread physical destruction, defeat at the hands of the Allies, and subsequent social and economic chaos. Furthermore, for an industry recently dominated by Goebbels's propaganda ministry, this call for a clean break would have rung with a particularly piercing urgency.

Since the late 1940s, critics and scholars have compared Germany's rubble-films—films made between 1945 and 1951 that were about contemporary issues and often shot in the postwar rubble—to Italian neorealist films, not least because Roberto Rossellini's *Germany, Year Zero* was shot in the Berlin rubble (as well as in Roman studios) in 1947.[3] Though there were certain obvious similarities between the films—

Germany, Year Zero (Roberto Rossellini, 1947)

engagement with the contemporary context, shooting on location, and generally avoiding film stars—most scholars conclude that rubble-films fell miserably short of neorealist works. Most critics merely contrast the two genres via the differences in the political interests of the films' auteurs and ostensibly the filmic content.[4] A second group of scholars admits that rubble-films have some of the same tendencies as neorealist films, but then argues (usually without much documentation) that rubble-films violate them in their lack of social commitment and in their refusal to engage directly with the protagonists' participation in Fascism.[5] Both groups claim to make a comparison but then rely on neorealism's traditional political content to distinguish the films.

Although such political differences may be important in distinguishing between the genres, it has become common practice to question whether the conspicuous political content of the plot or even "realistic" film techniques constitute the core of Italian neorealism.[6] Symptomatic of this trend, Marcia Landy, in her book *Italian Film,* avoids these recurring questions about neorealist films' political content or commitment by adopting a largely Deleuzian model to explain the transformation undertaken by neorealist films.[7] In his dense and rich *Cinema* volumes,

Gilles Deleuze emphasizes not so much neorealist political content or film technique but rather a new "cinematic image," that is, the "time-image" that had been evolving throughout the history of cinema up until that point, most prominently (and, one must admit, quite apolitically) in early Hitchcock films.[8] Previously, in the historically (and commercially still) dominant action-image, the part and the whole, of both movement and perception, were "organically" related in an easily comprehensible unity. In the action-image, the characters can absorb the situation, synthesize understanding, and act effectively, for example, in the conventional action film, in which the protagonist faces a series of challenges, quickly understands the obstacles, and acts effectively to overcome or circumvent them in both part and whole. In the time-image, however, these links between part and whole become "serial" rather than organic; they grow dispersive and are difficult to comprehend. In this newly uncertain and unpredictable cinematic situation, the characters are left struggling to read and comprehend the image rather than merely absorbing it and reacting to it.

Like Landy, I find Deleuze's analysis of Italian neorealism convincing, in large part because it successfully circumnavigates the dead-end questions about neorealist films' overt political content or their deployment of specific techniques. But in shifting the terms of the debate about what constitutes the core innovation of neorealist films, it is also important not to adopt Deleuze's account wholesale. In another context, I have taken explicit issue with Deleuze's analysis of neorealism and tried to demonstrate how sensitivity to the gendered aspects of these films can augment his analysis of the emergent time-image.[9] By considering how neorealist films dismantle the traditional masculine protagonist of feature films, one opens up neorealism to a different type of politics, one more fundamental to the cinematic image than the putative political commitments of the neorealist plot or filmmakers.

If one understands that a gendered social crisis contributed to the emergence of what Deleuze calls the time-image, then one has uncovered another common ground between the early postwar cinemas in Italy and Germany that likewise circumvents conventional questions about their overt political content. By revising Deleuze's description of a postwar cinematic crisis, I hope to introduce a nuanced comparative study of canonical Italian neorealism and a marginalized genre. In many neorealist as well as rubble-films, the male child plays a central role in representing the humiliated males, whose presence and fate refigure the traditional masculine action-image. Both cinemas were concerned with what Kaja Silverman has termed marginal males, men who were com-pelled—in the wake of the war and the social crises surrounding it—to embrace lack and inadequacy.[10] Italian and German postwar films reveal that one of the most effective ways to represent this lack was via the male child. They deploy such children in very specific ways to rework some of the constitutive elements of the Deleuzian action-image, including the system of masculine specularity, the relation between character and space, and the filmic duel that grounds the conflict-centered narrative. In the innocent figure of the male child, the two cinemas show mark-edly similar narrative and technical strategies: the child solves specific representational problems that arise from the surrender of the heroic male protagonist.

Partisans, Workers, and the *Heimkehrer:* Masculine Trauma after the War

In describing the emergence of the time-image in postwar Italy, De-leuze resorts—uncharacteristically for his *Cinema* books—to historical context. Generally, his very auteurist history of cinema focuses on film-makers and films that he regards as advancing the development from movement-image to time-image, which for him seems to be primarily a development internal to the history of cinema, so it is indeed unusual that he explains one of the most important developments in his book with the historical crisis of World War II. However, the crisis central to Deleuze's cinema history was both wider and deeper than his study suggests. Even if the pure optical and sound situation manifested itself most importantly in the Italian films, the widespread social crisis pro-duced similar images in Germany around the same time. Though it is difficult to establish that one cinema adopted themes or techniques from the other, they manifest remarkably similar approaches—thematically as well as technically—to the representational challenges they shared in the postwar period. The similarities in cinematic images that I shall be investigating arise because of something widespread in the postwar ex-periences of Italy and Germany: what Silverman has described as mas-culine trauma. The postwar cinematic crisis Deleuze elaborates unfolds not only in a cinematic register (as his philosophy and history of cinema implies), but also in a gendered fashion that I want to underscore as fun-damental to the politics of these films, both Italian and German.

In times of historical crisis, Silverman theorizes, marginal males lose their faith in the dominant fictions of society. In normal, or at least socially stable, times—that is, when rapid social upheaval does not threaten or alter social roles as they are passed on from generation to generation—subjects are, à la Althusser, interpellated to their positions and live out their lives in ways that more or less align with preordained roles. For this system to function, these subjects must believe in society and their roles, and thus in the "dominant fiction" of a given society. One key dominant fiction in western European and U.S. society is the denial of, lack, or inadequacy of the masculine subject, whose privilege and relative authority generally seem certain. At moments of historical crisis, when the male subject becomes overwhelmed or "ideologically fatigued," this dominant fiction grows labile, and the disavowal of lack starts to fail. Silverman suggests that the trauma of the wartime experience made it difficult for men to reintegrate into the dominant fictions of the family, community, and nation that, as George Mosse observes, the family underpins.[11] In postwar Germany, for instance, historians have documented how the domestic/familial sphere became uncannily alien for the returning man,[12] and rubble-films depict how marginal males fail to reassume the roles allotted to them by the dominant fiction. In certain historical moments, then, the discourse of masculinity can operate differently; it can expose male lack, introduce it as alterity, and invert the normal specular relations that underpin it.[13]

Postwar Italian and German films feature just such marginal males in place of the traditional protagonist. In canonical films like *Rome, Open City* (1945) and *Paisan* (1946), the traditional masculine heroes are overpowered or even killed by pacifying forces, often the occupying Germans. Not only are they killed, but their deaths are conspicuously humiliating.[14] Even when Italian neorealist films are not explicitly concerned with wartime and postwar issues, their male heroes demonstrate the kind of lack rampant during the occupation and the postwar period. For example, in other canonical films like *Bicycle Thief* (1948) and *Umberto D* (1952), the humiliation of the male protagonist rests in his precarious socioeconomic status, which invariably prevents him from fulfilling the role of economic provider and protector ascribed to men by the dominant fiction. Whether or not they are conspicuously concerned with wartime or postwar issues, all of these films chart how male characters—especially the male protagonist—forfeit their position of social authority and privilege. The similar figure that German rubble-films invariably follow across the desolate postwar landscape is the Heimkehrer, or "soldier returning home."[15] The Heimkehrer likewise does not correspond to the desiring male usually postulated in fiction films or psychoanalytic film theories.[16] Much like his Italian counterparts, the Heimkehrer constitutes a passive, marginal male who is neither active nor central, and who ends up complicating—often inverting—differences that traditionally serve the male's privileged social status.[17] The films are infused with the sense that the Heimkehrer is now superfluous to the society whose center he once occupied—and without this traditional center, the films depict a kind of dephalliation, a weakening of traditional social relations that generally privilege the male.[18] Such a sociocinematic shift requires a rethinking of key differences regarding the male protagonist, which should include both generational and gender differences.

Twilight of the Masculine Action-Image in the Early Postwar Period

A sensitivity to this interruption of conventional masculinity yields a fundamental rereading of Deleuze's radical transformation in the cinematic image. Though some of the terms of Deleuze's analysis might be familiar from either his own work or recent applications of it like Landy's *Italian Cinema,* I would like to recast certain aspects of his ungendered model in light of the postwar crisis of masculinity, especially how his rich analysis might yield a more nuanced reading of the male child and its role in the postwar crisis in masculinity. The role of the male gaze in the conventional specular system, the relation of character to setting and space, and the duel form in his theory help lay the foundation for a differentiated approach to the child in both Italian neorealist and German rubble-films.

In Deleuze's film theory, the war and its aftermath galvanize a break from the action-image that underpins the movement-image to the pure optical-sound situation that soon yields the time-image. At the core of the traditional (and commercially still dominant) action-image, Deleuze posits the "sensory-motor link," a relation co-constitutive with ideal masculine agency. The sensory-motor link asserts how a character senses the situation or setting, synthesizes some kind of understanding from this perception, and then acts on it, such that the action follows consequentially from this synthesizing understanding. Stimuli and the perception of them become in this model merely instruments of getting to the action. The sensory-motor schema corresponds to masculine agency and its gaze because the sensory-motor link suggests a coordinated, instrumental, or reified perception, a kind of perception that helps

30

constitute the privileged specular position of the male. Once the male subject sees something, he can act against and dominate it, the core of the male position in the dominant system of specularity.

According to Deleuze, however, this cinematic system—which is also a general social system for perceiving and synthesizing stimuli into understanding and action—undergoes a fundamental transformation in the 1930s and 1940s. At the end of *Cinema 1,* Deleuze explains how, in Hitchcock and even more fully in neorealism, the action-image starts to disintegrate because confusingly dispersive situations emerge and subvert the clear teleological logic of the sensory-motor link. For example, in Hitchcock's films, the protagonists are often left not only struggling to understand (as in conventional detective or crime films) but also staring at an image trying to comprehend it (as in *Rear Window* [1954]), such that spectatorship and the struggle to perceive and comprehend in an uncertain and unpredictable situation come to the fore. Narratively speaking, I would submit that this dispersive situation corresponds to the postwar meltdown of masculine agency and its replacement by a confusing manifold of gender, familial, and socioeconomic relations.[19] At the beginning of *Cinema 2,* Deleuze offers that which initially arises from the ruins of the action-image, the "pure optical-sound situation" that replaces the action-image and sensory-motor link.[20] In this emergent cinematic image, the situation completely outstrips the protagonist and his attempts to synthesize perceptions of stimuli into action. The protagonist's gaze no longer leads teleologically to understanding, action, and mastery: there is instead passive searching, sometimes confused observation of the character's surroundings. Such a development undermines the core of the action-image and subverts the male's privileged position of specularity: the male protagonists become spectacles while women and/or children, the formerly observed, now watch, synthesize, and act.

The transformation of the viewer modifies the inanimately viewed as well, in a complementary inversion of a formerly stable specularity. After Luchino Visconti's *Obsession* (1943), "objects and settings take on an autonomous, material reality which gives them an importance in themselves" (*Cinema 2* 9). The protagonist often finds him- or herself on a meandering voyage in which the character records space and objects but is unable to synthesize them into understanding or to act upon them.[21] Landscapes in neorealism and the rubble in the rubble-film, for example, take on meanings of their own and begin to symbolize something autonomous from, even resistant to, the dominant fiction—in fact, when stared at passively by a male subject who has been dislodged from the action-image, the landscapes and rubble begin to expose his hitherto hidden lack and inadequacy.[22]

Central to the traditional action-image and the sensory-motor link model is a duel at some point, in which the action-image arranges a clear and logical conflict between its protagonist and some force outside himself.[23] In the duel, the protagonist is able to reify, in understanding and in action, his animate and inanimate surroundings, thereby enacting the traditional subject/object duality constitutive of conventional knowledge and mastery. As this sensory-motor link becomes unglued, however, the duel form starts to grow dispersive, such that the subject/object split and conventional identification with the protagonist become less certain.[24] This mode of the oblique or dissolving duel leads the pure optical-sound image out of the conventional dialectic of visual domination: formerly, when the spectator's identifications were firmly with the male subject, what was seen by him was soon conquered by him and, vicariously, by the spectator. Now the dispersive situation destroys that hierarchy and introduces the male to his lack and inadequacy. This formerly perceiving, synthesizing, and acting figure now becomes a mere observer, a recorder of that which surrounds it. The alterity of what ought to be familiar develops because once the viewer is displaced from the formerly monolithic presence of the male subject, that subject can become other. Unveiling male lack and alterity, Deleuze's antidualism of the cinematic image subverts the relations of specularity, reification, and conflict underpinning conventional masculinity.

The Child in the Disintegration of the Action-Image

In the transition from the action-image to the pure optical-sound situation, Deleuze suggests that the child suddenly appears as a central figure. This child figures prominently in Deleuze's theorized transformation of the relation between protagonist and setting because the child acts differently vis-à-vis setting: the child is marked by a certain "motor helplessness . . . one that makes him all the more capable of seeing and hearing" (*Cinema 2* 3). The child feels less at home in the world than the traditional protagonist who, in the action-image sketched above, more often arranges and dominates it. When the child looks at the setting, the spectator is often left uncertain as to what the child understands and, subsequently, has fewer expectations as to the child's ability to act on its spatial or cinematic situation. The child thus serves the trans-

formed specular and spatial relations perfectly: it becomes an indispensable means for the film to depict a powerlessness reflecting the wider
wartime and postwar social crisis while still offering a site for spectator
identification.

This passive child, however, is only part of the story: Deleuze's concept of the child as a naturally weak observer reeks of an imaginary discourse about youth, particularly because children, even in Italian neorealism, are anything but simply weak or passive. Both Italian neorealist and
German rubble-films depict a revealing oscillation of the child between
active agency and passive observation: at times, the child is inscrutably
and passively observant, manifesting the acquiescent behavior suggestive
of the current meek state of the male. At other times, however, the child
acts in a manner markedly more effective than that of the male protagonist, such that its activity elucidates male lack and even threatens the
central male figure. In both cases, the presence of the child highlights the
limits of the male, the horizons of his effective agency, and the twilight of
his conventional role in the masculine action-image. The fact that neorealist and rubble-films offer overwhelmingly male children confirms the
film's concern with the link between the child and masculinity in particular.

As the duel of the action-image grows oblique and traditional confrontations fade, the male protagonists begin to encounter the male child
as the enemy. In one of their most important narrative innovations, both
neorealist and rubble-films deliberately disperse the duel form in which
the protagonist would conceive of, confront, and conquer the enemy
(with the spectator identifying with the character throughout these teleological thoughts and linkages). Now a third element, the child, enters
the dualistic form of filmic confrontation and diverts the film's formerly
goal-directed movement. As neither simple subject nor object, neither
clear ally nor enemy, the child dilutes the purer dualism of the action-
image duel, effectively rendering its form opaque.

These films dismantle the formerly clearly drawn duel, in large part
because they set out to stage the somewhat nebulous struggles within
their protagonists or other key figures, including films like *Rome, Open
City, Bicycle Thief,* and *Paisan,* which I shall analyze in more detail later.[25]
These internal struggles—to synthesize stimuli into understanding and
then to act on it—are co-constitutive with the postwar crises in the
masculine action-image suggested above. For Italian neorealist films,
the main characters repeatedly struggle with heroism, often with reconstructing effective agency after the German and Allied occupation;[26]

in German rubble-films they struggle with the past and reconstructing decimated psyches as well as cities. In order to stage such internal struggles, the films consistently confront their protagonists with a male child who is at once parallel (in its passivity) to the masculine protagonist as well as mocking (in its activity) that figure. Generational nexuses now predominate where duels formerly reigned.

The Duality of the Child in Italian Neorealism

To demonstrate how male children can function in these crises of masculinity, I would like to offer a few short examples from some master texts of Italian neorealism before moving on, in more detail, to lesser-known German rubble-films and their representations of the decimated postwar male. In *Rome, Open City, Bicycle Thief,* and the famous second episode of *Paisan,* the male protagonist finds himself in a crisis of effective agency that is conveyed by the oscillation of male children between passivity and overactivity. In *Germany, Year Zero,* a similar oscillation of the child structures the narrative, though I shall not be focusing on that film because it concentrates on young Edmund, rather than rendering the child a key complement to the adult male protagonist. As a constitutive aspect of the shift from action-image to pure optical-sound situation, this oscillation of the male child galvanizes a shift in the film's specular system, the characters' relations to the setting and space, and the duel form that rests at the core of traditional narrative conflict.

Rome, Open City

Many analyses of Rossellini's renowned film focus on the duality of the masculine hero in Manfredi and Don Pietro or on the strong emotional force emitted by Pina. Part of the film's remarkable cinematic innovation, one that foreshadows the more radical revision of narrative form in *Paisan,* rests in the multiplicity of centers that replace the conventional concentration on a single protagonist. Both Don Pietro and Pina diminish the masculine action-image by offering strong figures beyond the film's ostensible protagonist, Manfredi, with whom the spectator can identify. I would argue, however, that another key aspect of the decentering of the male protagonist in *Rome, Open City* is the presence of and parody provided by male children. Much of *Rome, Open City*'s dismantling of the "heroic" masculine center rests in the oscillation between the radical activity and passivity of the child that communicates, perhaps more than anything, the transformation of the cinematic image.

Manfredi serves as a marginal male in part because of the ineffectual agency he represents throughout the film. Over the course of the film, from the first to the penultimate scenes, the ostensible hero Manfredi is hunted down and killed, and he seems almost incapable of any positive agency. The very few moments of effective resistance to the Germans seem calculated to shift activity away from Manfredi: either through the passive handoff of the priest Don Pietro; the nameless partisans who liberate Manfredi and Francesco; or the surprise bombing by Romoletto and his gang of children. If the film can be said to afford only three effective anti-German actions, then one of them is conspicuously organized and executed by children. As in many neorealist and rubble-films, this scene of child-generated action is immediately followed by a sequence that emphasizes their tenuous agency, their oscillation between active and passive: they return home from the bombing only to be castigated by their parents for returning so late. Ultimately, however, their moment of activity proves central to the negative trajectory of the plot: their attack leads Bergmann to their apartment building and yields the roundup that kills Pina. When the male children provide the motor for activity in a cinematic environment where the main male figures become increasingly marginal, their overactivity simultaneously threatens the film's masculine figures.

The children likewise disrupt the conventional specular system of the masculine movement-image. Like the narrative system, the specular system in *Rome, Open City* seems to function in a decentered fashion that is more radically realized in later neorealist films. If a constitutive aspect of the masculine action-image is the ability to synthesize stimuli into understanding and action, then Don Pietro certainly represents a mockery of this masculine gaze and embodies a conspicuous kind of male alterity. As a celibate, he interrupts the normative desiring male gaze, for instance, when he turns the statue of the saint away from the nude female figure. In the final incarceration and torture sequence, *Rome, Open City* focuses on Don Pietro's compromised gaze, first in his glasses that break when he is thrown into the cell and then in his witnessing the torture and death of Manfredi. This coincidence of gaze and humiliation—of not only violence to comrades but also being compelled to watch the violence—is actually prefigured by the child Marcello, who has to watch the Germans gun down his mother in the film's celebrated roundup sequence. Marcello's burying his head in his mother's dead body provides one of the film's most memorable images and enforces the oscillation between the children's extreme activity (in the gang's successful bombing shortly before) and passivity (in their helplessness amid adult violence). In the last sequence, the film makes the link between the passive gazes of priest and children explicit: in a stark parallel to Don Pietro's watching the torture of Manfredi, the children must watch Don Pietro's execution. Don Pietro's marginal male gaze is effectively handed off to the children who have surrounded Don Pietro since the beginning.

The film's final sequence also establishes the confluence between Don Pietro's relation to space and that of the children. As they slowly wind their way back down to the city with St. Peter's Basilica looming in the background, the deep focus shot of diminutive characters disappearing into an overwhelming urban maze revisits Don Pietro's celebrated voyage through the city. This sequence, in which Don Pietro slowly walks to an appointed meeting with an unnamed partisan, is remarkable for its lack of action and its passivity. As Deleuze has described, a protagonist becomes a mere observer, a recorder for stimuli, rather than a synthesizing and transacting agent. But it is important to observe how this image of the voyager, of the meanderer, is likewise linked, even handed off, to the male children at the end. After Don Pietro's death, the children become the voyagers, those who meander—without the guidance of father, mother, or priest—down into an uncertain future.[27] The children likewise fulfill this passive image of the duel and dismantling of heroism: in the final sequence, they watch the German officer shoot Don Pietro but are helpless to do anything about it. The only heroes surviving at the end of the film are those left to watch the action.

Bicycle Thief

Even more than *Rome, Open City*, Vittorio De Sica's *Bicycle Thief* deliberately deploys the alternative gaze of the child to subvert the masculine antihero. The film's basic strategy confirms the link between masculine humiliation and the child's impact on the conventional specular system. Though Landy has productively emphasized the importance of precocious Bruno's looking in the film, I would emphasize above all how Bruno's gaze refigures the masculine gaze at the heart of traditional cinema.[28] By introducing the gaze of the son upon the father, De Sica foregrounds the transformation of the traditional male *subject* of the gaze into a humiliated *object* of the gaze. The film signals that this revision of the specular system is deliberate and self-reflective in early sequences when Antonio is working: while still in possession of his bicycle and job, Antonio expertly navigates the maze of the city to hang posters of the voluptuously larger-than-life Rita Hayworth. In these early sequences, with their conventional relation of male protagonist to setting and to cinematic objects of desires, Antonio embodies the masculine action-image and its constitutive gaze.

Once his bike is stolen and his son starts to track him, however, Antonio is slowly objectified by the gaze of the male child. Bruno's recurring point-of-view shots subjugate the male point of view and open the way for others in the cinematic situation to watch, and thereby subdue, Antonio. In conventional cinema the spectator identifies with the travails of the protagonist, with the obstacles he faces, and with his subsequent, usually successful, goal-oriented action. Here, however, the viewer's identifications are now routed through the child, a third element inserted between the protagonist and the cinematic environment. Bruno triangulates the relationship of protagonist to his environment and, in occupying this position of the third term, marks Antonio's transformation into the object of contemplation.[29] In part because the child implies a certain normative social role for the male subject—as provider and protector—the gaze of the child becomes a cipher for the social order to judge the actions of the male: a vigilant agent of the social order (a representative reminiscent of Lacan's big Other) is imposed between the spectator and masculine hero.[30] In this way, a powerful new regulative force is introduced directly into the film's specular system in which the male is now the object of the socially disciplining gaze.

The two climactic duels in the film are figured precisely through the impact of this rerouted gaze on the would-be masculine hero. When Antonio finally confronts the thief who has stolen his bicycle—sporting a German army cap, symbolic of the failed duel with the German occupiers[31]—he becomes overwhelmed and overpowered by others' observing and judging of him. Throughout the sequence, the film undercuts Antonio's agency as male protagonist by subjecting him to the gaze of strangers, especially women and children: he chases the thief into a brothel full of women who look at him aggressively, and then ends up in a lengthy, unwinnable argument with the mother of the thief. While seeking the stolen bicycle in her apartment, Antonio is framed next to a window through which a neighboring woman and child—in strikingly clear deep focus—watch his hopeless search. The long-awaited confrontation degenerates as Antonio is shot as the object, rather than subject, of the point-of-view as well as deep focus shots.

In the climactic end of the film, Antonio has one more duel to fight, that with a lonely bike beckoning to him like any traditional object of desire. But this duel also degenerates because of his inability to control the gaze of the child upon himself. When Antonio decides to steal the bike, he tries to send Bruno away so that the child does not witness the crime of the father—and so that the gaze of the social order that Bruno embodies does not once again regulate his behavior. But Bruno, in his motor helplessness, misses the tram, goes looking for his father, and then watches his father commit the crime. As in the confrontation with the thief, Bruno's witnessing of Antonio's crime anticipates the rest of society's seeing him do it as well: soon the newly minted bicycle thief is apprehended by the crowd and the bike's rightful owner, effectively rendering Antonio the passive object rather than subject of the gaze. In the end, it is only the action—literally, the lachrymose eyes—of Bruno that saves his father, an utter inversion of both the specular and authoritative systems of the film.

Paisan

In *Paisan,* the famous second episode—the encounter between the African American G.I. Joe and the Neapolitan boy Pasquale—deploys a similar oscillation between the active and passive youth while revealing another representational facet of the child: that of the gamin at the margins of society who can be deployed to reinscribe that society. The alterity of the child functions in *Paisan* as a social other, an outsider to remake the boundaries of the familiar. Pasquale leads the drunk Joe through the hostile and often unfathomable maze of a city—this time Naples—and mediates the relationship of the adult male to this intrusive setting. Pasquale takes Joe first to a puppet show that the adult misunderstands, then to a symbolic pile of rubble, and finally to a series of caves and shantytowns whose poverty shocks the American soldier. Like Romoletto or Marcello in *Rome, Open City,* Pasquale introduces Joe to a hostile context that threatens to overwhelm him. Pasquale does not personify, as Deleuze claims, a motor helplessness; rather, he serves as a kind of caricature of putative masculine agency that foregrounds the precariousness of that agency. The potential of children to cross borders, to navigate spaces both familiar and foreign, plays an important role in a context in which the cinematic situation and setting intrude upon and overwhelm protagonists. In light of their conflict, the spectator might expect a showdown between Joe and the boy who stole his boots, or at least between Joe and Pasquale's parents, but the duel form is dissolved in the haunting space of the caves. In his border-crossing abilities, Pasquale introduces Joe to a space at which Joe can only gape: the child-

galvanized dawning of understanding replaces the planned confrontation. The child, oscillating between overactivity and passivity, teaches his generational superior Joe, who sees, observes, and then understands that he should not act. In *Paisan,* as in *Rome, Open City* and *Bicycle Thief,* the male child subverts the film's climactic duel, recasting the masculine action-image as passive observer.

Coming to Terms with the Past and Reconstruction in *Somewhere in Berlin*

As only the second German feature film of the postwar era, Gerhard Lamprecht's *Somewhere in Berlin* (*Irgendwo in Berlin;* 1946, Soviet licensed) enjoyed enormous publicity and was praised by film critics. They often compared it to the first postwar feature film, *The Murderers Are among Us* (*Die Mörder sind unter uns;* Wolfgang Staudte, 1946, Soviet licensed), and approvingly underscored *Somewhere*'s shared realism, its similar attention to the contemporary social context, and its likewise lack of any film stars.[32] Critics, however, also indicated how *Somewhere* improved on *The Murderers,* even if they avoided judging which was better. One critic contrasted *The Murderers* to *Somewhere* precisely because the latter engaged a "collective" problem, "the lives of our young ones."[33] These critics recognized *Somewhere in Berlin*'s basic strategy: the key conflicts are not confrontations with the past or the challenges of reconstruction, though they pervade the cinematic environment; they rest rather in generational duels staged at decisive moments of the narrative.

Somewhere in Berlin follows a friendship between two (initially) fatherless boys, Gustav Iller and Willi. Gustav's father has yet to return from a POW camp, while Willi has lost both of his parents in the war. For the first twenty minutes of the film, the boys engage in delinquent behavior that symptomatizes the dispersive postwar crisis. But the boys' familial fates are ultimately split: Gustav's father, Iller, returns and then—traumatized by the war—struggles to reassume the masculine role in the family and film, while Willi's situation under a depraved adoptive father, Birke, degenerates into open antagonism. In order to make a welcome-home gift for Iller—who is constantly, literally and metaphorically, hungry—Willi steals some food from Birke, who then throws Willi out. Orphaned again and taunted by other boys, Willi decides to climb a ruined building, from which he falls and is killed. With the abrupt loss of his friend, Gustav reconciles with his father and turns his energies, along with his father, to reconstruction.

The first part of the film depicts the kind of dephalliated social crisis just described. As in *Rome, Open City* or *Paisan*, the fathers are missing, and in their place reign a series of decentered, marginal figures: shady black market dealers, ineffective mothers, and, above all, overactive children. In the absence of a strong, benevolent masculine force, the first quarter of the film is dominated, thematically and visually, by Willi and Gustav, who prove, as in Italian neorealism, the motor for the film's action-image. Most important in this regard is a long sequence in which the children play war games. The scene commences with their break from the film's adult world, as Gustav runs from his mother and a policeman to join the company of other kids. The scene is set on a huge field of rubble, where the children hide, shoot rockets, and march around in formation. The film cuts unpredictably among the different groups of kids, such that the anarchical games mock the absurdity of adult wars. Like the image of Pasquale and Joe in *Paisan* or Edmund in *Germany, Year Zero*, the sequence links children to rubble as a central image of social degeneration and masculine crisis.

When the masculine protagonist does appear, Iller the Heimkehrer cannot exert himself in the vacuum of effective male agency—his entrance only emphasizes the prevailing lack of any conventional social role for the masculine protagonist. When he walks into the frenetic war games, he is confused and disturbed by the make-believe violence, and his own son fails to recognize him. He sits down, dejected, on a pile of rubble, overcome by generational overthrow and dispersion. His look around the rubble and at his son is devoid of authority over the boy and of any real understanding of what he sees. He seems fascinated by the rubble, on a Deleuzian voyage where he is more prey than predator to the cinematic context. The passivity of his gaze contrasts with the determined looks and subsequent action of the children as they gleefully destroy what is left of the enrubbled neighborhood, including carrying out a rocket attack on a shell-shocked veteran whose eye was, literally and symbolically, mutilated in the war.

This alternative gaze of the war veterans reflects the transformed relation to the cinematic situation and especially the setting. The next day, Iller and Gustav set out to return a lost wallet to its rightful owner, the manager of a local bar and revue show. When father and son appear at the bar, the wallet's streetwise owner realizes he can accuse this haggard figure of stealing and slyly rejects giving Iller any reward. Befuddled, Iller stares dumbly at the rehearsal of the revue show while the son looks on, confused about the fact that his longed-for father has proven utterly ineffective. The spectator's view of the inadequate father is routed, as in *Bicycle Thief*, through the male child. The acquiescent submission to the atmosphere of a bar, a kind of passive absorption in one's surroundings, is a recurring image in the rubble-film (as well as in *Bicycle Thief*): everything has become alienating and therefore fascinating.[34] The bar invites the complete surrender to an environment that breeds self-forgetting, the utter abrogation of the formerly privileged masculine position.

The recurring images of Iller blankly staring and contemplating his surroundings remind the spectator of the internal struggle of the defeated postwar male. Since his own past is that which haunts and weighs upon him, the film cannot simply arrange a duel with the enemy. At a historical moment when traditional cinematic confrontation has become oblique—which enemies could a traumatized German soldier fight after Nazism and the unconditional surrender?—the narrative shifts its constitutive duels to generational conflict. In the first generational encounter above, the masculine hero cannot even command recognition from his feral son, whose threatening action-image parodies traditional masculinity. But the film then deliberately stages another confrontation, between the passive patriarch and the most overactive of the children, in part to jump-start the stuttering adult male.

Willi performs the role of the overactive, threatening youth not only because he is a central figure in the frenetic war games but also because he links Gustav, who has a family, to the social crisis of orphaned children. A figure originating like *Paisan*'s Pasquale in the margins of society, Willi might pull Gustav from the domesticated family into the belligerent and overactive youth gang. He threatens to rewrite the traditional boundaries of the family, a metaphor for the boundaries of postwar society. He is the most powerful figure of masculine lack because he represents, in contrast to Iller, active and effective agency but remains undisciplined and unhoused. His parody of the patriarch is even more pronounced when he seeks to play the provider to the moping Iller: he steals food from his own adoptive father for the always hungry but ineffective Iller.

After being banished from Birke's house for his theft, Willi wanders around the rubble and eventually scales a ruined building to demonstrate his courage to some boys who are taunting him. In an image parallel to Pasquale in *Paisan* or Edmund in *Germany, Year Zero*, Willi the orphan looks at the rubble in one of the film's starkest symbols of the general social crisis that has jettisoned the boy from the shattered domestic sphere. But in contrast to the men's passive rubble-gaze, Willi is all too determined to conquer the rubble to prove himself to the youth mob. As in *Germany, Year Zero,* a kind of vulnerable agency—orphaned but overactive—highlights the social dispersion underpinning the film. Because his youthful action-image parodies the (absent) active male, the traditional social and generational order, the film deems Willi a threat against that which it must defend: Willi falls from the rubble and dies soon thereafter.

In the film's climactic generational confrontation, Iller goes to Willi on his deathbed. Here, the despairing and inadequate father learns from the overactive child, recalling the generational lessons of *Paisan* and *Bicycle Thief.* Visually, the image of the now caring father attending to the child revisits and revises Iller's earlier appearance in the film, when his own son did not recognize him and the father could only look inward to his traumas. Iller tells the dying Willi he appreciates what he did and that now "we'll build it back up again," an announcement toward which the film has been driving since its beginning. In this second generational duel, Iller inherits faith in the dominant fiction from the dying Willi in another world-upside-down generational inversion: the man of lack learns from the child of the action-image.

German Children, East and West: *And Someday We Will See Each Other Again* and *In Front of Us, There Is Life*

Somewhere in Berlin deploys its male children, their gazes, and their alternative relationship to cinematic space and conflict to represent and resolve the postwar crisis of the masculine hero. For Germany, foremost among these crises were coming to terms with the past and reconstruction. *Somewhere's* children embody both challenges: their war games symbolically convey a battle at a moment when German audiences had grown tired of war, and Willi's and then Gustav's faith in the father help him "build it back up again." In this way, the film's children mediate two of the most important postwar German themes, *Vergangenheitsbewälti-gung* (coming to terms with the past) and *Wiederaufbau* (reconstruction), preoccupations that have dominated German culture since the end of the war. While *Somewhere in Berlin* was made in the Soviet-occupied sector, films in what would become West Germany also resorted to male children to negotiate the burdensome past and reconstruction. I would like to offer an overview of two similarly concerned films made in the western sectors, one that utilizes children to come to terms with the problematic past and another that deploys them to navigate the challenges of reconstruction.

And Someday We Will See Each Other Again (*Und finden dereinst wir uns wieder;* Hans Müller, 1947, British licensed) attempts to confront what must have been one of the most difficult postwar cultural tasks: disavowing, almost immediately, carefully conditioned dedication to the Nazi movement. While many rubble-films put forth an image of odious Nazis, understandably few offered convincing Nazis with whom the audience might identify: likable protagonists who also had Nazi leanings were as difficult and problematic to script as they were necessary. The representational solution to this dilemma was to offer children or young people who were dedicated Nazis but who also seemed passive enough to be "reeducated" by the end of the film. The consistent oscillation between overactivity and passivity could thus serve to represent one of the central challenges of the postwar period, both the fanatical dedication that Nazism inspired as well as the potential for rapidly forgetting it. Some of the most compelling films of the period, including Wolfgang Staudte's *Rotation* (original title, 1949, Soviet licensed) and Josef von Baky and Fritz Kortner's *Der ruf* (released as *The Last Illusion* [literally, "The Appointment"]; 1949, U.S. licensed), relied on precisely this device, a young Nazi with whom, in his innocence, the audience could nevertheless identify. The figure of the young Nazi offered the films a locus of fanatical overactivity that threatens the male protagonist while also presenting a threat that was ultimately manageable. The convinced Nazi as young person provides these films with a form of ferocious yet surmountable fanaticism.

In *And Someday We Will See Each Other Again,* a group of pupils has been sent in the last few months of the war to the countryside for safety. They learn, however, of the battle of Berlin and demand to help defend the tattered remnant of the thousand-year Reich. While the children devote themselves to their rapidly anachronistic ideals, their humanist teachers try to prevent their flight to Berlin. Throughout the film, most of the adult characters are either avowed anti-Nazis or highly skeptical about the Nazi movement. In the generational logic of the film, the fanatic followers of Hitler are invariably young people. While it is certainly true that Nazis effectively rode the enthusiasm of the young until the last days of the Reich, it is also of course ridiculous that only young people were convinced Nazis (teachers, in fact, were among the most notoriously coordinated professional groups of Nazis).

Like Italian films in this period, *And Someday We Will See Each Other Again* utilizes its male children to represent the transformed cinematic situation in which the characters have different relations to the specular system and the setting. Over the course of their determined trip back to

43

Berlin, the film offers a series of pure optical and sound situations from which the pupil is to learn. In one particularly telling scene, the pupils disembark from their train only to see the rubble of what was a station, and a voice-over asks Wolfgang, the fanatical leader of the group, "Why don't you look around, Wolfgang? These images belong [to the Reich], too. What do you see? Do you think they still believe?" The film cuts from a close-up of a gaping Wolfgang to a long pan around the ruined room and over huddling refugees and soldiers delighted to have escaped the front. The voice-over continues, "Do you not want to see what you see? . . . Open your eyes, my boy!" The film thereby wrests visual control from the most convinced Nazi in the film, whom the camera compels to observe the situation and to relinquish his fanatical fervor.

The narrative follows a journey not only from Germany's outskirts to its geographical capital but also from extreme dedication to Nazi ideals to core truths about Hitler and his "movement." The film likewise dismantles the possibility of a climatic conflict at its core: as they draw closer to the front, the boys grow less and less zealous about fighting. As in many neorealist films and in *Somewhere in Berlin*, a meandering journey to understanding replaces the climactic duel. The duel that the film does offer is, typically, a generational confrontation: the boys eventually encounter a benevolent soldier who is delighted to have escaped the fighting and helps the boys find their way back to their families instead of to the führer. Reminiscent of both *Bicycle Thief* and *Somewhere in Berlin*, long shots of this soldier with the smallest of the boys reinforce the overwhelming setting. In such a milieu, even Wolfgang eventually abandons his dedication to the Nazis and returns to his mother.

Like *Somewhere in Berlin* and *And Someday We Will See Each Other Again*, many rubble-films avoid the past altogether in favor of an overdetermined focus on the problems of the present and future reconstruction. But even in these more optimistic films, male children serve as an indispensable means for depicting the subversion of the masculine action-image. For example, in the U.S.-licensed *In Front of Us, There Is Life* (*Vor uns liegt das Leben;* Gerhard Rittau, 1948), a harbor town suffers under traumatized and ineffectual males: an opening collage associates the literal ruins of a ship with the metaphorical rubble of the former sailors, who now mope around local bars bored and drunk. In this realm of dephalliation and masculine lack, as in *Rome, Open City, Germany, Year Zero*, and *Somewhere in Berlin*, the marginal social figures play the role of economic providers. When their family needs a new goat to provide adequate milk and cheese for their son, Jürgen the father cannot

Germany, Year Zero
(Roberto Rossellini,
1947)

scrape together the required funds, so his wife, Renata, like Antonio's wife in *Bicycle Thief*, has to sell some fabric she was saving. Humiliated by his wife as provider, Jürgen meanders into the bar where he, in another explicit echo of Antonio in *Bicycle Thief*, morosely reviews the prices of various items that now overwhelm him in the changed cinematic environment ("10DM for a small Schnapps, 20DM for a large, 100DM for the coat fabric" needed to trade for the goat). In this world remade against the traditional paternal provider, the children again generate most of the film's effective agency: they are the ones, while their fathers sit around in the bar, who set sail, fish, and sell their catch on the black market to obtain other coveted foodstuffs. One son even supports his father's addiction to cigarettes, Germany's postwar currency and a clear symbol of the phallus that has floated away from the patriarch to the overactive children.[35]

Jürgen's abrogation of his paternal responsibilities culminates in a parental nightmare: after fleeing to the bar again, this time in the wake of an argument with his wife, Jürgen broods alone, shot in expressionistic shadows reflecting his tumultuous struggles to come to terms with his new landlocked life. At the same moment as the marginal male Jürgen looks inward—abandoning the formerly commanding gaze upon objects of desire or supervision—his son and his young friends sail too far out to sea in the midst of a storm, another journey into a hostile setting resulting from the overactivity of the children. The film intercuts the moping male protagonist who has to forfeit the supervisory gaze of the father with the children's determined voyage to another figurative phallus, a lighthouse promising a rich bed of mussels and crabs. As the only determined sailors in the film, the male children are the purveyors of the action-image in the vacuum created by the masculine hero's inadequacy. *In Front of Us, There Is Life* offers not only rubble but also the tumultuous sea as the changed cinematic environment.

As in many neorealist and rubble-films, the crisis of the male protagonist does not ultimately yield a duel that activates the defunct action-image. Rather, the traumatized male learns to come to terms with his diminished status: the man has to learn to embrace the lack conveyed by the changed cinematic environment and its children. In *In Front of Us, There Is Life,* Jürgen comes to accept his life on land because, as his son ventures out with his young friends, the father admits that he has discovered how awful it can be to wait for loved ones who are out to sea. The overactive children of the film locate Jürgen in the traditionally landlocked feminine position of waiting for her sea-tossed man. As in *Somewhere* or *Paisan,* the adults learn an important postwar lesson about lack and loss from children. In *In Front of Us, There Is Life* as in other films, children serve as the perfect social reeducators for adults: they enlighten the adults while only mildly threatening them in a context that was certainly already overwhelming enough.

Children of an Immanent Critique

Somewhere in Berlin, And Someday We Will See Each Other Again, and *In Front of Us, There Is Life* provide only a few of the many rubble-film examples in which male children contribute to the altered cinematic environment. Sometimes the children manifest open rebellion against and hostility toward the traditional male authority, as they do in *Wege im zwielicht* (*Ways in the Twilight;* Gustav Froelich, 1948, British licensed), *Zugvögel* (*Birds of Passage;* Rolf Meyer, 1947, British licensed), or *Der ruf* (*The Last Illusion;* Josef von Baky, 1949, U.S. licensed). Sometimes children are oblivious to the role that such traditional authority formerly played, as in *1-2-3 Corona* (Hans Müller, 1948, Soviet licensed) or in . . . *Und über uns der Himmel* (*And the Heavens Above;* Josef von Baky, 1947, U.S. licensed). In all these cases, the rubble-film deploys the child to represent the cinematic crisis of the now marginal male.

It is not clear, and perhaps not even ascertainable, whether this deployment of the child was adapted from Italian neorealist films, as Bergmann implored. Many of the most famous Italian neorealist films were difficult to see in Germany in these years: *Rome, Open City,* for example, did not go into general distribution in Germany until the mid-1950s. In any case, neorealist films were probably too pessimistic for German filmmakers charged with reconstructing their devastated nation. Many rubble-films subsequently tacked on a happily reconstructive ending, in which children were often reconciled to the lacking patriarch. However, irrespective of their manifest political content, the Italian and German films shared remarkably similar strategies for representing the postwar social and cinematic crisis. They depict the co-constitutive breakdown of the conventional Deleuzian action-image and masculinity, in large part by deploying male children to transform the dominant specular system of the male gaze, the traditional relation to space and setting, and the narrative duel with which narrative films conventionally conclude. Though rubble-films do "reconstruct"—with all its postwar connotations—the male subject by rewriting it back into the patriarchal family, they also (and here the rubble-film is at its most radical) complicate, even dismantle, traditional masculinity. They end up privileging male subjects like Iller or Jürgen who have embraced lack over those who simply ignore it, that is, over the male heroes of the conventional action-image. Even if one cannot establish that these narrative and technical approaches were adapted from Italian neorealism, these shared images reflect parallel sociocinematic situations and filmic strategies for representing and resolving them.

Perhaps most important in this regard was the deliberate staging—real or not—of a break from the cinematic past of the Fascist film industries. The early postwar films in both Italy and Germany sought to go against the grain of what had gone before and demonstrate at least the appearance of a new kind of cinema. Many scholars have theorized what was innovative in the neorealist films, and I hope that this analysis of similarities in the postwar cinemas in Italy and Germany demonstrates an important element in both cinemas: the role of the child in refiguring the masculine action-image. The child functions for both as an "internal enemy," as Ashis Nandy has termed it, that could take the place of the conventional enemy against whom the duel was traditionally arranged.[36] An enemy that was internal afforded an ultimately controllable threat: it offered the grounds for a social critique that at the same time could be managed without fundamental upheaval. Neorealist and rubble-films exposed the contradictions within the dictates of heroic masculinity and the traditional patriarchal family, and deployed these contradictions to critique, dismantle, and reassemble the male subject that serves the family as a cornerstone. Though they inscribe lack into the man, they do not fundamentally recast the family or film form. Even neorealist films execute this kind of immanent critique: they are precisely not revolutionary. They lodge instead a critique from within their prevailing systems, for example, Rossellini's interest in the contradictions within the norms of heroism. And in these social- and filmic-critical, but ultimately not revolutionary, inclinations, the two cinemas shared a great deal.

Notes

1. K. H. Bergmann, "Quo Vadis Italia," *Neue Filmwelt* 3.1 (1947): 5–6. Though *Neue Filmwelt* was published in the Soviet occupational zone—the part of Germany that would become socialist East Germany in 1949—journals from the West similarly called for "realism" at this point. For an example from the English-controlled zone, see Beiermann-Ratjen.

2. For a detailed study of such continuities, see Ruth Ben-Ghiat, "The Fascist War Trilogy" (in Forgacs, Lutton, and Nowell-Smith 30–35), which analyzes Roberto Rossellini's films made during the Fascist regime and argues that Rossellini was, in that period, already experimenting with techniques that came to be described as "realist" in his postwar films.

3. Kaes 12; Elsaesser 250, 252; Fehrenbach 211; Glaser 279; Brandlmeier 34.

4. Brandlmeier 34; Kaes 13; Kreimeier 13. Shandley's recent monograph on the rubble-film—the first one to appear in English—resorts once again to the issue of politics and technique in distinguishing between neorealist and rubble-films. See Shandley 48–49.

5. For critical postures vis-à-vis the rubble-film in this regard, see Brandlmeier 34; Kaes 13. Despite these critiques, it is not true that these films never took up the question of Nazism—in fact, the films engaged with Nazism by self-servingly depicting it in young people.

6. For instance, Geoffrey Nowell-Smith traces Rossellini's elusive politics in his essay "North and South, East and West: Rossellini and Politics," in Forgacs Lutton, and Nowell-Smith 7–19.

7. "Rethinking neorealism from a mechanical formalism to changes in the cultural milieu involves a more flexible understanding of media effects that inhere in the cinematic medium from its inception to the present" (Landy, *Italian Film* 15). Millicent Marcus makes a similar argument when she asserts that neorealism should be considered beyond its technical aspects (23).

8. Deleuze, *Cinema 1* 200–205. Neorealism rests right on the cusp of *Cinema 1* and *Cinema 2*, affording it a uniquely privileged position in his history. See also Deleuze, *Cinema 2*.

9. Fisher.

10. Silverman 2, 47. Much recent film theory has deliberately incorporated masculinity, especially the humiliated and lacking male, into canonical feminist film theory. See Studlar and Shaviro, both of whom foreground "alternative" masculinities in theories of gender in cinema.

11. "The family gave support from below to that respectability which the nation attempted to enforce from above.... The family was supposed to mirror state and society.... Friedrich Ludwig Jahn, the founder of the Gymnasts and the fraternity movement, had called the family the foundation of the national spirit" (Mosse 19–20).

12. Both Robert Moeller and Hermann Glaser describe in great detail the difficulties men had reintegrating into their civilian lives, especially back into the domestic house and family. Moeller cites a number of testimonies from oral histories in which wives considered the return of their husbands "superfluous" (28). Even when there was not such apathy toward the return of the once heralded patriarch, there would often be an inversion in the old provider/provided for relation: "[My returning husband] thought that when he came home, he'd be able to care for us. And instead he had to let me take care of him. He didn't really feel like a man. He suffered because I did everything alone and because he couldn't help me much" (Moeller 29). Women's labor subverted men's provider status; often women's knowledge of the bureaucracy of rationing made men seem ignorant. Another witness testifies even more pointedly to the intersection of sexual difference and work: "[My husband] was afraid to go out, he didn't scrounge, he didn't do anything. I did the work that I had to do as a housewife and mother, but my husband didn't want to do his job, namely getting wood.... I'd rather be alone. I got divorced." The breakdown of the gendered division of labor in the domestic sphere could split that formerly sacred sphere both metaphorically and literally (Glaser 63).

13. Parallel to Silverman's "ideological fatigue" vis-à-vis the dominant fiction, Peter Brunette senses a prevailing "lascivious exhaustion" in *Rome, Open City*, especially in the person of Marina, "that will become generalized onto the whole German people in *Germany, Year Zero*" (*Roberto Rossellini* 46).

14. There was a good deal of debate about how much to show of Manfredi's torture and death, but eventually the voices supporting showing more won out: the torture and death of the film's "hero" became more of a spectacle than was standard in such films. See Gallagher

139 for details of this disagreement between Rossellini and the main writer of *Rome, Open City*, Sergio Amidei. In *Paisan*, there is a similar spectaclarization of the male protagonist's death. In the first episode, the sudden sniper attack on "Joe from Jersey" is shot in slow motion so that the moment of death is augmented. In the final episode of *Paisan*, not only are the partisans killed but they are labeled with large signs declaring them partisans, providing one of the film's most memorable images.

15. For a contemporary critic's negative evaluation of the recurring and often redundant theme of the Heimkehrer, see E. R.

16. For these theories, the male, though (as all subjects) lacking and castrated, remains the constructed site of wholeness and plenty through his denial of lack, his compensation for it via his controlling and desiring position vis-à-vis gender difference. See Laura Mulvey, "Visual Pleasure and Narrative Cinema," *Film Theory and Criticism: Introductory Readings*, ed. Gerald Mast, Marshall Cohen, and Leo Braudy, 4th ed. (New York: Oxford UP, 1992) 751. She and other theorists tend to concentrate on the way in which women are voyeuristically or fetishistically objectified to firm up the juggernaut of male subjectivity.

17. Most influential feminist psychoanalytic film theory emphasizes gender difference as the fundamental difference for language and society and subsequently feature film. See Mulvey 751. Though I do not dispute the superlative nature of these claims, other differences seem pivotal in the construction of patriarchal hierarchies, among them generational difference.

18. A revealing image of dephalliation occurs in *Germany, Year Zero* when Edmund plays a recording of a Hitler speech while the camera pans wildly over the ruins. The voice of the former national-paternal figure drones over an image of utter destruction. The cut to an old man with a boy confused by the disembodied but familiar voice confirms the dismantling of the male subject that ends in generational chaos.

19. Many postwar sociological studies and oral histories document the widespread inversions of traditional gender and parent-child relations: discussions of "half families," "incomplete families," "mother families," and women's "forced emancipation" appear in postwar women's magazines as well as in the studies of leading postwar German sociologists. Moeller 33; Glaser 63.

20. The cinema of the pure optical-sound situation is fundamentally different: "This is a cinema of the seer and no longer of the agent" (Deleuze, *Cinema 2* 2).

21. Rossellini's comments on his technical approach to shooting a scene confirm this deliberate confusion of space: "Usually, in the traditional

film, a scene is composed as follows: a long shot, we see the milieu, the character, we approach it; then a medium shot, a three-quarter view, a close-up; and then the story of the character is told. I proceed in the opposite way: a person moves and his movements make us discover his surroundings. I begin always with a close-up; then the movements of the camera, as it follows the actor, reveal the milieu. The actor must never be left alone; he must move in a complex and comprehensive way" (in Eduardo Bruno, ed., *Teorie e prassi del cinema in Italia, 1950–1970* [Milan: Gabriele Mazzotta, 1972] 42; also in Liehm 69).

22. Marcia Landy has a very useful chapter, "The Landscape and Neorealism, Before and After," on the function of landscape in the narrative in her *Italian Film,* and takes a Deleuzian approach to the refigured relation of character and its cinematic environment (121–48, esp. 133–38).

23. Deleuze, *Cinema 2* 3.

24. Though not writing in a Deleuzian framework, Peter Brunette confirms this altered system of identification in *Germany, Year Zero:* "One *is* emotionally involved in this film, but the relation seems to occur not so much between the spectator and the characters as between the spectator and the film's formal elements, thus enhancing the sense of stylization" (*Roberto Rossellini* 84).

25. See, for instance, Landy's perceptive remarks on *Rome, Open City:* "Though the wanton torture and killing of the priest and the engineer can easily be read as an affirmation of the Italian resistance to political oppression, and though the Nazi behavior can be identified with the unmitigated evil of the Germans, there are many ambiguities and unresolved issues that provide another level of interaction with the film beyond the familiar narrative trajectory. This involves the complexity of Rossellini's style, which makes less determinate and transparent any understanding of motive and action" ("The Landscape and Neorealism" 134). Though she senses that the duel form has been dismantled in the film, she does not link it to the duel form in Deleuze's model.

26. As many critics note, heroism is a recurring theme of Rossellini's war trilogy: Manfredi dispels the concept of the hero in *Rome, Open City; Paisan* problematizes the concept of the hero in the liberating American forces; and in *Germany, Year Zero,* Rossellini said that he wanted to pose a particular question: "The Germans were human beings like everybody else. What could have led them to this disaster? ... the abandoning of humility for the cult of heroism, the exaltation of strength rather than weakness, pride against simplicity." Robert Rossellini, "Dix ans de cinema," part 2, *Cahiers du Cinéma* 52 (Nov. 1955): 5; also in Brunette, *Roberto Rossellini* 76.

27. The film likewise deliberately associates the movement of the children with that of the priest in one of the film's recurring visual gags, the constant genuflecting before the altar in Don Pietro's church. A zone of immobility in a war zone that generally warrants running, the altar constantly interrupts both Don Pietro and the children's movement. It becomes therein a recurring symbol of their compromised agency, literally and figuratively prostrate before the setting.

28. Landy, *Italian Film* 252–53.

29. Peter Brunette is very perceptive on this issue of neorealism's altered system of spectatorial identification, though he does not address the aspect of male humiliation or the child in this system of refigured identification. In his analyses of both *Paisan* and *Germany, Year Zero,* he emphasizes how the films narratively and technically interrupt standard identification. See Brunette, *Roberto Rossellini* 71, 84.

30. For an analysis of the big Other and its role as a third term in the system of specularity, see Žižek 72–77. For Žižek, the gaze is never direct and is always mediated by a third figure. Though I am not convinced of the universality of this model, I would submit that these films deploy the child as this third term in the system of the gaze.

31. The missed or lost duel with the Germans is likewise implied when Antonio and Bruno seek refuge from rain under an overhang they share with a group of German-speaking priests. Both Antonio and Bruno look confused, presumably for different but parallel reasons.

32. L. M.

33. Lenning.

34. Bar scenes in which characters abrogate their positions in the dominant fiction abound in both Italian neorealist and rubble-films; such scenes play key roles in *Bicycle Thief, Obsession,* and *Rome, Open City.* Besides *Somewhere in Berlin* and *Before Us, Life* (1948), Germany's first postwar film, *The Murderers Are among Us,* opens with and returns to a bar in which its protagonist, Mertens, drinks away the painful past.

35. The importance that cigarettes assume in many rubble-films also reflects the dual social and cinematic crisis. What were once the most casual, manipulatable symbols of phallic power—as Richard Klein has explained—now elude the male protagonist. As conduits of power away from the male subject, they become one of the most important postwar units of currency and exchange. While children deal in them—for example, Edmund in *Germany, Year Zero*—adult males often end up staring at them, passively and pensively.

36. Ashis Nandy's seminal study, *The Internal Enemy: Loss and Recovery of Self under Colonialism,* describes a symbolic code that was developed

in the colonies but amounted to a symbolic negotiation between ruler and ruled. Nandy examines not only the well-known racial but also the gendered and generational aspects of the colonial narrative, in which the colonized were both feminized and infantilized. Nandy spends a good half of his groundbreaking essay on the colonial mechanisms of generation and age, and describes how the child functions as just such an "internal enemy" (15–16, 33).

Chapter 2

Aesthetics or Ethics? Italian Neorealism and the Czechoslovak New Wave Cinema

LUBICA UČNÍK

> A man who has no conscience, who doesn't die, who cannot laugh, who is unaware
> of personal responsibility—such a man is of course the perfect unit needed in a
> manipulated, bureaucratically regimented system. In contrast, Man as portrayed by
> Czech culture of the last decade is a potential revolutionary, because he finds life in
> such a manipulated system unbearable.
>
> Kosík 399

According to Mira Liehm, neorealist films were often described in terms
of film consciousness, and despite differences among filmmakers, "all
these artists, one so unlike the other, brought to life a phenomenon with
clearly defined technical and moral components that influenced almost
all subsequent film trends in the West and in the East" (5, 129).[1] Describing the work of Roberto Rossellini, Liehm explains that neorealists
were not concerned with true pictures of facts or slices of life. What they
were interested in was an *impact on the viewer* of a life as represented in
film; neorealism was "a moral weapon aimed at the artistic conventions
of the past" (71). Reality is not an independent, autonomous phenomenon that exists outside representation; it is always a construction of the
filmic text. André Bazin and others argue that the style of neorealism
can be traced to the Soviet montage cinema.[2] Yet neorealists did not aim
to represent life as the people's struggle against the bourgeoisie, as Soviet
filmmakers did, but as the individual's struggle against an overwhelming
reality. As Liehm notes, "Zavattini's theory of the 'necessity to render
facts as they are'" was his recognition that reality is constituted through
"the relationship between men and reality" and is always open to "on-

tological cognition" (73). Instead of concentrating on aesthetic properties of neorealist films or enumerating techniques that supposedly define
neorealism, I will argue that neorealist filmmakers' ethical-political engagement with the everyday (understood not as a mode of aesthetics but
as a method) is their lasting legacy for world cinema, and in particular
for Czechoslovakian cinema.

Critics and filmmakers have persistently questioned neorealism's
"actuality" as a coherent movement.[3] Some critics suggest that neorealist
films were not economically successful and that the aggressive commercial war of images by Hollywood hastened its death.[4] Yet as French nouvelle vague, Czechoslovak New Wave cinema, or, more recently, Iranian
films indicate, neorealism in different guises seems to form a constant
return of the repressed: despite the triumph of Hollywood, dedicated to
the production of films with guaranteed financial return, some filmmakers understand their role to be more than just the production of entertaining and commercially lucrative films. For example, Alistair Whyte
proposes, as Liehm did when speaking of Italian neorealism, that the experimental nature of the Czechoslovak New Wave of the late 1950s and
1960s is ineluctably tied to "serious moral and social problems" (94). He
suggests that filmmakers intermingle humor and tragedy by manipulat-
ing stylistic techniques that create a certain element of fantasy in order
to produce "more serious, more experimental, more socially critical films"
(124). Likewise, Václav Macek claims that in the late 1950s, under the
influence of Italian neorealism with its ideals of social truth, young filmmakers attending the film academy in Prague rejected as lies film sche-
matism and the socialist realism of previous years to assert their right to
authenticity, originality, and a meaningful artistic standpoint. The most
important criteria became truthfulness, the desire to show human emotions, and conflicts rather than class-defined narratives and schematic
sketches. In a certain way, this claim is the same as that made by Liehm
when she argues that Italian neorealism was a moral weapon to be used
against artistic conventions of the past.

One of the attributes of neorealism—from its defining moment in
Italy through the French nouvelle vague, the Czechoslovak New Wave,
and Iranian film, for example—is the creation of a space by and for filmmakers to account for the ethical freedom of the individual in the face
of the overwhelming reality of globalization.[5] In this essay I will look at
Italian neorealism's appropriation by filmmakers of Czechoslovak New
Wave cinema, keeping in mind Simona Monticelli's claim that neorealism is not a singular event but an extension of earlier Italian film pro-

duction. Similarly, Czechoslovak New Wave cinema did not materialize in a vacuum; it was a continuation of a longer literary history beginning in 1898.[6] I will attempt to weave together two stories: one is a kind of history of Czechoslovak cinematic politics; the second is a claim about ethics. I will outline various filmmakers' efforts to negotiate the political reality they faced and their attempts to transfer ethical concerns about the present into their work, following their endeavors through parallels between Italian neorealism and Czechoslovak New Wave cinema.

The point of this essay is not so much to offer a historical account of Czechoslovak cinema or an outline of Czechoslovak New Wave cinema; rather, by comparing Italian neorealism and Czechoslovak New Wave cinema I highlight the importance of art that provokes its public with the possibility that reality is never neutral.

Czecho-Slovakia

Properly speaking, we can locate the Czechoslovak film industry only after World War I. Until 1918, there was no Czechoslovakia. The post–World War I period marks not only the establishment of Czecho-Slovakia but also the beginning of the production of Czecho-Slovak or, rather, Czech films. It was not until 1921 that the first Slovak narrative film, *Jánošík*, was produced, and not by filmmakers from Slovakia but by a Slovak American film company. (Jánošík is the Slovak counterpart to Robin Hood, although Jánošík came from a poor family and was captured and hanged.) The director Jaroslav (Jerry) Siakel and the camera operator Daniel Siakel, Slovak brothers living in America, produced the film in two versions: one with the hero hanged at the end (as Slovak folklore has it), targeted at Czech and Slovak audiences, and a second version—made for American audiences—with a happy ending (Jánošík runs away from the gallows into the mountains with his love and lives happily ever after).[7]

The first Czech encounter with neorealism is found in the book *Náš Film* (Our film) by Luboš Bartošek. According to Bartošek, the film *Šťastnou Cestu* (*Farewell;* 1943), directed by Otakar Vávra, was almost a neorealist drama. He explains that Vávra shot the film at a dynamic pace, reverberating with the everyday tempo of modern life. The narrative was linear, yet, by way of documentary stylistic techniques, the space constantly changed, following the multiple activities of the characters. Bartošek claims that the style of neorealism, if not the name, was already employed by Vávra in the early 1940s.

World War II was "kind" to the Czechoslovak industry, if not by granting freedom of choice where subject matter was concerned, then at least in providing industrial possibilities. Antonín Liehm notes that Germans not only preserved but upgraded the film studio Barrandov. The idea behind this was that Prague would become the film capital of the Third Reich.[8] In 1945, the film industry was nationalized by the government of President Eduard Beneš, which meant that the Slovak film industry, with the help of Czech technicians and specialists, was established in Bratislava. The year 1947 marks another international success for Czechoslovakia. A film produced before the imposition of Andrey Zhdanov's socialist realist formula, *Siréna* (*The Strike*), directed by Karel Steklý, received the Golden Lion—the grand prix of the International Film Festival in Venice.

Also in 1947, in the last democratic election in Czechoslovakia, Communists won control of the government. In 1948 they ousted Beneš and other non-Communists and a single-party government was established. From then on, socialist realism became the only stylistic norm for filmmakers. The new working-class hero was born. In practice, as David Paul explains, it meant that films were about "how disciplined workers overcome imperialist sabotage; interpersonal conflicts that are resolved through the common struggle to fulfill production plans; peasants discovering the virtues of collectivization and so forth" (16). In short, any representation of the personal life of an individual was seen as an attack on the Communist Party. Not only did depiction of contemporary life disappear from film screens, but struggling, feeling, emotional individuals and their personal problems were simply eliminated. The overall outcome of the imposed cultural policies in Czechoslovakia (and other European socialist states) was twofold. According to Paul, films were produced that shunned present-day topics. Instead, films concentrated on famous events of Czech history or portrayed the lives of former Czech public figures. This was a route taken by many filmmakers who wanted to avoid the extremity of the socialist realist prescription. The other route was the socialist realist formula per se, a principle taken from Soviet cultural policy.

In 1946, the Central Committee of the Communist Party of the Soviet Union legislated so-called Zhdanov decrees that reinforced the control of artistic production by the legislative state apparatus. This legislation was simply an extension of Zhdanov's earlier position. In August 1934, the Congress of the Soviet Writers' Union had instituted the doctrine of socialist realism as the only way to depict reality in the Soviet Union. Zhdanov, using Stalin's definition of writers as engineers of human souls, defined the responsibility of a writer or filmmaker as representing reality not in a dead scholastic way, not simply as objective reality, but in its revolutionary development. Zhdanov explained that "the truthfulness and historical concreteness of the artistic portrayal should be combined with the ideological remoulding and education of the toiling people in the spirit of socialism. This method in belles lettres and literary criticism is what we call the method of socialist realism" (in R.S.F.S.R. 21). Martin Ciel—drawing from the journal *Náš Film*—notes that from 1949 on, all photographs from abroad disappeared and strong pro-Soviet and anti-American propaganda began. Hollywood became the leading exemplar of ideological fraudulence, and the socialist realist mode was set as the only mode of artistic expression. Ciel explains that socialist realism's formula was pure and simple—the creative illustration of life. Films could not, under any circumstances, be about life here and now. According to Zhdanov, society was in transition; its interpretation should follow the official line that prescribed the *ideal* society as it would be one day in the very near future (14). In Czechoslovakia, there were some efforts to resist socialist realism and to produce films outside its prescriptive mode, as Alfred Radok's film *Daleká cesta* (*Distant Journey;* 1950) demonstrates. However, the official ideologues labeled the film existentialist, and because of the censorship regulations its screening was blocked.

The situation changed slightly after 1956 when the Twentieth Congress of the Communist Party in the Soviet Union took place. Revelations about the distortion of socialism under Stalin's leadership made many reassess their political conscience and look at the past and present from a different perspective. In Czechoslovakia, struggles between the Soviet-backed old guard holding onto power and new democratic forces among the party's leadership combined with the cultural forces trying to break from socialist realism and its imposed optimism culminated in Prague in the spring of 1968. The path was then cleared for new artistic representation in cinema.

The Film Academy of Music Arts

Neorealism's influence on Czechoslovak filmmakers can be traced to the founding of the Film Academy of Music Arts (FAMU) in Prague on October 25, 1945.[9] It is generally acknowledged that Czechoslovak New Wave cinema was a cinematographic movement made up of mostly young, university-educated (at FAMU) filmmakers reacting to the imposition of a Soviet blueprint of socialist realist form and style. Galina Kopaněvová notes that in the 1960s the most important stimulus for the resurgence of Czechoslovak cinematography came from the Prague film school.[10] At first, the university curriculum stressed the "correct" educational model for new socialist filmmaking,[11] which meant that only some of the films from Soviet montage cinema were shown. The theory of this school was "improved" by Zhdanov's prescriptive formula of socialist realism. In 1950, the first generation of film graduates entered the industry. Kopaněvová praises Vojtech Jasný and Karel Kachyňa for overcoming the indoctrination of the early film school's curriculum based on "illusive, compromised" aesthetics of Zhdanov and for successfully competing with younger graduates, who were spared such didactic practices (22).

Later, as in many other Soviet satellite countries, Italian neorealist cinema was added to the film academy's curriculum.[12] Under the influence of professional filmmakers who taught at the film academy, students evaluated films made in Italy and France, especially works of Italian neorealism, French New Wave cinema, and cinema verité. They were also introduced to works of their Polish counterparts from the Polish Film School. A similar account is given by Jan Žalman mentioning Chaplin, Pudovkin, Fellini, and Truffaut as important inspirations for young cinematographers (*Films and Film-makers* 18). In light of stringent restrictions imposed on foreign films that originated from capitalist countries, Italian neorealist films were allowed by the party because of their ability to serve as examples of the deprived life of the proletariat living under capitalism. According to this logic, Italian neorealist films revealed the unethical capitalist exploitation of the masses to lucky workers living under socialism (Žalman, "Umlčený Film, Part 5" 385).

To return to the claim of neorealists that there is no "neutral reality" independent of representation, we can see how the films' meaning can be read differently. For the party's representatives, Italian neorealism revealed the corruption of the capitalist mode of production. Not so for the young filmmakers. For them, neorealism offered a way to present "socialist reality" critically, without the glossy promise of a bright future. As Mira Liehm suggests, "Neorealism holds a special place in the development of East European cinema. In the mid-fifties, its influence in Hungary, Poland, and Czechoslovakia was crucial, merging with the endeavour of these productions to free themselves from Stalinist aesthetics" (131). For the students of the film academy, neorealism represented the ethical-political possibility of an engagement with the everyday. Thanks to the film practitioners cum pedagogues—such as Milan Kundera, Elmar Klos, Otakar Vávra, and Otomar Krejča— the school offered critical and not demagogic evaluation of films. Macek also reminds us that A. M. Brousil invited well-known film practitioners to speak to students; unofficial visits by Cesare Zavattini, Giuseppe de Santis, and others were the rule rather than the exception (15–16). Later on, students were also exposed to many Western films produced and sent to Prague to be sold. Most of these films were never bought—shielding the population from the "vicious propaganda" of the West—but students saw them in the specially organized projections for study purposes only and engaged in critical discussions afterward.[13] Hence, the future filmmakers of the New Wave drew their inspirations from Italian neorealism, Soviet montage cinema, French nouvelle vague, and cinema verité.[14]

Patrick Cattrysse writes that "the Czech New Wave . . . shows formal analogies with . . . Italian neorealism and with the French New Wave movement . . . [and] a *cinema verité* style. [Films were] generally shot on location. They used natural light and nonprofessional actors who often spoke improvised dialogues" (229). According to Macek, filmmakers enthusiastically adopted Italian neorealist theoretical aspiration in order to portray people's everyday lives. Films ceased to represent the ideal picture of society and began to show reality, including all the problems people encountered daily. Macek poetically writes that "the spark from Italian Neorealism lighted a small flame that was starting to warm up" (13–14).[15]

Italian Neorealism and Czechoslovak Cinema

The similarities between the situation in Italy after World War II and in Czechoslovakia after 1956 give credence to Bazin's observation that "neorealism is [neither] the exclusive property of any one ideology nor even of any one ideal" (87). In the case of Italy, Monticelli argues that "Neo-Realist films provided an immediate response to the desire to wipe out the material and ideological legacies of fascism" (in Bazin 71), while in the Czechoslovak context, Mira Liehm reinforces Monticelli's claim, pointing out that "the neorealist experience . . . symbolized the yearning for truth and freedom that obsessed the East European filmmakers as much as the early neorealists" (131). As mentioned above, in the case of Italy the postwar situation prompted a search for new values and, in the case of Czechoslovakia, this search was triggered by the Twentieth Congress of the Communist Party in the Soviet Union.

Miloš Fiala explains that the Twentieth Congress and its revelations allowed a distinction between socialism and its distortion by the Stalinist cult of personality. Revelations prompted filmmakers to reassess their experience, revealing at the same time the moral conflict of the period (62–63). Hence Italian postwar experience reverberates in Czechoslovakia. Rossellini can be used here to extend this qualification. The period after World War II prompted Rossellini to confront moral and emotional uncertainties of the time. Alfonso Procaccini suggests that historical circumstances force the writer (or filmmaker) to ask different questions, and through this process compel a redefinition of one's relationship to society. The important point for Procaccini is that neorealism is not only a manifestation of a subjective state, but "a disclosure which exposed a particular objective reality" while directing viewers' attention toward a specific social issue and voicing, "even if indirectly, a judgment on that reality" (43, 5). Thus in both cases, in Italy's prewar as well as postwar situation and in Czechoslovakia in the late 1950s and early 1960s, there was a need to reexamine the question: What is reality? For Italian and Czechoslovak filmmakers, the question belonged more to the ethical-political category than to the aesthetic one. In a similar vein, Bazin argued that "neorealism is more an ontological position than an aesthetic one" (66). Likewise, in 1974, Lino Miccichè said that "Neorealism was 'an ethics of aesthetics.' It was the answer of a generation of filmmakers to the question asked by Vittorini: 'Shall we ever have a culture capable of protecting people against suffering instead of just comforting them?'" (in M. Liehm 129). Thus, as Bruce Hinrichs observes, "the realist concept was purposely altered and reconceived . . . to portray the personal, emotional truth experienced in the everyday lives of ordinary people . . . [and strove to represent] . . . some fundamental truth of the human condition" (9).

To follow the comparison between the two countries, in Czechoslovakia the partial revelation concerning Stalin's policies was also a question of personal conscience (Škvorecký 45). Žalman speaks of works that raised social and moral questions and thus addressed themselves to the public conscience (*Films and Film-makers* 18). Films such as *Tři přání* (*Three Wishes;* [1958]) and *Smrt' sa volá Engelchen* (*Death Is Called Engelchen;* [1963]) by Ján Kadár and Klos represented a reaction against and denunciation of the archetypal worker struggling with class enemies. They represented a shift toward the representation of idiosyncratic individuals and their personal problems. Film narratives were altered from a prescription of an ideal life to a personal depiction of people struggling with their mundane chores. As Siegfried Kracauer observed, "[W]hen history is made in the streets, the streets tend to move onto the screen." Echoing Bazin's view that ideology is not the exclusive property of a certain style, Kracauer stresses that neorealist narratives serve to dramatize social conditions in general (*Theory of Film* 98–99). Žalman points out that Kadár and Klos frequently emphasized that "the only art . . . is art concerned with the key problems of the time, art that adopts a frank moral and social standpoint" (*Films and Film-makers* 17).

For Kadár and Klos, films cancel out the view of art that had dominated the socialist world under Stalinism. The point is not to withdraw from society to the imagined life of the individual existing as a self-subsisting atom; the aim of filmmakers is to help strengthen man's faith in common sense, in moral certitudes, in the permanent values of truth and life. The focus *is* on the individual, but it is his life as embedded in society where he must confront his choices as always choices informed by his responsibility toward oneself and the society in which he lives. Concerning man's relationship to society, Žalman notes, the purpose of the individual's actions concerns "not 'whether' but 'how' to become committed" (*Films and Film-makers* 17–18).[16] Žalman explains that the link connecting films made by Kadár and Klos, for example, is "the morally philosophical theme of compromise" ("Umlčený Film, Part 5" 201). Thus the film *Obchod na Korze* (*The Shop on Main Street*), made in 1965 and directed by Kadár and Klos, can serve as an example of the ethical dilemma of responsibility that an individual potentially faces.[17] The overall framework in which the story unfolds is World War II and the context arising from the Nazi Nuremberg racial laws. The Nazi era comes to represent an authoritarian government. The historical setting allows the filmmakers to explore freely contemporary society and the moral predicaments faced by people living under totalitarianism.

Different stylistic methods are employed to highlight the central theme of ethical responsibility.[18] The opening scene of the film is constructed as a montage of various motifs that are developed throughout the plot. Accordingly, the opening shot relates to the last scene in the film. While in the first scene, a stork seems to dance and fly as he wishes, in the last scene, faced with the ethical impasse caused by a Jewish shop owner's unintended murder, the protagonist, Tono, hangs himself. Another motif is the subjective point of view (POV) shot. The first scene is constructed as the stork's POV taken from the high, sharp angle revealing prisoners walking in a castle yard and then panning over city roofs to show people promenading on the main street. It is as though we are encouraged to see that we all are prisoners of some sort of order.

The Shop on Main Street (Ján Kadár, Elmar Klos, 1965)

This high, sharp angle shot is repeated and varied throughout the film. The first repetition occurs in Tono's living room—the family dinner with Kolkocký. It is thus related to the opening shot, the supposed POV of the stork. Thus the scene of the family dinner is designed to show, by inference, that Tono is the prisoner of the family order and, in a larger context, a prisoner of political order as well, since his brother-in-law is the commander of Hlinka's guards, which makes him the head of the city. The shot is taken from a high, sharp angle, later used in connection with long shots, denoting Tono's subjective POV when he is not sure about himself, as, for example, in the shop he comes to appropriate as the new "Aryan" owner. His moral conscience causes him to feel uncomfortable with the role into which he was forced by his wife. He simply does not know what to say to Mrs. Lautmanová, the Jewish owner of the shop.

An interesting variation of this motif takes place at the end of the film. In front of the shop, the Nazis are rounding up Jews destined for a work camp. At this moment, Lautmanová suddenly sees what is happening outside the shop and realizes the implication of the Jews waiting for transportation. Here the same angle is used but this time as *her* subjective POV. Her lack of knowledge compels her to scream, "Tono, what is going on? I don't understand!" Terrified, Tono tries to stop her. The problematic nature of responsibility he felt toward her until then turns into panic for his own life. The final moral decision seems to be out of Tono's control.

The Shop on Main Street (Ján Kadár, Elmar Klos, 1965)

Tono's relief when the Jews are taken away turns to horror when he unlocks the door of a cellar into which he pushed Lautmanová. She does not respond to his calls. A high, sharp angle implies Tono's subjective POV as Lautmanová's dead body is revealed. Marked by her Jewishness, Lautmanová can be free only when her soul leaves the body. The angle never levels (as has happened in all previous variations of this motif) as if to suggest that this time, there is no way back. Tono's moral potential is exhausted. At the same time a connection with the opening scene is established and foreclosed: a soul trapped in a body (like a bird closed in a cage) is able to fly free like a bird only when it frees itself from the "prison" of the body. The angle motif is concluded in the same scene when Tono, sitting on the chair in Lautmanová's bedroom, is framed from above, with a high, sharp angle, for the last time. By this time, his inner war and indecision have ended. The camera suggests that perhaps it is Lautmanová's soul (finally free) that looks down on him. The film closes with a dream sequence. Tono's dance with Lautmanová in front of people is only possible after death. Her Jewishness and his "Aryanism" were incompatible. Only death gave them freedom.[19]

The film is structured around Tono, an atypical hero who talks to us through a struggle with his conscience as he faces everyday moral questions.[20] The film does not offer answers but presents the everyday life of this antihero trapped in the totalitarian order by showing that moral decisions are not heroic choices that take us outside the mundane level of our lives. On the contrary, they are accumulations of banal, everyday events, never significant in themselves. And this non-conclusion is prefigured when various protagonists (like the Jew Katz, when he receives a summons to go to the camp; Lautmanová, when she sees most of her friends summoned outside the shop; and Tono on a few occasions) simply state, "I do not understand." It is left up to viewers to engage with the film's meaning and to face the ethical possibilities that we can miss, as did Tono. The filmic reality is presented to viewers not as a fait accompli, not as something that simply mirrors the existing world. It is up to viewers to make sense of Tono's ethical dilemma.

In a parallel endeavor, as Rossellini suggests, "neorealism involves a greater interest in individuals . . . through the investigation of reality" in order to "reach an understanding of things, and to give them their true value" (in M. Liehm 137). Italian neorealist filmmakers as much as New Wave cinematographers strove to produce films that would present reality anew; the film simultaneously will reveal and compel spectators to get involved with the social and ethical issues explored. Czechoslovak filmmakers—as much as those in Italy after the war—recognizing spectators' involvement in the text's construction of meaning, attempted to face up to ethical issues that confronted people in their respective political circumstances.[21] Procaccini suggests that neorealism "serves a double function: to be diagnostic as much as prognostic. . . . To bridge the two is to form a political consciousness" (52–53). In the end, the ideal achievement of this new art will be when the film's ending prompts viewers to engage in a new understanding of the world around them. It was precisely this possibility of critique triggered by new artistic expressions that the old-new communist guards feared the most. As Liehm and Liehm argue, "[E]very advance, every experiment, as well as any attempt to establish contact with native or European artistic tradition of the twentieth century, was considered to be an expression of opposition and rebellion—and in effect, really was" (231).

Dirty Linen

We can see here another parallel between the Italian and Czechoslovak experiences: films that answer the question "What is reality?" by suggesting that it is all around us, embodied in the small problems we struggle with every day and in the authorities who reject this idea. In 1949, the Italian government's response to a neorealist vision of reality was a censorship law for films. This so-called *legge Andreotti* withheld financial support from the state and severely limited production of films representing struggling people in Italy. Neorealist films were blamed for "washing dirty linen in public" and for "slandering Italy abroad." Giulio Andreotti wrote an open letter to Vittorio De Sica, demanding that he "assume his social responsibility, which cannot be limited to a description of the poverty and abuses of a system" (in M. Liehm 57, 91). Similar charges were laid against filmmakers in Czechoslovakia.

In February 1959, the First Film Festival of Czechoslovak Films opened in Banská Bystrica. Contrary to general expectations, the occasion was used by the government to publicly criticize and condemn certain trends in Czechoslovak cinema, especially films that attempted to look critically at socialist praxis. This event marked the strongest criticism of the cinema by the Communist Party since 1948. The official speaker asked a number of rhetorical questions, such as, "What are the themes of our films, which should talk about contemporary society?" (in Fiala 68). Josef Škvorecký explains that Václav Kahuda, the minister of culture, blamed directors because they represented themes taken almost exclusively from private life that were not sufficiently optimistic. Moreover, reminiscent of Andreotti's accusations, Kahuda mourned that films showed "contemporary settings exclusively among old decrepit tenements, where life goes on in corridors and dirty flats" (in Škvorecký 60).[22] Andreotti would have been delighted to hear Kahuda's indictment and condemnation. In particular, according to Škvorecký, Kahuda condemned the impact of Italian neorealism. As far as the Communist Party was concerned, it was one thing to approve films that reveal the exploitation of people in capitalist countries but quite another to apply the same treatment to the socialist society of Czechoslovakia. In conclusion, Kahuda asked the question, "When will we see our positive, proletarian, contemporary hero, political and public worker in our cinemas? How will our film help to change life for the better; how will film help to enrich our citizens with ideals, morals, and aesthetic values?" (Fiala 68). Thus, Italian neorealism turned out to be a blessing as much as a curse for Czechoslovak filmmakers.

Clearly, the party's moral and political ideals were incompatible with those of filmmakers. The speaker (and the party) called for a continuation of, or rather a return to, the socialist realism that had dominated cinema screens since 1948. Again the call was for cutout, bright-eyed heroes who change history and build socialism, whose only problem was figuring out how to fulfill the five-year plan and produce more steel than any other country in the world. Socialist heroes had no personal problems; in fact, they had no personal lives at all. Here the personal was always tied to Stakhanov's ideal; an imaginary representation of society not yet here but coming soon: the "land, where tomorrow already means yesterday."[23] The only problem with the present (1959) was that tomorrow seemed a long way off and yesterday was the Twentieth Congress. Given this state of affairs, Škvorecký reminds us that because of the revelations of the Twentieth Congress, charges against filmmakers could not be formulated any longer as "intentional enmity, or of plotting schemes injurious to socialism; [and] the Jews, [directors] Kadár and Jasný [could not be conveniently] accused of a Zionist plot; and even the well-worn CIA failed to get into speeches." All in all, two main culprits were identified: the Italian neorealist formula, wrongly applied to an otherwise bright socialist life, and "the remnants of bourgeois thought, represented by Yugoslav revisionism" (62). Clearly, Zavattini's method of rendering facts as they are was dangerous when applied to representations of Czechoslovak life. The party was interested only in "ideal" facts, how things would ideally be sometime in the future. As Škvorecký notes, "the socialist-realist critics tolerated [neorealism] in Italian films, but were allergic to it in Czech cinema" (44).

Unlike the Italian situation, criticism was not the end of the affair in Czechoslovakia. In Italy, Andreotti could refuse to give money to film production and the Andreotti laws could make foreign distribution of certain films difficult, if not impossible. In Czechoslovakia, however, at least until a regime change, the party could outlaw already produced films forever. The film *Tři přání* (*Three Wishes;* 1958), directed by Kadár and Klos, was singled out and banned because of its "nihilism, petty bourgeois scepticism and defeatism" (Fiala 68).[24] Films such as *Tři přání, Zde jsou lvi* (*Here Are Lions;* Václav Krška, 1958), *Konec jasnovidce* (*The End of a Clairvoyant;* Vladimír Svitáček, 1958), and *Hvězda jede na jih* (*The Star Goes to South;* Oldřich Lipský, 1958) were prohibited and withdrawn from distribution. Furthermore, Kadár and Klos could not work in the film industry for the next two years. Reorganization at the top level of the Barrandov film studio followed, and censorship was reinforced through the so-called autocensorship of an author. As Žalman observes, "Nobody seems to wonder why this young generation was blamed and punished; the generation, which grew up and was educated during the socialist era, which knew and experienced only the socialist system and further on, never looked for solutions to the problems beyond this system, but always within it" ("Umlčený Film, Part 1" 146). As a result of the First Film Festival of Czechoslovak Films and the criticism of the film industry by the Communist Party and government officials, cinema was thrown back to the optimistic socialist realism era.

In the first half of the 1960s, the struggle reopened with the party still managing to keep films from the domestic market using censorship regulations and its bureaucratic apparatus. Although censorship became less stringent, there was one final act of conspicuous open interference by the party, which resulted in the condemnation of films by Jan Němec and Ewald Schorm and prohibitions on the distribution of *O slavnosti a hostech* (*The Party and the Guests;* Němec, 1965) and *Každý den odvahu* (*Courage for Every Day;* Schorm, 1964). In January 1968, Alexander Dubček came to power and on March 1, 1968, censorship was lifted. Media openly engaged in debates about freedom, democracy, and "socialism with a human face." Films locked in the party's vault were released but not for long. On August 21, 1968, all this came to an end. The invasion of Czechoslovakia by the armies of the Warsaw Pact ended artistic freedom. It took another year, but the ensuing normalization process—that is, the reintroduction of censorship and the reapplication of the Soviet model with central power over the economy, politics, and culture—became facts of life in Czechoslovakia until the Velvet revolution in 1989. These events meant the end of Czechoslovak New Wave cinema. Many filmmakers of the New Wave, such as Věra Chytilová, Miloš Forman, Juraj Herz, Jaromil Jireš, Juraj Jakubisko, Jiří Menzl, Němec, and Schorm, were forbidden to make films, while others chose to leave Czechoslovakia. Among those who left were Forman, Herz, Němec, and Schorm. Alternately, some turned to the realm of fairy tales for children.

Czechoslovak New Wave cinema attempted to do what Liehm suggests Rossellini did when he finished *Rome, Open City* in 1945. According to her, "Rossellini already saw film as an instrument of a modern vision, a way of seeing things '*with one's own eye*'" (63, italics added). I suggest that it is this idea—to represent life through one's own eyes and challenge moral and political complacency—that Czechoslovak filmmakers appropriated from Italian neorealism. They attempted to formulate new ways of understanding reality.[25] They endeavored to challenge their audiences to face up to the moral and political landscape of their lives. The message of the New Wave cinema was enunciated as an ever-present need to confront the everyday in order to lead meaningful lives. This is what Italian neorealism attempted for the first time in film, and it is this heritage that is taken up anew by filmmakers whenever reality needs to be renegotiated.

Notes

1. See also Sorlin, "Neorealism."
2. See Bazin 42; M. Liehm 5–6. See also Nichols, who writes, "constructivist art, Soviet montage theory, and the European avant-garde stood in accord: the world as it offers itself to us provides the starting point for both political and aesthetic acts of transformation" (596; see also nn. 21, 38, 53).
3. See, for example, M. Liehm; Sorlin, "Neorealism"; and Furhammar and Isaksson (especially 87–92). For a critical appraisal, see Deleuze, *Cinema 2* 1–6. For a critical account of literary neorealism, see Procaccini.
4. See Mattelart, "European Film Policy" in Hill and Gibson.
5. Richard Corliss—noting the influence of "Italian postwar neorealism"—writes that "Iran is today's one great national cinema. Not since the Czech New Wave of the mid-60s has a country made such a lovely noise at the big festivals and in Western capitals. . . . Directors Abbas Kiarostami (*A Taste of Cherry*), Jafar Panahi (*The White Balloon*) and . . . Mohsen Makhmalbaf (*Gabbeh*) are . . . revered in the world of film" (85).
6. See Bartošek; Škvorecký 54ff; Whyte 91ff.
7. Bartošek. See also Brož.
8. See Piech 38; A. Liehm, *Closely Watched Films* 84; Liehm and Liehm 26–27.
9. M. Liehm 6. The importance of film education to the success of filmmaking can be traced to the first film school, the Soviet State Film School, which was established in 1919. The formation of an Italian film school in 1934 in Rome had a similar effect. The school graduates included Roberto Rossellini, Michelangelo Antonioni, Giuseppe De Santis, and Luigi Zampa.
10. See M. Liehm 6; Kopaněvová 22. For a different reading, see Hames 81.
11. See Kučera.
12. Iordanova writes, "The stylistic influences over Balkan cinema can be located mostly within Europe—the Italian Neorealism and the French *Nouvelle Vague.* . . . The visual style, however, was mostly influenced by the dynamic camerawork seen in Czech cinema of the 1960s, and by the elaborately staged takes of directors such as Hungarian Milkos Jancso and Russian Andrei Tarkovsky, as well as by the tableau-style of Georgian Sergei Paradjanov" (23–24).
13. See A. Liehm, *Closely Watched Films*; A. Liehm, "Miloš Forman"; Liehm and Liehm; Macek 15–16; Žalman, *Films and Film-makers*; Škvorecký.

14. See, for example, Ciel 18; Trančík; Brož 54.
15. Bazin and Gilles Deleuze claim that Italian neorealism also influenced the French nouvelle vague; I will concentrate only on Italian neorealism's impact on Czechoslovak filmmakers.
16. The idea that ethical norms can be derived unproblematically from the social life of the community had already been questioned by Hegel. It follows then that in the absence of the prescribed mode of the good and virtuous life, it is the question of responsibility that comes to the fore. The "ethics of responsibility," to use Adorno's expression, becomes linked to an individual's acting in the world. This moral attitude of an individual forged by taking up different options is the theme running through these films.
17. The film received an Academy Award in the foreign film category in 1965.
18. The treatment of the story is a mixture of Kafkaesque desperation with the satirical undertones of Hašek.
19. In his first dream sequence, while still alive, he does not dare promenade with her in public.
20. If the narrative of the film had been couched in a socialist realism mode, Tono would have acquired a proletarian consciousness and engaged in an underground struggle against the Nazi occupants with other unsatisfied workers, probably sacrificing his life for his country and Communist ideals along the way.
21. For a discussion of the spectator's activity in reading film text, see Kracauer, *Theory of Film* 308–09. See also Bordwell, *Narration;* Bordwell and Thompson; Sobchack.
22. See also Fiala 67–68.
23. This quote refers to the title of a book about the Soviet Union in which changes happen so quickly that the tomorrow of other countries is a yesterday in the Soviet Union.
24. Most condemned the film without actually seeing it. See Fiala; Škvorecký.
25. Some of these directors and their films include Věra Chytilová: *Pytel blech* (*A Bagful of Fleas;* 1962), *O něčem jiném* (*Something Different;* 1963), *Sedmikrásky* (*Daisies;* 1966); Miloš Forman: *Černý Petr* (*Peter and Pavla;* 1963), *Lásky jedné plavovlásky* (*Loves of a Blonde;* 1965), *Hoří má panenko* (*Firemen's Ball;* 1967); Juraj Herz: *Spalovač mrtvol* (*Cremator;* 1968); Elo Havetta: *Slávnosť v botanickej záhrade* (*The Party in the Botanical Garden;* 1969); Juraj Jakubisko: *Kristove roky* (*Crucial Years;* 1967), *Zbehovia a pútnici* (*Deserters and Pilgrims;* 1968), *Vtáčkovia, siroty a blázni* (*Birds, Orphans and Fools;* 1968); Ján Kadár and Elmar Klos: *Smrť sa volá Engelchen* (*Death Is Called*

Engelchen; 1963), *Obžalovaný* (*The Accused;* 1964), *The Shop on Main Street* (1965); Jiří Menzl: *Ostře sledované vlaky* (*Closely Watched Trains;* 1966), *Skřivánci na niti* (*Skylarks on a String;* 1970); Jan Němec: *O slavnosti a hostech* (*The Party and the Guests;* 1966); Evald Schorm: *Každý den odvahu* (*Courage for Every Day;* 1964), *Návrat straceného syna* (*Return of the Prodigal Son;* 1966), *Farářův Konec* (*The End of a Priest;* 1968); Štefan Uher: *Slnko v sieti* (*Sunshine in a Net;* 1962), Organ (*The Organ;* 1963).

Chapter 3

In the Mirror of an Alternative Globalism: The Neorealist Encounter in India

MOINAK BISWAS

While many third world "national cinema" traditions have been cata-lyzed by a dialogue with Italian neorealism, in the Indian case, historians have seen the experience of neorealism as somewhat radical—they have associated it with a break with tradition. The actual encounter has a date, 1952, the year of the first International Film Festival, which brought a clutch of neorealist films to India. That we also put a date to the realist break in Indian cinema follows from a similar logic. Satyajit Ray made his first film, *Pather Panchali*, in 1955. It was and still is largely seen as a departure from Indian film traditions. Its realism is sometimes thought to have heralded the true form of cinema in India, establishing a modern practice in a medium that had been functioning until then under pre-modern compulsions. The criticism that made this distinction between realism and conventional forms of cinema in India—one that extended into a distinction between "art" and "popular" cinema—appeared around the release of Ray's film. Although a modern form of criticism seems necessary to make such a distinction, one finds that this type of theo-retical discourse is older than *Pather Panchali*. It is crucial for a reread-ing of Indian film history, somewhat indelibly marked by the distinction in question, to remember that the discourse did not necessarily emerge from the minority cineaste sector but from mainstream film criticism.

Pather Panchali established as a fully formed aesthetic what was only partially operative in earlier Indian cinema, that is, the realist textual principle. The success of this aesthetic was measured in terms of its abil-ity to free itself of impulses characteristic of traditional Indian cinema—textual heterogeneity, lack of individuation, nonsecular narrative logic, and the predominance of spectacle over narrative. After *Pather Pan-chali,* these same impulses were associated with popular cinema. A "world cinema standard" has often been invoked by Indian critics with respect to Ray's contribution. However, the creative method that connected a local (and minority) practice to world cinema has often also been associated with methods of a national cinema. In discussions of Italian neorealism the idea of national cinema is of major conceptual importance. As Franco Venturini pointed out in an important essay, Italian film criticism between 1940 and 1943 could be seen as laying the basis of neorealism in envisioning a "national" style, "the style to be formed" (in Overbey 171–78). According to Venturini the idea of national style was meant to connect Italian cinema, lost in the mire since the demise of the early regional styles, to the mature realism developed in French, German, and British cinemas in the 1930s. But creating a national cinema also meant reclaiming a national landscape for the screen—destroying the veil of lies that covered the domain of representation during the Fascist rule, collecting details of a ruined map as well as the trivia of the everyday life that was supposed to defy the rupture imposed by Fascism. This was the ethical ground that naturalism occupied for the moment, the organic source of an aesthetic which, in the words of Cesare Zavattini, showed not the abstract "historical man" but the "real . . . hidden man who acted," the anonymous humanity of a nation who now have to appear with "first and last names" (in Overbey 68, 72).

The contours of a national Indian cinema then became visible through the encounter with another national cinema, one not much removed in time. The encounter proved all the more creative since neither was a crystallized tradition; both were historically localized, largely amorphous projects, taking root in a medium that appeared to be free of the weight of age-old conventions.[1] At this point the contention about the realist narrative being exogenous in relation to Indian traditions, a point often made in postcolonial criticism, has to be freed from the binary distinction of tradition and modernity. If the modern critical discourse launched in the 1950s upheld realist Indian cinema as the expression of modernity against the so-called backward practices of popular cinema, the criticism that succeeded it in India (following the decline of art cinema itself) has expressed skepticism about the very authenticity of the realist enterprise. Realism's historical implication in the production of a national form is seen in terms of its collusion with nationalism as ideology, rendering modernity itself somewhat unauthentic as a project. This is part of a general critique of modernity that addresses the prob-

Pather Panchali
(Satyajit Ray,
1955)

lem of modern forms in non-Western societies. Along with (and often as a formal ground to) nationalism, the nation-state, discourses of secularism, science, and development, narrative form has been targeted critically. For example, it is possible to see the realism inaugurated by Ray as ideologically implicated in the same project of modernization that the Nehruvian regime in India is identified with. This criticism, serious in intent, has found an echo in the populist position on Indian cinema that is getting increasing international attention. The populist critic presents a certain model of Hindi film as the authentic Indian film; its resistance to realism is presented as a matter of ethnic difference.

What can the historical event of the encounter with neorealism tell us about this problem? In as much as authenticity is measured against the difference from globalized norms, it should be remembered that the model Ray and his contemporaries found in the Italian films was itself a reaction against such norms. There is nothing "neo" in neorealism, critics often argued; but one way of justifying the appellation is to point to its difference from the realism enshrined in Hollywood. Neorealism was forced to remain a minority cinema in Italy, and its popular success was limited compared to that of American films that flooded the market after the war and to the Italian home production that followed the commercial logic of Hollywood. Thus one might point to the overlap between the editing styles of *Bicycle Thief* (1948) and the Hollywood classical film,[2] but such analytic procedure does not explain why the generic divide between the two cannot be bridged, why the globalized grammar of Hollywood would resist some of the basic principles of neorealism. India, like many third-world countries, negotiated its cinematic modernity through the connection with a practice that socially extended bourgeois realism into a domain of reality that the latter disavows.[3] An internally conflicted model of cultural modernity is needed to put such transactions in perspective, where borrowing is seen not in terms of a binary of West and non-West but in terms of a global movement that acts against the globalization of ossified commercial forms. As the Indian realists of the 1950s entered into a dialogue with Italian cinema they shared an internationalist project built on the basis of local enterprises.

If Italian neorealists were rearticulating the novelistic tradition dating from Giovanni Verga and Alessandro Manzoni, the Indian realists were forging a link with the Indian novel of the twentieth century. Realism and its pervasive embodiment, the novelistic discourse, are formations that a modern society must negotiate. Rather than measuring their authenticity for a non-Western culture, it is more worthwhile to study the specific results yielded by the importation of modes such as the novel or the perspective system of image-making in that culture. The literary critic Franco Moretti has suggested that a "world-system" of literature can be imagined in terms of the novel emerging from the center in the West and taking on various shapes on the semi-periphery and periphery.[4] Such a systemic view will yield, he believes, a conception of the novel which in its "original" form is hardly found outside England and France. The world-system of the novel is "one and unequal," but inequality also means a predominance of the non-ideal form of the novel fostered by the difference that capitalist modernity encounters in its own global utopian expansion. Without a concept of the ideal form (or the paradigm), however, it would be impossible to map difference. It has been argued that in non-Western societies nonmodern modes of narrative and subjectivity have informed the novel, but these local histories of literature will also record the coming of a novelistic break, when such modes will be framed within the novelistic discourse as embodiments of difference.[5]

It becomes necessary to imagine a realist paradigm of cinema that will encompass moments of classical and neorealist narration since both have demonstrated an ability to spread globally, albeit with different ideological momentum and effects. The encounter with realism was radical enough to transform the whole field of Indian cinema. A new popular film emerged around the same time that the new realist cinema arrived. It incorporated neorealist elements even as it launched an advanced dialogue with Hollywood—the 1950s films of Raj Kapoor and Guru Dutt are good examples. The Indian critic Madhava Prasad has connected the distinction between the two modes of realism with the idea of representing a national space in the following way: nationalist realism falls within the project of the state trying to represent the nation. The land and the people make up the substance of this realism, a substance that is organized into narrative by the "vertical" gaze of the state as it were, not so much by a principle immanent in the substance itself. Realist cinemas of peripheral modernities, where the state undertakes the modernization of society, would bring together diverse life worlds or semiotic orders into one narrative working through a metanarrative positioned above the represented material. The realism identified with Hollywood, on the other hand, arises not so much at the level of the political but at the level of a social reality that is considered desacralized, contractual, and runs on the basis of a uniform law.[6]

For Prasad, the new cinema of the 1970s, especially the films of Shyam Benegal, exemplify the kind of nationalist realism mentioned here. But this type of social theory of form—where the form's own history is provisionally kept out of critical purview—poses problems when applied to the years around 1955, when something like a realist encounter seems to inform the transformation of Indian cinema as a whole. Fundamental distinctions have to be made between the cinema represented by Ray and the popular form represented by many others, and one distinction can be drawn along the lines suggested by Prasad. While the neorealist impulse is stronger in the former kind, Hollywood realism forms the dominant horizon of realist negotiations for the latter. The popular film is characterized by a heteronomy of addresses, but so far as it functions as a modern narrative mode it works primarily with elements drawn from Hollywood realism. The problem, however, appears when the question of continuity of forms is posited. It becomes necessary then to see the realist break visible in *Pather Panchali* in relation to a dynamics in the *Social* film dating back to the early 1940s on the one hand, and in relation to the Indian novel on the other. In order to make a link between *Pather Panchali* and earlier realist narratives, one needs to bring back a general conception of realism—a paradigm that helps one read a certain process theoretically as a realist negotiation.

There are parallels between the popular optimism of the postwar national reconstruction that formed a backdrop to the Italian experiment and the postindependence fervor of national reconstruction in India. It has been noted that a political climate of consensus supports the kind of humanist realist project that emerged in these contexts. In the Italian case it was the consensual legacy of the Resistance that was sustained through the 1940s and went into decline after the coalition of the Christian Democrats and the Communists broke up. In India the period of early reconstruction under the leadership of Nehru was one in which the hopes of nation building, of development, could produce a coalition of sorts between ideologically divergent groups. The limitations of such a consensus are well known, just as the limitations of the humanism they tend to produce are. Ray is a good example of the crisis that his brand of humanism faced when disidentification with the nation-building project became widespread, when a new political language of dissent appeared in the mid-1960s. He found it increasingly difficult to fashion a response to the radical and violent apprehension of the present that imposed itself on the contemporary artist.

One of the most exhaustive critiques of the humanism form within Italian neorealism came from Mario Canella. The anti-Fascist consensus in Italy, often characterized as the popular front aesthetic in art, was an expedient strategy. It ultimately led to a compromise with the bourgeoisie since it continued to speak in terms of defending "civilization" and "culture" against Fascist barbarism, giving up on the critique of the very culture in question. But Canella was astute enough to direct his criticism not so much against neorealist cinema as against neorealist criticism, against the model of cinema emerging through a certain critical discourse. By the mid-1930s, international affiliation became an articulate program for the Indian arts. As the Indian writers organized themselves into an anti-Fascist and anticolonial movement in 1936 (through the Progressive Writers' Association), they gave themselves an agenda that echoed the Dimitrov thesis. They sought to extend the progressive, rationalist trends in nationalist culture into a critical and socialist direction. Realism was conceived of as an ethic that could oversee this "progress." The movement largely merged into the Anti-Fascist Writers' and Artists' Association formed in the wake of the Nazi invasion of the Soviet Union. The consensus was now more openly negotiated on the basis of the united front of nationalists and Communists against Fascism and imperialism that Dimitrov suggested. In 1943, the leaders of these earlier organizations founded the Indian

People's Theatre Association (IPTA). It lent its name to a movement that in the next ten years or so would directly or indirectly influence almost every important artist in the country. Its political engagement was effective enough to go beyond the urban middle-class coterie and produce a brilliant crop of working-class artists. The social realism that distinguished the artistic output of the movement can be viewed against the perspective of a popular front consensus of sorts. But to see it as an art of ideological compromise would obviously be wrong. Realism came to perform a radical critique of society that was bound to cross the limits of a nationalist humanist consensus. In the sphere of politics itself, one saw a mass revolutionary upswing in 1945–46, which defied the protocols of nationalist politics.

The transformation set in motion in the *Social* films of the 1940s cleared the space for the reception of neorealism in 1952. It was not solely the postindependence imperative of "developmental" nationalism that provided the impetus for this assimilation.[7] As one follows this history, a neorealist aspiration in Indian cinema becomes apparent at certain crucial points. We are looking here at a historical moment when realism became critical, transformative, and creative—a generalized understanding of realism in terms of its humanist or nationalist compromise would not do justice to its varying historical functions, nor to the diverse functions of the moments within it.

The subjects of rural poverty, urban unemployment, and working-class politics became increasingly visible in the genre that was called the "studio *Social*" beginning in the late 1930s. Mehboob Khan's *Aurat* (*The Woman;* Hindi, 1940), the first version of his more famous *Mother India* (Hindi, 1957), and Tulsi Lahiri's *Thikadar* (*The Contractor;* Bengali, 1940)[8] are important early examples of social realism in the *Social*. By setting the family melodrama against a broad and detailed background of labor and economic exploitation and integrating location into the story, these films expanded the mode of representation established in the early sound era. Exploration of real locations, visualization of labor, and use of community as the social perspective set in motion a dynamic that came into conflict with the codes of the *Social*. As the IPTA was preparing *Nabanna*, the play about the Bengal Famine of 1943 that signaled a new era in Indian drama, New Theatres, one of the biggest studios, was engaged in the production of *Udayer pathey* (*On the Ascent;* Bimal Roy, Bengali, 1944). The film uses the familiar pulp fiction theme of cross-class romance—a trade union leader falls in love with the daughter of his boss—but the difference with a film like *Samadhan* (*The Solution;*

78

Premendra Mitra, Bengali), made a year earlier, is immediately visible. Unlike *Samadhan*, which also tells the story of the romance between the working-class hero and the factory owner's daughter, there is no restoration of the class status of the hero. The hero of *Udayer pathey* remains a political activist; the romantic couple renounces wealth and family, and sets out on a trip to a colliery town to organize a workers' strike. The hero sheds his surname to get rid of the basic marker of social privilege in India—caste identity—and calls himself a "writer." The middle-class reformer was the typical protagonist of the *Social*, but here the character is an intellectual, his weapon his verbal wit, and he states as his aim a socialist change of society. K. A. Abbas, an important director of the realist school, introduced the intellectual hero in his *Naya sansar* (*New World*; Hindi, 1941) as a journalist struggling against the established press. By 1953, the *Social* had become complex enough to use the same protagonist in *Foot Path* (Zia Sarhadi, Hindi) in his tragic incarnation: fighting the black market and corruption, the hero ends up selling himself to his enemies—the story of his betrayal and solitude is set against the dark and sordid background of urban slums.

A major thematic shift is visible by the time of *Udayer pathey*. Contemporary history has begun to enter the frame of representation; the need for a reorientation of style to respond to the cataclysmic events of the decade was already apparent. The Quit India Movement, the Bengal Famine, the revolutionary uprisings of 1945–46, the Hindu-Muslim riots, Partition—wave after wave of mass action and mass suffering swept through the decade. The scope of representation had to be "extended" to respond to a reality in visible ferment. The new content came into conflict with the style of the studio *Social;* the visual and narrative demands of extension could not be met without inflecting that style in a realist direction. The problem was not so much with importing the full gamut of codes of the Hollywood decoupage; the *Social* had largely adopted the codes though not the whole narrative system. The challenge seemed to lie in introducing techniques we now associate with neorealism. Space, for example, had to be constructed on the basis of an integration of location into the text, the contact with locations had to inform even the constructed sets; the existing studio codes of art direction became impediments to this development. By 1940, these codes had become more or less stable across India. The mise-en-scène was marked by flat, high-key lighting and a regularity of mid-long to long shots capturing characters grouped laterally in the mid-ground. The perspective beyond the stage of action was presented in painted backdrops in which not details

Pather Panchali
(Satyajit Ray, 1955)

but notations would stand for objects ordered into one flat plane (for example, the space beyond the courtyard boundary in rural domestic settings or the cityscape beyond the balcony in urban settings). Outdoor
scenes, most frequently the street corner, the garden, or the woods, followed restrictive use of board and cloth surfaces, painted or blocked sky,
and props of wilting trees. A palpable restriction would be imposed on
the space of action (*Samadhan* is an example where strict entry and exit
by characters continue through more or less static frames of action).
There was also a set of regulated relations established between actors
and objects like the piano, the staircase, and the doorway. And there was
a strong tendency to turn dialogues into frontal deliveries—a tendency
stemming from the spatial system itself. This visual style resulted in aesthetic and semantic impoverishment, not necessarily because it shunned
realist codes but because it stemmed from a nonnegotiation of those
codes.

One should add to this another hallmark of the Indian studio style:
a narrative procedure where the action is more or less "blocked" off into
set locations, and an alternation between a limited number of such locations is developed to set the narrative in motion.[9] The space tends to be
divided along the lines of contrasts that the plot follows; the intermedi-
ary spaces are dropped. *Udayer pathey* tries to work out various socially
stratified locations and changes the scene of action rather frequently, but

it avoids mapping out the spatial relations between the main locations of action. The use of space and narrative shores up in films like *Udayer pathey,* the impression of a new content trespassing into the generic domain of the *Social.* When we come to *Dharti ke lal* (*Children of the Earth;* K. A. Abbas, Hindi, 1946), the very conditions of the film's production will come to underline this tension.

Dharti ke lal was an independent venture undertaken by the IPTA. The idea was to bring the impact of *Nabanna* onto the screen. Based partly on that play, the film tells the story of a peasant family's experience during the Bengal Famine. It makes no sustained attempt to break away from the codes of the studio *Social*—codes that stick out so far as characterization, performance, and even dramaturgy follow the impulse of the new realist theater. As the peasants arrive in the city images appear that hint at a representational shift. The scenes of starving people on the street, for example, seem to emerge out of not only the new idiom of the stage (dance, drama, and shadow plays) but also the photojournalism and graphic art that the Bengal Famine of 1943–44 inspired. When the IPTA report on the film used the expression "documentary feature" it was not simply a misnomer; the word "documentary," one remembers, was frequently applied to the neorealist films in Italy to point to their method of working outside the usual limits of narrative and performance (in Pradhan 12). A breaching of generic boundaries between fiction and nonfiction was certainly at issue. But *Dharti* does not extend this potential of the image into a filmic principle.

The next independent venture where IPTA workers became involved, *Chinnamul* (*Uprooted;* Nemai Ghosh, Bengali, 1950), laid out the problem more clearly—the old style and the emerging alternative occupy two episodic spaces in the film. Ghosh and his colleagues at the Calcutta Film Society (the first film club in India, formed in 1947) had yet to see neorealist films, but a neorealist style was anticipated in such contexts. This anticipation and the afterlife that neorealism enjoyed in various national cinemas through the rest of the century show that its global reach is not to be understood solely through the model of "influence." In *Chinnamul,* a group of peasants, uprooted from their ancestral homes in the wake of the partition of India, find their way into Calcutta as refugees. A young couple gets separated and reunited in the process, but their story is not meant to discipline the larger portrayal of a community passing through the tumult of dispersal and regrouping. The first part of the film, set in a village in East Bengal, was largely shot in the studio and mixes the most conservative aspects of the studio style with documentary exposition (for example, voice-over narration) and agit-prop visual modes (allegorical pantomime) without much success. As the peasants arrive in Calcutta, however, the cityscape invades the frame of representation and works to disperse the narrative line. It is not accidental that the principles of filmmaking mentioned by the director, Ghosh, echo those of neorealist filmmaking.[10]

Chinnamul, in its failure to adhere to the limits of the *Social*, made it apparent that a realist threshold had to be crossed before one could rework the elements of the *Social*. By 1955, such reworking would produce a genre of classic melodrama—the most successful to date from either Bombay or Bengal—classic in the sense that melodrama functions in it through an active dialogue with realism. *Chinnamul*'s flaws were obvious, but its contribution to a realist transition was immediately noted. A popular magazine, praising the venture, used the word "documentary" to describe its effect.[11] This was not an unusual position at all; film criticism in the popular press throughout the period of ascendancy of the *Social* in the 1930s and 1940s was consistent in its critique of the convention. As the major sound studios were established and literary practitioners joined the industry in large numbers, film criticism became a regular feature in literary magazines. Film magazines were also published in substantial numbers (only a handful existed before 1930). Sound cinema brought questions of language, literary input, and regional specificity to the center of the critical discourse.[12]

In 1952, the editorial page of the popular magazine *Chitrabani* speculated that Indian cinema would die in its current form and would be reborn, the implication being that the new cinema would be realistic.[13] In the same year, Manik Bandyopadhyay, a leading writer, noted in a rare reference to cinema that he could see "fundamental changes" coming to "the Bengali and Indian cinema." He had been feeling that way for some years, but "this impression has gradually become stronger and clearer."

> The change of consciousness among common people is bringing this transformation about. . . . The common audience may not apply conscious judgement, may not consciously grasp this, but with the times their taste is changing. They want the story of real life and living humans in film. . . . I . . . took to literature . . . because I felt a major transformation was coming in literature, and at that epochal moment there was no point wasting time in other pursuits. The *Kallol* era was in its heyday then, but I sensed that the *Kallol* literature was just an early symptom of the new

turn. The real change would come in a different shape—literature would gradually become realistic. I have been feeling for
some years now that a similar fundamental change is due in
cinema. The main point about that change is the same—cinema
cannot satisfy people any longer by resorting to romance, thrills,
mythology and religion—they want real life, real characters.[14]
(490–92, my translation)

During the war years the Indian studio system faced a crisis from which
it never recovered. One of the likely causes was the influx of "black
money" earned from wartime speculation and supplies, which propped
up the independent producers. The institutional crisis, however, created
the space for independent experimentation. In the early 1950s, realist
experiments were taking place increasingly on the fringes of the studio
system. The demise of that system, incidentally, more or less coincided
with the arrival of *Pather Panchali*.[15] In addition, many artists and directors groomed in the IPTA joined the film industry around this time.

The impact of these changes can be gauged from the career of Debaki Bose, a director renowned for his *Devotionals* (a subgenre of the
Mythological) and not known for any involvement in the left cultural
movement. In 1949 he made *Kabi* (*The Poet;* Bengali), based on a novel
by Tarashankar Bandyopadhyay, a major realist writer of the period.
From the lives of medieval poet-saints he turns to the story of a peasant
poet, a *kabiyal,* and his social milieu. The exploration of *bhakti,* the de-
votional movement that he had portrayed before, was now placed in the
context of the social existence of a people whose artistic and emotional
life is infused with the bhakti idiom. In 1953, Bose adapted a play by the
leftist playwright and screenwriter Tulsi Lahiri, *Pathik* (*The Wayfarer;*
Bengali). The writer-activist figure of *Udayer pathey* reappears in the film
as if continuing the journey suggested at the end of the 1944 film. The
hero arrives in a colliery township and gets involved in a miners' dispute.
The use of locations and exploration of community life, the complex
camera movements, and the new performance style supported by a cast
dominated by the IPTA artists come into visible conflict with the studio-built outdoor sets that are also used. This stylistic mix is found in realist experiments launched in the years following independence in films
by Jyotirmoy Roy, Ardhendu Mukherjee, Salil Sen, Satyen Bose, and
others in Bengal, and Bimal Roy, Zia Sarhadi, K. A. Abbas, and others
in Bombay.

The conservative popular magazine from Bombay, *Filmindia,* la-
mented that in *Pathik* Bose "has not gone the whole hog for realism,

but for a blend of realism and idealism."[16] The cultural and institutional change such criticism signifies prompts us to abandon the idea that realist cinema was a project of minority cineastes and the developmental regime. State initiatives negotiated the debates coming from the public sphere. In 1949, the government instituted the Film Enquiry Committee to assess the problems of the industry and make recommendations. It submitted its report in 1951, and it remains the most valuable document on the film institution from the period. In their depositions, people inside and outside the industry seemed to agree that escapism, predilection for unreal spectacles, and so forth were problems dogging Indian cinema. The industry people defended their practices, arguing that the masses needed such things, whereas those outside pointed to the moral culpability of the practitioner. But the report is subtle enough to render the very terms of this debate problematic. It says that by believing people need escape from reality both sides end up mirroring each other; the entertainment versus art debate does not help cinema per se.[17] The report envisions a cinema where the "story" as well as aspects of production would be rationally organized and socially committed. Artistic material should be able to entertain, it felt, and one did not need to shy away from the creative aspects of "fantasy." While it recommended plurality of forms and practices rather than putting a premium on a single aesthetic, it broached the question of social commitment through a general critique of the existing cinema that echoed the critical discourse of the popular press, as well as that of the cineastes.[18] Social commitment was tied to the question of ethical commitment to reality, to reality seen in terms of "social problems." This was not far from the sentiment of ethical arguments made in favor of the Italian neorealist movement.

While there are certain critics who condemn the film as "escapist" or "unreal," others have considered this a justification for excluding its motifs from the scope of critical examination. . . . While there can be no objection to a fantasy which helps to divert the mind from immediate problems or from conflicts that cannot be quickly resolved, we cannot tolerate a film which leaves the audience subsequently in a mental state that sustains or ignores the conflict or prevents future readjustment. Providing an "escape" into an "unreal" world should be condemned when that world is based solely on wish-fulfillment, and enables the subject not only to escape his responsibilities but to enjoy the sensation of having discharged them.[19]

By the time the Italian neorealist films arrived in India the movement was in crisis in Italy. The 1953 Congress of Parma gave filmmakers and critics a scope to reflect on realism's ten years, but it also signaled its end in many ways. A year before, some of the well-known specimens of the movement came to India at the International Film Festival organized by the Films Division, a body set up in 1949 by the government to sponsor developmental filmmaking. Films came from twenty-three countries, but the impact of *Bicycle Thief, Miracle in Milan* (1951), and *Rome, Open City* (1945) far surpassed that of others. The impression of witnesses from Bombay, Calcutta, Delhi, and Madras, the cities the festival toured, prove this. Reports in popular magazines (like *Chitrabani* and *Filmfare*) singled these films out for praise. A preparedness for the style was clearly in evidence.

Satyajit Ray had seen *Bicycle Thief* a couple of years earlier in London and "knew immediately that if I ever made *Pather Panchali*—and the idea had been at the back of my mind for some time—I would make it in the same way" (9).[20] He saw this film and other neorealist films again in 1952. For his colleagues in the new cinema—Ritwik Ghatak and Mrinal Sen among them—the festival was crucial. But the fact that the mainstream *Social* also underwent a significant change after the exposure is less discussed. In the work of Bimal Roy, Prakash Aurora, Sarhadi, Amar Kumar, Kapoor, and Abbas one can see the more easily identifiable aspects of the realist shift. Lower-middle-class poverty, unemployment, homeless children on the street, and the experience of the urban subalterns formed a regular thematic repertory. In style, the change is visible in the use of location, space, and light. A new breed of cinematographers emerged in the industry whose contribution to the new shooting style has yet to be properly assessed. One can name among them V. K. Murthy, V. Ratra, Bimal Roy, Ramananda Sengupta, Dinen Gupta, Asit Sen, Ajoy Kar, and Dilipranjan Mukhopadhyay.

Cultural and institutional grids played a role in the assimilation of neorealism in India. The dialogue with neorealism, as we have suggested, was one of the ways in which Indian cinema entered a global affiliation; it found an alternative mode of becoming part of world cinema—a globalism different from the one created across nations by Hollywood. The global spread of the novel form provides a broad horizon against which this dynamics of cinematic modernity could be understood. But at a more specific level, one can suggest that the internationalism in cultural production that the Progressive Writers' movement sought to introduce provided the context for the assimilation in question.

The new phase of absorption of the generic conventions of Hollywood in the early 1950s was also informed by the neorealist encounter. Its mature specimens appeared around 1953–54 in the work of Dutt, Bimal Roy, Chetan Anand, Kapoor, and others.

The new content of the romantic melodrama, the dominant genre of the period, was characterized by a romance with modernity. The city, its modes of living and belonging, not only provide a horizon of action but a motivation of form in this cinema. It is beyond the scope of this essay to explore the relation of location and narrative procedures that becomes evident, a relation that neorealist cinema turned into an aesthetic principle with far-reaching influence. But let me mention a director from outside the mainstream genres: Ritwik Ghatak. Ghatak is considered a major representative of the new art cinema with Ray, but his cinema has also been considered antithetical to the realism that Ray and the art cinema stood for. Ghatak's self-consciously critical attitude toward realism has been duly examined, but without enough attention to the fact that it was a *relationship* with realism. In 1953, after his experience as an assistant director and actor in *Chinnamul,* he made his first film, *Nagarik (The Citizen;* Bengali), with self-raised finance, never to be released in his lifetime. The film opens with a first-person voice-over, the camera sweeping over the cityscape in a series of pans, invoking a figure that is both the city and an anonymous dweller of the city. But the film does not develop the method that could integrate the city as location into the narrative. It has the problem of working with a content developed much beyond the stylistic scope of the studio *Social.*

In its portrayal of a lower-middle-class family facing proletarianization, *Nagarik* does away with the melodramatic determinations of personality, kinship, and accidents and moves onto a sociological plane of inquiry. By pointing to socialist political action as the redemption of this suffering, Ghatak comes close to the short stories that authors like Manik Badyopadhyay wrote in the 1940s. Within the walls of the hero Ramu's home he often develops compositions where bodies interact with a sharp sense of struggle and pain, the images infused with the dramatic intensity that characterizes his later films. But drama mostly remains confined to the dialogue, and interactions are sometimes laid out flatly as if the characters are on a stage. As the action extends beyond the confines of the house, almost inevitably we are taken into another studio-built, notational scene. The self-conscious realist departure Ghatak proposes is circumscribed by the codes of the set, makeup, composition, music, and performance that make the subject extricable from the filmic material. The advanced content comes from Ghatak's artistic and political education (he became close to the Communist Party around 1945, and to the IPTA around 1948, which he joined shortly afterward), but a cinematic model was still not available to him to work through.

In Ghatak's second film, *Ajantrik* (1958), a realist break is immediately apparent. The director is already poised to take on realism as a discourse after having assimilated it. He is working with an enhanced vocabulary, complex syntax, and multiple means for the constitution of his content. It is no accident that he chose a story of outdoors and one about an automobile. The vast, undulating plateau outside the western borders of Bengal, its rough-hewn texture, and its combination of barren tracts and forests offered him the freedom to explore a spatial articulation of content, to explore the tonality and repertoire of compositions that would become his stylistic hallmark. The landscape allowed him to explore the "landscape principle," fundamental to realist representation, and introduce fissures into it. Ghatak could move into the complex historical exploration his films are known for on the basis of this dual ordering. On the first level, the basis of narration and articulation of the visible world stand on the landscape principle; on a second level, the principle is interrogated. The second register has drawn more critical attention, but it does not make much sense if one discounts the other moment, the realist moment. This is why Ghatak wrote that Ray showed the way to him and his contemporaries.[21]

If with *Ajantrik* Ghatak made a second realist beginning, Ray can be said to have made a second beginning of sorts with his second film, *Aparajito* (1956). Arguably his most powerful work (and the one closest to Ghatak's heart), *Aparajito* failed with audiences and critics. The latter felt it lacked coherence and narrative logic.[22] This shows that even in Ray's work realism was not embraced as a finished and unitary form.

I would like to return to a point I raised earlier about the question of naturalism in connection with *Chinnamul.* If the Italian movement was criticized because of its humanist compromise, its naturalist tendency was thought to be its other source of weakness. In an essay in *Sight and Sound,* Eric Rhode used Georg Lukacs's distinction between realism and naturalism to explain what he thought was the flawed aesthetic of neorealism.[23] Lukacs cast this distinction as one between narration and description. *Pather Panchali* comes closest to neorealism in the frequent passages where no apparent dramatic development takes place; the rise and fall of a moment, the passing of a day, and the change of seasons are captured in their concrete unfolding. Ray called this "rambling"; "Life in a poor Bengali village does ramble," he wrote (33). He reminds us that the original novel raised similar questions; the author, Bibhutibhushan Banerji, was turned down by publishers because his work lacked a proper story (Ray 32). It is well known that Ray's viewers, especially in the West, had difficulty accepting his rhythm.

Ray seems to suggest that what he learned from Renoir and Vittorio De Sica was already there in the Bengali novel, and his style was somewhat dictated by his material—life in a poor Bengali village. This legacy does not sound paradoxical if we consider the spread of the novelistic discourse across national contexts. That discourse was not confined to novels but became a more generalized mode of capturing experience. This narrativity, as a mode of modernity, had become part of the Indian consciousness. But so far as realism is concerned its constitutive moments can perform varying functions according to specific historical contexts. The "description" in question is part of the naturalist moment within realism. Describing against the imperative of narrative can render the realist closure problematic. Functioning on the boundary of fiction and documentary, it can render the generic rules unstable and help create new rules. The dialectical possibilities of such description, for example, can be seen to connect two divergent trajectories of neorealism and the nouvelle vague.

In Ray's Bengali village, property is meager and commodity circulation is minimal. His art of detailing engages with objects that merge easily into nature, and with nature itself as a horizon never absent from the stage of human action. He works through a contact between the camera and the horizon. The leaves, the grass, the raindrops, the wind, the sparse objects of possession—all breathe and linger; space is sentient in a way that lends it a voice. It is a translation of what is sometimes suggested in the novel and its sequel—a voice emanating from the surroundings speaking to the protagonist. Ray extends this voice into a principle, making and connecting images along an axis of contact between the natural horizon and the eye of the camera. The former speaks to the latter. To the argument that Ray's protagonist Apu signals the institution of a subject in Indian cinema built on the universalist modern model one should add the qualification that the deep investment in details, in description, often displaces the individual as a sovereign consciousness in these films.[24] It is typical of many Indian novels of the time: the possibility of individual evolution and that of ahistorical circularity of time are recognized in the same narrative movement. The principle of contact we mention here could not emerge before aesthetically processing the contact between the camera and real location. This does not mean that one had to follow the neorealist shooting style as a prescription, or that real location is more real than sets. It is to say that the principles learned from the movement helped Indian cinema break away from a set of restrictions and lay the basis of modern ways of working with its own material. The material in question was not only its reality lying outdoors, or its people living out there, but also its novels, poems, and pictures.

Notes

1. In this sense neorealism could be seen as staging a return of cinema to its origins in the venture of the Lumiere brothers; see Luigi Chiarini in Overbey.
2. See Thompson 203–17.
3. I borrow the idea of social extension from Raymond Williams, who warned against a simple ideological distrust of realism by pointing to the history of extension of representation into reality excluded from bourgeois art. See Williams, "A Lecture on Realism," and "Realism, Naturalism and Their Alternatives."
4. See Moretti.
5. The novelistic predecessor of Satyajit Ray, Bibhutibhushan Banerji, is one of the many examples of this development; an ahistorical impression of time is underlined by a historical movement in his *Pather Panchali* (1929) and *Aparajito* (1931).
6. Colin MacCabe called this textual model the "classic realist text." Accordingly, the metanarrative is enmeshed in the horizontal order of the narrative in this case. The realist text in this sense corresponds to bourgeois hegemony in society. See, for instance, Prasad 61–62.
7. The ideological connection between Indian film realism, nationalism, and the developmental regime has been suggested by critics like Geeta Kapur and Rajadhyaksha. See entries on Ray and *Pather Panchali* in Rajadhyaksha and Willemen. See also "India: Filming the Nation" and the "Special Feature" on Ray in Nowell-Smith. In a different vein, see Chakravarty chap. 3.
8. The director of the film was Prafulla Roy, but the writer Tulsi Lahiri was mainly responsible for the realist experiments.
9. This somewhat parallels the narrative style found in Griffith at the transition from early cinema to classical narration. See Jacques Aumont, "Griffith—the Frame, the Figure," and Raymond Bellour, "To Alternate/To Narrate," in Elsaesser and Barker. Ravi Vasudevan has

discussed the technique of sequencing the tableaux into narrative in the *Social.*

10. Ghosh wanted his film to be experimental in not using professional film actors, using actual refugees in the cast, little or no makeup, everyday dialogue, concealed camera, and in avoiding songs; see Ghosh, in Banerji. Pudovkin and Cherkassov saw the film in Calcutta in 1951, and later wrote to Ghosh, "[I]n your work you are carrying out a great and noble task in confirming a realistic trend in Indian cinematic art. . . . Cling steadfastly to the realistic path you have chosen. Develop and deepen its foundation" (142-43).

11. See *Chitrabani* 3.4 (1952).

12. See Biswas.

13. See *Chitrabani* 4.11–12 (1952).

14. The letter was originally written on August 2, 1952. The literature produced in the 1920s and 1930s in periodicals like *Kallol* and *Kalikalam* by Premendra Mitra, Achintya Sengupta, Sailajananda Mukhopadhyay, and others was thought to have started a literary movement away from Tagore. The group joined the film industry in the 1930s and made their contribution to the early developments in the *Social.*

15. The three most important studios, Prabhat Film Company, Bombay Talkies, and New Theatres, stopped production in 1953, 1954, and 1955, respectively.

16. *Filmindia,* August 1953.

17. *Report of the Film Enquiry Committee* chap. 4, para. 143, p. 49.

18. The cineaste criticism of the industrial practices came mainly from the writers associated with the Calcutta Film Society at that time.

19. *Report of the Film Enquiry Committee* chap. 4, para. 130, p. 42.

20. See also Ray, *My Years with Apu* 25.

21. Ghatak 107.

22. Eric Rhode, Robin Wood, and Chidananda Das Gupta, for example, found the film flawed on these grounds. See Rhode, "Satyajit Ray" 133–36; Wood, *The Apu Trilogy* 40; Das Gupta 40. Rhode is the most brutally dismissive, finding it "all very embarrassing" (134). While the novel *Pather Panchali* has been translated more than once into English, *Aparajito* has not been translated, probably for similar reasons. See Mukherjee chap. 5.

23. See Rhode, "Why Neorealism Failed" 30–31.

24. For an important critique of the Apu trilogy in terms of the institution of a normative Indian subject, see G. Kapur.

Chapter 4

Alphaville: A Neorealist, Science Fiction Fable about Hollywood

DAVID ANSHEN

> One must get to the extreme point where things speak for themselves. Which does not mean that they alone speak, but that they speak of what they really are. When you show a tree, it must speak to you of its beauty as a tree, a house of its beauty as a house. . . . Men and animals too.
> Roberto Rossellini, quoted by Jean-Luc Godard

> The question is: how to give human life its historical importance at every minute.
> Cesare Zavattini

> They can all be broken down into the following components: documentary reality *plus* something else, this something else being the plastic beauty of the images, the social sense, or the poetry.
> André Bazin

> Reality becomes too complex for Oral Communication. But legend gives it a form that pervades the whole world.
> Jean-Luc Godard, from the opening of *Alphaville*

The quotes above are polemics. The first three are partisan statements defending the postwar Italian cinematic movement termed neorealism and the fourth comes from the opening words of Jean-Luc Godard's New Wave film *Alphaville* (1965). The passages share a common conviction: Oppositions traditionally associated with cinema are possible to transcend. The contrast between striving to reproduce reality and the counterposed goals of making films of beauty, poetry, and the imagination are denied. Consequently, the dominant values of cinema, which at least by the end of World War II were associated with Hollywood as a so-called dream factory, are challenged in these quotes. The "dream factory" label ironically captures the worst of all worlds. It describes what critics of Hollywood felt the need to escape from: both escapism (anti-realism) and the conformity of the studio system as the dominant mode of Hollywood practice. In the first three quotes above the path to the aesthetic seems to come from history and reality, not mere flights of fancy. The quote from *Alphaville* suggests that reality needs legend and myth to attain form, but they all share confidence that real objects and events can be aesthetic and creative without losing truthfulness.

Film theorists, from at least Siegfried Kracauer on, have traditionally divided film into "two tendencies." From the birth of cinema, according to Kracauer's influential argument, filmmakers have gravitated toward either a "realist tendency" or a "formative," aesthetic tendency.[1] Though this distinction has never been absolute, it seems reasonable. It makes sense that a filmmaker must decide if the goal is to report or to create. In addition, film critics and theorists must decide whether to support aestheticism, claiming that films focusing on history and politics reduce to journalism and reportage, or to champion only realist films, claiming films motivated entirely by pleasure are irrelevant in the face of the horrors of history.

One goal of Italian neorealism, at least according to Rossellini and Zavattini, and the French critics and budding filmmakers in the early *Cahiers du Cinéma* circle, is that such oppositions can be transcended. While many critics focused on neorealism as a set of formal devices or "social reportage," a certain tendency claimed something much more radical. Bazin and his colleagues at *Cahiers*[2] stressed the "phenomenological" features or attention to "appearances" in this new brand of "realism" while paradoxically finding "humanism" and "love" as the basis of Italian neorealism. At the same time, according to Zavattini (one of the theorists of neorealism as well as the scriptwriter for several key films), focusing on "banal dailiness" leads to "great adventures." This strange mixture of attention to human life from the outside, almost impersonally, and love of humanity is explained by Bazin's conception of love and "poetry" as deriving from the same source—human life.

The conviction that divergent values can be merged in films that are true to life and attentive to everyday detail, while remaining magical, beautiful, and interesting, defied standard attitudes. Further, it was argued that neorealist films create great human drama without structuring narrative around traditional dramatic principles. This effort to break down the traditional division between documentary-like realism and poetic expression was first put into practice (in the postwar period) by Italian neorealism. However, the impetus carried through to the French New Wave, even after neorealism was considered a thing of the past. Another, perhaps more well-known aspect of neorealism is the way such films challenge the values and logic of capitalist film production (with its tendencies to produce grand, capital-intensive, mechanized spectacles) by stressing the value of simplicity in film production: simple experiences of daily life are valued as realistic and stimulating. The film that follows such an approach in neorealism's immediate French "afterlife" most closely is Jean-Luc Godard's *Alphaville.*

Little or no critical attention has been given to the connections between *Alphaville* and the stylistic, formal, political, and aesthetic features of postwar Italian cinema. This is true despite the fact that much of the New Wave style was influenced by Italian neorealism in many obvious ways, such as employing an unorthodox narrative structure that avoids classical conventions of continuity, scaled-down sets, and location shooting—not to mention the more complicated question of being concerned with real life. Jim Hillier comments in his edited collection of *Cahiers* essays that "Italian cinema [neorealism] represented something which new French film-makers could aspire to . . . which suited both their tastes and the production conditions and possibilities in France" (177), making the point that however much Hollywood auteurs were defended, Italian neorealism was practical as a model. It must be remembered that the French New Wave as a movement was formed in critical hostility to the "tradition of quality" standards of postwar French cinema, with its literary approach and technically sophisticated film construction and design—conditions unavailable for the young critics and would-be filmmakers such as Godard and his comrades—making the rough-and-ready Italian style attractive and necessary. Indeed, how could it not be? In Godard's case, he has never made secret his deep admiration for the artistry of Rossellini in particular and the Italian style in general. Indeed, in a famous interview Godard spoke of his earlier film, *Une femme est une femme* (1961), as "a neo-realist musical. . . . a complete contradiction," stating that "this is precisely what interested me in the film" (*Alphaville* 182). Godard's interest in such "contradictions" remained.

As mentioned, the critics around Bazin at *Cahiers* focused on certain unorthodox features they found in Italian neorealism. The "realism" they ascribe to neorealism is composed of elements that stand beyond merely social concerns and reportage that others had ascribed to neorealism.

Indeed, even Bazin, who earlier focused on the "ontology of the photographic image" as the basis for realism in cinema, stresses the aesthetic selection process behind the films of Vittorio De Sica, Luchino Visconti, and Rossellini. What neorealism adds to "realism," in this view, is the way the events of the plot lack dramatic links: events just follow events. This lack of plot linearity, combined with the absence of detailed character development, creates a sense of looking at life from the outside. On-screen, people act in reasonable ways, but we have no interior insight into their psychology or motivations. However, these "realist" features are combined in neorealist films with what Bazin stressed was a revolutionary humanism, defined as "the most sweeping message of love that our times have heard since Chaplin" (71). He goes on to explain, "I have used the word love. I should have used the word poetry. . . . Poetry is but the active and creative form of love, its projection into the world" (74). This understanding of neorealism and its components among the developing French New Wave closely parallels Zavattini's theoretical ideas that Italian neorealism "requires us, in effect, to excavate reality, to give it a power, a communication, a series of reflexes which until recently we had never thought it had" (217). In both cases, reality is seen as an aesthetic project.

Zavattini stresses the beautiful underneath the "banal 'dailiness'" and the "adventure" that comes from the "spectacular," which comes from "normal qualities" (221) of everyday life. This perspective—shared by Bazin in sensing that the poetic in neorealism arises from the real and the quotidian—is precisely the dialectic that Godard takes to its logical extreme in his fantastic legend, *Alphaville*. Godard also employs similar formal means found in the quasi-documentary films he so admired by Rossellini. Indeed, even the "estrangement" techniques in *Alphaville* (which shall be discussed shortly) have their counterpoint in Rossellini. In fact, the "realism" of *Germany, Year Zero* (1947), which is about a little boy who inhabits a world of unexplainable violence, gratuitous sexuality, and inexplicable behavior among adults, set against a backdrop of ruined buildings, rubble, sewers, and overall decay, is no more immediately comprehensible than the world of *Alphaville,* to which we turn.

The Legend and the Reality of *Alphaville*

Alphaville is one of the most popular of Godard's films. It is sometimes seen as a period drama, a quaint and charming piece of pop art, simple surrealism, or playful camp. However, it is an enigmatic film that is not appreciated fully in terms of its revolutionary implications. As such, it needs to be evaluated carefully in terms of its ongoing political and aesthetic significance. Its complexity is disarming because the film masks itself as uncomplicated science fiction.

Legend has it that Godard considered titling *Alphaville* "Tarzan against IBM." The title is insufficient, however, since the term "IBM" signifies computer technology, which might imply the film merely concerns a struggle against technology. While the tale does involve a struggle against a master computer, as Robin Wood points out in an early essay on the film, *Alphaville* is not merely another *1984, Brave New World* (1932) projection of a bleak totalitarian future. To sum up the film this way consigns it to a stable, familiar genre, reduces the film's significance, and misses the experience of watching the film, which is itself a deceptive experience.[3] *Alphaville's* real contribution to cinema is the way that it extends the values and approach of neorealism by capturing real but intangible features of modern society. The film accomplishes this by building on a unity of seemingly impossible elements: the traditions and concerns of Italian neorealism and the seemingly opposite traditions of science fiction and film noir.[4]

Part of the strangeness of the film is the way in which it is ostensibly concerned with the future but reveals objects of the present (1965) by making them look futuristic. Wood cites Godard describing the main character, Lemmy Caution, as "not a present-day human transported into the future, but as a man from twenty years ago who suddenly finds himself in the world of today" (85). Situating history is made more difficult because *Alphaville* employs familiar objects to represent a world of technologically mediated, prepackaged experiences that dominate real life, blurring the boundaries beyond the real and the fictional. Godard's solution to "presenting the unpresentable" is properly postmodern: he breaks down and merges formerly fixed categories, boundaries, and oppositions in search of something new. The tendencies described and given form by the computer in the film, Alpha 60, did not merely prefigure the future but gave form to tendencies that were already present in cultural expression.

Many of the most pressing issues concerning postmodern life are staged in the film, despite the fact that many of the technological advances cited therein (the Internet, virtual reality, computerized controls of information flows, and Hollywood as digitized spectacles that ignore subtle expression of emotions) existed only in comparatively primitive forms. In this regard, *Alphaville* was a response to the existing logic of

Hollywood processes, never complete, that were described by Theodor Adorno and Max Horkheimer as the "culture industry." Indeed, these same processes within film production correspond to what Zavattini criticized as "the American Style."

Does GE Bring Good Things to Life?

To summarize the plot of *Alphaville* is deceptively easy. *Alphaville* concerns a secret agent, Lemmy Caution (played by Eddie Constantine), entering the tightly controlled city of Alphaville from the outside. Alphaville appears as the enlightened, rational, perfect city that promises the values shown on the sign that greets visitors as they enter the city: "Silence, Logic, Safety, Prudence." Caution's mission is to kill the architect of the city-state, Professor Von Braun. Upon Lemmy's arrival he knows nothing of the functioning of Alphaville; he is put in the spectator position analogous to that of the audience watching the film. However, the rules of the town are quickly learned. The city is apparently successful in its calculated effort to eliminate all variability, all emotions, and all randomness from the life of its citizens. This is being accomplished by a giant computer, Alpha 60, which continuously eliminates words from the vocabulary of the citizens. In an early discussion between Lemmy and Natasha, Von Braun's daughter (Lemmy's love interest and guide through the city), she explains that "nearly every day there are words which disappear because they are no longer allowed. In their place, one must put new words to correspond to new ideas. And you know . . . in the last few months . . . some words have disappeared that I liked very much" (*Alphaville* 59). Words disappear because the computer keeps deleting words from the Dictionary/Bible that dictates what can be spoken. Presumably this determines what can be thought. In response to Caution's inquiry as to which words have been lost, Natasha replies, "Robin redbreast . . . to weep . . . Autumn light . . . Tenderness also" (*Alphaville* 59). These missing words give clues to the real subject of the film: Can artistic expression survive the dominant tendencies of society? Has the world become so "rational" that emotions and simple beauty are things of the past? The words being eliminated have been chosen carefully. On the one hand, they express simple emotions and beauty, corresponding to the priorities *Alphaville,* as a film, shares with the direct unmediated poetic reality Italian neorealism is known for. On the other hand, these words serve as more direct references. They suggest well-known literary references: "Autumn light" brings to mind *Light in August,* the William

Alphaville (Jean-Luc
Godard, 1965)

Faulkner masterpiece, while "tenderness" suggests *Tender Is the Night* by
F. Scott Fitzgerald. Indeed, the film constantly makes explicit literary
references to, for example, Sophocles, Paul Elouard, and the myth of
Orpheus.

It is clear that the computer, representing the logic of the society, is
intent on getting rid of personal and idiosyncratic language—all traces
of poetry—as a means of assimilating particularity and originality into
mechanical conformity. If things are made orderly and controlled, if information serves rational, predictable purposes, anything poetic becomes
unstable and therefore political. However, if even the banal can become
adventurous—as Zavattini was convinced it could—and if *Alphaville* can
use documentary techniques to make the familiar beautiful and strange,
then poetry can be reinvented and political critique of the existing order
can return. The computer divides the world into the real and the poetic.
This is what Lemmy Caution struggles against.

The film continues with a series of loosely connected episodes as
Lemmy wanders around. In this manner, the film also echoes neorealism with its temporal ordering that avoids traditional dramatic, narrative
principles.[5] As Lemmy moves through Alphaville he meets various characters, including the dying fellow secret agent Henri Dickson who tells
him that Dick Tracy and Flash Gordon are dead. Ultimately, Lemmy
discovers that Natasha has repressed her ability to express love (she cannot form the words), and Lemmy engages in a test of will with the computer Alpha 60. At the end of the film, Lemmy has caused Alpha 60 to

implode by posing a riddle it cannot solve: what exists as simultaneously unchanging continuity and movement toward the future—the answer is love. Again within the logic of the film, love is both romantic, in terms of the love affair between Lemmy and Natasha, and serves, as Bazin claimed, as the equivalent to poetry. We know that love and poetry are equivalent in the film because of the particular form that Caution uses to reawaken love in Natasha, reading Paul Elouard's *The Capital of Pain*. And it is the paradox of love/poetry that destroys the system of rationalized representations typified by the computer as Platonic Guardian of the city of Alphaville. This allows Lemmy and Natasha to drive off into the night as she haltingly but effectively articulates the final words of the movie: "I love you." She regains the lost capacity to express herself and feel love when Alphaville lays in ruin.

By Godard's standards this ending is almost uniquely optimistic (contrasting as it does with his other movie from the same year dealing with similar themes, *Pierrot le fou* [1965], which ends in the deaths of the lovers). *Alphaville* investigates whether the motifs of Italian neo-realism (externalized treatment of characters and locations combined with poetic strangeness derived from the familiar) can serve as effective resistance against the fact that (post)modern life threatens to exhaust any authentic feeling, emotion, expression, or nonprogrammed behavior. The film achieves contradictory objectives: it shows things as they are by depicting ordinary locations and objects, and from these props it creates the beautiful, poetic, and, in this case, the futuristic and strange. Why the turn to science fiction? Because the features of contemporary life that cannot be easily represented get displaced to an imaginary future.

The Realism of *Alice in Wonderland*, or Why the Culture Industry Fails

Godard once explained that he began his breakthrough movie *À bout de souffle* (1960) as realism but ended up in Wonderland. A reverse process develops in *Alphaville*. The unbelievable paradox is how effectively alien Godard is able to make the real Paris look. Even by today's post–*Star Wars* (1977) standards, with a high-tech, digitized universe of extreme technological image-spectacle (exemplified by films like *The Matrix* [1999], *Moulin Rouge* [2001], and the various *Star Wars* sequels), Godard accomplishes a high degree of futuristic feel. And he does this in ways that should not be possible in terms of contemporary film generic divisions. A documentary look at city life in Paris should need extra staged construction to become futuristic. Instead, in *Alphaville,* there are no technological spectacles, just people in their environment recorded directly.

The effect of the film is created through a mixture of approaches to film technique starting with shots in which the characters and locations are placed within the backdrop of real urban life in the manner that has been associated with the cinematic language of neorealism. Medium and long shots characterize any neorealist film, in an urban setting, where the character is planted in an atmosphere of buildings and architecture that seem to impose upon the individual. A similar use of real settings works in *Alphaville,* but to the opposite effect. Flashing shots of the Paris cityscape are what make *Alphaville* feel alien. However, as Kristin Thompson effectively argues in her essay on *Bicycle Thief* (1948), there can be no a priori, natural approach to the reproduction of reality; just conventions and choices.[6] Indeed, even Bazin, often taken as the arch champion of realism as the teleological essence of cinema, notes in his treatment of Italian neorealism that one set of realist choices are made at the expense of other conceivable approaches, which suggests that there is always something beyond the real that remains. Therefore, when a film with such a seemingly unrealistic narrative employs conventions of realism to create a world that at first glance seems so alien, something remains to be explained. Why isn't a sense of the real promoted? Rather than discounting the presence of realism in *Alphaville,* which seems logical at first glance, instead the dialectic of the real and the fantastic needs to be revealed.

Another way to consider this question is to ask: Why has *Alphaville,* which has been compared to pop art, surrealism, comic books, and dystopic science fiction, never been understood in light of its closest film antecedents and traditions? Even the label "avant-garde" that has sometimes been applied to the film makes sense only in terms of the ways *Alphaville* rejects traditional Hollywood norms—formally and stylistically—along the same lines as Italian neorealism.

To understand the deep political and aesthetic significance of the film, an imaginative leap is required—the leap of seeing the present historically, as *Alphaville* does through neorealist techniques made strange. The strangeness of the film and its realism coincide when banal features of everyday life become filled with beauty and wonder. In this regard, the film builds on Zavattini's conviction that film should "astonish us by showing so many things that happen every day under our eyes, things we have never noticed before" (MacCann 221). *Alphaville* does this; but more, it also builds on one of Godard's central theoretical foundations—that whether you begin with documentary or fiction, the two categories inevitably switch. This conviction, which Godard has repeatedly affirmed in all stages of his variegated career, is of the utmost significance for a postmodern, commercialized, capitalist present because it is precisely this dialectic—the movement between the imaginative and the real this film strives for—that allows the survival of realist and aesthetic aspirations in the face of the dominant tendencies of contemporary Hollywood that become increasingly universal. The importance of the film lies in the means it uses to break down the barriers between recording and creative filmmaking to offer an immanent critique of what exists.

The Documentary Techniques of Estrangement

To begin, the film is shot with simple camera work. Shots are made of various locations in Paris. The film's images begin with a technologically simple reproduction of external, unmediated reality. There are shots of buildings, electrical power stations, hotel rooms, elevators, phone booths, streets, traffic lights, and so forth. Indeed, these shots are similar to the opening shots in *Germany, Year Zero*. Lemmy is placed in Alphaville, just as the boy is placed in Germany. These images are unaltered, striking, and offer visual pleasure to the spectator. To receive visual pleasure from simple reproductions harkens back to the birth of cinema with the actualities of the Lumière brothers, when the camera was simply placed in some situation and left running. These shots also correspond to what Bazin labeled "faith in the reality of the image" since they are unmediated by "plastics" (lighting or sets). In addition, the shots are taken without artificial lighting except the normal electrical lighting of Paris. Real outdoor lighting was used by the Italian neorealists, but Godard took it one step further and employed this technique at nighttime. Indeed, one of the salient features of Italian neorealism is the journey through Italy (one thinks of *Bicycle Thief, Paisà* [1946], *Rome, Open City* [1945], and even post-neorealist films like *Viaggio in Italia* [1953] or the opening shots of Michelangelo Antonioni's *L'Avventura* [1960]), where the images of city life form a metonymic backdrop to the action at hand,[7] setting the tone and contributing to the "realism."[8] This is also true, of course, of *Alphaville,* in which every scene is shot—outdoor and indoor shots alike—in real locations with a minimal amount of staging.

It is not merely the scaled-down, visual camera work that this film shares with Italian neorealism. Godard's continuity assistant from this period pointed out that during his filmmaking Godard refused to edit out natural sounds, even if they at times drowned out dialogue.[9] Though on the face of it this might seem the opposite of the Italian tradition of post-synchronized dubbing, the film theorist P. Adams Sitney argues that Rossellini's use of dubbing German and English in *Paisà* is a gesture toward realism. He argues that since lack of aural understanding is a common feature of reality and linguistic misunderstandings were part of the problems of the military conflict in Italy, real confusions were being captured by Rossellini. Godard also valued extraneous sounds corresponding to something real outside the film (nondiegetic street noises).

The comparison of sound does more than highlight similarities—a common attempt to accurately capture oral and aural confusion. The very nature of the different types of confusion is historically situated. In one case, in the immediate postwar occupation people cannot understand each other because they speak different languages. In the other case, the fast-paced, chaotic world of multiple simultaneous actions and reactions creates an overwhelming spectacle in which the individual cannot screen out background noise. Similarly, Godard shows city life, as do Italian neorealist films, but he decontextualizes the images as a means of creating an alien feel in the present. This is a poetic attempt to capture the reality of a historical moment in all its strangeness.

The Historical Reality behind *Alphaville*

It is well known that immediately after World War II, Italy was left economically destitute. Elaborate film studio traditions were associated with Fascism, which made them politically suspect. In this context, filmmakers wanted to make films associated with common people in ways that required few resources and little technical equipment. This was seen as the proper approach to the subject of daily life. *Alphaville* is centered on the value of daily life as aesthetic and meaningful, and these values are shared with Italian neorealism. Godard also struggled with this film against the official conventions of filmmaking. Indeed, the possibility that cinematic originality could be killed off from commercialism that threatens to force it into formulaic molds only intensifies as the historic moment of Italian neorealism recedes. It is not surprising Godard produced a beautiful and original film based on simple filmic means to show the continuing possibility of resisting the "culture industry." Alphaville appears to be nowhere and yet it represents a real place. It makes visible the real "dream factory" that shapes our dreams. Its location is not "zero-ville," to quote Lemmy Caution, but a real, mysterious place, impossible to find on maps but freely moving across space in a globalized world. Alphaville is actually a set of coordinates known by various names but called by some "the culture industry" and by others Hollywood.

The term "culture industry" was coined by Horkheimer and Adorno in 1944 in "The Culture Industry: Enlightenment as Mass Deception" (Adorno). They claim that culture has become assimilated to the logic of capital, as cultural production becomes an industry producing mass standardized products. The goal is to reduce investment risk. Culture has become a commodity and the production of cultural commodities involves rationality, which breaks products down into simple interchangeable units that proliferate. This process automatically works to eviscerate all traces of personal, social, or cultural autonomy just as craft production with all its personal traces becomes replaced by mass production. Cinema is singled out for special condemnation in this analysis, since film production—particularly under studio conditions—is shaped by huge industrial concerns requiring large amounts of capital. The effect of such conditions does more than shape the production of mass art objects into safe, tried-and-true products. Powerful corporations that largely control exhibition and distribution integrate what millions of people around the world visualize and experience. This system, which is intangible but real, is precisely what Godard allegorizes in *Alphaville*. Alpha 60, the computer determined to eliminate chance human responses, is nothing more than a way of presenting such conditions that govern film and culture making.

One objection might be that to reduce a totality of social processes into a singular figure moves away from the literalism of Italian neorealism. However, I find persuasive Sitney's claim that neorealist films were always situated in a tradition of symbolism and iconography. Sitney argues that iconography (defined as "meaningful images and image types that tend to recur" [11]) functions as an "interlocking" that "constitutes an allegory" (13) within postwar Italian cinema as a whole leading from neorealism to the extreme fable-like films of Pier Paolo Pasolini. In addition, Sitney stresses that images of city life in Italian cinema are metonymic in function, furthering the allegorical process. If we take his argument seriously we recognize new ways that the conventions of Italian neorealism function as political allegory as well as realism, and we gain new understanding of the seemingly absurd features of *Alphaville*. The film uses direct images of Paris metonymically to construct an allegory—an allegory of the present given historically, that is, in unfamiliar fashion, made distant and strange.[10]

The connection between this film and its documentary-like attention to Paris has already been stressed. This also links the film with Italian neorealism, which shared a fascination, almost an obsession, with situating characters within the landscape. However, when Adorno and Frankfurt School critics describe the dominant tendencies within urban architecture we get descriptions that sound like the mise-en-scène from *Alphaville.*

> Even the aesthetic activities of political opposites are one in their enthusiastic obedience to the rhythm of the iron system. *The decorative industrial management buildings and exhibition centers are much the same as everywhere else. The huge gleaming towers that shoot up everywhere are the outward signs of the ingenious planning of international concerns,* towards which the unleashed entrepreneurial systems (whose monuments are a mass of gloomy houses and business premises in grimy, spiritless cities) were already hastening. (Adorno 120, italics added)

In this passage, architecture serves a functional, rationalized purpose beyond beauty or ornament, and everything looks the same. The architectural descriptions above claim universality and yet literally match the images of city life in Alphaville, strengthening the bleak analysis. In the film we have recurrent medium and long shots of the exterior of "management buildings," "towers," "gloomy houses," and so forth, and they are "gleaming" and "grimy" and "spiritless." This can be mere coincidence if the film were completely fictitious or if the claim that urban architecture is dominated by "enthusiastic obedience to the rhythm of the iron system" didn't seem persuasive. But given that the visual features of Alphaville are real images of 1960s Paris, shot in minimalist style with little staging, alteration, or special effects, it appears that the (anti)aesthetic described above has been successfully incorporated into daily life. If this is true, then the realism of the film comes from its close fit with critical theory at its most pessimistic. The world struggle between capital and labor, art and commercialism, the human and the machine are all over and the bad guys have won. However, to draw this conclusion from the visual features of *Alphaville* would be to miss the film's profound affirmation and optimism. This comes directly out of the film's central enigma and dialectic. The trick of the film is the way familiar images of city life are made to *not look the same.* This is what sets in motion both the film's charm and its politics. To understand how this is done is to lay bare the mechanics of the film.

David Anshen

The Prison House of Representation:
An Escape through Film Form and Film History

Lemmy's adventures in *Alphaville* are a love story among all else. His love interest, Natasha Von Braun, is a prisoner, analogous to the struggling maiden bound to a train track. What binds her is language and what threatens to be taken from her is purity of expression and feeling (a legitimate anxiety for our times). She is the victim of a monster (society, cultural tendencies, impersonal economic forces—all personified by a computer) that has systematically worked to eliminate words and emotions. Each word dropped from the Dictionary/Bible of Alphaville is another knot tied. She is trapped in a closing circle of language that prevents her from speaking with subtlety, or poetry, and this leads to the dimming of her life force, preventing her from remembering the words of love. At the same time she loses her ability to speak the truth or the beautiful, when language has a purely referential function, conversations seem empty and formal. Natasha is placed in a prison of language that holds her trapped within ugly bonds that prevent her from accessing anything but shadows on the wall.

As a film, *Alphaville* strives to overcome the same tendencies that put Natasha in danger. Her struggle becomes an expression of the film's struggle to create new and expressive cinematic forms against the dominant and restrictive language of Hollywood (another parallel with neo-realism). The film employs a relationship between words and objects that breaks down the unthinking acceptance of the way meaning is produced. It does this through focused attention to the language employed for common objects of daily life. To term a phone a "telecommunicator," an elevator a "teleporter," the area outside Paris "the Outlands," and even refer to a book as alternatively "Dictionary/Bible" calls into question our relations with banal objects. The objects remain the same, they look as they literally did at the time of filming, but they attain a different significance. A telephone is revealed for the strange object it is by giving it a new name. And the new words reference invented terms of the science fiction genre with its "tele" things. This process of making the familiar into the property of science fiction reaches its limits when the image of a spinning window fan becomes Alpha 60. Combined with a voice garbled by mechanical speech equipment, the fan convinces as a monster.

The arbitrary nature of language is underscored while the distinction between what a word means and what it implies is heightened. The denotation and connotation of words create an alien feel—a kind of literal

Alphaville (Jean-Luc Godard, 1965)

alienation effect. The hidden features of language are employed to create a sense of the future in the present. It should also be noted that Godard has created a new kind of Kuleshov effect—the Russian filmmaker determined that audiences perceive the same image of a face differently depending on the shots surrounding it. Here, Godard shows we perceive an image differently depending on the words surrounding it. These non-technical "special effects" break the link between words and images, creating historical effect—making the present seem futuristic—which is a direct challenge to the oft-repeated ideological claim made by Alpha 60 concerning the nature of the human experience of time as eternal present beyond history. The world depicted in the film is one where language appears completely synchronic, a system and structure that work purely on closed relations, and it is this which traps the individuals, deleting their speech and imprisoning them in a repetitive, empty circle. Alpha 60 tells of this in the form of a riddle: "But no one has lived in the past and no one will live in the future. The present is the form of all life and there are no means by which this can be avoided. Time is a circle which is endlessly revolving. The descending arc is the past and the rising arc is the future. Everything has been said. At least as long as *words don't change their meanings and meanings their words*" (*Alphaville* 37, italics added). Lemmy refers to Natasha as "pretty sphinx" because she is the source of the riddle, even if Alpha 60 is the monster threatening the city. She believes she has never lived in the past and seems unable to live in the future, making her life an endless present. But such a condition is not living; she explains that she learned from Alpha 60 that "life and death exist within the same sphere" (*Alphaville* 38), which means there is no life. How does one escape the nullifying and endless present, an eternity of death, if "everything has been said"?

When Oedipus confronts the riddle of the Sphinx, he realizes the puzzle is self-referential by answering that man is the measure. Of course, Oedipus's tragedy is that he does not realize the degree to which he is the answer to the riddle of his life. In similar fashion, there is a simple answer, already provided to the riddle of the seemingly timeless nature of language and expression. The very way the question is posed, by a spinning fan posing as the last stage of the human, provides the answer. What the film demonstrates is precisely how words alter their meanings and meanings alter their words. The film is one large demonstration of this point. This applies on the level of words and even on the level of larger systems, such as the language of filmmaking, which can change its meaning. What the film shows is that even the traditional dichotomies between the real and the imaginary can change their position. It also shows, more specifically, that the formal conventions of Italian neorealism can be deployed in a project that both breaks and extends the gesture of realism, becoming beautiful and true while fantastic. The levels to which the self-referential and allegorical features of the film operate break out of the systematic constrictions that limit meaning and spiral to larger and larger reference points. For example, Natasha's inability to say "I love you" suggests the end of old sensibilities and the dying of romantic love. This then develops into a context for representing systems of language structure. But clearly the subject is easily taken to suggest film itself on a macrocontext through the ways this film specifically employs language to work at creating new forms of film expression. Of course, since the film is set in real Paris and self-consciously oscillates between familiar images and strangeness, the scope of the subject expands to encapsulate Paris as typical of modern society. And, finally, the way sexuality is depersonalized, which is expressed through the commodified, proletarianized, and robotic behavior of Alphaville's citizens (upon greeting someone people say, "Hello," "You're welcome," "Thank you"—the language of the service industry), suddenly becomes a critique of the system of equivalence and exchange. Godard is not the first to use prostitution as a metaphor for selling oneself in the capitalist marketplace (nor is this the first time he employs this metaphor). The power of Godard's representational politics in this film lies in the ways that the overlapping levels of meaning move back and forth, overcoming boundaries, and therefore in a "postmodern" allow the totality to become represented. As one of the men about to be executed for crimes against the state proclaims, "In order to create life, it is merely necessary to proceed in a straight line towards all that we love" (*Alphaville* 45). The line signifies direct movement through time and space, therefore history, as the answer to an absence of life and love. In this way, the solution lies in an approach to history that seems naïve and outdated. In the same way, history becomes the way out of the closed structure of language.

History is therefore demonstrated within the film whenever something familiar becomes strange. Becoming strange, however, is built out of close attention to real features and objects of daily life. Viewing the world impersonally and objectively suddenly creates poetry and adventure. Even more important, the historical nature of the present is revealed and maintained through the variation of visual experiences that allows temporal distinctions to be made by the film's spectators. A true victory of an all-pervasive sameness and repetitions would erase distinctions and dissolve the real, but this is not allowed in *Alphaville* for an instant. The political demand to make the real beautiful demands constant estrangement. The film, therefore, compels its viewers to consciously make sense out of the moments presented, in reference to time and what has been and will be. There is a struggle to keep up with a language of vision that reconfigures objects and restructures their context. This is the way film form escapes its own limitations.

Alphaville extends the framework of Italian neorealism from representing the economic devastation of postwar Italy to depicting the last decades of the twentieth century. The seeming rupture with realism mirrors a set of radically shifting cultural coordinates in real life. The subject of concern, in day-to-day life, changes from the economic destitution of a jobless worker and his son searching for a bicycle into the cultural destitution of a mass media standardizing and homogenizing systems of representation. The political and aesthetic problem Godard faces is twofold. First, due to the dominance of the culture industry, history appears to have mutated into a globalized, information economy that further calls into question any authentic daily life. The separation between daily life and poetry remains a threatening prospect. The second dilemma Godard encounters is how to depict such abstract concerns. Godard must reassert the possibility of dramatizing daily life in a poetic way, and this is made more difficult by conditions of increasing depersonalization and cultural standardization. These conditions have come to be associated with postmodernism. In this sense, Godard is a prophet of the post-modern condition through the science fiction world he creates in this film. However, he also develops a strategy of opposition. He draws on his forerunners—the Italian neorealists, and their conviction that daily life can be the subject of great beauty—and applies their approach to a new setting. The political/aesthetic value of *Alphaville* lies not merely in its depiction of struggle against a dominant culture that divides beauty from real experience but in the ways the film itself escapes such a division.

Notes

1. André Bazin, in his famous essay "The Ontology of the Photographic Image," privileges "faith in reality" over "faith in plastics," which divides filmmaking in a similar manner. However, as this essay will show, Bazin's later essays on Italian neorealism indicate that his perspective had shifted somewhat.

2. It seems reasonable to treat Bazin and the group around him as a relatively unified whole. Although over time Bazin developed aesthetic and political differences with his friends and younger colleagues, at the time of his essays on Italian others such as Amédée Ayfre, Jacques Rivette, Eric Rohmer, Francois Truffaut, and Jean-Luc Godard all praised Rossellini, Visconti, and Italian neorealism. They wrote defense and analysis of Italian neorealism along common lines and largely detected the same features in the films. Indeed, it is notable that many of their essays were directed against Italian filmmakers and critics who found the films of Rossellini, in particular, wanting. Therefore, when discussing Bazin's approach to Italian neorealism, it can be fairly called the *Cahiers* approach—although only from a certain period. It is well known that by the late 1960s *Cahiers* moved far away from interest in "humanism" or "realism," seeing such values as bourgeois.

3. Wood comments, "*Alphaville* cannot be dismissed as merely the sum of certain second-hand ideas; it is an intensely felt unity with atmospheric coherence to which the ideas contribute but whose value is by no means restricted to the value of ideas as ideas" ("Alphaville" 83).

4. Zavattini is not atypical in his hostility to what he termed the "American style" and to genre films. The exception, of course, would be the Visconti film *Obsession* (1943), one of the many variants of the noir classic by James Cain, *The Postman Always Rings Twice* (1946). The

only neorealist film that could be plausibly considered science fiction would be De Sica and Zavattini's *Miracle in Milan* (1951). However, this film is more of a "fable" than science fiction proper.

5. Gilles Deleuze argues in his two volumes on cinema that the fundamental rupture represented by Italian neorealism and the French New Wave concerned the shift from a "movement-image" to a "time-image," by which he means that rather than actions driving events in film, as in classical cinema, film becomes the depiction of time. Events are minimal, random, and do not structure film narrative. This is closely related to Bazin's observations that neorealism represents a different temporal ordering principle from earlier cinema and that its contribution to "realism" lies in a refusal to subordinate time to drama. Editors' note: See Thomas Stubblefield's essay in this collection for an extended discussion of Deleuzean theory, postmodernity, and Italian neorealism.

6. Thompson argues that "[w]e can see the absence of a natural relationship between the art work and the world in the fact that so many different styles have been historically justified to their publics as 'realistic'" (197).

7. Metonymy, using a part to stand in for a whole, has usually been seen as opposed to literalism since figures of speech are seen as distinct from direct representation. But if film can function as realism at all there is no reason to reject metonymy since film, at best, is inherently metonymic as it frames images. In addition, literary realism has often valued character types as a means to reproduce human life; therefore, images of buildings or computers can stand in for the system of buildings or computers if they are typical.

8. I have been arguing that perhaps the greatest direct influence on *Alphaville* would be *Germany, Year Zero,* which involves shots that situate the characters closely within the ruins of postwar Germany and shots that pan around the rubble in ways similar to the shots of urban Paris in *Alphaville.* The connection this film has with *Alphaville* is made explicit with Godard's sequel to *Alphaville* in which Lemmy returns and travels through post–cold war Germany, *Germany Year 90 Nine Zero* (1991).

9. This is mentioned by Richard Roud in *Jean-Luc Godard.* He quotes Godard's continuity assistant as stating, "Godard always wants to keep as much as possible of the actual shooting—if there are some unexpected noises off, they are retained. Unless, of course, the unexpected comes from the equipment and not from 'life': the noise of a camera or a tracking shot" (74–75).

10. By employing the Russian formalist approach of estrangement,

Godard is again borrowing from cultural modes of the past. He employs such techniques to reveal the commonplace as a historical construct similar to Shlovsky's famous citing of Tolstoy's horse narrator to reveal historical relations in all their absurdity. Godard does this within film using filmic means.

Chapter 5

Neorealism in Anglo-Saxon Cinema

Antonio Napolitano

Solo mantenendo, così, fede integrale al patrimonio della vita, si può essere certi che la lezione del Neorealismo conserverà il suo carattere nel sangue e nel corpo dei nostri migliori artisti.

Only by keeping such faith in the intrinsic value of life can one be sure that the lessons of neorealism will be saved/preserved in the blood and body of our best artists.
Camillo Marino, *Cinemasud* 1966

The 1966 issue of Cinemasud, *titled "Neorealism's Heredity," suggests an impulse to explore global cinema from the angle of Italian neorealism, a goal we find interesting for obvious reasons.[1] In an effort to recapture some of this impulse, we have chosen to reprint here for the first time in English an article from that issue.[2] As Paolo Speranza explains in the introduction to the 2002 reprint of the 1966 issue, there was an interest at the time in considering the "renewed creative wave [in global cinema] in the early 1960s and its possible tie with the lessons of the various works of Rossellini, Zavattini, De Sica, [and] Visconti" (5, our translation). This global perspective was in line with the journal's entire mission.*

The first issue of Cinemasud *appeared in January 1958 with the simple secondary title of "Rivista di cultura cinematografica" (Journal of cinematographic culture), a title that only loosely suggests its critical perspective. Edited and launched by the film scholar Camillo Marino, its stated goal was to create a critical dialogue about film within a southern Italian and Marxist framework, a framework that recognized links between southern Italy's history of disenfranchisement and colonization, and the disenfranchisement of national cultures well beyond Western Europe. Simona Dolfi in her "Il Cinema d'avanguardia neorealista di Camillo Marino" indicates that the journal had a "popolarità mondiale" (global popularity) (in Speranza 18, our translation). It seems that the southern feel of the journal in part conveyed this international interest as suggested back in 1966: "Flipping through the pages of* Cinemasud *one discovers the wish to export the true values of southern Italy; it's also not just a journal on Italian cinema but instead incorporates news about foreign cinema as well" (in Speranza 18, our translation).*

Marino and other filmmakers were likewise crucial in the development of the Festival del Neorealismo (1959–89), which took place in Irpinia and was backed by Pier Paolo Pasolini, among others.[3] This particular film festival was committed to showing the works of lesser-known filmmakers, in particular from Eastern bloc countries and Latin America. In the pages of Cinemasud *we see a look beyond regionalism, and a commitment to understanding the global landscape of film that resonates with our project.*

Thus we share with Cinemasud *a desire to investigate the connection between Italian neorealism, as it was originally cast by Roberto Rossellini, Vittorio De Sica, and others, and other national film traditions—a connection that traverses historical, political, and cinematic landscapes. With these goals in mind, the article we chose to translate and reprint here explores the links between 1950s–1960s British and U.S. cinema and the history of Italian neorealism. Napolitano argues that Hollywood and Great Britain's Rank Corporation, while seemingly both at odds with the understood goals of neorealism, have in fact produced films that stand out because they had, as he puts it, a "way of looking at reality that was different from their usual one," a way that was, in fact, in line with Italian neorealism.[4] Napolitano goes on to offer broad sketches of such films, from Tony Richardson's* Look Back in Anger *(1959) to Herbert Biberman's* Salt of the Earth *(1954). This essay expands on some of the discussions taken up in our introduction with respect to the supposed lack of neorealist influences within certain film traditions, the United States and Great Britain being two main locations where such influence is not self-evident.*

For starters, we should first clarify the meaning of the neologism invented for Italian cinema produced between 1945 and 1950. Having such a definition, we can then find the equivalent (not the identical) meanings in two cinemas, the British and the American, each of which has different cultural traditions and roots. It is clear that in neorealism—intended as one of the possible options for art to see and express itself—we see above all the refusal of complicated mythologies, of quasi-

Cinemasud cover photo, 1966

theatrical conventions, and of sophisticated searches for the bizarre. Therefore, its prevailing characteristic is a most immediate "capturing" of social, emotional, and historical realities enclosed within a very narrow time span. It becomes then almost evident that the influence of this "new style" has stimulated a new metabolism in various cinemas around the world, making them aware of a lively and current sense of the present (one that is not to be lost, but in fact remembered and analyzed immediately without letting it get cold or crystallized).

The major contributing factor in steering even the most honest moviemakers of Hollywood or of the Rank Corporation toward a way of looking at reality that was different from their usual one was the favorable acceptance, the positive, and at times enthusiastic, critique of works such as *Roma città aperta* (*Rome, Open City;* 1945), *Paisà* (*Paisan;* 1946), and others. Indeed, the duty to communicate—along with the ethical nature of a commitment toward the community and the spontaneity of the reactions that were already available in Anglo-Saxon cinema—led filmmakers to put aside formal, stale constructions and instead brandish in the most brilliant fire images of an inner experimental world, not just as a means of expression, but also as a way to communicate the totality of human relations.

Many British and American directors also suddenly understood that the news of everyday life must be brought up to the level of a story "in progress." They realized that only the speedy impact of a movie camera capturing simple angles and shots could convey the most ample meanings before they were lost and forgotten in a time without importance and resonance. Reality could not be a pretext to exercises of fantasy. Neither must reality be an excuse for a narrative play of sterile invention, but instead it must be a rule for the most direct visual orientation. Thus the director must accept a situation (one that becomes the film's subject matter) without judgment, filters, or spectacle. This type of acceptance can be seen in Italian neorealist movies such as De Sica's *Sciuscià* (*Shoeshine;* 1946), Luchino Visconti's *La terra trema* (*The Earth Trembles;* 1948), Federico Fellini's *I vitelloni* (1953), or Michelangelo Antonioni's *Cronaca di un amore* (*Story of a Love Affair;* 1950).[5] The transformation and the reflection of an ordinary experience into a feeling and then into an idea and an image were the most intrinsic aspects of neorealism, aspects found also on the other side of the Atlantic and on the other side of the Channel. This does not mean that at this point movies became practical and pragmatic; instead cinema became the outlet for a particular attitude toward tradition and the environment (with all its symbols, and positive or negative values).

Neorealism in England

In England, any invitation to acknowledge significant and insignificant facts of daily or direct experience was readily accepted. Remember that England was home to empiricism, the fight against axioms, social novels, 1930s engagé, and angry *ante litteram* poetry. This new realist trend could be modified only by being absorbed by and filtered through British culture, made jagged by its own insular nature or by its own cinematic conformism.

Sequence, a journal that debated the value of British entertainment cinema against realist trends, was launched at Oxford by Lindsay Anderson and Karel Reisz in 1947, the year following the explosion of neorealism in Europe. But even before the appearance of *Sequence*, director David Lean was able to discover in certain tonalities of dull gray, in outdoor takes, and in the understatement of a Chekhovian melancholy a taste for a tale embedded in a real environment (in his *Brief Encounter* [1945]). In fact, *Brief Encounter*, with its petit bourgeois, almost proletarian aesthetic, resonates with De Sica's 1942 film *I bambini ci guardano* (*The Children Are Watching Us*). Even the "comedy of manners" style began to be renewed following a spirit of observing everyday life; the little manias, the tics of the man of the street. Particular exploits, like those of Lean, were partially copied by Carol Reed and Anthony Asquith, but it was only through the influence of so-called Free Cinema[6] that realist cinematic terminology could be considered as more than a mere fad.[7] In 1953, Free Cinema ushered in the first successful attempts to stay away from conventional cinematic language: *Wakefield Express* (1952) and *O Dreamland* (1953), directed by Anderson, are shorts in which reality is assaulted in its full social context. Although these films evoke something of the documentary school of John Grierson, Basil Wright, or Paul Rotha, the strongest, sharpest stimulus toward a realistic revival comes from the Italian school.

For example, the mysterious Joseph Walton (Alias Losey), with his latest project, is looking for a narrative model that is less pretentious and more genuine. His style lies somewhere in the balance between a Rossellinian approach and the false beauty of the most antiquated type of box-office enticement. Other short films are infiltrating this cinematic resistance zone area and preparing for the launch of a new discourse. The titles alone point to a change in direction—Guy Brenton's *People Apart* (1957), Anderson's *Truck Conveyor* (1952), and Gavin Lambert's *Another Sky* (1954)—titles suggesting the many problems of everyday life, irreducible facts developed in the social sphere.[8] Lorenza Mazzetti, a young

115

Italian director, contributed to the evolution of neorealist cinema beyond the Channel. With *Together* (1956), based on a novel by Denis Horne, Mazzetti made a film of sharp reflections and burning contrasts. The story of two deaf-mutes, set against a painful and obtuse background of the shipyards, piers, and quays of the industrial river Thames, filled the National Film Theatre, reaffirming that taste and sensibility were maturing and maybe even going beyond the expectations of the supporters themselves. In any case, the Free Cinema group had decided in one of its programs to face and challenge without compromises "a movie industry which was still bound to class prejudices and refused the stimulus of the present-day life and the responsibility of self criticism. These ideas reflected a metropolitan or a provincial southern culture which excluded the rich diversity of traditions and personalities that are part of all of Great Britain."[9]

The challenge to go into the streets, to look at the surroundings was accepted by many young and not-so-young people—and not only metaphorically. *The Street Cleaners* (1956), *The Singing Street* (1957), *We Are the Lambeth Boys* (1958), and, more explicit in its political basis, *March to Aldermaston* (1958), were the less timid explorations of the everyday. They were shot without polish, concealments, special effects, or face makeup. So-called middle-class spaces became bloodied: from the Covent Garden Market (which *Every Day Except Xmas* [1957] has its most disenchanted portrayal) to the youth clubs, to London street sweepers, to the amusement parks, to the less respectable pubs. These films authentically captured people in their daily routines, in their *erlebnis*, a reality all the more baffling for its persistence. The "ordinary" person was discovered in the street, was filmed in his own habitat without being erased from the place were he lived all his life by statistics or other more or less abstract deductions.

The impulses of many directors were didactic, oratorical, exhortative, or indignant, but the substance of their films consisted of a warm attention to widespread everyday events, events forgotten exactly because they were accessible and obvious to all. Surely, the "new style" was like a river fed by many streams. For example, there was a gradual confluence of neorealism with the more distinctly British stream of "angry young men." And thus the vagabond antihero of the welfare state was arrogantly introduced on-screen. This character has his own way of viewing all that is wrong, challenging nostalgic rhetoric and the most anachronistic Kiplingism.

Because of this trajectory, we have films that examine in detail the psychical and physical world of exasperate sadness, shown as bursts of anger, anguish, erotic bad mood, from burdensome to moralistic, with a sardonic and irritated realism. Such films include the works of the Film Institute Experimental Committee, such as Michael Grigsby's *Enginemen* (1959) or Robert Vas's *Refuge England* (1959), as well as the first works of John Osborne, Arnold Wesker, and others (including Richardson's *Look Back in Anger*). In line with neorealism, this type of cinema insists on mistrusting the order of the establishment (with its old-fashioned slogans), which from Victorian and Edwardian predecessors morphed into a "modern" conservative identity. It shows bare, wretched surroundings, without drawing from the solace of fairy tales or panacea instilled into good feelings.

Often, however, the lack of collaboration in such films dissolves into a kind of uncomfortable fog without tangible structure or, at least, precise suggestions. However, the questions that arise and develop are those that touch deeply without stereotypes, outrageous attitudes, or rebellious or pained dramas. For example, *The Entertainer* (1960) by Richardson is clearly connected to an argument that undermines the basis of the "imperial" prestige of the United Kingdom. It shows mummies embalmed in austerity, adults who never grow up, old failed clowns: they are all at fault for the death of Mick, and not for a reason but for the horrifying presumption of modifying the course of events.

The progressive and leftish ideology of the angry men in *The Entertainer* intersects well with certain experiences of national self-criticism elsewhere—from a "defeated" nation like Italy.[10] Thus directors remove any leftover theatricality, opting instead to combine daily news and human problems in a manner that is not fictitious or prefabricated. For example, in *Sabato sera, domenica mattina* (1960) by Reisz (from Alan Sillitoe), in *A Taste of Honey* (1961) by Richardson, and in *Whistle down the Wind* (1961) by Bryan Forbes we see the same calm approach to the rent fabric of society and its individuals. *A Taste of Honey* is produced and directed by that solid and expert narrator, Richardson, who was able to give the bare yet cogent dialogue of the young playwright Shelagh Delaney appropriate gray tonalities and, sometimes, sharp suggestions of a Dickensian industrial city.

Richardson explores the English lower classes with a passion for a realism that is moderate, controlled, and without impulses that are too violent or too involved with the lower stratum of everyday life. In other words, a realism in which the figurative invention adheres closely to the squalid events that at times are also crossed by small comets of light. Richardson's subjects are traumatized, wavering between solitude and a pathetic search for dignity, between sincerity and the escape from a sense of life that is too conventional. Richardson fully demonstrates an effective control of cinematography that removes any remains of theatrics, and injects in the work a corrosive spirit of environmental and psychological analysis. A clear orientation toward the documentary can be detected (even in the way he shoots), but his is a style in which daily life and human problems are combined. His is a unity that is not fictitious or designed by a script, but brought to the screen through laborious struggle. The foggy Lancashire locations, the squalid homes of Chelsea, the unconventional facial features of the actresses, the surprising revelation of Rita Tushingham, a new actress already at the top of her expressive possibilities, and the renewed personality of an old "comedienne," Dora Bryan, are all the coefficients of this "empirical realism" that obeys poetry rather than a particular poetics. This realism, therefore, even though it does not reside in high temperatures, through well-calculated ambitions, is able to make a memorable impression and to follow a road that is not one of adventure, experimentation, or technical or aesthetic skill.

On another level, *Term of Trial* (Peter Glenville, 1962) is an inferior film precisely because it relies on supporting help, such as stiflingly well-known actors (Laurence Olivier and Simone Signoret). However, because the director is imaginatively eclectic and can be placed artistically among honest craftsmen, it can be seen as a product of dignified marketability. This work indulges in an exploitation of Anglo-Saxon virtues: modesty, privacy, and an obstinate belief in the less conspicuous values of life. It is exploitative because it evolves slowly among judicial traumas, unexpected scenes capable only of fracturing, if not shattering, that muted image of a common man with many qualities. This drama unfolds against a backdrop of clichés; it is a pseudo-heroic vision of the monotonous but not easy everyday reality, complete with stock characters, including the common man's wife.

In spite of the (critical) silence that surrounds the activities of English cineastes, we are favorably impressed by the fact that they continue to refer to a medium that they hope to realize by their honest seriousness of intentions (which is, at base, the most reliable approach to realism). As with any complex achievement, realism cannot be dealt with and exhausted through impatience or overprogramming. No longer do we have the strong revolutionary shouts of Behan or the wordy pleading of Hyde Park but the intense connections to reality, resulting from a consciousness that is also an obligation to denounce. Anderson says, "To fight means to commit oneself, to believe in what we say and to say what we believe. . . . [I]t is the nature of the artist to be in conflict with hypocrisy, meanness, reactionism."[11]

In this manner, the mundane, refined, cynical words of the British mid-cult are swept away and are replaced by words that reveal, attack, and cauterize the sure failures of the upper class, of the so-called Oxonian or Cantabrigian elite. (Colin Smith, the boy from Borstal, and main character in *The Loneliness of the Long Distance Runner* [1962] directed by Richardson, based on a novel by Sillitoe, defines them as "those grave-diggers who always have the whip by the handle.") Even in works such as *Sparrows Can't Sing* (1962) by Joan Littlewood (better known as a theater director) or *A Kind of Loving* (1962) by John Schlesinger, we have merciless portrayals of the middle-class "milieu." Such realism often leans toward the bizarre, with odd jumps and peculiarities that cover it with dry and bitter humor, taking on a particular hue, one that is always more clearly defined in its own elements. *The Kitchen* (1961), directed by James Hill, shows irregular and unconventional characteristics that are similar to those of Wesker's original play. In fact, woven throughout are heavy symbolisms, complicated practical jokes, and concentric recoils: the back shop of a London restaurant is populated like the navel of a Joycean memory—too many metaphors for realism to have anything to do with a well-delineated trend in its trajectory.

Instead, films made with the "Italian way of filming" reach the lyrical or the grotesque with less semantics: consider *The L-shaped Room* (1962) by Forbes, *This Sporting Life* (*Io sono un campione;* 1963) by Anderson, or *Girl with Green Eyes* (1964) by Desmond Davis. The visual focus in these works is on the minute urban reality, with a technique that is detached from affected snobbery or artificiality. If the perspective—as in the good English tradition—is directed toward an ordinary narrative pattern, while at the same time submerged under an obtuse, gray, and at times filthy surface, one notices a pathetic emotional underground that calls to mind the lyrical and bitter neorealism of Cesare Zavattini, De Sica, Fellini, or the first Antonioni.

Moreover, in more recent works (such as *West 11* [1963] or *The System* [1964] by Michael Winner, *The Boys* [1962] by Sydney Furie, or *Lunch Hour* [1961] by James Hill), the directors seem to be looking for "good courageous causes, which don't seem to exist any more."[12] In these films, neighborhoods (such as Notting Hill, Hamstead Heat, or Elstree and Threadmeedle) that have cultural, political, and emotional relevance are sought by the lens, which captures characteristics that differ from those of farther away and more common places of "relief," such as West End or Kensington Gardens. They are shot and painted in all their misery, in the gray, obsessive passing of days. This is all in perfect accord with the manifesto of Free Cinema, that is, without apologies for a brilliant and not-too-familiar "Metropolitan Southern England."

With respect to these projects, so strikingly different from past patterns, even certain men devoted to the movie industry (such as Jack Clayton) have found particular courage. Clayton gives Anne Bancroft a part that could have been given to a mature Anna Magnani in *Bellissima* (1951). I'm referring to Clayton's *The Pumpkin Eater* (1964), where the environment and the predetermination of certain problems follow a development, a rhythm, and a formal destiny that call to mind our most vivid Italian post–World War II cinema. A new and more solid generation of actors has emerged from this environment and they are in contact with this very particular revival; actors ranging from Albert Finney in *Sabato sera, domenica mattina* to Tom Courtenay in *Billy Liar* (1953), from Rita Tushingham in *A Taste of Honey* and *Girl with Green Eyes* to Richard Harris in *This Sporting Life* (1963). From these contributions and new ideas cultural immigrants such as Losey or Edward Dmytrik have likewise discovered their most serious self, confronting their technical resources with a need for authenticity, for lived and not fantasized experiences. Therefore, the paths between the "new style" (that is, neorealism) of Italian cinema and British Free Cinema have been buried, intricately but not impenetrably. They are part of the natural metabolism of ideas, of compression and contact with a whole society in motion, in all of its lowest and most humiliating strata. This fight against a "false reputation of authenticity" and the capture of a "living background" induced a scholar such as Ivor Montagu to define (in his book *Film World*) a good part of English film production as bona fide "British new-realism."

Neorealism in the United States

The same cultural, human, and sentimental wave coming from postwar Italy in 1948 also touched the United States. Screenings in New York and other cities of movies by Rossellini, De Sica, and later by Visconti shook up Hollywood and stimulated spiritual practices and new expressive attitudes. Finally a distinction was beginning to be made between glossy, impeccable, banal films and rough, imperfect but living films.

As a result the most conscientious, less sedated Yankees felt the excitement of real emotions, of problems that do not belong only to a particular people in a particular political and economic situation. They realized immediately that this new language is not a formula nor a formalism but a way to show human values, to face collective history and interior meanings without solipsism or oneiric evasions. In addition, the low cost, actors "taken from the street," the use of real choreography, and urban, on-location settings are not commercial methods but a way of looking at subjects without masks or frames, without abstractions or useless agoraphobia.

Even the well-known American producer Louis De Rochemont feels the importance of the newly imported discourse and his *March of Time* (1935–51) newsreel series and other movies show a clear neorealist imprint. Instantly capturing reality is a youthful way of looking; therefore young American cineastes embrace it. They fight not only to increase Italian film imports but also for projects that can come to fruition independently from cinema moguls. For example, the first "off-Hollywood" production was the 1948 film *The Quiet One* (*L'escluso*) by Sidney Meyers, a minute and touching analysis of a black neighborhood as seen through the long and difficult day of a young man, a man who is desperate, misunderstood, and unable to loosen the knots that tie him to his daily life. Every small event in this film represents the beginning and expression of all the *petits faits vrais* that happen to his race, amplified by a sense of inner torment. The resignation of the grandmother, the incoherent rage of his friend, the misery of the streets and of the homes are all lost in a kind of hall of mirrors that bounces around images of this world without end, images from a dark game or endless drama.

This film's white counterpart, *The Little Fugitive* (1953) by Morris Engel and Ray Ashley, is only remotely happier. The story may seem to have its own happy ending due to the fact that young Donald is found, but the same continuous neglect of small children, in addition to their tough, street education among children of the same age or more "hardened" older boys—the absence, in short, of a constant and loving adult guide—emphasizes the shortcomings of a society that has reached the maximum of its capitalistic expansion. Though there is only a hint of a contribution from Italian cinema, it nonetheless resonates with the vicissitudes of our *Sciuscià*, which above all shows victims of a painful loneliness who grow up in a risky, if not dangerous, place.[13]

On a more deliberately social level, *Salt of the Earth* by Biberman parallels the lyrically epic film *La terra trema*. In both films the spirit of rebellion and human dignity is identical even though the endings are aesthetically quite different. However, these neorealist-like attempts confirm that American cinema, due to the tenacity of its most honest artisans (or the stubborn endurance of a few artists), does not want to be labeled "a sausage-making machine," as Chaplin (himself not at all a sausage maker) called it. Moreover, the basis for this new American cinema had already been established by such men as Leo Hurwitz with *Strange Victory* (1948), Herbert Kline and Charles Korvin with *Heart of Spain* (1937), Pare Lorentz with *The Plow That Broke the Plains* (1936), and J. Hamid with *T.V.A.* (1940), namely the directors of the New Deal. But once again the catalyst for this group, a group always searching for the best, was neorealism rather than a revival in documentary filmmaking or the location of the filming itself (a topic that had suddenly become important to some American moviemakers).

As such, the film *The Savage Eye* by Ben Maddow and Sidney Meyers (1960), a long panoramic view of an affluent society, shows segmented sequences of street accidents, analyzes a certain alienated femininity (coiffeurs and nightclubs), and features long tracking shots of people running and hastily pushing each other in the street—all pointing to underlining neuroses. The film is comprised of master shots recomposed through careful editing, which offers a clear diagnosis of the age of anxiety mentioned by W. H. Auden.

Lionel Rogosin, in his *On the Bowery* (1957), an inquiry into the hellish aspects of New York City, offers a much sharper example of filmmaking, one made up of moral mud, sour defeat, and the strong, disgusting smell of cheap whiskey.[14] Rogosin moved to South Africa in 1959 in order to trace the equivalent or the metaphor of the racial situation in his own country. The result is a film in which a hidden movie camera explores the faces of black subjects with an impartiality not lacking in comprehension or benevolence. The film unearths, without dispute, the harsh treatments and abuses that make these men desire an impossible return to their old village or a descent into the chaos that arises from revenge.

John Cassavetes's *Shadows* (1959) parallels Rogosin's film. Here a parable likewise becomes clear (even if it is found in an open debate between various beliefs). The problem of overcoming "internal" limits between men—between a changed conscience and a faithful one—still remains. The exposition and introduction of the characters is perhaps a little weak (three hoodlums visit the Metropolitan Museum in a manner that is reminiscent of a high school prank), but the second part continues with many fine details: the relationships between Leila and Tony (the white boy) and between Leila and Jim, and, above all, the relationship between the brothers, are difficult, harsh, and oppositional but contain a hint of love. For these reasons the film is closer to the delicate humanism and good sentiment of neorealism rather than to the tones of uncontrolled beatniks whose posture is always abrasive and tense. With *Too Late Blues* (1961), Cassavetes seems to have been taken back into the fold of Hollywood, but with *A Child Is Waiting* (1963) he again presents courageous and nonconformist themes that are clearly derived from neorealism. Although urged by Stanley Kramer and Abby Mann (the scriptwriter), Cassavetes was able to maintain his personal point of view in penetrating the subhuman but existential lives of mentally disabled children. The camera shows a tender and sorrowful journey without digressions and concessions. The director seems to desire questions, themes, and moral conflicts from his spectators, confirming again that he has overcome banal "boy meets girl" narratives.

American independent cinema faces many obstacles, even from the unions. Small crews and the necessity of speedy production mandate that financiers are not the only ones concerned with the exploits of these directors, who seem to be convinced, like Zavattini, that "the emphasis on the story is the only, and often an unconscious, way to put a face on human defeat." Often these are extreme cases as Pandolfi says (C.N. 154), and in them "one can observe here and there some satisfactions that are characteristic of a certain 'miserable' neorealism."[15] But modesty, pity, and understanding are predominant therein. The plots are generally concerned with moral decision-making and a collective sensibility. These characteristics are found in more complicated and less conventional works such as *The Connection* (1962) by Shirley Clarke and *The Exiles* (1961) by Kent MacKenzie. These films are hallucinating documents concerning the double alienation of man (physical and ethical), bodies wasted by drugs and alcohol on Indian reservations. The shooting technique is confused and opaque, and the editing is rough, but the weight of human degradation and victimization puts a stamp "De profundis" on this testimonial and makes it not easily forgotten.

Stemming from both British and American cultural currents, but often crossing each other in an unclear union, is the magazine *Filmculture* and the new directors who emerge from it. Consider Jonas Mekas's *Guns of the Trees* (1964), in which a violent detachment reminiscent of Jack Kerouac, Gregory Corso, or Lawrence Ferlinghetti resonates with an intoxicated lamentation that feeds only on the objective energy of the image; or Jack O'Connell's *The Greenwich Village Story* (1963), which, despite the title, appears to derive from the French school, from Agnes Varda in particular. However, a general distrust of the "American way of life" is very evident in these films: art, according to all these filmmakers, should not undermine reality, even though in the end there are divergent interpretations of the term "reality."

Other films lie halfway between Italian investigative films (*polizze-schi*) and cinema verité. For example, Richard Leacock (British, but working in the United States) in his work *The Chair* (1963) offers a dramatic chronicle of a petition for a pardon made by a man sentenced to the electric chair; see also Mel Stuart's *The Making of the President 1960* (1963) or the inferior film *Primary* (1960) by Robert Drew and Leacock on the same subject. Jerome Hill's *The Sand Castle* (1961) is a less corrosive and more heroically lyrical film. In it one notices a misunderstanding of foreign poetics as they arrived on the other side of the Atlantic. The ending, with the painter who is unable to paint the beach because the people always assume a different formation (while the sand castle of the child gets bigger and bigger), seems to lean toward the apotheosis of abstractionism, the only shape—according to Hill—in which the daily confusion finds a faithful reflection, or at least one that is not in bad faith.

Productions such as *Pull My Daisy* (1959) and others show how a Yankee brand of neorealism immediately met, clashed with and embedded itself in an already existing, turbulent avant-garde movement. Such productions (characterized by a combination of Zen-style solipsism and nihilism) often end up losing the basic notion of rebellion, the basic social exposure, even if—in more successful examples—they contribute to introspection and an implicit criticism of an environment that is stagnant, conformist, and ready for any order. The sum of these experiences, full of polyvalent implications, can be found in works such as *The Cool World* (1963), directed by Shirley Clarke, Curtis Harrington's *Night Tide* (1961), and *The Inheritance* (1964), directed by Harold Mayer. The clash between the individual and society in these films seems taken to immature extremes. Often the characters appear only as symptoms of a morbid restlessness without escape. These films are often full of neurotic anxiety and border on the psychopathological where movie language is concerned (see, for example, *The Queen of Sheba Meets the Atom Man* [1963] by Ron Rice).[16] We eagerly await other Anglo-Saxon independent films, though we realize that direct influence from neorealism is getting lost in the current of a much more tumultuous river, enlarged by the complex cultural currents of present-day America.[17]

Notes

1. The epigraph comes from a 1966 issue of the Italian film journal, *Quaderni di Cinemasud,* with the special issue title of "L'eredità del

neorealismo." In 2002, Mephite Press reprinted this classic issue, which included an essay on cinema and literature by the prominent Italian film scholar Gianpiero Brunetta (who, in fact, first published in the pages of *Cinemasud*), as well as a piece on the relationship between writers and directors by the filmmaker Alberto Lattuada (lesser known outside of Italy). We have added notes, where appropriate (see "editors' notes" below), but have been unable to document all of the author's uncited quotes.

2. We would like to acknowledge Mephite Press, which assisted with the reprinting of this essay in English, and Anna Ruberto and Raffaele Ruberto, who worked on the first draft of the translation. In editing the translation of Napolitano's essay we have kept some of the poetic sensibility of the original. It reflects a European academic tone of a certain era, and we wanted to preserve the stylistic integrity of the essay; its metaphorical approach may at times be off-putting to the sensibilities of the early twenty-first-century scholarly reader.

3. Irpinia is a landlocked area southeast of Naples in the Campania region in and around Avellino.

4. J. Arthur Rank is the name behind the most powerful film corporation during the golden years of British cinema (1940s and 1950s). The Rank Organization is said to have owned five studios, two newsreels, several production companies, and around 650 cinemas in the United Kingdom. See Macnab and Wakelin.

5. Editors' note: Fellini's *I vittelloni* has been described as neorealist in its sensibility; in addition, Fellini broke into film by working on Rossellini's *Rome, Open City*. Nonetheless, most contemporary film historians would not consider Fellini a neorealist director. Likewise, some of Antonioni's earlier work has been called neorealist. In general, though, both directors are described as breaking from neorealism in their attention to a stylized cinematic experience, one that has more in common with Jean-Luc Godard than De Sica. For a discussion about the relationship between Godard and neorealism, see David Anshen's essay in this collection.

6. Editors' note: Free Cinema was first an event rather than a movement—a group of filmmakers brought their films together to be screened at the National Film Theatre in February 1956 in London (in all there eventually were at least six such film programs lasting until 1959). Included in the program was a printed manifesto outlining the need for an improvised filmmaking that sought to outline the realities of everyday England. The directors—Lindsay Anderson, John Fletcher, Walter Lassally, Lorenza Mazzetti, Karel Reisz, and Tony Richardson—were originally from various countries (Czechoslova-

kia, Germany, Italy, and England) but shared a documentary style of filmmaking and were influenced by earlier British documentarians as well as Italian neorealism. As their manifesto explains, "Implicit in our attitude is a belief in freedom, in the importance of people and the significance of the everyday" (Free Cinema manifesto, reprinted online at <http://www.bfi.org.uk>). Since 1959, Free Cinema events have occurred elsewhere, namely in France and Italy.

7. The proliferation of seeds imported from southern Europe was therefore lengthy and slow, as was lengthy and difficult the reversal of business propositions or the convictions of showmen like Alexander Korda and the Boulting Brothers or Del Giudice. Besides, Del Giudice was working in cultural areas beyond the pale of criticism: refined Shakespearean remakes with Olivier.

8. *Another Sky* was filmed mostly in Africa and shows a search for the roots of old diseases now surfacing without false pretenses.

9. Editors' note: The source of this quote is not offered in the original essay but presumably comes from one of Free Cinema's pamphlets distributed at its screenings.

10. Editors' note: The reference here presumably is to Italy's position in World War II.

11. Editors' note: No citation accompanies this quote in the original text.

12. Editors' note: No citation accompanies this quote in the original text.

13. One should likewise remember that the basis for *The Little Fugitive* comes from an interesting short film by Lewis Jacobs, who in addition to being a historian of the adventurous American cinema is the creator of the most expressive tendencies of independent cinema.

14. *Wedding and Babies* (1958) by Engel is less surgical and iconoclastic but no less bitter in its victories. This film consists of a reportage shaded with melancholy on the life of a photographer aspiring to an existence that is less repressed and limited, and therefore more human.

15. Editors' note: No citations accompany these quotes in the original text.

16. Leaning more fully toward reality is the film *David and Lisa* (1962), Frank Perry's pedagogic story of two young people who are victims of personality disorders. As with most medium-length films the subject matter here stays on track, refusing to fall prey to schizoid originality: see, for example, *The Language of the Faces* (1934) by the Sanders brothers (many years ago we praised their works, *A Time out of War* [1954] and *Crime and Punishment, USA* [1935]); *The Legend of Marilyn Monroe* (1963) and *Good Times, Wonderful Times* (1965), the last film of Rogosin, which, even though filmed in England and with

repertory materials taken from everywhere, remains the fruit of a new and vital "American" undertaking. This political pamphlet of unusual visual concentration was used by the director to collect evidence of uncommon testimonial vigor, the *corpora sceleris* of the most recent Nazi warmongers (but we do not want to repeat ourselves since we have already written at length about this topic in our report from Venice in number 37 of this magazine).

17. Consider *Day of the Nightmare* (1965) by John Bushelman; *Planet of Blood* (1966) by the already known Harrington; *The Snow Ball* (1966) by G. Clarke; and the last work of Jacobs, the veteran "experimentalist" who just finished, as he mentioned to us in Venice, *The Bird* (1966). This last film deals with racial problems and is framed by the symbolic life of saxophonist Charlie Parker, precursor of bop and, above all, precursor of a human solution for "colored men" not only in America but on any continent.

Chapter 6

A Stonecutter's Passion:
Latin American Reality and Cinematic Faith

Tomás F. Crowder-Taraborrelli

> So far the most powerful human beings have still bowed worshipfully before the
> saint as the riddle of self-conquest and deliberate final renunciation . . . the sight of
> the saint awakened a suspicion in them: such an enormity of denial, of anti-nature
> will not have been desired for nothing, they said to and asked themselves. There may
> be a reason for it, some very great danger about which the ascetic, thanks to his se-
> cret comforters and visitor, might have inside information. In short, the powerful of
> the world learned a new fear before him; they sensed a new power, a strange, as yet
> unconquered enemy.
> Friedrich Nietzsche

García Márquez and the Neorealists

Screenings of the first Italian neorealist films in Latin America coincided with an influx of young artists in the cultural camp, many of whom
became leaders of the cultural revolution some decades later. In Bar-
ranquilla, Colombia, Gabriel García Márquez, then a young journalist,
covered the 1950 premiere of *Bicycle Thief* (which had been released in
1948). He is said to have been deeply moved by this new style of filmmaking that encouraged the spectator to think critically about the recent
horrific history of World War II and seemed to have the power to ignite
a feeling of solidarity for the working class. With the triumph of the
Cuban Revolution in 1959 and the founding of the Cuban Institute of
Art and Cinematographic Industry (ICAIC), Latin American admirers
of Italian neorealism hoped to develop an industry that could rival, in
influence and ideology, the Hollywood studio system.

García Márquez's review of *Bicycle Thief* for *El Heraldo* begins as follows: "The production of Vittorio De Sica that is currently exhibited in

128

a theater of the city gives a lot of thought in regards to the advances and possibilities of the cinematographic art" (*La soledad de América Latina* 113).[1] In particular, García Márquez was especially impressed by the way in which De Sica and Cesare Zavattini turned a bicycle into a myth, calling it "a divinity on wheels and pedals with which—and only with which—man can be superior to hunger" (113). The cinematic representation of the relationship between the down-and-out worker and the bicycle expressed the anguish of not only the protagonist but an entire social class. Reality was represented with scientific exactitude. Roberto Rossellini suggested that in his own films, he tried to capture the "intelligence of things . . . because to give the true value to anything means to have apprehended its authentic and universal significance" (in Marcus 12). García Márquez suggested that the Colombian bourgeois, looking to pass time in movie theaters, would find the relationship between the worker and his tool insignificant; however, others would identify with the alienation of a worker without a community, labor union, or institution in which to find shelter. García Márquez ends his review praising De Sica's film as "the most human film that has ever been made" (113). Years later a young Argentine poet named Fernando Birri would travel to Rome to study film at the Centro Sperimentale di Cinematografia (CSC). Birri would posit neorealism as an early cinema of underdevelopment: "Neorealism is the cinema that discovers the Italy of underdevelopment, discovers in a country that apparently has the clothing, the tinsel, and what's more, the rhetoric of development, another reality, a hidden one, that of underdevelopment . . . it was the cinema of the humble and offended. It was possible everywhere" (Hess in King, Lopez, and Alvarado 110). As in the case of Birri, García Márquez was inspired by the films of De Sica to abandon his career as a film critic and travel to Rome to study scriptwriting with Zavattini.[2] There Birri, who had been studying in Rome and working at Cinecittá for five years, took García Márquez under his wing (Saldívar 335). Scriptwriting was not part of the CSC's curriculum but taught as part of the directing course. García Márquez enrolled in classes in 1954. He had hoped to have Zavattini as a teacher but ended up being one of many who only saw him from a distance. He found most of the courses too technical, as he was primarily interested in learning how to write a successful screenplay. His greatest achievement seems to have been working on one of Alessandro Blasetti's films, assisting the production team by holding a rope to keep curious onlookers from interrupting the shooting (337).

Although García Márquez's experience in Rome did not live up to his expectations, I suggest that his film studies helped define his literary career and his role as a leader of the New Latin American Film Foundation, which currently supports the San Antonio de los Baños International School of Film, Television and Video, founded in 1986. In the 1990s, García Márquez returned to his memories of studying at the CSC, taking the opportunity to reflect on the influence of neorealism on his work and on the Latin American film industry. For example, he suggests that, despite the letdowns in Rome, he was able to travel and accumulate material for stories that would become newspaper articles and, later, a collection of short stories titled *Strange Pilgrims: Twelve Stories* (1991).[3]

García Márquez's relationship to neorealism can best be understood by looking at "The Saint" from *Strange Pilgrims* and its precursor, a film he cowrote with director Lisandro Duque Naranjo titled *Miracle in Rome* (1988).[4] Both versions are based on a newspaper article García Márquez wrote in November 1982 titled "The Long and Happy Life of Margarito Duarte."[5] The story establishes a dialogue in which the problem of the miraculous nature of Latin American reality is debated between a group of characters, including fictionalized versions of García Márquez (a film student in Rome) and Zavattini (his instructor). What results from this fictional debate is a cultural impasse in which Europe renders Latin American self-representation dependent upon European sanctioning.

John Hess argues that because the Cuban Revolution had gone beyond what the Italian left was able to achieve, Latin American filmmakers had to go even further in depicting national struggles (including the struggle to be recognized in North America and Europe). He suggests that unlike Italian neorealists, for whom Fascism could be overlooked or footnoted in an effort to build a new society, colonialism and imperialism were not brief interludes that could be overlooked for Latin American intellectuals (such as García Márquez) but centuries-long struggles for self-representation. In Latin America and other regions of the underdeveloped world, this struggle is far from over. Colonialism, imperialism, and neocolonialism, phenomena characterized in our age by the term "globalization," have hindered the development of national cultural expression, restricting the ways in which the realities of different communities are imagined and represented. In Latin America, this has resulted in continuous experimentation with literature and film by artists working under the pressures of monopolizing industries, unified in the struggle for self-representation. A radical, contentious form of representation has been at the center of Latin America's search for independent expression.

No intellectual in Latin America has made film the center of his writing to the extent that Gabriel García Márquez has.⁶ An early penchant for neorealist film has informed his literary production and has constantly challenged his strategies for representing social reality. For example, he recounts that while writing *No One Writes to the Colonel* (1961) he had trouble describing something in the novel without imagining the story as a film in progress. He became conscious that in writing a text there are "literary solutions" and "visual or cinematographic" ones.

> For example: if we were dealing with a room, its size, the steps the character has to take to move inside the room, etc.; in other words, I worked like a filmmaker . . . when during my work as a novelist I find myself with a story in which I don't see literary solutions but visual, I leave them to the side because that is cinema and I sell them [the rights to the story] without intervening in the screenplay and without having to do anything else with it. (Torres in Rentería Mantilla 46, 48)

Miracle in Rome (1988)

The story of Margarito Duarte deploys the theme of conflicts arising from colonialism, imperialism, and development. In the previously mentioned article, "The Long and Happy Life of Margarito Duarte," García Márquez explains how in 1954 he met a man (Duarte) who had come to the Vatican, with the help of a collection of money from his country, to lobby for the canonization of his dead daughter. When he showed up at the consul general's office with this incredible demand, the consul asked his friend, a Colombian tenor, to find Duarte a room in the same pension where he and García Márquez were living. That same day, says García Márquez, Duarte told them his story. He had suffered great losses in his life; both his wife and daughter had passed away. Six months before his trip to Rome, he had been forced to remove their remains because the local cemetery was to be moved to create space for a new business. His wife had turned to ashes, but his daughter, retells García Márquez in this early article, was "intact" (160). When they opened the coffin, Duarte told his new friends in Rome, one could smell roses: "There was no question: the incorruptibility of the body had always been one of the most visible symptoms of sainthood and even the bishop of dioceses was in agreement that the news of this event had to reach the Vatican so that the sacred congregation of the rite could render their judgment" (160).

Duarte opened the lock of the cello case he always carried with him and made the tenor and García Márquez "participants in the miracle": "It was not a wilted mummy like you see in so many museums the world over; this one could have been confused with a child that kept sleeping after twelve years of being underground. She was the restful color of honey and the open eyes were clear and alive, and caused the irresistible impression that they had been looking back at us from death" (160). Duarte also carried a jar with the nails that had been cut from the saint's hands. The town had decided to cut them because they thought that long nails were a gruesome spectacle that would tarnish the girl's saintly image.

The film version of Duarte's story, *Miracle in Rome*, is an obvious tribute to De Sica's *Miracle in Milan* (1951).[7] In the film, the cemetery of the town of Finlandia must be moved not to give place to a dam but to a modern cemetery called Campos de Paz (Fields of Peace).[8] In one of the movie's most memorable scenes, the residents of Finlandia are shown digging up the remains of their relatives because they cannot afford a burial ground in the new cemetery. A middle-aged woman is seen putting her mother's skeleton in a plastic bag as she repeats to her husband that she is going to take the remains home until she can save enough money to rebury them. The camera follows Margarito through this battlefield of hollowed graves as he witnesses the sorrow of his community. A man crosses his path carrying a cross he had looted from a grave or had bought for a loved one. A threatening voice is heard through the loudspeaker warning the crowd that if they do not remove the remains of their relatives they will be thrown into a common grave. Margarito stares into one of the common graves, a gesture designed to remind Latin American audiences of the hundreds of mass graves that have been discovered throughout the continent after military repression and genocide.

When Margarito arrives at his daughter's grave, a section of the coffin reveals the untarnished feet of his daughter. Desperately, he opens the coffin hoping to find his daughter alive. At the same time, a strong wind rises, signaling the arrival of an untamable force. The indigent gather around Margarito and his daughter; a woman proclaims the sainthood of the child and the presence of a miracle. Some kneel down and begin to pray. The discovery causes great commotion in Finlandia. The archbishop is summoned and has to battle his way through a crowd that has gathered outside Margarito's pension to assess the situation. Upon seeing the girl he concludes, "Un curioso episodio de la vida real" (a curi-

Miracle in Rome
(Lisandro Duque
Naranjo, 1988)

ous episode of real life). He orders Margarito to bury the body because
it constitutes a public health hazard. Margarito respectfully refuses to
follow the archbishop's orders since he wants to keep her next to him
for the rest of his life. At that instant, the sky goes dark. Outside, the
mob is shaken by the eclipse, which they attribute to the saint's power.
A collection begins sporadically. A middle-aged man is the first to offer
his money: "I am very poor but I offer these thousand pesos so that Margarito can go to Rome to speak personally with the Pope." The scene
ends as a pile of money grows and then cuts to a shot of an Avianca
airplane carrying Margarito to Rome.

The power relation as it pertains to the miracle is depicted more
clearly in the film than in the short story, which followed the film. Finlandia's priest wants to convince the town that the miracle is a signal
from God that he approves of the building of the new cemetery, the
archbishop wants to deny the possibility of a small rural town having a
saint, and the Colombian ambassador living in Rome thinks it would do
their country a lot of good, politically speaking, to have a saint. At the
Colombian embassy in Rome, a majestic petit hotel, Margarito is shown
sitting peacefully, holding on his knees the strange case in which he carries the saint. As the camera pulls back, the image of Margarito becomes
smaller and the ambassador's voice is overheard through the telephone:
"Developed countries rarely need a saint. But the poor areas of the planet

. . . yes, exactly, like Colombia, need these stimuli. At least to relax social tensions." When the ambassador hangs up the phone and turns around, he finds that the chair where Margarito was sitting is empty.

In the end—and herein lies the biggest difference between the film and the subsequent short story—Margarito, threatened by the mortuary police who demand the body of the saint be buried, resurrects his daughter. *Miracle in Rome* ends with the image of father and daughter walking together to buy an ice cream. The "Hallelujah" of Handel's Messiah is heard in the background, sanctifying and vindicating the resurrection. In the short story, written some years after the film, García Márquez creates a fictionalized encounter with Zavattini, in which Zavattini considers García Márquez's idea of adapting Margarito's life story into a screenplay. García Márquez's idea for the screenplay follows the newspaper story that suggests that the girl is a saint. Zavattini argues that nobody would believe the idea of a Latin American saint and that the girl should be resurrected at the end. The end of the movie thus elicits two possible interpretations depending on whether one has read the short story: it can be seen as a form of Latin American resistance to European powers—the girl comes alive at her father's command to spite the mortuary police—or as a cop-out—in which García Márquez and Duque Naranjo follow Zavattini's suggestion for a type of closure that will be more understandable to Europeans. One could also argue that García Márquez found a way to make Zavattini's suggestion work, without diminishing the importance of the miracle of sainthood to Latin American self-representation, with this element of resistance on Margarito's part.

"The Saint" (1991)

In "The Saint," the short story based on the friendship between Duarte and García Márquez, the author retains an autobiographical tone (casting himself as the narrator) and allows his readers a glimpse back at his studies in Rome, his experience as an aspiring filmmaker, and the earlier filmed version of the story. Part autobiography, part fiction, part literary criticism, and part film criticism, the narrative—by retelling the story of Margarito—divides García Márquez's subjectivity and reflects on the relationship between neorealism and Latin American representation.

The narrator is a student at the CSC who wants to study screenwriting with Zavattini, described as one of the great figures of world cinema: "He tried to teach us not only the craft but a different way of looking at life. He was a machine for inventing plots. They poured out of

134

him, almost against his will, and with such speed that he always needed someone to help catch them in mid-flight as he thought them up aloud" (48).

By contrast the narrator says that his own amazing drive to write screenplays would wane when he had to finish them: "For he thought that on the screen they would lose much of their original magic" (48). The story begins with the voice of the narrator, who informs the reader that he has gone back to Rome and, in the streets of Trastevere, stumbles upon an old friend, Margarito Duarte: "[H]is hair was white and thin, and there was nothing left of the Andean intellectual's solemn manner and funereal clothes with which he had first come to Rome" (36). After a brief conversation over a cup of coffee, the narrator sees him as he used to be: "secretive, unpredictable, and as tenacious as a stonecutter" (36). Here the image of a stonecutter represents a positive quality, as it represents Margarito's unflinching drive for recognition.

Modern development and expansion in Latin America always bring tragedy in García Márquez's novels and short stories. In "The Saint," the construction of a dam leads to the relocation of a cemetery and its bodies. As in the newspaper article, when Margarito shows up to move his family's bones, he discovers that the body of his daughter is intact and has "no weight" (38). A public collection is then organized by the town and its local chieftains so that the miraculous case of Margarito's daughter can be taken to authorities in the Vatican. This is the beginning of Margarito's odyssey. He spends the rest of the story carrying the body of his daughter in a violoncello's case through the labyrinthine hallways of the Vatican's bureaucracy. But his continuous attempts to reach the right authorities to advance his daughter's case for canonization are in vain. In the offices of the secretariat of state, one of these bureaucratic functionaries verifies the weightlessness of the body and concludes that Margarito's is a case of "collective suggestion." Although constant rejection does not weaken Margarito's stonecutter's drive and resolution, it triggers the compassion and solidarity of his compatriots, García Márquez and Silva, the tenor. The constant rejections make them think that Margarito is becoming increasingly lonely.

The idea of the saint could be interpreted as the "magical realist" element in the story. Following Gerald Martin's suggestion, a more critical interpretation can render this occurrence an allegory of the political and social relationship between Latin America and Europe that García Márquez describes in his Nobel Prize speech. The three Colombians find solidarity in their own struggle for recognition, mirroring the efforts of Latin American nations to find cultural self-expression alongside the enlightened institutions of European culture. As Michael Palencia-Roth points out, García Márquez, both the writer and the implied narrator, demonstrates great compassion for Margarito. This compassion leads to a feeling of solidarity among the guests of the pension. Both García Márquez and Silva understand that something must be done to advance Margarito's cause, but they are not sure what to do. They are, after all, in a foreign country discovering for themselves how European institutions behave toward Latin Americans. In the same manner that Latin American culture must "travel" and seek recognition overseas, the saint must also travel, hoping to be recognized as a miracle by foreign authorities. European institutions do not see or do not want to see the miracle, and in the short story, the saint remains after twenty-two years (and many formalities) eternally in waiting. Her reality is condemned, to use García Márquez's famous expression, to "one hundred years of solitude."

But Margarito's quest is not simply a Latin American one. It speaks to a type of sympathy for, or solidarity with, those who continually chisel away at seemingly monolithic hardships. Margarito could have been a character in one of Zavattini's screenplays and could easily belong to postwar Italy. García Márquez suggests in his review of *Umberto D* (released in 1952) that the old pensioner is a character who could appear anywhere in the world, "walking the streets with his dog, with tremendous dignity that does not allow one to know his soul" (*La soledad de América Latina* 244). According to García Márquez, De Sica and Zavattini were able to divide the drama into miniscule everyday spaces: "[T]hey have laid out the tremendous pathos that there is in the simple act of going to bed, of returning home" (245). "The Saint" attempts to render the pathos of stonecutters such as Margarito and Umberto D, individuals who relentlessly hammer away at bureaucratic institutions in order to chisel out the form of a community's hope. Palencia-Roth points out the neorealist aspect of Margarito's character when he says that the style in which "The Saint" is written "emanates a breath of the sacramental both in things and in people" (84). This "breath of the sacramental" surrounds the whole story and becomes the central point of the argument between Latin Americans and Europeans. A difference in sensitivity to and understanding of what the saint is and represents becomes the cause of a breakdown in communication.

In "The Saint," the first European character to challenge the originality of the miraculous event that constitutes Margarito's daughter is Bella Maria, the owner of the pension. During a dinner party, Bella Maria says that in Palermo there is an exhibition in a museum of "the incorruptible corpses of men, women, and children, and even several bishops, who had been disinterred from the same Capuchin cemetery" (44). Margarito insists that his friends take him there, but when he walks through the museum's galleries he dismisses these corpses on the grounds that one "can tell right away they're dead" (43). Later in the short story, on an autumn night in a trattoria in Trastevere, the students of the CSC gather with the students of Silva's singing teacher. One of the students, Lakis, an "intelligent, amiable Greek whose soporific discourse on social injustice is his only fault" (47), sees Margarito carrying the case and asks him if he plays the violoncello. Margarito, to the embarrassment of his Colombian compatriots, opens the case to show the saint to everyone. The incorruptible body causes a great stir in the trattoria, to the point that one of the cooks falls to his knees and begins praying.

After a long discussion, Lakis declares that he wants to make a movie about the saint, justifying his intentions by saying that Zavattini would "never let this subject get away" (48). The students rush to call their maestro on the phone to tell him their idea. Zavattini asks them to come over to his house so that he can see the miracle with his own eyes. Upon opening the case himself, Zavattini exclaims, "It's no good for the movies. . . . Nobody would believe it" (49).

For Zavattini, the "magical realist" event threatens the credibility of the story in the eyes of European audiences. They would not believe the story on film, even though in life, nobody could negate the verisimilitude of the saint. The students leave Zavattini's house disillusioned by his reaction and try to figure out why he discarded the story. But when they arrive at the pension, Bella Maria tells them that the maestro wants to see them right away. Zavattini has found a way to render the story credible on the condition that Margarito performs a miracle and brings Margarito's daughter to life. The narrator (García Márquez), revealing his faith in the miracle, asks Zavattini whether he wants to have the father resurrect his daughter "in the picture or in life." Initially, the Italian maestro finds his student's comment irritating, as if this level of faith challenged his authority, but the possibility of resurrection in film moves him to begin assembling scenes and dialogue right in front of his students. In Zavattini's version, Margarito, frustrated after being rejected so many times, one day opens his daughter's coffin and, echoing the words of Jesus Christ, says, "For love of your father, my child, arise and walk" (53). And the girl rises and walks.

The students feel cheated by the master's solution to the story. Lakis is the first to offer criticism, saying that the maestro's resolution is unbelievable. Zavattini accuses the Greek of being a Stalinist, implying that his fanatic devotion to social realism does not allow him to believe in reality itself. One could view Zavattini as angry at Lakis's refusal to accept his cheap and easy solution to insert the saint within the parameters of the miracle of Lazarus's resurrection. The transposition of the girl's miracle onto a Christian topos robs the event of its communal solidarity and its allegorical power.

The importance of this incident in relation to the other elements of the story is not in the way the polemic is resolved but in the hesitation Zavattini exhibits when confronted with the saint. This hesitation is one of interpretation. Zavattini cannot insert the saint within the structure of his moral narrative. He is faced with the ultimate challenge of finding a way to make the miracle "work" within the "realist" narrative tradition of neorealism.

In *Beyond Good and Evil* Friedrich Nietzsche states that the powerful "still bowed worshipfully before the saint as the riddle of self-conquest and deliberate final renunciation" (65). The saint is an unsettling phenomenon for the powerful. It unsettles what we consider existence because it appears to belong to a realm outside nature. Nietzsche goes on to explain that the powerful discover before the saint a new kind of fear: "[T]hey sensed a new power, a strange, as yet unconquered enemy" (65). In relation to García Márquez's story, Zavattini's drive to render life into screenplays finds itself at a loss when confronted with the saint. His success at representing in film the relationships of power that give rise to a concept of life and reality is upset. After this incident, the short story shifts its focus, and the reader is left with no resolution. Margarito continues with his plight, a neorealist version of his story is not filmed, and twenty-two years later when the narrator returns to Rome he discovers that Zavattini's fame was a passing thing. When he runs into Margarito in a street in Trastevere, he is surprised by how old he looks and how persistent he remains: "Then I had no doubt, if I ever had any at all, that the saint was Margarito. Without realizing it, by means of his daughter's incorruptible body and while he was still alive, he had spent twenty-two years fighting for the legitimate cause of his own canonization" (53).

Although the polemic around the filmic credibility of the saint is not resolved, what comes through in the story is the myopic vision of Zavattini, who cannot accept at face value the miraculous event that constitutes the saint and does not care to understand its allegorical power. As Martin says in relation to the "incomplete readings" of *One Hundred Years of Solitude*, Zavattini does not take into account the historical context that gives rise to the miracle or the myth of the saint: for "those who do not know the continent, the novel is more abstract, and the incidents are recognizable as vehicles of universal experiences of truths distorted by Latin American eccentricity" (G. Martin 102). It is the narrator, García Márquez, who demands that a "critical movie" about the theme of the saint should be made. The use of the term "critical" signals the importance of establishing the political and social issues related to the phenomenon that Zavattini is not interested in or willing to discover.

García Márquez, Latin American Self-Representation, and the Search for Solidarity

In his Nobel Prize lecture (1982), García Márquez argued that the cause for the solitude in which Latin Americans live is a result of the lack of conventional mediums to represent their lives in a credible form. He points a finger at Europe and suggests that in ecstasy over the contemplation of their own cultures they have been unable to develop the necessary "method" with which to interpret Latin American culture.

> It is understandable that they would insist on measuring us with the same stick that they measure themselves, without remembering that the struggles of life are not the same for everyone and that the search for one's own identity is as bloody and hard for us as it was for them. The interpretation of our reality with foreign schemes only contributes to make us more unknown, less free, and each time more solitary. (*La soledad de América Latina* 508)

García Márquez encourages Latin Americans to invent a utopia of opposition, one that finally will allow these communities "condemned to one hundred years of solitude" to express their reality within their own parameters. But he also points out the incredible hurdles that artists of the continent have to face because of a lack of conventional resources to render their lives in a credible way. From the first steps in his film career, García Márquez has had to deal with this absence of conventional resources. His experience in Rome anticipated the enormous difficulties he would have in developing a national film industry that would answer the call to invent a "utopia of opposition" that has been the guiding force in his intellectual career. His life in Rome, his relationship to Zavattini and other students of the CSC, and his autobiographical writing about his first work in the film industry highlight compromises that Latin American artists must make.

While working in the film industry, García Márquez learned that the relationship between the screenplay writer and the director is often one of conflict and that the role of the writer is simply to be a source of ideas for the director (Torres 48). The nature of these conflicts usually centered on the fact that directors had a different vision of the screenplay, often opting to sacrifice the ideological and solidarity-building content of the work for more commercial content: "[I]t was then that in 1966 I said to myself: shit now I'm going to write against cinema!" (in Torres 47). García Márquez has tirelessly repeated that his relationship to film has been troublesome, and that the lack of control the screenwriter has over the material once it is in production threatens the allegorical, symbolic, and political content of the original story.

> The film director's destiny is in the glorious secret of darkness, and only the one who resigns himself to this interior exile has a possibility of surviving without bitterness. No work demands greater humility. Moreover, it should be considered a transitory factor in the creation of a movie and is a living test of the subaltern condition of the art of cinema. As long as cinema needs a writer, in other words the help of a fellow art form, it won't be able to fly on its own. This is one of its limits. The other one, and even more important, is its obligation to the industry. (*La soledad de América Latina* 489–500)

García Márquez uses the language of cinema to critique cinema from a literary point of view. In this way, he hopes to recover some of the allegorical power of his stories and preserve his characters' search for solidarity in a continent condemned to exist in solitude. García Márquez's film studies at the CSC in Rome were a crucial starting point for his search for representation. The question of solidarity that screenplay writers and directors were debating in Rome remains at the center of his literary preoccupations. Neorealism showed him a way to turn the alienation of an individual into the allegory of a nation.[9] Both Ricci in *Bicycle Thief* and Umberto in *Umberto D* spend most of their time searching for someone who can identify with their struggles and lend them a hand.

This depiction of the need for human solidarity resonates strongly with García Márquez's work. In *One Hundred Years of Solitude* the individual quest becomes a continent's quest, and the struggle to achieve solidarity is constantly jeopardized by internal and external forces. This search becomes the driving spirit of the continent and expresses its urge to achieve cultural independence.

Today García Márquez is known in literary markets as one of the exponents of "magical realism." As Gerald Martin points out, the term has done nothing but contribute to the exoticization of Latin American artistic expression and the reality that art represents. Martin accuses critics of not having perceived that *One Hundred Years of Solitude* is about "the myths of history and its demystifications" (99). Thus critical perspective is eschewed, explains Martin, because most critics ignore the historical and literary context in which Marquez wrote the novel. García Márquez reiterated these ideas during an interview when the interviewer told him that he thought European readers "see the magic of the things" he presents in his stories but fail to see the "reality that inspires them." García Márquez replied as follows: "For sure, because their rationalism doesn't let them see that reality does not end in the price of tomatoes or eggs. Daily life in Latin America demonstrates to us that reality is full of extraordinary things. . . . It is enough to open the newspapers to know that among us, extraordinary things happen every day" (*La soledad de América Latina* 592).

According to Martin, García Márquez positions his omniscient narrators in such a way that the religious beliefs and myths the characters hold dear are taken very seriously. Thus, García Márquez avoids passing judgment on the reality of the miraculous events his stories present. As Martin points outs, he accomplishes this by positioning his narrators at the center of events but at the same time separated by an "abstract plain of analysis" that allows the narrator to draw important metaphysical conclusions at the end of the story. The relationship between the narrator and the characters is one based on solidarity, the solidarity of being able to recognize in each other specific imprints of history and trauma brought on by colonialism, imperialism, and development.

The resolution of *Miracle in Rome* is disappointing from a Latin American perspective. The miraculous event, which represents the faith of a whole community, is inserted into a familiar narrative of Christian resurrection. In a sense, García Márquez betrays his earlier Nobel Prize speech, in which he celebrates a Latin American ability to search for new ways of representing reality and to search for utopias of opposition. I suggest that the polemic between Zavattini and his students presented in the short story can be read as García Márquez's self-critique of the film version of "The Saint," in which he initially failed to make any reference to the bohemian atmosphere of the trattorias and the passionate polemics about cinematic representation between students and their Italian instructors. Such polemics were central to the debate about film and representation, and yet they are absent from *Miracle in Rome*. We can imagine that aspiring Latin American filmmakers (like the ones depicted in the short story) would surely have benefited from the inclusion of scenes of the debates between students at the CSC about the miracle. These types of debates might have even been central to the imagining of new forms of expression in Latin American film that could push the boundaries of neorealism, transforming it for a Latin American context. Instead the film offers a happy ending, one that might garner more sympathy with international art-house audiences. Margarito and his daughter are reunited, providing simple gratification on an individual level but leaving larger, more complex community matters (ones that comprised the establishing shots of the film) in the dust. The film recoils from experimenting with alternative forms of film narration that might have echoed the allegorical powers of the miraculous event and addressed its significance for Margarito's community. Margarito's struggle for recognition, as depicted by García Márquez in various incarnations (newspaper article, film, and then short story), enacts the struggle of Latin American self-representation in the face of European hegemony. In the short story version, García Márquez brings us back full circle to the sentiments expressed in his Nobel Prize acceptance speech, namely, that nothing has more value in the struggle for rendering believable the lives of Latin Americans than a deep commitment to the exploration of innovative forms of representation.

Notes

1. All translations from Spanish are mine unless otherwise noted.
2. See Saldívar's "La Penumbra del escritor de cine" in *La soledad de América Latina* 491. He states that the reasons why the young journalist decided to leave Bogotá and travel to Europe are still debated. Some suggest that he left for political reasons, a sort of "forced exile," over the controversy that *The Story of a Shipwrecked Sailor: Who Drifted on a Life Raft for Ten Days without Food or Water, Was Proclaimed a National Hero, Kissed by Beauty Q* (1955) ignited during the government

of Rojas Pinilla. Saldívar, however, says García Márquez moved to Europe for personal reasons: "[H]e wanted to study cinema in Rome and he needed to broaden his cultural horizon and have a sufficient perspective of Colombia and Latin America" (323). That was not the only motivation; he also wanted to gather the knowledge to create a film institute in his own country. See Miguel Losada in Blesa 719.

3. See García Márquez's introduction to *Strange Pilgrims* (14).

4. Palencia-Roth points out that there are five versions of this story.

5. This article appears in García Márquez's *Notas de prensa*.

6. In interviews, García Márquez has repeatedly acknowledged the enormous influence that film has had on his narrative style. See Torres, "El novelista que quiso hacer cine," in Rentería Mantilla.

7. *Miracle in Milan* is a postwar narrative about displaced, homeless people. Ironically, the film was criticized by contemporary filmmakers for indulging in the fantastical in its style, which might seem to contradict Zavattini's idea that "the true function of the cinema is not to tell fables" (in Bondanella, *Italian Cinema* 93). García Márquez's depiction of Zavattini's myopic perspective, where metaphysical elements in scriptwriting are concerned, in his short story "The Saint" seems to underestimate the significance of these qualities in his script for *Miracle in Rome*.

8. The name "Finlandia" can refer both to its literal translation in Spanish as "the land at the end of the world" and to the European country.

9. André Bazin also recognizes the importance of solidarity in neorealist films. For him, neorealism contained a message of fundamental human solidarity fostered by the anti-Fascist Resistance. See Bondanella, *Italian Cinema* 31. Marcus echoes Bazin when she states that if one goes beyond technical consideration to the ethical impetus behind neorealism, one is apt to discover far more of a consensus (23). Marcus emphasizes what De Sica stated about his work: "All my films are about the search for human solidarity" (in Sitney 79).

Chapter 7

From Pensioner to Teenager: Everyday Violence in De Sica's
Umberto D and Gaviria's *Rodrigo D: No Future*

KRISTI M. WILSON

In an essay titled "Neorealism and New Latin American Cinema," John
Hess criticizes what he sees as Italian neorealism's lack of social responsibility. Though he acknowledges the powerful influence of Italian neorealism on directors like Tomás Gutiérrez Alea, Julio García Espinosa,
and Fernando Birri, who studied at the Centro Sperimentale di Cinematografia in Rome, Hess claims that neorealism did not go far enough
politically in its attempts to change society: "Neo-realism had its own
ideology, one that helped it break through conventional film-making
and gain the status that Kolker [*The Altering Eye*] and others give it,
but that also limited it by preventing film-makers and contemporary
neo-realist intellectual culture from carefully studying its own past or
current context" (in King, Lopez, and Alvarado 105–06). Hess's critique
echoes those of Latin American filmmakers such as Fernando Solanas
and Birri, as well as Communist Party members in Italian artistic circles
who faulted neorealist filmmakers even earlier for a lack of revolutionary
insight that prevented them from interrogating their country's Fascist
past and from effecting real social change. While this may or may not
have been the case for certain neorealist directors, Vittorio De Sica (in
collaboration with scriptwriter Cesare Zavattini) was not one to sidestep
what he saw as Fascist residue in postwar Italian society. In *Umberto D*
(1952), Umberto and his dog, Flick, fall victim to a type of brutal, everyday fascism that seems to have settled into Italy's bureaucratic institutions.[1] The protracted scene at the dog pound, for one, demonstrates De
Sica's use of the theme of institutionalized cruelty to address ongoing
fascistic treatment of the elderly and the poor, two social groups de-

144

picted in the film as having no valuable role in Italy's postwar economic recovery.

Marcus suggests that *Umberto D* was meant to be understood in dialogue with Roberto Rossellini's *Rome, Open City* (1945); she positions the two films at opposite ends of the optimistic beginning and pessimistic finale of the neorealist era of Italian filmmaking (96).[2] In this essay, I argue for the continued relevance of De Sican neorealism to a Latin American context. I look at De Sica's *Umberto D* alongside Víctor Gaviria's *Rodrigo D: No Future* (1990) to show how the film that critical consensus claims ended the neorealist movement in Italy is a starting point for the twentieth-century Colombian poet and filmmaker Gaviria, who relies on neorealist techniques to create a neo-neorealist aesthetic of urban despair very much rooted in the type of urban despair that characterizes many parts of De Sica's Italy.[3]

Although they are from different eras and different social classes, Umberto and Rodrigo (the respective protagonists of *Umberto D* and *Rodrigo D*) can be considered twentieth-century flaneurs, insofar as they find themselves trapped in the urban ruins of different stages of the postindustrial age.[4] Both films explore the brutal consequences for protagonists who attempt to traverse and understand city streets that seem to hold no place for them. Building on Gilles Deleuze's discussion of the open qualities of many neorealist films, Landy suggests that in neorealist films "actions and situations are no longer governed by purposiveness but by aimlessness characterized by the stroll, the voyage that can occur anywhere" (*Italian Film* 14–15).[5] The dispersive quality of Umberto's and Rodrigo's particularly alienated style of urban wandering resonates with the open-endedness (almost purposelessness) of what Benjamin understood as the flaneur's outsider journey through the modern European city.

In his notes for the *Passagen-Werk* (Arcades) project, Benjamin describes large-scale nineteenth-century urban modernization campaigns in European cities that rendered many city dwellers homeless and jobless. He was especially drawn to Hugh Walpole's 1933 description of the machines exhibition at the Crystal Palace for its clarity in pinpointing the decadent aspects of progress and technology: "In this hall of machines there were automated spinning machines ... machines that made envelopes, steam looms, models of locomotives, centrifugal pumps and a locomobile; all of these were laboring like crazy, whereas the thousands of people who were beside them in top hats and workers' caps sat quietly and passively, and without suspecting that the age of human beings on this planet was at an end."⁶ Walpole's quote, which depicts people whose way of life will soon be destroyed by modernity, corresponds to Benjamin's attempts to discover a historical theory that would unmask Fascist tendencies in the age of mechanical reproduction. He suggests that the first shopping arcades were early forms of public housing for an increasingly large public that needed to be awakened through revolutionary action from what he considered a collective dream state.⁷ The contradictions inherent in an age that produced a class of workers who could window-shop but not afford to buy most of the products in the public marketplace were embodied for Benjamin in the figure of the flaneur, a city street stroller and loiterer whose intellectual object of contemplation was modernity—more specifically, the modern crowd. Flaneurs were perpetual outsiders who lived on the edge of economic extinction.

Gaviria's 1986 film (released in 1990) about a group of teenagers in the slums of Medellin, Colombia, is more than just an homage in title to *Umberto D.* In particular, Gaviria relied on such neorealist conventions as natural lighting and street locations, nonprofessional actors, a collaborative scriptwriting process, diegetic sound in many scenes, an emphasis on colloquial, regional speech, and a story line that emphasized a day in the life of the underclasses. Thus, traditionally neorealist in form, fusing fiction and social reality, *Rodrigo D* signals the ongoing importance of the neorealist mode of production to contemporary Latin American depictions of poverty, underdevelopment, and global capitalism. Gaviria's film is best understood in dialogue with *Umberto D.* Where De Sica's film has been understood as an attack on the "new Italy" of the postwar economic "recovery" years, Gaviria's film can be seen as an attack on the social displacement and alienation that result from neoliberal economic policies in Latin America and their accompanying rhetoric of development.⁸ *Umberto D* depicts an Italy whose Fascist past has not been entirely eliminated in the wake of postwar democracy and capitalist economic restructuring, a situation that has resulted in a large class of working poor without opportunities or hope for survival. *Rodrigo D* depicts a community in which the empty promises of top-down liberal capitalism contribute to the restlessness of a class of impoverished, unemployed youth who are aware that the price for first-world consumerism (and access to the spaces and structures of that world) is always violence and sometimes death.

The central protagonist of De Sica and Zavattini's narrative is a pensioner named Umberto D. Ferrari, whose efforts to keep up his longstanding middle-class appearance confront the specter of homelessness. Ironically, it is Umberto's desperate effort to avoid life on the public streets (in a boardinghouse) that drives him into the streets for a solution. The dangerous quality of Rome's city streets for men like Umberto is established in the opening scene of the film in which a crowd of pensioners stages a protest for an increase in their government stipends. Military jeeps full of police officers arrive almost immediately to harass the marchers. A bird's-eye angle of the crowd's dispersion adds a sense of the pensioners' inability to affect change in their situation. Dialogue between Umberto and another old man reveals that although the protesters had tried to get a permit for the march (presumably their right as citizens), the government turned them down. Thus, in the first few shots of the film De Sica establishes an aura of everyday Fascist cruelty in public institutions like the police and the type of bureaucratic offices that grant permits to stage public events. Umberto embodies the lived contradiction of many members of his generation as he is both a disenfranchised pensioner and a former civil servant of the ministry of public affairs, one who spent thirty years of his life working quietly as a cog in Mussolini's bureaucracy. His exhaustive efforts to keep up middle-class appearances bleed into a more blatant struggle for survival, exposing the bleaker aspects of social relationships. Interestingly, De Sica denied that Umberto's economic situation was of special interest to him: "The economic condition of Umberto is not what concerns us. What concerns us is his moral and human relationship with society. What concerns us is the loneliness of an old man. Men do not communicate with one another; how then can they communicate with Umberto, who, moreover, is an old man? . . . Human beings have this primitive, perennial, ancient fault of not understanding one another, of not communicating with one another" (in Sitney 107). But perhaps De Sica is being coy here—after all the film is at its most basic level about poverty, economic deterioration, and the moral and human elements that are shaped by that fundamentally economic fact. In its exploration of the dangerous side of human nature, *Umberto D* both embodies a critique of capitalism and moves beyond it to suggest ways in which a Fascist residue can settle onto any economic or bureaucratic system—or, as Benjamin might suggest, that an industrial, bureaucratic drive of any type seems to emerge out of Fascist tendencies.

Umberto D is shot largely in deep focus, which has the effect of locking Umberto into his urban environment and not permitting audiences to distance themselves from the social conditions surrounding the main character. Any interpretation of the character's actions also involves an interpretation of the way in which he moves through space and is situated in the environment. For example, deep focus shots with densely packed mise-en-scènes emphasize the stifling magnitude of the problem of poverty in Rome when Umberto visits the soup kitchen and public hospital. In these and many other instances, Umberto is shot as one of thousands of men in his situation. Umberto's interior environments consist of spaces that suggest alternately cold bourgeois ambition (the landlady's apartment) and institutionalized ambivalence to the plight of those not able to make ends meet in the postwar economy (the public hospital, the public cafeteria, and the dog pound). Exterior shots of Umberto's environment depict him wandering down lesser-known city side streets as well as among impressive Roman ruins such as the Pantheon and the obelisk at the Piazza del Popolo.

Though De Sica's use of certain ancient sites is in keeping with a neorealist aesthetic of using outdoor city locations as opposed to studio sets, there are enough shots of ancient ruins to suggest their strategic importance in the film. Brunette points out that the ruins are always in focus and suggests that they provide a visual link between Umberto's dire predicament and the human condition that "stretches back centuries" ("When Neo-Realism Collided with Reality" 33). I suggest that the ruins, rather than speaking to the idea of timeless quality shared by all human beings, serve as allegorical references to two specific periods of empire: Augustus's ancient Rome and Mussolini's Fascist Rome.[9] Citing the Italian painterly tradition as it informs iconographic depictions of Christian motifs, Sitney suggests that the traditions of iconography and allegory are intertwined in neorealist films (12–13). Accordingly, if one considers architecture allegorically, monuments, skyscrapers, and ruins can tell their own stories in film.

Scholem defines allegory as "something which loses its own meaning and becomes the vehicle of something else . . . arising out of the gap between form and meaning" (in Buck-Morss 236).[10] Classical ruins functioned accordingly in Mussolini's Rome. As Wyke and others have pointed out, in his efforts to foster a connection between early twentieth-century Italians and Italy's grandiose imperial past, Mussolini made use of ancient imperial ideology and large-scale cinematic epic productions.[11] For example, Italy's colonization efforts in Africa ushered in a series of historical films about ancient Romans, which were designed to foster a modern nationalistic collective consciousness.[12] Mussolini's Fascist attempts to recall the glorious days of the Roman Empire involved an Augustan-style strategy that combined authoritarian rule and large-scale visual reminders of that rule with republican rhetoric that attempted to elevate the Roman populace from a state of social illness and frailty to a grandiose place in history. In a speech commemorating the anniversary of the mythical founding of Rome on April 22, 753 BCE, Mussolini proclaimed:

> We dream of a Roman Italy, that is to say wise, strong, disciplined, and imperial. Much of what was the immortal spirit of Rome is reborn in Fascism: the Fasces are Roman; our organization of combat is Roman, our pride and our courage are Roman: *civis romanus sum*. Now, it is necessary that the history of tomorrow, the history we fervently wish to create, not represent a contrast or a parody of the history of yesterday. . . . Italy has been Roman for the first time in fifteen centuries in the War and in the Victory: now Italy must be Roman in peacetime: and this renewed and revived *romanità* bears these names: Discipline and Work. (in Bondanella 176)[13]

Mussolini masks the new and innovative aspects of Fascism by suggesting that they are simply a reincarnation of ancient history. The practice of citing historical forms out of context is a particularly modern phenomenon, according to Benjamin, that attempts to contain fear of the rapid, exaggerated pace of social change. Mussolini's brand of Fascist neoclassicism in film and architecture conforms to what Benjamin would call nineteenth-century neoclassical idealism in that it helps to ease the anxiety of modern transience through images and structures that suggest permanence. However, as Mussolini's speech suggests, Fascist neoclassicism accords even more closely with the concept of human omnipotence over nature; the director and film studio (a closed system) over the spectator. In its emphasis on creation and immortality, rather than historical parody or a nostalgic imitation of the past, Mussolini's speech equates modern domination with permanence and suggests that tomorrow's history will be rewritten in a way that shows no gap between the ancient and modern empires of Rome.

Although he was originally trained in Fascist studios under Mussolini (and it's perhaps a reaction to this), De Sica depicts ruins in a new light in *Umberto D*. Unlike Mussolini, De Sica does not quote the past in a seamless fashion that suggests certainties about the human experience. Instead, he uses the image of the displaced flaneur to comment on the inevitable failure and dangerous consequences of attempts to resurrect the past. Umberto's wanderings through the city unmask the interrelated qualities of ongoing Fascist tendencies in Italy and the country's economic recovery.

Marcus calls *Umberto D* "at once a celebration of neorealism and a lament for its death, a pure embodiment of its ideals and the terminus beyond which the movement could not go without lapsing into repetition or mere self-embroidery" (96). Marcus's words capture the sense in which the film is about decadence on many levels. Roman ruins function allegorically in the film to tell the story of the official fall of Fascism and its lingering effects on everyday life.[14] After the breakup of the pensioners' strike that opens the film, Umberto is shown walking with a new acquaintance he met at the strike. Umberto's drama has begun in medias res, his desperation made obvious by the fact that he can speak of nothing other than his dire economic situation to the stranger. Following a bit of lighthearted conversation, Umberto stops and offers to sell his gold watch to the stranger for a good price; this is the first of numerous times we see Umberto try to sell his personal belongings to pay off his debts.

In this scene Umberto is framed in a deep focus medium shot with a neoclassical statue gleaming, but diminished by Umberto's size, in the background. The composition of this scene works against the grain of nineteenth-century ideals of beauty that equated good bourgeois taste with "classical" Greco-Roman style, an aesthetic staging of history that promoted an idea of time-honored truth and lent itself well to Fascist rhetoric and ideology.[15] The "time-honored" aspect of neoclassicism as an aesthetic of truth and stability is undermined completely in this scene. Umberto's desperate offer visibly offends the sensibilities of his acquaintance, who was under the impression that he was among well-mannered social equals. Umberto is rebuffed with embarrassed, casual conversation as the acquaintance politely takes his leave. Umberto, however, in his efforts to maintain his previous middle-class lifestyle at all costs, is oblivious to the fact that he has offended the man in any way. Ironically, the acquaintance's reaction seems to underscore the fine line of propriety that separates him from Umberto's impoverished situation. The two elderly characters are members of the same socioeconomic class of pensioners who need more money than they receive from the government to survive in postwar Italy.

Shortly after this scene, one of Rome's many obelisks (the aforementioned obelisk at the Piazza del Popolo) serves as the site for the first instance of petty thievery in the film, magnifying the problem of poverty as it has been set up by the pensioners' strike and Umberto's attempts to peddle his watch. Traditionally a symbol of Roman victory over the powerful empire of Egypt, the obelisk now serves as the background for a scene in which the same swindler who pulls out a handful of cash and shortchanges Umberto for his gold watch poses as a beggar immediately thereafter. The swindler looks a bit younger than Umberto, suggesting that the problem of poverty in postwar Italy crosses generational lines in a dangerous way that threatens to turn Italians against one another.[16] De Sica's depiction of Maria, the young, pregnant maid who works for Umberto's landlady, reinforces the magnitude of this problem. She will soon be turned out of her home (the hallway of the landlady's apartment) when her pregnant state becomes too obvious to hide, demonstrating that the impoverished streets of Rome are beckoning women, children, and the elderly alike, while interior spaces in the film house and shelter everyday Fascists.

The triangular relationship between Fascist cruelty, neoclassicism, and blind economic ambition presents itself clearly in *Umberto D* in the scenes between the landlady and Umberto. The interior space of the apartment resembles something between a boardinghouse, brothel, and nineteenth-century bourgeois salon, although the salon decor of the apartment is rapidly taking over, with neoclassical knickknacks and drapery spreading from their cramped quarters at the back of the apartment forward into Umberto and Maria's domain, a small area of space at the front of the apartment. Marcus calls the landlady an "empire builder" and her bleached blond, stylized coif adds a Nazi aesthetic to her particular brand of cruelty (108).[17] In fact, the shots of the landlady's nouveau riche salon call to mind the Nazis' makeshift lounge that shared a wall with their torture chamber in Rossellini's *Rome, Open City*. Here, a thin wall still separates victims from torturers, but the form of torture is more mundane and insipid. We learn, for instance, that Umberto cared for the landlady like a daughter during the war. According to the logic of familial relations, she should now care for him by keeping him off the street, which no longer represents a space of freedom but a lack of protection. Instead, Umberto's private struggle to remain off the streets (and firmly within the bounds of middle-class society) takes the form of a territory war with the landlady over the space of his rented room, blurring the boundaries between friends and enemies that were once clear-cut in *Rome, Open City*. Umberto's status as a flaneur in the film is tied to his image as the loser of the battle for a place in the new city of Rome. His wanderings through the city produce nothing but an increased sense of alienation, which culminates in the literal destruction of his living space.

Umberto returns from the streets to find the wallpaper hanging from the walls of his former room and, in fact, a giant hole in the wall that separates his living quarters from the street. The landlady's relentless remodeling plan has reached all the way into Umberto's room and turned it into a ruin. The symbolism of this scene is unmistakable: Umberto is out; the bourgeois, upwardly mobile set is in. The significance of this message is underscored by the fact that a fancy evening party is in full swing in the apartment and Maria is now dressed in a French maid's uniform. De Sica leaves no stone unturned in his efforts to expose the dangers of empire building in the name of economic recovery. Even the spectator, by the simple fact that he or she has sought the interior space of the movie theater, is forced to identify with the landlady's boyfriend, a movie theater owner who is also the indirect cause for Umberto's expulsion from the apartment. Umberto's point of view when he first sees the hole in the wall becomes the eye of the camera, which moves all the way through the wall to look out onto the street. Umberto becomes synonymous with the neorealism here. De Sica offers a bleak vision for the future of Italian film production in which neorealism will be squeezed out.[18]

Understanding the struggle between the landlady and Umberto as a metaphor for the struggle between "new" postwar middle-class values and traditional, humanitarian values, respectively, makes Umberto's status in the film as a continual hindrance that much more plausible. Umberto is quite simply always in the way. He stands in the way of the landlady's expansionist plans for her apartment (or empire), and he is frequently in the way when he is in the streets; he is almost run over by a jeep at the pensioners' protest and almost run down in front of the hospital. In a Benjaminian sense, Umberto's expulsion from the apartment is necessary as he represents age, decay, and, most importantly, a transience that bourgeois ideals attempt to mask. Marcus suggests that the end of *Umberto D*, like *Bicycle Thief*, offers no visible solution to the social problems represented in the film and ends on an even more pessimistic note (at least there is solidarity between Bruno and Antonio at the end of *Bicycle Thief*).[19] She argues that the absence of a discernable future for Umberto at the film's end highlights the way in which the film violates the neorealist mandate for artistic transparency (116). I suggest that we read this lack of a future for several characters in the film (Umberto, Maria, and the dog, Flick) as an artistically transparent gesture that supports De Sica's belief that *Umberto D* was, in fact, his most neo-realist film (Sitney 87). The film foreshadows the absence of a future for many of the characters who will perish in the wake of Italy's ruthlessly burgeoning economic "recovery."

This projected absence is the present state of affairs in *Rodrigo D: No Future*.[20] In fact, the lack of a social corrective so prevalent in De Sica and Zavattini's films is one of the most exportable aspects of Italian neorealism where Latin American cinema is concerned, as it encourages audiences to look for the larger causes of social problems beyond the film. In this sense, tidy closure and corrective measures only serve to block macrocosmic reflection on larger issues after the film is over, keeping audiences in the realm of spectators rather than activists. One of the tenets for new Latin American cinema was that there be open endings in the films. Social work was theorized as beginning *after* the film ended.[21]

A disenfranchised and helpless form of wandering characterizes the young men who make up the cast of characters in Gaviria's *Rodrigo D*. Although a large part of the narrative is devoted to Rodrigo's frustrated and unproductive existence in the slums of Medellin, his story unfolds as a microcosmic example of the lives of most young men in his neighborhood. In essence, all of the characters in *Rodrigo D* are born futureless (as the title suggests) and are aware of the fact that life holds no opportunities for them. Time passes grudgingly, and all of the characters are bored and restless. This disturbing lack of purposiveness creates a climate of violence and unpredictability in which we can detect Gaviria moving beyond the warnings in De Sica and Zavattini's brand of neorealism toward extreme conclusions.

The film opens with shots of Rodrigo walking through what looks like an empty upper-class apartment building in the process of being painted. No one is around, and Rodrigo wanders through the rooms quickly before he is caught by the building's armed guard. Explaining that he used to work in the building and was looking for his bag, Rodrigo is promptly thrown out. We learn shortly thereafter that Rodrigo was laid off because of work-related headaches. Rodrigo's suicide at the end of the film revisits this aesthetic of ghostly ruin. Once again, upon entering the lobby of the high-rise from which he will jump, Rodrigo is confronted by a guard who wants to know where he is going. He claims to be visiting someone in the building and is allowed into the elevator where he is interrogated again, this time by a maid who gets out of the

Rodrigo D: No Future (Víctor Gaviria, 1990)

elevator with her mop and pail on a floor that is entirely unfinished and empty. Here Gaviria comments on the inability of the city structures to generate work. The maid, equipped with the tools of her trade, ostensibly on duty, has no work to do. In fact, "real work" versus activity that kills time is an important theme in the film. A conflict exists between Rodrigo's gang of punk rockers who refuse to work as a form of killing time and other characters in the film who do odd jobs to help one another in the community or to help their parents. Rodrigo looks down on those who work without real pay and calls them "freebies," akin to slaves. Rodrigo's mother has recently died and he shares a house with his father, two brothers, and a sister. His older brother works, his younger brother studies, and his sister does housework.

Rodrigo's unemployed status and his refusal to help around the house create tension between him and his family. He has several arguments with his sister, who accuses him of being worthless and lazy, and at one point his father suggests that he stay with a family friend to "get his head straightened out," to which Rodrigo replies, "I'm not sick." Rodrigo seems to be the only one in his family who understands the futility of trying to improve his status in life. Accordingly, a punk soundtrack follows his wanderings with lyrics that link his life to greater systemic problems: "dinero, problemas, dinero, systema" (money problems, money system).

Throughout the film, the politics of boredom born out of poverty that initially fueled the punk rock movement in Europe (generating such lyrics as "another year with nothing to do") provide the musical backdrop for Rodrigo's activities. Rodrigo and his friends are either playing punk songs on cassettes, listening to local punk bands in houses, or trying to figure out what the lyrics to English punk songs mean. The title of the film combines an homage to De Sica and Zavattini with an homage to the Sex Pistols. On the use of the slogan "No Future," Gaviria had the following to say:

> NO FUTURE is a punk maxim all over the world. It points to the threat of nuclear war, but above all, to the abandonment in postindustrial society of all that is not in the image of a consumable, devourable product. NO FUTURE is the maxim of that which has been called postmodernism . . . the world of advertising where everything has been reduced to an enormous dump site. Time has been detained in an ingestible present, in the imminence of consumption. The present in which the product lives, enclosed in its vacuum-sealed packaging, which, at one time or another, will be eaten, consumed, and will then become trash in the trash can of all things . . . the past and future are abolished. (in Kantaris 4)
>
> Benjamin suggested that although Balzac was the first to enunciate the ruins of the bourgeoisie in Europe, surrealists were the first to experience truly what he called the "field of debris left behind the capitalist development of the forces of production."
>
> But it was Surrealism that first opened our eyes to them. These ruins became, for Surrealism, the object of a research no less impassioned than that which the humanists of the Renaissance conducted on the remnants of classical antiquity. . . . This unrelenting confrontation of the recent past with the present moment is something new, historically. Other contiguous links in the chain of generations have existed within the collective consciousness, but they were hardly distinguished from one another within the collective. The present, however, already stands to the recent past as the awakening stands to the dream. The development of the forces of production, in the course of the previous century, shattered that century's wish symbols even before the monuments representing them had collapsed, and

before the paper on which they were rendered had yellowed. (in Buck-Morss 13, 898)

Where De Sica's Umberto contemplates suicide but is not able to go through with the act, Rodrigo ends up committing suicide.[22] Rodrigo's suicide is the result of such unfulfilled wish symbols and the profound sense of boredom, alienation, and restlessness that comes from wide-spread, perpetual unemployment and the absence of a person to care for him (there are several shots in the film that indicate Rodrigo misses his mother). His death establishes the film's context and the overall insig-nificance of Rodrigo and his friends to Colombian society. Accordingly, Rodrigo's suicide is shot as a momentary blip on a radar screen. We see him looking out from behind a wall of windows on the twentieth floor of a building that he has lied his way into, over a busy city thoroughfare surrounded by tall buildings. As if looking into a void, Rodrigo is con-templating his death. In the next shot we see a split-second image of a body falling quickly past the same window. Our point of view shows what occupants in the building might have seen if they happened to be looking out the window the moment Rodrigo's body passed by.[23] Just as De Sica forces his audiences to acknowledge their positions as sheltered film spectators and thus somehow complicit with the landlady's expan-sionism in *Umberto D*, Gaviria positions his spectators to witness a death that might be missed (depending on whether one blinked) from behind a high-rise window, leaving them completely impotent to change the action. There is no follow-up reference to Rodrigo's death in the film. In a flash, the character of Rodrigo is gone. There is no postscript narrative about the impact of his death on others. He simply disappears.

The effect described in the above quote by Benjamin and depicted in Gaviria's film (best illustrated in Rodrigo's suicide scene) would only later be theorized by postmodern critics like Lefebvre and Harvey as the dangerous effects of accelerated time under capitalist accumulation and the increasingly abstract notions of space that affect (and often render invisible) lived communities. In his essay "Allegorical Bodies and Visions in Colombian Urban Cinema," Elia Kantaris suggests that the city itself in *Rodrigo D* is filmed as an allegory for a spatial politics that disappears or renders invisible marginal bodies under the aggressive flows of flexible accumulation. In contrast to depictions of buildings in *Umberto D* (like Umberto's apartment building and the public hospital), which threaten to throw bodies out onto the street, this process has been accelerated in *Rodrigo D*. City buildings appear to be empty, mirroring the hollow, listless nature of many of the boys in the film whose bodies will, in death, become spent commodities, *munecos* literally thrown to the streets as discarded waste.[24]

The cityscape of *Rodrigo D*, as in the case of any urban space, is layered by different moments of historical change.[25] Gaviria's portrait of Medellin takes into account the modern history of urban overpopulation and the subsequent diminishing of salaries and increased unemployment in Colombian urban centers, a result of large-scale migration to the cities following the destabilization of the government in the mid-1940s. The violence of the 1940s and 1950s was contained for almost two decades by an alliance of conservative and liberal leaders called the National Front, a group dedicated to (but ultimately unsuccessful at accomplishing) agrarian reform in the impoverished rural zones. Over time, as the National Front disintegrated, Colombian guerrilla groups such as the FARC (Colombian Armed Revolutionary Forces), the ELN (National Liberation Army), the EPL (Popular Liberation Army), and the M-19 (April 19th Movement) began to consolidate their power and to feel increasingly alienated from the concerns of the National Front. The 1980s saw a rise in violence among competing guerrilla political groups and an increase in *narcotrafico* to the United States. Although narcotrafico began in the 1970s, cocaine's value as an exportable commodity that overshadowed the economic potential of all other Colombian products was not fully realized until the 1980s, an era that saw an increase in political assassinations, everyday guerrilla and gang warfare, kidnappings, and the rise of powerful drug cartel leaders. But unlike such glamorous depictions of drug kingpins as one finds in a film like *Scarface*, Gaviria's film borrows from neorealist technique and thus gazes through several layers of dramatic history at the everyday lives of the underclasses who have lived and continue to live through such moments of epic change. Commenting on his own "cartography" of the region of Medellin, Gaviria had the following to say:

> The pulse of the cartographer is made from many hands. Each one makes his mark, each one teaches the lines of their hand and, in this way, contributes to the configuration of a collective invisible map. Up there on the screen, we hear everything that we hear now without paying attention: school songs, noises from the patio, declarations of love in the neighborhoods. . . . One day, I think, we will hear minor words on the screen. The purring of the trucks that move down the freeway toward the

coast, yellow lights that advance, speaking out loud. (in Gomez
79, 86)

Gaviria's cartography in *Rodrigo D* (and his later film *The Rose Seller,* for
that matter) involves a form of allegorical storytelling that incorporates
an internal soundtrack of everyday sounds. Like most Italian neorealist directors, however, Gaviria breaks Zavattini's prohibition of external soundtracks by including a variety of imported and national songs
that speak to social and generational differences between the characters.
Tango and punk rock, in particular, seem to represent a divide between
lost tradition and a new code of general disrespect that pits older parents against a younger generation that rebels against low-paid work and
unemployment.

But Rodrigo is far from lazy. Like all of the characters in the film,
he moves constantly, almost in sync with the frenetic soundtrack that
suggests that while there may be nothing for people in Rodrigo's community to do, movement does not stop. Rodrigo's friends are stealing
motorcycles to sell, listening to music, smoking marijuana, running from
the police or vigilantes in unmarked jeeps, going to the "hills" to hide
out, or dying. Gaviria plays down the adventurous qualities of this type
of renegade lifestyle by stressing the degree to which Rodrigo and his
friends are motivated by boredom. Several of the characters comment
on how bored they are throughout the film. Even when they are on the
run for their lives, the boys in the film are bored. They miss their families
and neighborhood. Rodrigo's boredom is emphasized by the fact that
when he walks around (in search of a cheap drum set so that he can start
a punk band) he kicks cans listlessly, throws rocks, and spits. Rodrigo
deals with his boredom in a manner somewhat different from that of his
friends. For example, he is less interested in stealing than are his friends.
At one point in the film, he is invited to steal a motorcycle but refuses.
The following dialogue ensues:

> Friend: "Look man, that bike is up for grabs. If only we had a
> gun to heist it."
> Rodrigo (to himself): "I'm the one up for grabs, and all the rest
> of us, too."

With a stone-faced delivery, Rodrigo theorizes his boredom as a result
of the futility of *all* action, legal or illegal.[26]

Rodrigo D:
No Future (Víctor
Gaviria, 1990)

As in the case of Umberto, the city structures appear to shun Rodrigo. He is constantly either walking on the outside of fenced-in areas looking in or framed as if behind bars, suggesting that prison—or worse—awaits him should he try to break into the space that locks him out. For example, in one scene, Rodrigo walks with his little brother to school to pay the school fees, only to find that the gates have already been locked because he is late. Only the shadows of the boys are shot, creating the illusion that they are behind bars. Rodrigo is framed in a similar manner just before his suicide in the high-rise later in the film. Gaviria uses city structures again to emphasize Rodrigo's marginal status when he shoots him walking precariously under a giant billboard depiction of a man's dress shoe. Rodrigo is figuratively at risk of being crushed by a consumerism of which he is no part. Repeated shots of guard dogs barking from behind fences or from atop balconies reiterate Rodrigo's marginal status in the city.

I have argued that De Sica and Zavattini's form of neorealism offers a strategy for historical unmasking that has continued relevance for late twentieth- and twenty-first-century filmmakers like Gaviria. This connection sheds light on Gaviria's use of modern ruins as his mise-en-scène for *Rodrigo D*. Accordingly, the sad telos of the narrative is, at the same time, the hollow state of affairs that establishes the everyday context of the drama; the ghostly urban ruins of a bourgeoisie whose structures anticipate an existence that becomes obsolete before it is born. Gaviria creates a parallel between the hollow image of development in Latin America (in his shots of empty offices and buildings) and the empty, bored lives of the boys in the film. The effect of the urban ruins in *Rodrigo D* conveys an overall sense of incompletion. Not only are buildings built but not filled, or not completed at all, but young lives both on- and offscreen are cut short. An epilogue and dedication at the film's end inform audience members that several of the actors in the film were killed by the same type of violence depicted on-screen before the film was ever released. Their collaboratively written story is told posthumously. The film lies somewhere between fiction and documentary, and is perhaps more neorealist in its adherence to such neorealist conventions as collaboration, the use of nonprofessional actors, colloquial language, everyday themes, and stories of the underclasses than are many of the Italian neorealist films that influenced its style.

Notes

1. Drawing on the work of Pier Paolo Pasolini and Paul Ginsborg, P. Adams Sitney suggests that De Sica and Zavattini, in their tendency to emphasize a breakdown of social solidarity in their films, illuminate various ways in which the state structure and administrative aspects of postwar Italian society had never broken ties with Fascism: "During both the Parri and De Gasperi governments the traditional state structure and administration inherited from Fascism was quietly being consolidated. . . . No serious critique was made of the many semi-independent special agencies created by Fascism for the purpose of social assistance or intervention in the economy. . . . In 1960 it was calculated that sixty-two out of sixty-four prefects (the central government's principal representatives in the provinces) had been functionaries under Fascism. So too had all 135 police chiefs and their 139 deputies. Only five of these had in any way contributed to the Resistance" (Sitney 81). With respect to the opening protest scene in *Umberto D*, Sitney suggests that Italian audiences would have been reminded of a workers' demonstration in Modena two years earlier (1950) in which six workers were killed (106).
2. I would add that De Sica's animal slaughter scene in *Umberto D* recalls a scene from *Rome, Open City* in which two Nazi soldiers shoot the sheep that will be their dinner in the street in front of a restaurant.
3. Implied in my argument is a critique of the tendency by scholars like Hess and Ana López to conflate Italian neorealism with other Eu-

ropean postwar cinema movements like the French New Wave and New German Cinema. Such arguments group all European cinema movements together and suggest that they are limited by the fact that their unity as movements is based solely on, as Lopez puts it, "the desire for national expression and differentiation from the Hollywood 'pleasure machine'" (in Martin 137).

4. Here I borrow from Kracauer's discussion of the flaneur as it relates to *Umberto D*. Accordingly, the flaneur is described as one "intoxicated with life in the street—life eternally dissolving the patterns which it is about to form. . . . [T]he street in the extended sense of the word is not only the arena of fleeting impressions and chance encounters but a place where the flow of life is bound to assert itself" (*Theory of Film* 72).

5. See Deleuze's *Cinema 1: The Movement-Image*. See also Fisher's essay in this collection for a more extensive discussion of Deleuze and neorealism.

6. Walpole's quote comes from Benjamin's notes for his never completed Arcades project. See Buck-Morss 400.

7. In his essay "The Work of Art in the Age of Mechanical Reproduction," Benjamin discusses film as a tool that has the power to reach the masses in their dream state (for better or worse): "The distracted person, too, can form habits. More, the ability to master certain tasks in a state of distraction proves that their solution has become a matter of habit. Distraction as provided by art presents a covert control of the extent to which new tasks have become soluble by apperception. Since, moreover, individuals are tempted to avoid such tasks, art will tackle the most difficult and most important ones where it is able to mobilize the masses. Today it does so in the film" (*Illuminations* 240). The collectively dreaming public, for Benjamin, was in a position to be claimed cinematically by Fascism or Communism. Kracauer further analyzes the power of film to affect large-scale spectator action in his chapter, "The Spectator," in *Theory of Film*. Similarly, Kracauer argues that the experience of watching a film creates a lowered consciousness that "invites dreaming" and that certain elements of film may be "sufficiently dream-like to launch the audience into reveries and perhaps even influence their course" (163).

8. See Marcus for a discussion of the way in which *Umberto D* launched a critique against the new Italy of the postwar years (101).

9. Peter Bondanella explores Mussolini's refashioning of ancient Roman history to suit his own nationalist plans in *The Eternal City: Roman Images in the Modern World*. He argues that Mussolini's use of architecture as propaganda was especially modeled on Augustus's style

(201). However, as Landy points out, "while there is some agreement about the ways the Fascist regime in Italy sought to create consensus through institutional structures and participation through the uses of the moving image, there is less unanimity about the regime's success in achieving its aims" (*Italian Film* 10).

10. Peter Burger suggests similarly that the modern "allegorist pulls one element out of the totality of the life context, isolating it, depriving it of its function" (in Buck-Morss 225).

11. Like most monumental architecture, ancient Roman structures were conceived of as highly politicized, ideological acts designed to manifest visually Rome's imperial power. Rome's first emperor, Augustus (27 BCE–CE 14), in his efforts to double the size of Roman territorial holdings, both exported the look of the city of Rome to the farthest reaches of its empire and celebrated his power at home with a long-term urban plan that sought, in his own words, to turn a city of brick into a city of marble. The exact meaning of imperial, monumental architecture often had little to do with the function of the building. For example, amphitheaters for gladiator games, tombs, altars, and temples built under Augustus's reign had very different functions but were linked together as part of his civic beautification policy. Each structure thus had both an individual function and a shared overriding political and ideological function as examples of Augustus's patronage of the city. Public buildings during Augustus's rule were, in effect, already serving an allegorical function in that they told stories of his apparent success as a peacemaker and as one who brought prosperity to the Roman populace.

12. For an extensive analysis of these films, see Wyke 20–24.

13. The original was translated by Bondanella from *Il popolo d'Italia*, April 22, 1922, and cited in his *Eternal City*.

14. Marcus looks at *Umberto D* alongside *Rome, Open City* to argue that the excitement over anti-Fascist activism and progressive social action that we see in the latter film is sadly exposed as having failed the test of time in the former.

15. See Buck-Morss 147–54. See also Bondanella for a discussion of the architectural struggle between tradition and modernism under Mussolini that culminated in the design for the Palace of Italian Civilization, now renamed the Palace of the Civilization of Labor (*Eternal City* 204–05).

16. Marcus cites the opening scene in which the pensioners' strike is broken up by the police as evidence for the fact that society is depicted as being at war with itself (97).

17. The film subtly suggests that the landlady's desperate struggle to survive the war (working as a prostitute) has corrupted her and made her as hateful as a Nazi (hence her cruel aesthetic). The landlady's connection to prostitution does not die with the end of the war, however. It simply transforms into a more respectable guise, as she now occupies the role of Madame, renting out rooms to respectable people while she is in the midst of adulterous love affairs.

18. This vision is foreshadowed in *Bicycle Thief* (1948) in the many shots depicting Ricci hanging posters of Rita Hayworth's latest film, *Gilda*.

19. This lack of a programmatic solution is noted by several critics and scholars, but there is disagreement about whether the end of the film offers an optimistic or pessimistic message.

20. The title (*Rodrigo D: No Future*) refers both to *Umberto D* and the British punk group the Sex Pistols. The subtitle was suggested by one of the film's nonprofessional actors and alludes to a state of affairs predicted by *Umberto D* and soon thereafter incorporated into the identity of the Sex Pistols, who were perceived as subcultural icons: "God save the Queen / The Fascist regime / They made you a moron / Potential H-bomb . . . We're the future, your future. . . . / No future, no future / No future for you / No future, no future / No future for me" (in Kantaris 3, 9).

21. Solanas and Gettino argue this point in *Cine, Cultura y Descolonización*.

22. The script for *Rodrigo D* was inspired by the failed suicide attempt of a nineteen-year-old that was reported in the local press. Originally, Gaviria's script followed the real-life story, and the protagonist's death was prevented by the intervention of a bystander. However, the nonprofessional actors who worked on the film suggested that death was a more plausible end to the story. See Fernandez.

23. Rodrigo flirts with death earlier in the film after he walks by the mangled corpse of a woman who has just been run over by a bus on a busy street. As he passes by the gruesome scene, he moves from the side of the road to the center of the busy four-lane highway, seemingly challenging cars to hit him.

24. Kantaris points out that the image of the commodified doll (muneco/ muneca) appears repeatedly in the film. This blanket term is used to represent the great number of anonymous dead bodies found on rubbish heaps or on the side of the road. The commodified, grotesquely casual nature of this term also points to a disembodied relationship to death on the part of the boys in the film (5).

25. In the case of *Rodrigo D*, it is important to keep in mind that the term

"cityscape" includes the city of Medellin and its surrounding slums, where most of the action takes place in the film.

26. Fernandez argues that one of the reasons Rodrigo chooses not to be a gangster but hangs out with them is that he is, from the start of the film, on a journey toward death. Taking a slightly different view of the spatial politics of the film from Kantaris, Fernandez suggests that the movement upward in the film (going up to the hills, being on roofs, and going up to the top floors of skyscrapers) represents an attempt to reach celestial space (49).

Chapter 8

Migrations of Cinema:
Italian Neorealism and Brazilian Cinema

Antonio Traverso

It's a sunny day in Rio de Janeiro. A group of children dive, splash, and laugh at a public fountain. Buildings, consumption, and violence surround them: these are the icons of third-world corporate capitalism and of an adult world so absorbed in itself that it has neither time nor compassion for these children, who have recently escaped from a reformatory and now live on the streets. In order to survive they smuggle drugs and steal from passersby in the city. Soon they will have guns to kill and will die. These children are the characters in Brazilian filmmaker Hector Babenco's *Pixote* (1980). Almost three and a half decades earlier a young boy walked alone on the streets of Berlin. He encountered other children: some chased each other joyfully, running around a monument in a city square, while others played football on a road. To survive children smuggled goods in the black market and stole from commuters in busy train stations. The city around them was a ghostly mise-en-scène of ruins: a desolate landscape of skeletons of concrete that had survived the recently ended Allied bombings. The complete destruction of the architectural space metonymically reiterated the moral collapse of its inhabitants, who, as in *Pixote,* could not perceive the greater plight of the children. The boy, who walked playfully and childishly toward a self-inflicted death, was the central character in Roberto Rossellini's classic of Italian neorealism *Germany, Year Zero* (1947).

The differences between these two films may seem obvious at first sight: clearly, the surreal look of a hollow, death-stricken Berlin at the end of World War II seems dissonant with the crowded vitality of Rio de Janeiro in the 1980s. However, there is an undeniable continuity in theme, style, and production approach, not to mention a less tangible authorial sensitivity when dealing with the subjectivity of children's experience in the midst of torn worlds. These cinematic reverberations may be described by the expression "migrations of cinema," as they denote the diasporic movement of people, politics, ideas, and practices of cinema. This essay proposes that the study of both the history and the texts of political Brazilian films demonstrates unambiguously an inspirational influence exerted by Italian neorealism since the 1950s. More specifically, neorealism entered Brazil via the direct intervention of filmmakers such as Nelson Pereira dos Santos and Glauber Rocha, both of whom studied film in Europe and became precursors of a lasting tradition of political filmmaking in Brazil.[1]

Both "neorealism" and "Brazilian cinema" will be treated as open and plural categories, and this essay will seek to identify specific continuities between the two cinematic moments. Such continuities will be considered through an examination of the historical, ideological, and theoretical context of the films and filmmakers involved, and the film texts' central themes and concerns, whereby the centrality of children stands out. To achieve this, the essay will consider some of the classics of Italian neorealism in relation to Brazilian films that have stood out both in Brazil and internationally, such as the above-mentioned *Pixote* and Walter Salles's *Central Station* (1998). The renewal of neorealist aesthetics in Brazilian cinema will be scrutinized in terms of three main areas of analysis. Accordingly, the essay will first discuss the films' observational and often raw documentary style; next, the filmmakers' commitment to the exploration of political, sociological, and historical themes; and finally, the production approaches, which often include the use of scripts based on true life stories, authentic locations, and nonactors playing themselves.

Italian Neorealism and Cinema Nõvo

If in the first decade of the twenty-first century one is to talk about the death of the plural cinematic expressions that emerged in Latin America, especially in the 1960s and 1970s, and that came to constitute the New Latin American Cinema, then this *end* should be understood as an effect of this movement's self-defined historical specificity. As revolutionary filmmakers, principally the exponents of the Brazilian movement of Cinema Nõvo, viewed themselves as ideological catalysts in the broader project of socialist revolution in the Latin American region, the end of their unique cinematic strategy was marked by the collapse of a broader political project. With the emergence of lasting military dictatorships in the continent between the 1960s and the late 1980s (in Brazil the military took power as early as 1964), political filmmakers were arrested, assassinated, or forced into exile. The revolutionary spirit of the movement, however, did not die. On the contrary, the fact that it has been unrelenting in its ongoing capacity to energize politically charged filmmaking in the continent will be demonstrated in the second half of this essay when I analyze recent Brazilian films. Thus Cinema Nõvo, like neorealism, has found an "afterlife" in new generations of filmmakers. This is true of numerous recent Brazilian films that continue to engage with Cinema Nõvo's project of cultural decolonization, identity politics, and narrative and stylistic experimentation, while simultaneously aspiring to their own place in the global networks of exhibition and distribution regulating film consumption today.

By extending the metaphor of migration in this essay's title, it is possible to appreciate the fact that international cinema audiences have more recently witnessed the renewal of neorealist aesthetics in contemporary Brazilian films. In this sense, the political elements in neorealism are most clearly expressed in Brazilian films. Though this political aspect has often been related to leftist politics, in the case of Brazilian films it did not regress to simple propaganda. Rather, neorealism's influence was embodied as an ethical stance that sustained an ongoing exploration of the nature of class divisions and the human condition in the face of oppressive circumstances, be this a dictatorship or the suffering caused by war or capitalism. The case of Rossellini is a good example. His reported "betrayal" of neorealism after *Germany, Year Zero* was explained by his critics as a departure from politics: as a moving away from the struggle of the working classes against Fascism and capitalism toward a bourgeois interest in individuality and spirituality. However, as Geoffrey Nowell-Smith has argued, later Rossellini films, especially those notoriously attacked by Marxist critics such as Guido Aristarco (namely those of the Bergman cycle), are extremely political. "[P]olitics," stresses Nowell-Smith, "far from being a distraction, throwing off course [Rossellini's] essential, spiritual, human quest, was actually a major source of consistency in his career. Throughout his career, Rossellini was a profoundly political artist" (9). Two examples of this political bent are *Stromboli* (1950) and *Europa '51* (1952). In the former, Ingrid Bergman plays a woman who faces consecutive stages of oppression: from the war to a refugee camp, and from her forced marriage to an Italian soldier to an unbearable life on an isolated island within a hermetic and hostile fishing community. In the latter film, Bergman plays a high-class woman who becomes increasingly aware of and involved with the suffering of the poor after the death of her only child. Thus, she renounces her class status and family and as a result has to suffer their retaliation, which comes in the form of imprisonment in a psychiatric hospital. Apart from the attention given in these films to the trope of individual spiritual enlightenment, which is undoubtedly a central theme, it is obvious, first, that these films continue Rossellini's concern with human existence in a world marked by oppression and suffering as a result of war, Fascism, poverty, or social convention. Second, it is also apparent that the individual of these narratives is gendered as female, and as the Bergman character struggles against structures of patriarchal power, eventually achieving a sense of personal discovery and transcendence, the film functions to expose these oppressive structures. Attention also needs to be given to the fact that Rossellini's "Bergman" films addressed gender politics, thus anticipating a key direction of later political filmmaking by several decades. Similarly, recent Brazilian films, *Central Station* being the primary example, engage with political themes that involve power, oppression, poverty, and violence and do so from the view of female characters, thus gendering their exploration of the political.

The echoes and continuities identified between the two scenes of filmmaking described at the beginning of this essay demonstrate the lasting impact of Italian neorealist films on cinema emerging from Brazil. Furthermore, any examination of the neorealist influence on Brazilian cinema requires a consideration of the specificity of the tradition of political cinema in this country. As a source of cinematic influence and inspiration, neorealism entered Brazilian film via the revolutionary filmmaking of the late 1950s and 1960s. However, such an examination also requires that it be situated historically within the broader context of the regional movement of political cinema that came to be known as the New Latin American Cinema, an analytic category that describes a heterogeneous, multiple, and changing range of cinematic practices and theoretical endeavors occurring more or less simultaneously in most Latin American countries (but significantly in Cuba, Brazil, Argentina, Bolivia, and Chile) between the late 1950s and mid-1970s. Salles's recent film *The Motorcycle Diaries* (2004) calls our attention back to the theme of a unified and liberated Latin America through the film's depiction of Ernesto "Che" Guevara's experience of travel through the continent and his recognition of the commonality of the tribulations of all

Latin American peoples. Salles's own understanding of the project of filmmaking in Latin America responds to what the film scholar Zuzana Pick has called a "continental project," that is, a common creative activity directed toward cultural decolonization, identity search, and political unity through the cinematic expression amid the continent's countries (in Elena and Días López 11).

Historically, Brazilian cinema has suffered from an endemic poverty in its production and distribution infrastructure. This poverty is further augmented by the lower appeal of local production to local cinema audiences in relation to Hollywood and other commercial cinemas. Such circumstances are sometimes explained as an effect of the alleged later advent of cinema to third-world countries. This assumption is mistaken, however, since the new cinematic technology arrived in most non-Western countries soon after the first Lumière screenings in Paris. Randal Johnson and Robert Stam remind us that "[c]inema reached Brazil only six months after Lumière revealed his *cinématographe* in Paris in late 1895" and that the first filmmaking equipment was introduced to Brazil as early as 1898 (19).[2] Few are aware that many Latin American countries can claim as the golden age of their national cinemas the first decades of the twentieth century, before the transnationalization of Hollywood's monopolies succeeded in strangling local production. Johnson and Stam explain that in Brazil "from 1900 to 1912, Brazilian films dominated the internal market, reaching an annual production of over one hundred films [which] fostered a public habit of frequent movie going [and] intense filmmaking activity" (20). Unfortunately, these histories are often only the domain of film historians. Sadly, an overwhelming majority of the contemporary Brazilian film audience, especially the young, have never seen a locally made film after several generations of sustained Hollywood consumption.

It was Hollywood's dominance that the experimental and activist films of Cinema Nõvo rose against in the 1950s, very much like postwar European movements, from Italian neorealism to the new waves.[3] This neorealist countercinematic emphasis was later replicated in other film movements in several Latin American countries.[4] As in the rest of Latin America, in Brazil this project of cinematic countercultural war was legitimately believed to be one of many fronts in a more general process of ideological decolonization and social revolution. Retrospectively, the four decades between the 1950s and 1980s—dramatically marked by revolution, dictatorship, and exile—came to constitute what the cinema of Brazil has most generally been identified with both in world film exhibition and in Latin American film studies in English.

The similarities between the historical and ideological context in Italy from the mid-1940s to the 1950s and that in Latin America from the mid-1950s to the 1970s may explain the popularity of the neorealist approach among politically committed filmmakers. Like Italian neorealism, Cinema Nõvo's radical critique of both Hollywood and local Hollywood-like cinematic production was expressed not only in its focus on themes and stories representing the lives of working people but also on an extreme experimentalism in production methods and film style. Through these innovations Brazilian filmmakers both embraced and expanded the tenets of neorealism—as well as those of other progressive film approaches—eclectically adapting them to the specific requirements of their particular political and cultural contexts. As a result, they produced revolutionary films that subverted not only classical Hollywood formats but also the European stress on individualism and intellectualism. Cinema Nõvo film was essentially an ideological weapon of cultural and ideological decolonization. In this context, the neorealist interdependence between themes (real life stories, working-class and everyday people, and the broader social and historical context), forms of production (use of real locations, nonactors, and authentic participants), and experimental realist aesthetics was a crucial element triggering and inspiring political filmmaking in Brazil.

Therefore, the echo of neorealist themes and aesthetics in political Brazilian films is unmistakable. The visual poetics that describe the life of the dispossessed, political conflict, oppression, the experience of childhood in the midst of social breakdown, and the tangible historicity of cinema migrate from the long black-and-white sequences of Rossellini's and Vittorio De Sica's classics to the observational long takes in the films of Pereira dos Santos and Rocha.[5] However, the immediacy and urgency of the relationship between a film and the historical context of its production and exhibition was a defining aspect not only of Cinema Nõvo but most broadly of the new political cinema being nurtured throughout Latin America. In this context, it is important to pay attention to a significant event that functioned as a catalyst for the diverse experiences emerging from different countries. The First Film Festival of Viña del Mar, Chile, in 1967 became a moment of convergence of the new continental cinematic vision. The festival allowed Latin American filmmakers to become aware of political film production outside their national borders, and this awareness was expressed in enthusiastic terms in a statement of principles for politically motivated filmmaking in the continent. These principles addressed the need for filmmakers to join ef-

Bicycle Thief
(Vittorio De Sica,
1948)

forts on a continental scale, developing critical national cinemas that opposed cultural imperialism and expressed the realities of the peoples of
Latin America. The festival saw the presentation of not only the earliest
films of the New Latin American Cinema but also the key theories and
manifestos that gave the new film movement its heart (Mouesca 32).
Among the participants was Rocha, who presented his highly influential
thesis "Eztetyka da fome" (Aesthetics of hunger), which contains the
theoretical foundations of Cinema Nõvo.[6] Johnson and Stam point out
that "the truly seminal contribution of this essay was to call for a style
appropriate to the real Brazil, to articulate a social thematic together
with a production strategy into a truly revolutionary esthetic" (68). Both
Rocha's theory and his film *Black God, White Devil* (1955) made a great
impact at the festival. Remembering the occasion, the Chilean director
Raúl Ruiz commented on their response: "Unexpectedly, we discovered
a self-confident cinema that in the most natural way. . . was being made
with very scarce means . . . and with a freedom that . . . European cinema did not possess" (in Mouesca 33).[7] Yet at the same time Brazilian
filmmakers were also influenced by the theoretical and cinematic presentation of other Latin American filmmakers. In every case, neorealist
aesthetics circulated in both ideas and films.

The contribution of Brazilian cinema toward developing critical national cinemas was an exemplary case. Brazilian filmmakers were also
deeply impressed by their encounter with Italian neorealism in the 1950s

and 1960s, which became a central source of influence for the filmmaking of that period. Not all Brazilians discovered neorealism on the occasion of the screening of Italian neorealist films in Brazil; some of them, as in the cases of Argentine Fernando Birri and Cubans Tomás Gutiérrez Alea and Julio García Espinosa, found it directly in Europe. Salles, for example, spent his childhood in Europe as the son of a diplomat. It was during this period that he became acquainted with Italian neorealism and other key European film expressions. On his return to Brazil in the early 1960s he found himself as an adolescent returnee who knew more about European film culture than Brazilian film culture. Salles reflects, "I admired Rossellini and Visconti and the early films of Godard and Truffaut. . . . On taking the camera to the streets and showing the faces and lives of ordinary people [they] had fomented a true ethical and aesthetic revolution in films" (in Elena and Días López xiii).

The lives of the characters in Salles's *Foreign Land* (1995), codirected with Daniela Thomas, reflect his own experience. The film explores the culture of exile that followed the period of dictatorship in Brazil and the revival of Brazilian cinema in the 1990s. For the two main characters in the film, Alberto Elena explains, the distance and strangeness characteristic of the experience of exile fail to offer solutions to their confusion and rootlessness, as they subsequently question their place in both their home country and the world to which they departed and from which they have returned (Elena and Días López 211). However, this confusion did not last long for Salles as he discovered Latin American film through the militant films of revolutionary Cuba and the Cinema Nõvo of Rocha. Salles describes his first viewings of Cinema Nõvo films.

> On returning to Brazil, while still an adolescent, I had the privilege of watching *Deus e o Diabo na Terra do Sol* [*Black God, White Devil*] . . . together with a Brazilian psychoanalyst named Hélio Pelegrino. When the film was over, we sat there, ecstatic, overwhelmed by an emotion that is difficult to describe. Hélio turned to me and said: "This film hits the heart of Brazilian-ity." And so it did. It was a dazzling experience. And the same thing happened when I discovered *Vidas Secas* (*Barren Lives*) by Nelson Pereira dos Santos and *São Paulo S.A.* by Luis Sergio Person—an extraordinary and sometimes overlooked film of the Brazilian Cinema Novo (in Elena and Días López xiii–xiv).

While Italian neorealism had been a source of inspiration for Cuban and Brazilian directors in the early to mid-1950s, throughout the 1960s both Cinema Nõvo and neorealism were simultaneously "discovered" by filmmakers both inside and outside Brazil, people who had not been aware of these movements until then. In a highly politicized context, however, Cinema Nõvo took priority as a model of filmmaking for Latin America. Indeed, while the Brazilian film movement included the central neorealist features, it adapted and expanded them into forms deemed more flexible and appropriate to the Latin American reality. Rather than simply imitating principles learned in Italy, key Brazilian filmmakers who had been exposed to neorealism in Europe (namely, Pereira dos Santos, Rocha, and Ruy Guerra), on returning to Brazil, reflected on the Brazilian cinema that preceded them.

The so-called father of Cinema Nõvo, Pereira dos Santos, spent two months in Paris in 1949, where he was exposed to Italian neorealism through the French Cinémathèque. During the screenings he was also impressed by the documentary style and leftist humanism of John Grierson and Joris Ivens. Thus, neorealist and documentary elements would later be decisive in the production of his films (San Miguel in Elena and Días López 71). In the early 1950s Pereira dos Santos and other young intellectuals overtly rejected the films being produced in Brazil, which uncritically reproduced Hollywood conventions. They supported the notion of a new national cinema that would represent the reality of Brazil "from the poverty of the *favelas* to the drought of the *sertão*" (72). In Heliodoro San Miguel's view, the urgent desire of young film-makers such as Pereira dos Santos to change the substance of Brazilian cinema "called for a film-making style devoid of the ties of an industrially crafted cinema in favour of an aesthetics of urgency and poverty in which technique was secondary to content" (72). This active search for an alternative model helps explain the rapid yet critical adoption of neorealism as an appropriate and useful filmmaking and philosophical approach. San Miguel adds,

> Like other Latin American countries, the adoption of neorealist tenets was formal, and not based on mere imitation. The themes were purely Brazilian, but neorealism provided a method and a tool to depict and denounce the different social conditions of the country. It also opened the doors for the possibility of making low budget artisan films that could be made in the streets without professional actors, and that could address popular themes and social problems, making clear their authors' political inclinations and intentions. (72)

The making of Pereira dos Santos's *Rio, 40 Degrees* (1955), which was facilitated by a cooperative model of production, suffered in and of itself the endemic poverty affecting Brazilian society that the film set itself to represent. All things considered, *Rio, 40 Degrees* was a very innovative film for its time. This innovation was expressed through a new film aesthetic depicting the marginality and oppression of Rio de Janeiro's poor. From the point of view of structure, it experimented with narrative form, presenting its content through a semi-narrative collage. San Miguel observes that the film already contains all the features of the new cinema of the 1960s and that although it can be seen as an extraordinary anticipation of Cinema Nōvo its significance as a film in its own right should not be underestimated as it continues to grow in the historiography of Brazilian and Latin American cinema (71).

In *Barren Lives* (1963), argue Johnson and Stam, Pereira dos Santos anticipated Rocha's aesthetics of hunger in his "soberly critical realism." Johnson and Stam stress that "[r]arely has a subject—in this case hunger, drought, and the exploitation of a peasant family—been so finely rendered by a style. Rarely have a thematic and an esthetic been quite so fully adequate to one another" (120). Yet "hunger" defined not only the film's theme and style but also its production methods, and in this sense, as stated above, Italian neorealism offered Pereira dos Santos the most adequate model (Johnson and Stam 121–22). Johnson and Stam continue,

> *Vidas Secas*, then, has certain affinities with Neo-Realism, affinities that extend even to a thematic level. Like many Neo-Realist films, *Vidas Secas* makes the story of a few ordinary individuals the springboard for a discussion of a larger social problem. Just as the lone bicycle thief of *Ladri di Biciclette* "speaks for" the armies of the unemployed in post-war Italy, so the single peasant family of *Vidas Secas* sums up the lives of the millions of northeasterners who migrate to the cities of the south. (122)

It is important to note that Pereira dos Santos himself both acknowledged and qualified neorealism's influence on his generation's enthusiastic and energetic filmmaking: "The influence of neorealism was not that of a school or ideology, but rather as a production system. Neorealism taught us, in sum, that it was possible to make films in the streets; that we did not need studios; that we could film using average people rather than known actors; that the technique could be imperfect, as long as the film was truly linked to its national culture and expressed that culture" (in Johnson and Stam 122). The commitment to authenticity in the representation of reality meant that many filmmakers would experiment with a hybrid textuality working at the limits between documentary and fiction. This is, indeed, the case in *Barren Lives* when a segment alternates shots of the main character in jail with documentary shots of villagers celebrating a traditional ceremony (Johnson and Stam 123). The use of documentary segments interspersed within the narrative to enhance the text's realism, common in Brazilian cinema, was also a typical feature of Italian neorealism. For example, in *Stromboli* there is a memorable scene in which the Bergman character, after being taken out to sea with the island's fishermen, faints during the mesmerizing fishing sequences in which the contents of full nets are deposited in the boats.[8] Similarly, the opening sequence of *Pixote* that precedes the narrative film proper is a documentary segment shot in São Paulo in which the director, Babenco, stands in front of the camera and points at the favelas that fill the frame behind him, while giving statistics about destitute children in Brazil. One of the film's central characters is shown standing next to his mother in a favela. Babenco explains that the characters of this film are played by children who actually live in this place. More recently, *The Motorcycle Diaries* contains a segment in which the main characters enter a food market in southern Chile, and while they talk and joke with the vendors the film acquires a documentary mode. Another, more subtle, approach to realism can be found in *Barren Lives,* whose long opening shot, in which "[a] static camera records the slow progress of four human figures and a dog across an inhospitable landscape," represents the temporality of peasant life and, as a consequence, marks the cultural difference between the perspectives of the peasant characters and the film's middle-class urban audience (Johnston and Stam 126).

Despite Pereira dos Santos's importance, the principal legacy for Brazilian activist filmmaking has undoubtedly been the work of the legendary director and film theoretician Glauber Rocha. Apart from *Black God, White Devil* Rocha is best-known for films such as *Anguished Land* (1967) and *Antônio das Mortes* (1969). In her discussion of Rocha's *Black God, White Devil* Ivana Bentes shows the formal experimentation and political commitment energizing the Cinema Nôvo project in terms of the ideological and stylistic principles of Rocha's aesthetics of hunger. In reference to these principles, Bentes describes Cinema Nôvo as "a cinema movement that rediscovered and gave visibility to the social and human landscape of the country's Northeastern region while creating a cinematic language in which aesthetics and politics could not be dissociated" (89). In this context, *Black God, White Devil* became a sociological study through the archetypal narrativization of two of Brazil's most visited mythical themes: the *sertão*, the harsh expanse of territory in the Brazilian northeast, and the *cangaço*, cycles of banditry that thrived in the northeast from 1870 to 1940 (Bentes 90).[9] Both the *sertão* and the *cangaceiros* are explored by Rocha as figures that represent a past revolutionary force, which, although destined to disappear in modern Brazil, signal a great change to come. Bentes discusses Rocha's dialectical combination of documentary, avant-garde, and Brechtian elements, including an abundance of long takes, raw and abrupt editing, and thematic repetition and reiteration. The cinematic vision, Bentes adds, oscillates between realism and subjectivism, with the camera itself at times entering the trance that energizes the characters (93). Rocha's assault on Hollywood's cinematic conventions destroys any vestiges of naturalism; his realism is constructed instead on a new aesthetics. His aesthetics of hunger and violence, therefore, attempts to represent the world from the perspective of an antibourgeois consciousness; using Brechtian techniques of distanciation it refuses to mediate the world of his characters for a middle-class, intellectual public. In Rocha's film, according to Bentes, "not a single character is an intellectual, a legitimate representative or mediator of the people" (96). Instead, bandits, *beatos,* and mercenaries "deprive the intellectual of the privileged position as an agent of change" (96). This ideological strategy of Cinema Nõvo can be clearly identified in later Brazilian films, such as *Pixote* and Fernando Meirelles and Kátia Lund's *City of God* (2002), in which the middle-class viewer can escape neither the shock of the crudeness of the social reality depicted nor the fact that the subjectivity of the film coincides with that of the violent children and youth who constitute the films' characters. Although the Cinema Nõvo of the 1950s was heavily influenced by Italian neorealism, the movement continued to evolve theoretically and stylistically, not abandoning but expanding the neorealist precepts (Hayward 56).

Political Cinema in Brazil after Cinema Nõvo

In recent Brazilian films it is possible to see the departure from the radical aesthetics of hunger proposed by Rocha as filmmakers, in order to produce films that appeal to both national and international audiences, have been required to engage once again with the classical narrative structure and visual glamor associated with commercial cinema. Nevertheless, the persistent commitment of recent Brazilian films to the social and historical reality of destitute people characterizes Cinema Nõvo's legacy and, in this way, comments on the lasting influence of neorealism. The films I would like to devote some attention to here, namely, *Pixote, City of God, Central Station*, and Carlos Diegues's *Bye Bye Brazil* (1979), represent both the rupture and continuity with the ethical, political, and aesthetic priorities of neorealism and Cinema Nõvo.

Diegues's *Bye Bye Brazil* explores the transformation of a traditional Brazil into a contemporary one at the end of the twentieth century by focusing on the technological and capitalist penetration and destruction of indigenous cultures and their natural Amazonian habitat. The film, not unlike *Central Station* and *The Motorcycle Diaries*, is structured as a road movie in which the journey of a troupe of circus artists through changing landscapes functions allegorically to expose the macro structures and processes at play in contemporary Brazilian society. In the absence of Rocha's aesthetics of hunger, the polished style of the film does not completely silence the echoes of Cinema Nõvo's experimentalism, which is visible in its use of allegory, the sporadic attainment of a documentary register in the fiction, and the presence of a *magister ludi* character, a character whose function is to mediate the narrative (in Elena and Días López 161–67). However, Joao Luis Vieira emphasizes that unlike the films of Cinema Nõvo, *Bye Bye Brazil* "offers no omniscient political analysis"; rather, it "displays a Renoir-like tenderness for all its characters, without completely forgetting the social contradictions in which they are enmeshed" (167). Renoir's poetic realism was also a strong influence on Italian neorealism (Thompson and Bordwell 318) and, indeed, this caring for the characters is a strong feature of Rossellini's and De Sica's films. This is clearly an attitude that reverberates in Brazilian cinema.

There is a commonality of elements in the ways in which Italian neorealism and Brazilian political cinema, respectively, have approached the representation of social reality. Two of these elements include a controlled observational approach and a focus on the figure of children against the landscape of historical events in a way that subverts the Western myth of the innocent child. Sociological observation is seen in Rossellini's *Rome, Open City* (1945) through its detached narrative description of forms of clandestine resistance and counterinsurgency methods, including torture. This aspect of *Rome, Open City* anticipates the more systematic descriptions and elaborations about the workings of insurgent cells in *The Battle of Algiers* (1965). Sociological reflection through visual examination is also an approach used in Brazilian films. In *Pixote* and *City of God* it is the narrative itself that is conceptualized as a sociological study, since the acts perpetrated by the children and youth, no matter how abhorrent they may appear to a middle-class audience, are depicted as matter-of-factly from a detached perspective, without being underpinned by moral judgment. In *Pixote* this is further enhanced by the documentary opening sequence, already mentioned above, in which the film's director offers statistics about Brazil's destitute children. *City of God* provides a voice-over description of gang life from the perspective of a young boy who lives in the neighborhood, which is impressive because of the detailed insider's knowledge and its chilling reification of these extreme conditions.

The second realist representational element that I want to highlight as a common element of both Italian neorealist and Brazilian political films is their shared interest in the theme of children amid sociohistorical turmoil and their subsequent subversion of the Western idea of the innocent child. Indeed, as in the case of many Italian neorealist classics, many contemporary Brazilian films challenge the myth of the innocent child, itself a concept based on a binary opposition between the moral citizen and the amoral criminal. When children are represented in these films, their deprived lives are articulated within a discourse that is critical of the idea of childhood. For example, both in *Rome, Open City* and *Germany, Year Zero* child characters are brought to the foreground as the narrative engages with their experiences in the face of war and destruction. Surely, the images these films are best remembered for are, first, the group of children walking back to their homes after having witnessed the execution of their neighborhood's priest, in *Rome, Open City*, and, second, the lonely boy who playfully climbs a dilapidated building before jumping to his death, in *Germany, Year Zero*. Following Rossellini, Gillo Pontecorvo also explored the theme of children as political activists in a war scenario in *The Battle of Algiers*, while in *Bicycle Thief* (1948) De Sica focused on the relationship between childhood, labor, and poverty. Similarly, *Pixote, Central Station,* and *City of God* represent childhood as a state that requires the negotiation of homelessness, violence, sexuality, and survival.[10]

Ismael Xavier argues that a thematic continuity exists between the Brazilian cinema of the 1960s and that of the 1990s, as recent films continue to be motivated by central questions concerning cultural and national identity. The continuity remains in spite of the fact that, as Xavier claims, there has been a general shift in focus from the social to the

178

individual dimension. And, in this sense, the figure of the child as an agent of adult redemption has occupied a central position in recent narrative films, for example in *Central Station* (in Nagib xx–xxi). However, I would suggest instead that Brazilian filmmakers' attention has not so much shifted away from politics as it has reinscribed individual, psychological, and spiritual dimensions against a mise-en-scène of social and political figures. This is an important distinction, because through such a perspective Brazilian cinema of the 1990s can in fact be reconnected with neorealist influences of the 1960s. That is, the representation of children, in this sense, continues as a central allegorical narrative that further reconnects the classics of Italian neorealism to recent Brazilian cinema. In Murillo Salles's *How Angels Are Born* (1996), for example, a group of favela children become involved in violence and crime and end up killing each other. Similarly, an orphaned child unexpectedly met in a train station changes a lonely, middle-aged woman's life in *Central Station* (in Nagib 44–46).

Such representations of children in recent Brazilian cinema reflect similar depictions found in neorealist classics such as Rossellini's *Paisà* (1946) and De Sica's *Bicycle Thief*. In one episode of the former we follow a black American military police officer, Joe, going about the streets of Naples with a small shoeshine boy, Pasquale. In the latter film, Antonio (the father) and Bruno (the son) also walk about the streets of an impoverished Italian city. According to Christopher Wagstaff, it is illuminating to compare the man-boy pairs in these films. This is because the visual contrast of the body height between man and boy is further emphasized by the opposite psychological and spiritual imbalance between an adult who is anxious, lost, and in despair and a young boy who is alert, intelligent, resourceful, and streetwise (in Forgacs, Lutton, and Nowell-Smith 42–43). While this dual figure can be read as an allegory of the spiritual decay of an old Europe against the hope of a better future, it may also be understood as a subversion of a bourgeois conception of the child as vulnerable and innocent. Indeed, in war and postwar periods children are forced to be like adults while adults may regress to a state of utter vulnerability. While Brazilian films insist on the figure of the autonomous, parentless child, Italian neorealism explored the weaknesses and strengths of the familial. Neorealists focused on the severed and yet still surviving ties between fathers and sons, as in *Paisà* in which Joe represents a father figure even though he lacks the knowledge and capacity to protect. In Brazilian films, by contrast, it is not the aftermath of a war that causes the downfall of the family but the permanent war on the individual by capitalism: poverty produces a war-like scenario for orphans and homeless children who have to learn to become survivors by themselves. Wagstaff also notes that in both *Paisà* and *Bicycle Thief* "the adult is too self-absorbed to notice the needs of the child" (43). In Brazilian films such as *Pixote* and *City of God* the adult world is altogether absent from the children's lives, as they are left alone to learn and develop their own survival strategies. In these films adults and older kids exist for the children in so far as they are a source of threat, abuse, and exploitation. Furthermore, in *Central Station* the orphan child is very much like the children in *Rome, Open City, Paisà,* and *Bicycle Thief,* that is, more resourceful and determined than the adult, leading the way for the adult and setting a challenge and a standard of moral values, which in the end will result in the spiritual transformation of the adult.

Thus, in these films the adult-child relationship is marked by ambiguity. The traditional view of the child as vulnerable and the adult as protector is presented in the surface of the narrative. However, as the complexity of the characters and their relationship is progressively revealed, the traditional logic is reversed, and the child becomes not just a guide and support but a spiritual source of redemption for the adult. In *Paisà* the police officer is black and, as he explains, a "slave back at home." Meanwhile, in his poverty the boy is resourceful and knowledgeable, thus triggering a form of enlightenment in the soldier. In *Rome, Open City,* while the child's father is tortured and killed and the priest executed, it is actually the children who successfully organize clandestine acts of sabotage, such as bombings, without being found or punished. In *Bicycle Thief* the boy is an efficient employee at a petrol station and becomes an enthusiastic assistant during the search for the bicycle, being able to calm his desperate father. While the figure of an autonomous, knowledgeable child who enlightens an adult is expressed directly in *Central Station,* films such as *Pixote* and *City of God* signify instead the spiritual decay and guilt of the adult capitalist world, which is the cause of the neglect and abuse the children suffer, as well as the cause of their life of crime and violence.

The unromanticized engagement with the theme of childhood in *Pixote* is already prefigured in the title of the book the film is based on: José Louzeiro's *Infância dos mortos* (*Childhood of the Dead*). From the start and throughout the film the narrative sustains an ambiguity about the characters and the spaces they occupy: Are they children or small adults? Is their world a home and a family or an ineffective substitute? In the first scene, set in a children's reformatory, a group of children are watching television before being ushered to bed by the center's director. The suggested ambivalence oscillates between the paternal tenderness of the father figure's "bed time" and the violence and abuse that will follow, especially because the main perpetrator will be this very man. Pixote (his nickname means "little kid") is a small, homeless orphan who is spending his first night at the reformatory. One night is enough to teach him the kind of home he has come to: from behind the bars of his bunk bed he witnesses a group of older boys rape one of the newcomers. At the same time, there is an adult discourse of caring around him that contradicts his experience and renders this discourse incomprehensible to him. One man says to the children, "You don't have anything to worry about. Children are protected by Brazilian law. You are immune from punishment." After a riot in the reformatory in response to the killing of one of the kids by the police, a government minister asks the children, "Why the destruction and violence? This is your home," while failing to get anyone to point a finger at those responsible for initiating the riot. Once again the adult world's contradiction between abuse and care renders the gap between the middle-class intellectual consciousness and the children's subjectivity unbridgeable. In just a few days at the reformatory Pixote has been exposed both through dialogue and action to glue sniffing, drug smuggling, promiscuous sexuality, rape, bullying, bashings, killings, riots, self-mutilation, and the narrative of escape. In fact it is Pixote himself who finally says, "Freedom is outside." Soon a group of children, including Pixote, escapes the center, and the remainder of the film follows their life on the streets of São Paulo and Rio de Janeiro. They work in groups as city pickpockets. Various scenes show the kids running through the crowds, stealing people's bags and wallets, a direct link to *Germany, Year Zero*'s depiction of children stealing in train stations.

In the final segments of *Pixote*, the children have moved into a prostitute's apartment and formed a profitable partnership with her. In one scene, they all lie in the woman's bed watching television. The woman becomes a mother figure, but this image is soon made to collapse by her successive shifting of roles between mother and lover. In the final scenes, after one of the children has been killed and another has left, the woman holds a sick Pixote in her arms against her chest while sitting on her bed. Pixote seeks her breast and she bares it for him, creating a metonymic oscillation of absence and presence between a mother breastfeeding a child and a woman making love to a man. However, the impossibility of this act makes the woman push Pixote away, yelling,

"I'm not your mother, she's dead! I hate children!" This ambivalent man-boy stands up with a look of defiance while placing his gun against his waist inside his trousers. In the final shot we see the first light of the sunrise: Pixote walks away childishly balancing himself on the railway line. This man-boy ambiguity is strongly reminiscent of the image of the children walking away in the final shot of *Rome, Open City* as well as the last sequence of *Germany, Year Zero,* in which the German boy walks on the street just before his suicide.

The pessimistic realism of *Pixote* is continued and expanded in José Joffily's *Who Killed Pixote?* (1996), a film that shows the extent to which reality and representation blend together in Brazilian cinema. The film is based on the true story of Fernando Ramos da Silva, who as a child played the character Pixote in Babenco's award-winning film. *Who Killed Pixote?* relates Ramos da Silva's short life of shifting between petty crime and fruitless attempts at earning an honest income. In the process the film depicts disconcerting features of Brazilian society that are presented as the causes of the high levels of crime affecting the country, such as the lack of opportunities for unemployed youth, corruption, and the police's use of torture and execution as coercive methods. The film also portrays a society that does not show any concern for the young Ramos da Silva. This includes Babenco himself, whom the young man has to beg in order to get a role in a television soap opera. Unable to pursue a career as an actor because he is illiterate, despite the international success of *Pixote,* Ramos da Silva goes back to a life of petty crime and ends up being set up and murdered by a corrupt police officer. He was nineteen years old at the time (R. Kapur).

Central Station

Walter Salles's *Central Station* is one of the most successful Brazilian films of recent years. It was a Golden Globe winner for best foreign-language film in 1998 and Fernanda Montenegro, as Dora, one of the two central characters, was nominated for an Academy Award as best actress. The film narrates the unlikely friendship between a recently orphaned boy, Josué, played by Vinícius de Oliveira, and Dora, a bitter and cynical middle-aged ex-teacher who earns an income writing letters for illiterate passersby at Rio de Janeiro's main train station, Central do Brasil. Starting in Rio the film shifts to road movie format when the two characters take a bus trip to northeastern Brazil looking for the boy's estranged father. The road narrative highlights the precariousness of the travel and is intersected by the growing friendship between Josué and Dora. The journey, as in the classical road narrative, transforms Josué when he finds his brothers instead of the mythical father he has been looking for. However, the journey mostly involves the radical transformation of Dora, who ceases to be a selfish, uptight woman and experiences a process of spiritual redemption and cleansing. This redemptive movement is further enhanced by the contrast the film articulates between the big city and the sertão, a mythical space that Brazilian cinema has engaged with throughout its whole history, as discussed earlier in relation to films such as *O Cangaceiro* (1953) and *Black God, White Devil.*[11]

The film's focus on a small, orphaned, homeless boy is reminiscent of the children in neorealist films. This is a story about the life of the poor, and it involves themes of desperation, survival, illiteracy, alcoholism, crime, child abuse, child neglect and abandonment, street life, and violence. Most of the scenes are shot on location. At the train station we see everyday scenes of crowds coming and going, buying food and other products in the many small shops and stalls located inside. This segment also includes a scene involving a shoplifter who is chased and shot dead by a security guard. There are also many images of Rio de Janeiro, a city that is presented as a jungle of concrete and metal where the law of survival of the fittest prevails. After the segments on the bus in which Dora and Josué travel to rural Brazil, we see their destination: a housing development with hundreds of recently made, identical, simple, small houses. However, it is mainly the mise-en-scène representing the life of poor, struggling people that links this film to the Italian neorealist classics, especially when this is conveyed through documentary-like sequences that act as a counterpoint to the narrative.

There is also a certain neorealist sense of detachment through which we gain insights into the characters' subjectivity, not through artificial revelations of their thoughts, memories, or dreams but through a mode of "objective" looking at their movements and actions and gestures in the context of challenges, threats, and fears. For this reason, our insight into the characters' psyche is always tentative, merely suggested. This is perhaps one of the key denominators of neorealism that reverberates in political Brazilian films. For example, the suicide of Edmund at the end of *Germany, Year Zero* has been explained away as the effect of his guilt after having poisoned his sick father. However, this is only a plausible interpretation because the film contains enough clues that signify a generalized state of collapse of Edmund's world, where adults continue to give him contradictory messages. In the film's final sequence his suicide occurs almost as an unpremeditated, sudden act, which is not substantially different from any of the many games he played until that last, fatal minute. Clearly, Rossellini's film does not allow us to know what is happening inside Edmund's mind and heart just before he jumps, just as we cannot know what goes on in the minds of children from war-ravaged territories. Despite such dark influences, the optimistic ending of *Central Station* seems to point toward an unusual locus in Brazilian cinematic representation: the space of hope. As Xavier puts it, "Walter Salles' allegory of hope can be taken as a rigorous counterpoint to the collection of bitter experiences enacted in many Brazilian films of the 1990s [and] 1980s" (in Nagib 60). However, Salles's suggested direction for Brazilian cinema has been defied by subsequent international Brazilian hits, such as *City of God*, which have reclaimed their place in a powerful tradition of harsh realism.[12]

Although many differences exist between Italian neorealist classics and Brazilian political films, a neorealist influence continues to energize contemporary political filmmaking in Brazil, an influence that marks an undeniable continuity in theme, style, and production approach. Indeed, as I have argued herein, Italian and Brazilian directors' shared sensitivity to the experience of children in the midst of collapsing worlds remains one of the more powerful links between the two cinematic traditions.

Notes

1. The neorealist influence circulated both inside and outside Brazil through a process of cross-fertilization in the midst of the broader movement of revolutionary filmmaking known as the New Latin American Cinema.
2. Similarly, in Mexico the early introduction of the Lumières' movie technology immediately triggered both the practice of filmmaking by local enthusiasts and massive moviegoing by an eager public. This enthusiasm, in fact, launched the national cinema tradition before or soon after the turn of the century (Gómez 131).
3. Susan Hayward points out that "[a]lthough cinema nõvo is more readily associated with its 1960s' manifestations, it is important to remember that it pre-dates most of the 'new wave' movements that occurred in Europe. It is also important to recall that it was far more radical in its purpose than any of its European counterparts" (56).
4. For example, Cine Imperfecto in Cuba, Tercer Cine in Argentina, Cine Combativo in Bolivia, and the New Latin American Cinema,

184

which emerged as an overarching category that described progressive cinematic practice broadly in Latin America. According to Julianne Burton, neorealism appealed to young Latin American filmmakers as a cinema that was more authentic, urgent, and real than Hollywood: "Turning their backs on local commercial efforts, which they condemned as alienated and alienating [they] undertook to produce films [exploring] national identity" (*Cinema and Social Change* x–xi).

5. This is also true of other Latin American cinemas. To name just some of the period's key titles: *Throw Me a Dime* (1960) by Birri, who studied film in Italy in the mid-1950s (see Burton, *Cinema and Social Change* 3–6); Chilean Patricio Guzmán's *The Battle of Chile* (1975), a title that harkens back to Pontecorvo's *The Battle of Algiers* (see Ortega in Elena and Días López); *Valparaiso My Love* (1969) by Chilean Aldo Francia, who, acknowledging the direct influence of neorealism, defined his film as a "document of denunciation of social injustice" (see Mouesca 37–38); and *Memories of the Underdevelopment* (1968) by Gutiérrez Alea, who studied at Rome's Centro Sperimentale di Cinematografia between 1951 and 1953 with Cuban director García Espinosa and Colombian writer Gabriel García Márquez (Berthier 101; for Cuban cinema, see Myerson; Benamou; Burton, *Cinema and Social Change* 116–31).

6. Rocha's essay is reprinted with an introduction by Johnson and Stam, in which they explain that it was initially presented in Genoa, Italy, in January 1965 as part of a retrospective of Latin American cinema. Then it was published in *Revista Civilização Brasileira* in July 1965 and subsequently translated into French and published in *Positif* as "L'esthétique de la violence" (68–71).

7. All translations of Mouesca are mine.

8. While *Stromboli* has been described as a film produced after Rossellini's neorealist period, this scene is arguably strongly neorealist. As discussed earlier, I conceive of neorealism as less a group of films in a given time period and more a cinematic approach with a specific style and range of preoccupations. In fact, the expression "migrations of cinema" makes it possible to talk about neorealism as emerging in other latitudes and periods.

9. An antecedent of Cinema Nōvo's interest in the figure of the *cangaço* was Lima Barreto's *O Cangaceiro*. Rocha, however, drastically criticized Barreto's film, even though it had won two awards at Cannes in 1953 and had been distributed to twenty-two countries by Columbia Pictures under the title *The Bandits*. For Rocha, Barreto's film presented a stereotypical image of Brazil through a Hollywood-like format, avoiding an engagement with the real, historical phenomenon of

the cangaço (in Elena and Días López 66). Breixo Viejo notes that *O Cangaceiro* did not reflect any of the central features of the New Latin American Cinema: leftist politics, rejection of the Hollywood model, and adoption of neorealist aesthetics (66). Nor did it avoid transforming what it was in principle—a dynamic historical reality—into static narrative types, thus continuing the mythmaking of commercial cinema (69).

10. In most of the films discussed in this essay the children depicted are boys negotiating an early manhood. Editors' note: See the essays by Fisher and Ruberto in this collection for further discussion of children and gender in neorealist films.

11. For analyses of the significant place that the contrasting myths of the *sertão* and the *favela* occupy in Brazilian cinema, see essays by Ivana Bentes, Luiz Zanin Oricchio, and Lúcia Nagib (Nagib 121–72).

12. The same year (2002), another Brazilian film that explored the gritty aspects of social reality in Brazil was well received by critics and audiences overseas: *Madam Satã,* by first-time feature director Karim Aïnouz.

Chapter 9

"A Poetics of Refusals": Neorealism from Italy to Africa

RACHEL GABARA

> I would very much like to ask Sembène what he thinks of Rossellini. Does he mean anything to him? Has Rossellini had as much influence on Sembène's cinema as on mine, for example?
> Rouch 94

Scholars have tended to write about African film as though it exists in an odd sort of isolation, only reacting against and rejecting the themes and styles of colonial and neocolonial European cinema rather than participating in international cinematic traditions. Even within discussions of non-Western cinema, connections between African and Latin American or Indian films and filmmakers have rarely been drawn in any detail. In what follows, I will ask what legacy Italian neorealism might have left African film, tracing a political and aesthetic cinematic project as taken up in different national and historical contexts. I cannot answer the question posed above by the French ethnographic filmmaker Jean Rouch, and Ousmane Sembène has never directly answered it himself. It is not only possible but productive, however, to read Sembène's work as well as that of a younger generation of African filmmakers for a response to Roberto Rossellini and the neorealist movement.

This project, a consideration of neorealism's impact on African film, is quite literally a twisted one. There is little evidence of any direct influence of Italian cinema in Africa, whether in the form of assertions by filmmakers or allusions within their films. We will get from Italy to Africa, therefore, via Latin America and the concept of a revolutionary

Third Cinema. Italian neorealism in the 1940s and 1950s, New Latin American Cinema from the late 1950s to the early 1970s, and sub-Saharan (mainly West) African film from its beginnings in the early 1960s share the search for a radically new way to make films that would be strikingly unlike the American ones flooding their markets. All three were based on a political and stylistic rejection of Hollywood that film-makers, film historians, and theorists alike have characterized as realist, but these realisms look very different and serve different ends. Neoreal-ism was formative for non-European filmmakers with respect to both production methods and thematic concerns, but it is crucial to address the stakes involved in the establishment of such a genealogy. The other side of influence is innovation. Latin American and then African film-makers built on and developed aspects of neorealism while rejecting others in favor of strategies and styles they felt were more authentic as well as more effective. In doing so, and as a result of their particular his-tories and experiences with film, they engaged a theoretical discussion about realism in cinema that had been largely absent in Italy.

Italian directors including Rossellini, Vittorio De Sica, and Luchino Visconti accomplished a certain realism, or, to use Roland Barthes's words, a "reality effect" via a blurring of the traditional distinction be-tween documentary and fictional genres, using one (documentary) to inflect the other (fiction). Latin American and African filmmakers also mixed these genres in their quest for a realist cinema, but they strove to go beyond a neorealist construction of the illusion of reality within fic-tion. Argentinean, Brazilian, and Cuban filmmakers such as Fernando Birri, Nelson Pereira dos Santos, Tomás Gutiérrez Alea, and Julio Gar-cía Espinosa chose ultimately to focus less on a "documentarizing" of fic-tion as practiced by the neorealists and more on a "fictionalizing" of the documentary. The work of the Senegalese filmmaker Ousmane Sem-bène, which has been characterized as both neorealist and "social realist," seems at first to be closer to the Italian model, whereas recent documen-taries by David Achkar, Jean-Marie Teno, and Mahamat Saleh Haroun, from Guinea, Cameroon, and Chad, respectively, employ techniques and tactics of fiction to bring into question the nature of documentary real-ism itself.

In 1943, as Benito Mussolini's regime fell and Italian society be-gan to reimagine and rebuild itself, the film critic Umberto Barbaro de-scribed a group of 1930s French films as "neorealist" and called for a new realism in Italian cinema as well (Bondanella, *Italian Cinema* 24). Italian filmmakers sought to create a realist cinema that would stand in stark contrast to the "white telephone" comedies and lavish productions of the Fascist period. Neorealism attempted, like earlier realisms in the Soviet Union, France, and Great Britain, to represent the everyday lives of the poor or jobless, ordinary citizens who had been invisible in mainstream studio films. Cesare Zavattini, screenwriter and filmmaking partner of De Sica and self-appointed theorist of neorealism, asserted that the artist's task was to "excavate reality" (217). Zavattini never clarified the nature of this underlying or hidden reality, however, and instead specified a method—neorealist films should be made not in a studio but in the streets and without professional actors, in fact, without the entire "technical-professional apparatus, screen-writer included" (225). Moreover, films should remain unresolved, with no plot closure, because "this is reality" (223). The French critic André Bazin took most of his cues from Zavattini, praising neorealist films and especially those of De Sica for being "full of realism," for their "concern with actual day-to-day events, . . . an exceptionally documentary quality, . . . [and] this perfect and natural adherence to actuality" (18, 20). Bazin claimed for neorealist filmmakers a mystical connection to a reality that he went so far as to apostrophize, "'My little sister reality,' says De Sica, and she circles about him like the birds around Saint Francis. Others put her in a cage or teach her to talk, but De Sica talks with her and it is the true language of reality that we hear" (69).

Both Zavattini and Bazin advocated an absolutely realist cinema while avoiding any analysis of reality or cinematic realism. De Sica and Rossellini, however, spoke quite differently about the neorealist filmmaker's goals and connection to reality. De Sica denied not only the absolute hold on reality attributed to him by Bazin but even one of the cardinal characteristics of the movement's films: "[N]eorealism is not shooting films in authentic locales; it is not reality. It is reality filtered through poetry, reality transfigured. It is not Zola, not naturalism, verism, things which are ugly" (De Sica 31).[1] For Rossellini, neorealism was "a need, appropriate to modern man, to speak of things as they are, to be aware of reality, in an absolutely concrete manner," yet he continued that "for me, it is nothing other than the artistic form of truth" (in Overbey 89). Like De Sica, Rossellini acknowledged and even stressed the art implicit in any representation of reality, stretching his definitions to the point that a neorealist film could be almost anything, any truth in any artistic form. His characterizations of neorealism were consistently vague, from "above all, a moral position from which to look at the world" (in Overbey 1) to, famously, "following a human being, with love, in all its discoveries, all its impressions" (in Armes, *Patterns* 90).

Returning to Bazin, moreover, we find that despite his unqualified praise for a seemingly miraculous realism, he recognized that "realism in art can only be achieved in one way—through artifice" (26). He called De Sica's *Bicycle Thief* (1948) "one of the first examples of pure cinema. No more actors, no more story, no more sets." Bazin continued, "[I]n the perfect aesthetic illusion of reality there is no more cinema" (60). In this almost perfectly contradictory statement, pure cinema equals no cinema, yet it can be accomplished only by aesthetic means, by creating, cinematically, a perfect illusion. Neorealism, for Bazin as much as for De Sica, was ultimately a question of style. Bazin concluded that "we would define as 'realist,' then, all narrative means tending to bring an added measure of reality to the screen" (27); this new style was not a magical convergence of film and reality but a result of strategic filming and editing. Neorealist filmmakers tried to make us think that their artifice is reality; they made the artificial *seem* real. Bill Nichols has eloquently described neorealism as an "art of artlessness," one that "provides a repertoire of techniques for giving the formal effect of representing a reality that evades the control of the filmmaker" (169). Realism defines reality, not the reverse.

Neorealism was, then, as has been every literary or filmic realism, a style, and in this case a style based on what the Soviet semiotician Jurij Lotman called a "poetics of refusals."

> Its active elements were always "refusals": refusal to use a stereotypical hero or typical film scenes, refusal to use professional actors, denial of the "star" system, refusal to employ montage and an "ironclad" scenario, refusal to use a "prepared" dialog or musical accompaniment. Such a poetics of "refusals" can only be effective against a remembered background of cinema art of the opposite type. Without cinematography of historical epics, film operas, westerns or Hollywood "stars" it loses a good deal of its artistic meaning. (20–21)

The "adherence to reality" invoked by Zavattini and Bazin was not the result of any perfect coincidence between a film and the reality it represented, but rather of a rejection of certain filmic conventions in favor of others. Peter Brunette follows Lotman to remind us that neorealism's "'reality effect' seems to stem from the ironic fact that we think an event or image is more real precisely because we have not seen it before on the screen" ("Rossellini" 38). It is important to remember, however, that we *have* seen these filmic conventions before—in newsreels and other documentary productions. Neorealist films rely on a spectatorial familiarity with the codes of documentary, which have been imported into fiction; although we have not seen this particular combination of documentary and fiction before, we must recognize its parts for the whole to be effective. Neorealism refused a certain kind of fiction filmmaking, but not the conventional realism associated with documentary.

Yet more than style was at stake in the critical insistence on neorealism's realism. Franco Venturini wrote in 1950, at perhaps the height of the movement's popularity at home and abroad, that just as the prewar French films were "unmistakably French," Italian neorealism was a result of the search for "our ethnic realism . . . an original Italian style, the real beginning of an Italian film culture" (in Overbey 175, 191). An essential element of this indigenous film style was the use of nonprofessional actors, even if Visconti's *La terra trema* (1948) was the only neorealist film that completely adhered to this principle (Overbey 13). Angela Dalle Vacche has noted that these nonactors, these "supposedly 'typical' Italians, . . . allegorize an imaginary nation called 'Italy'" (256). They lent authenticity to neorealism and postwar Italy became known around the world in their image. Zavattini, De Sica, Rossellini, and Visconti wanted to show a previously invisible Italy in a newly Italian way in a style that would reinvent Italy artistically. One of the best proofs of their burgeoning success was the reaction of Vittorio Mussolini in 1942 to Visconti's *Ossessione*, the Italian film perhaps responsible for the coining of the term "neorealist."[2] One year before the end of his father's Fascist dictatorship, Mussolini left the screening angrily declaring, "This is not Italy!" (Bondanella, *Italian Cinema* 28). He meant, of course, that this was not *his* Italy, and he was absolutely right.

Neorealist filmmakers, seeking to represent a new national reality, created one. They did so by using stylistic elements traditionally emblematic of documentary film—rough composition, "real" people and locations—without strictly documentary content. Despite his seeming desire to strip all that was fictional from film, Zavattini was not interested in making documentary films but documentary-like fictions. Neorealism documentarized fiction to tell stories that seemed real, producing authentic illusions and the illusion of authenticity. The filmmaker Giuseppe De Santis considered this innovative mixing of genres itself a potential national characteristic; as early as 1941 he had written that "we should stop considering the documentary as a genre apart. It is only by blending the two elements that, in such a landscape as our own, we will find the formula for a true and genuine Italian cinema" (in Overbey

127). Martin Scorsese has confirmed De Santis's hope in *Il mio viaggio in Italia* (2001), his personal history of neorealism and its impact on his life and filmmaking, concluding that "the Neorealists had to communicate to the world everything their country had gone through. They needed to dissolve the barrier between documentary and fiction, and in the process, they permanently changed the rules of moviemaking."

This change in the rules of filmmaking was of profound importance to filmmakers in Latin America, who were themselves trying to resist both Hollywood cinema and domestic national film industries. From the mid-1930s to the mid-1950s, production in Argentina, Brazil, and Cuba, the countries on which I will focus for lack of the space even to gloss the whole story of the New Latin American Cinema, consisted mainly of genre films adapted from Hollywood models. Argentina, the largest producer of films in Latin America before World War II, had its gaucho films and Brazil its *chanchadas,* popular musical comedies. The Vera Cruz Company, with studios in São Paolo, was created in the 1940s to make films that would compete on the international market, but it hired for the most part foreign technicians and filmmakers. The self-titled "New Cinema" arose in the late 1950s and 1960s in reaction to the state of affairs following the 1959 revolution in Cuba and in the wake of neorealism. Several of the filmmakers at the forefront of the movement studied in Italy, and many acknowledged the direct influence of neorealism on their work. We will see, however, that Latin American filmmakers soon rejected neorealism and felt the need to go beyond it to create a realist cinema of their own. Unlike the Italian neorealists, they wrote manifesto upon manifesto proclaiming their political and aesthetic goals, establishing a theoretical framework for an inquiry into the nature of cinematic realism.

There were many direct connections between Italian neorealism and the New Latin American Cinema. Birri studied in Rome at the Centro Sperimentale di Cinematografia in the early 1950s, as did Gutiérrez Alea and García Espinosa. García Espinosa went to Italy after having seen neorealist films in Havana, and Zavattini himself then visited Cuba before the revolution to work with him on *Cuba Dances* (Chanan 116). One of the first feature films made after the revolution and within the framework of the Instituto Cubano de Arte e Industria Cinematográficos, Gutiérrez Alea's *Stories of the Revolution* (1960), was filmed by neorealist cinematographer Otello Martelli, whose camera operator was Zavattini's son, and used an episodic structure similar to that of Rossellini's 1946 *Paisan* (Chanan 111). As early as 1953, Alex Viany's *Needle in the*

Haystack constituted a first attempt at a Brazilian neorealism (Johnson and Stam 32).

Gutiérrez Alea has said that "from the beginning of the Revolution, our artistic foundation was in fact essentially Italian Neorealism" (in Burton, *Cinema and Social Change* 123). Pereira dos Santos also claimed that "without neorealism we could never have begun," and many other Latin American filmmakers, including Humberto Solas and Ruy Guerra, have stressed the importance of neorealism for their early work. According to Dos Santos, "[N]eo-realism taught us . . . that it was possible to make films in the streets; that we did not need studios; that we could film using average people rather than known actors" (in Johnson and Stam 122). There were many reasons for the importance of neorealism; Latin American filmmakers were working outside of and against any dominant studio system with a comparable lack of resources. The only kind of film they could possibly make would be a low-budget production using post-synchronized sound and no movie stars, and Italian directors showed them that this was not only possible but laudable. The "classics" of the New Latin American Cinema, however—Glauber Rocha's *Terra em transe* (1967), Fernando Solanas and Octavio Getino's *Hour of the Furnaces* (1968), Gutiérrez Alea's *Memories of the Underdevelopment* (1968), and Jorge Sanjinés's *Blood of the Condor* (1969)—date from the late 1960s, by which time these filmmakers' enthusiasm for neorealism had waned.

Rocha, one of the leaders of Brazil's Cinema Nõvo movement, recognized the importance of neorealism for Latin American film yet resisted any easy acceptance or imitation: "Our bourgeoisie has been colonized by Neo-Realism and the *nouvelle vague*. . . . Fox, Paramount, and Metro are our enemies. But Eisenstein, Rossellini, and Godard are also our enemies. They crush us" (in Johnson and Stam 88). We will see that this antagonism becomes crucial to conceptions of cinematic realism not only in Latin America but in Africa. Yet why would Rocha put Rossellini in the same bag as Paramount? In 1962, a group of Latin American filmmakers, including Rocha, met in Italy for the Festival of Latin American Cinema. Their discussions resulted in a series of resolutions titled "The Cinema as an Expression of Latin American Reality." Another meeting six years later similarly resulted in the affirmation of filmmakers' dedication to "a cinema committed to national reality . . . which creates works permeated by realism, whether they be fictional or documentary" (in M. Martin, *New Latin American Cinema* 147, 149). The New Latin American Cinema would be a realist one and, as with the neorealism that so influenced it, this meant that it would have to deal in national reality. Argentineans Solanas and Getino proclaimed, moreover, that "any form of expression or communication that tries to show national reality is *subversion*" (in M. Martin, *New Latin American Cinema* 37, 39).

In manifestos and theoretical texts from the 1960s, Latin American filmmakers advocated a revolutionary cinema that was both art and action, a transformational social practice, an instrument of change and consciousness-raising. Solanas and Getino declared that this cinema of the struggle of third-world peoples against first-world imperialism was "the most gigantic cultural, scientific, and artistic manifestation of our time," representing "the decolonization of culture" (in M. Martin, *New Latin American Cinema* 34, 37). Julio García Espinosa coined the term "imperfect cinema" to signify a new "consciously and resolutely 'committed' cinema" (in M. Martin, *New Latin American Cinema* 79), which would avoid the slick perfection of classical Hollywood seamless editing and character-driven narrative. First used in a Cuban film journal in 1969, Third Cinema designated an anticolonial (and anti-neocolonial) cinema, set in opposition to a capitalist "first cinema" and an artistic, intellectual, auteurist "second cinema." Rocha stated that "we cannot make films to express Brazilian or Latin American content using North American [or European] language" (in Burton, *Cinema and Social Change* 107). Not only did filmmakers desire to show a Latin America that had previously been hidden because it had been oppressed from within and without, but they needed to develop a new filmic language in which to do so.

The national reality at stake in Latin America during this period is distinct from the one that Italian directors had been negotiating. Although national submovements such as Cinema Nõvo did exist, Argentinean, Brazilian, Cuban, Chilean, and other filmmakers felt themselves to be part of a larger movement, which they described as Latin American and, moreover, popular. Italian filmmakers had been fighting a primarily internal battle, searching for an authentic Italian identity somehow untouched by Fascism, what Venturini called an "ethnic" realism. Latin American filmmakers, attempting to throw off centuries of European and then North American political, economic, and cultural colonization, advocated multiethnic solidarity among the so-called underdeveloped. Theirs was in fact a regional realism, and the concept of a Third Cinema allowed them to band together with filmmakers from other nations within Latin America as well as those from other "underdeveloped" parts of the world against dominant cinematic traditions.

The linkage between realism and "national" reality meant, then, somewhat ironically, that Italian neorealism, based within a very different (and, importantly, European) national reality, would have to be rejected in its turn and relegated to "second cinema" status. Lotman's description of neorealism's "poetics of refusals" seems to apply to the New Latin American Cinema as well, and neorealism itself joined the refused "background of cinema art of the opposite type." Prior national cinemas were also rejected, also in the name of a more authentic reality and realism. Birri, a theorist, documentary filmmaker, teacher, and founder of the Escuela Documental de Santa Fe, argued that earlier Argentinean films had presented "unreal and alien" images of the country, and the task of the new documentary was to provide a true image "by showing how reality *is*, and in no other way. . . . By testifying, critically, to this reality—to this sub-reality, this misery—cinema refuses it. It rejects it. It denounces, judges, criticizes, and deconstructs it" (in M. Martin, *New Latin American Cinema* 87, 94). Birri concluded that the task of the filmmaker was "to confront reality with a camera, and to document it, filming realistically, filming critically, filming underdevelopment with the optic of the people" (90, 94). The common denominator of the New Latin American Cinema was "a poetics of the transformation of reality"; it "aspire[d] to modify the reality upon which it is projected" (96).

From the Bazinian "showing how reality *is*" Birri moved immediately to the refusal and then to the transformation of this reality. Reality was no longer what it had been for Zavattini, something one "walk[s] out with a camera to meet" (226) and records in real time—reality was to be confronted, attacked, and changed. Solanas and Getino similarly stressed that a "revolutionary cinema is not fundamentally one which illustrates, documents, or passively establishes a situation: *rather, it attempts to intervene in the situation* . . . it provides *discovery through transformation*" (in M. Martin, *New Latin American Cinema* 47). Gutiérrez Alea has described the development of his theoretical conception of revolutionary realist filmmaking.

> So when we began to make films in a postrevolutionary situation, that Neorealist mode of approaching reality was very useful to us because in that early stage we needed little more. . . . All we had to do was to set up a camera in the street and we were able to capture a reality that was spectacular in and of itself. . . . But our revolution also began to undergo a process of change. Though certainly not the same as that which occurred in post-

war Italy, the meaning of external events began to become less obvious, less apparent, much deeper and more profound. That process forced us to adopt an analytical attitude towards the reality that surrounded us. (in Burton, *Cinema and Social Change* 124)

García Espinosa has also stated that the progression of the revolution had led filmmakers "beyond neorealism": "straightforward neorealist ideas could not really catch the speed and depth of revolutionary change" (in Chanan 128). Their new cinema would not only record images of historical and social import but analyze and interpret them so as to enable a corresponding change in reality. Bazin considered continuity "a fundamental quality of reality" (28), and both he and Zavattini rejected montage as antirealist. For Gutiérrez Alea, on the other hand, montage was a central element of any realistic cinema, since "cinematic realism does not lie in its alleged ability to capture reality 'just like it is' (which is 'just like it appears to be'), but rather lies in its ability to reveal, through associations and connections between various isolated aspects of reality—that is to say, through creating a 'new reality'—deeper, more essential layers of reality itself" (in M. Martin, *New Latin American Cinema* 122). This new realism was one of critical reflection and not mirror reflection or poetic adaptation; critical realism can be achieved only in the creation of a new reality that transforms the old.

Nichols has called neorealism a "fictional ally" to documentary realism, since it "melded the observational eye of documentary with the intersubjective, identificatory strategies of fiction" (167). Unlike the Italian neorealists, most of the Latin American filmmakers I have mentioned preferred the documentary genre to fiction, but never with an observational eye; their documentary was intersubjective without being identificatory. New Latin American filmmakers wanted spectators not to sympathize with suffering characters but instead to maintain a critical distance conducive to the initiation of transformative political action. Birri stressed the "documentary support" of their new cinema, yet continued that a strict distinction between fiction and documentary was no longer relevant: "A characteristic that has been progressively accentuated is the rupture with traditional genres: with what is traditionally understood by documentary; with what is traditionally understood or understandable as narrative" ("For a Nationalist" 96). Neorealism had "dissolved the boundary" between fiction and documentary, but had relied on a conventional understanding of the relationship between reality and documentary style to create documentary-like fiction. Latin American filmmakers wished, on the other hand, to break the easy illusion of reality associated, by force of convention, with documentary roughness, on-location shooting, unresolved plot lines, and nonprofessional acting. Beginning with neorealism, they ended up rethinking realism itself to remake both Latin American film and Latin American reality.

As opposed to the example of Latin America, Italian film in general and neorealism in particular rarely figure in discussions of African cinema. Although N. Frank Ukadike writes that "the appropriation of neorealist techniques by Third World filmmakers has been well documented" (*Black African Cinema* 279), he does not cite a single example or reference, and De Sica, Rossellini, and Visconti are completely absent from the book. Their names are equally absent from the first survey of African film written in French, *Le cinéma Africain: Des origines à 1973* (1975) by the Senegalese filmmaker and critic Paulin Soumanou Vieyra, and the first in English, Manthia Diawara's *African Cinema: Politics and Culture* (1992). Not one of the twenty African filmmakers interviewed in Ukadike's more recent *Questioning African Cinema* (2002) mentions neorealism or any neorealist director. Ukadike, Vieyra, and Diawara have focused on the ways in which African filmmakers, working within a tradition of oral narrative, have established a distinctively African cinema; all three avoid any investigation of the influence of European or even Latin American cinematic movements.

If we return to the epigraph to this essay, we see why the question of influence has been such a critical one for African cinema, why it has been important to refuse European influence and assert the newness of African film. Jean Rouch, whom Ousmane Sembène has famously accused of filming Africans as if they were insects, wonders what Sembène might think of Rossellini and asks, "Est-ce que pour lui ça veut dire quelque chose?" which I have rather badly translated as "Does he mean anything to him?" The "ça" here, though, is almost a "tout cela," and seems to refer not only to Rossellini but to the special place in the history of European cinema held by the director of *Rome, Open City* (1945), the breakthrough neorealist film. To retranslate, then: "Doesn't all of this (the tradition of realist art cinema in Europe) mean anything to him (this African filmmaker, on whose continent I have spent so much time making innovative documentary films, which he insists on rejecting as patronizing)?" Rouch, who coined the term "cinema verité" after Vertov's *kino-pravda*, sees himself as belonging to a European tradition of new cinematic realisms that includes Italian neorealism. For

197

Sembène, Rouch is the latest in a long line of European anthropologists and ethnographers who came to film Africans in Africa; their realism just another arm in the colonial weaponry.

Realism, then, has particular stakes in Africa, which like Latin America has long been defined by the images created of it and its people by exploring, conquering, and colonizing Europeans. Ukadike has stated that "from the beginning, the major concern of African filmmakers has been to provide a more realistic image of Africa," more realistic than the images provided in films such as *King Solomon's Mines* (1937) or any of the numerous ethnographic documentaries (*Black African Cinema* 3). Films shot in West Africa before independence were made by European and North American directors using an imported crew and for their home audiences; Africa served as an exotic backdrop. The only exception to this rule were the so-called educational documentaries produced by the colonial film units of France, Belgium, and Great Britain, which were shown to nonelite (and often illiterate) African audiences and designed to shore up colonialism by shaping the practices and ideology of the colonized. Against these foreign representations of Africa, filmmakers desired to create authentic images of a previously hidden regional and national reality. In the collective statement published in *Présence Africaine* after a 1974 seminar meeting in Burkina Faso titled "The Role of the African Film-Maker in Rousing an Awareness of Black Civilization," we read that film content should grow from African history and literature, and reflect "African realities" (16); African cinema should "nourish our people's reflection on their own destiny, by presenting *African human, social, and cultural realities*" (62). A year earlier, the Third World Film-Makers' Meeting in Algeria had united North and sub-Saharan African filmmakers with several from Latin America, including Birri. As had Birri for the New Latin American Cinema, African filmmakers declared that their goal was a critical and transformative realism, the production of "films reflecting the objective conditions in which the struggling peoples are developing, . . . which bring about the disalienation of the colonized peoples at the same time as they contribute sound and objective information for the peoples of the entire world" (Bakari and Cham 20).

Sembène's short film *Borom Sarret*, released in 1963, three years after Senegalese independence from France, was the first film shot by a sub-Saharan African director in Africa. Considered the father of African cinema, Sembène is also the filmmaker most often associated with the development of an authentically African cinematic realism. The hour-

Mandabi
(Ousmane
Sembène, 1968)

long *Black Girl* appeared in 1966, his first long feature in color, *Mandabi*, in 1968, and eight more feature films in the years since then. Sembène's early films, like those of the neorealists and New Latin American film-makers, were shot with little equipment or funding and without studios, professional actors or actresses, or synchronized sound. He has consistently represented the everyday lives and problems of ordinary Africans, rejecting classical Hollywood editing and plot resolution. Sembène has always described himself as a realist filmmaker: he has tried to show "the true face of Africa" (Vieyra, *Sembène* 173) and has "never tried to please [his] audiences through the embellishment of reality" (Pfaff 40). His films have also been repeatedly described as realist by reviewers and critics; Ukadike, for example, claims that they exhibit an "undiluted realism" ("The Creation" 109).

It is surprising, at the very least, to discover that not a single study of Sembène's work in relation to neorealism exists. It has been quite common, on the other hand, for European and North American critics to call his films "neorealist" in passing, a shorthand that gestures toward the superficial similarities I have noted above. French reviewers of *Mandabi* at the time of its release, including Louis Chauvet and Jean Rochereau, described Sembène's work as "neorealist" (Vieyra, *Sembène* 221, 231), as have more recently William Van Wert (214), Françoise Pfaff (52), and Roy Armes (*Third World* 291). Speaking with the Mauritanian film-maker Med Hondo in 1970, a reviewer with *Positif* claimed that "Sem-

Mandabi
(Ousmane
Sembène, 1968)

bene Ousmane is just more Zavattini-De Sica" ("Entretien" 24). None
of these critics has analyzed or reflected on the comparison. This labeling
limits the terms of discussion to the vocabulary of the European canon
and, whether as praise or critique, functions to pull Sembène toward it.
He becomes part of the "ça" or "tout cela" invoked by Rouch, without any
investigation of the ways in which he, like Gutiérrez Alea and Rocha,
might have transformed neorealist aims, methods, or style in and for an
African context.

When an African critic has tagged Sembène as "neorealist," however, it has been to a different end, if based on an equally limited reading of his work. In 1968, the journalist Bara Diouf harshly criticized
Mandabi for presenting an unflattering image of Senegal.

> Its faults arise from the philosophy of Ousmane Sembène, bor-
> rowed from Europe. It is a question of this neorealism which is
> very fashionable . . . it is absolute pessimism. Yet it is not with a
> pessimistic morality . . . that we will build a nation. . . . Ousmane
> Sembène must disengage himself from European moral codes
> in order to adopt the true ideology that responds to our situa-
> tion as an underdeveloped country. (in Vieyra, *Sembène* 217)

"Neorealism" here once again stands for a European cinematic tradition,
which now should be rejected in the search for an authentic African
cinema, national morality, and reality. Sembène has responded to this

reproach with a reassertion of his commitment to realism and, moreover, by allying himself with the neorealist project to "excavate" an often unpleasant reality: "It's curious that certain spectators don't want to look reality in the eye. There are, for example, slums in Senegal. The scandal is in their existence and not in showing them. Certain people would like to mask the truth. . . . We already saw this in Italy with the Neorealist films" (26). And, in fact, in 1951, Giulio Andreotti, then Italy's undersecretary of public entertainment, wrote an open letter to De Sica, condemning *Umberto D* (1952) as too pessimistic and thus harmful to the nation (Bondanella, *Italian Cinema* 87). Like the French and North American critics, however, Sembène does not further elaborate his cryptic comparison.

In the one mention of neorealism in his history of African film, Diawara points to a fundamental difference between the two traditions. He argues that the Fédération Panafricaine des Cinéastes, when formed in 1969, was "less a cinematic movement aimed at deconstructing traditional film narratives . . . and more a politico-economic movement committed to the total liberation of Africa" and therefore had more in common with the pan-African Organization of African Unity than with film movements such as the French New Wave or Italian neorealism (*African Cinema* 45). African cinema was born with independence from Europe and has thus, even more than the New Latin American Cinema, been associated with the work of nation building through the representation of national reality. Like the New Latin American Cinema and joining the Third Cinema movement, it has been a regional rather than strictly national movement, grounded, for both ideological and financial reasons, in an anticolonial pan-African solidarity.

Diawara's opposition of political and narrative or stylistic concerns recalls Latin American filmmakers' classification of neorealism as a Second rather than Third Cinema. Yet for Birri, Gutiérrez Alea, and Rocha, the political aims of the New Latin American Cinema were to be achieved precisely by the deconstruction and then reinvention of film narrative. High praise of Sembène's realism has all too often relied on such an opposition and has often been accompanied by analyses of his films as only political acts, as if they lacked an aesthetic dimension. Describing Sembène's body of work as "fastidiously realistic," Michael Atkinson writes that "from the first mini-feature . . . Sembène's work has ached with austerity—as an artist he is virtually style-free, almost unprofessional, but possessed of a voice as clear and uncomplicated as sunlight." The birds of reality flutter around Sembène's head as they had

around De Sica's, and we seem to have forgotten that realism is always a result of artifice, whether it be De Sica's "reality filtered through poetry" or Birri's "poetics of the transformation of reality."

Burkina seminar attendees had emphasized the importance of creating a cinema in African languages ("Séminaire" 11), and Sembène's *Mandabi* was the first feature film to be shot in an African-language version. Filmmakers and critics also called, however, for the development of an African cinematic language, "a language properly adapted to Black Civilization" (171). This would entail, as we now might expect, another refusal: "a true African cinema can only be built by breaking away from the Western cinema" (14). The Burkinabé filmmaker Gaston Kaboré has asserted, concluding with almost exactly the same words used by Rocha, that "we have a perception of space, a certain notion of pacing and rhythm, and a narrative tradition that we can invest in our films . . . we can't be Africans and make films like Americans" (in Petty 6). Sembène has been praised for his realism and he has also been praised for having shaped "a truly indigenous African cinema aesthetic" (7), but these two aspects of his work are strongly linked.

Sembène's films are neither "style-free" nor "almost unprofessional"; over the course of his career, he has consistently experimented with the structure of filmic narrative in order to represent a previously hidden African reality in a newly African manner. African realism, like neorealism and the New Latin American Cinema, is a question of style. Sembène has repeatedly described his role as that of a griot, and many critics have traced the ways in which he and other filmmakers have worked to adapt the structures of the African oral tradition.[3] Although Mbye Cham characterizes Sembène's realism as seamless and continuous, modeled on the linearity of oral narrative tradition (27), Diawara notes that the oral tradition is not linear but rather "abounds in digressions, parallelisms, flashbacks, dreams, etc." (*African Cinema* 11). And, in fact, Sembène has used flashbacks and flash forwards in most of his films, including *Black Girl*, *Ceddo* (1976), *Camp de Thiaroye* (1987), and *Guelwaar* (1992), as well as reflexive techniques such as the nondiegetic and anachronistic music of *Ceddo*.[4] In his attempts to depict contemporary African social and political reality, Sembène has worked toward an artistic and critical realism.

In a 1979 interview, the Senegalese filmmaker Safi Faye described her artistic goal to be a particularly African cinematic realism: "What I try to film [are] things which relate to our civilization . . . a typically African culture. . . . I make films about reality." When then asked to

comment on the mixing of documentary and fictional genres in her films, she replied, "For me all these words—fiction, documentary, ethnology—have no sense. . . . At the end of my films people wonder if there is *mise en scene* or not" ("Four Film Makers" 18). Faye, who acted for and then trained with Rouch, was all too familiar with a certain tradition of ethnographic realism. She rejected the division between fictional and documentary in terms analogous to Birri's and refused, as had he and the other New Latin American Cinema filmmakers, documentary's easy claim on reality by blurring the boundary between the genres. Sembène has similarly been aware of the risks involved in putting too much trust in documentary codes. Working against the unrealistic images of Africa and Africans put forward in fictional as well as documentary films, he has avoided a neorealist use of documentary conventions to create a seemingly transparent reality effect. In *Camp de Thiaroye*, for example, documentary-like black-and-white flashbacks break up the linear and engrossing dramatization of the events leading up to the French murder of Senegalese *tirailleurs* just returned from fighting in World War II, and remind us that neither is a direct recording of reality.

Sembène's innovative realism is evident in another aspect of his work that distinguishes it from neorealism. His films have fictionalized the reality of everyday life and contemporary social crises within African society, but he has also filmed stories of crucial events in African history. From *Black Girl*, based on a *fait divers* found in a newspaper, to *Emitai* (1971), which recounts the destruction of a village that had refused to give its rice supply to the French army, to *Camp de Thiaroye* Sembène has sought to reveal the truth of African history against colonial accounts. In a short comparative study of neorealism and the New Latin American Cinema, John Hess criticizes the Italians for having ignored history in their representations of national reality, for having narrated only in the present tense (in King, Lopez, and Alvarado 115–16). Teshome Gabriel claims that Third Cinema, on the contrary, in Africa as well as in Latin America, has taken on the past "to redefine and to redeem what the official versions of history have overlooked" (57). Sembène, who has said that "the artist is there to reveal a certain number of historical facts that others would like to keep quiet" (in Gadjigo et al. 101), has accomplished the goals set forth by Latin American filmmakers in an art without the "artlessness" of neorealism. Unlike the Latin Americans, however, who fictionalized documentary, he has documentarized fiction and avoided the documentary genre.

Documentary, given its history on the continent, has not been a popular genre for African filmmakers. Although Latin Americans and Africans have together participated in the discussions and debates surrounding Third Cinema, Vieyra was one of very few filmmakers of Sembène's generation in West Africa to make more than one documentary. In one of the surprisingly rare direct links between the New Latin American Cinema and African cinema, Ruy Guerra, who was born in Mozambique but became one of the best-known Cinema Nõvo directors in Brazil, returned to his place of birth in 1978 to help create and run the National Institute of Cinema. From independence through the late 1980s and under his guidance, the Mozambican as well as the Angolan cinema consisted mainly of documentary films, but this situation has been unique to Lusophone Africa. In the 1990s, however, there was a relative "boom" in documentary production, especially in francophone West Africa.

I would like to close by pointing to the development of a fascinating new genre within African cinema, a genre that mixes genres: the reflexive documentary film. A group of young filmmakers, including Jean-Marie Teno, David Achkar, and Mahamat Saleh Haroun, has made films that layer autobiographical, biographical, and historical (both national and international), and first-, second-, and third-person narratives, combining photographs, newspapers, newsreels, and home movies with reenacted scenes and interviews to retell both colonial and postcolonial African history.

What we might call the New African Documentary shares the concerns and some of the characteristics of New Latin American Cinema documentary films, and has similarly involved an experimentation with form, particularly the use of montage, in the pursuit of a critical realism. Teno, who is from Cameroon, responding to a question about cinema and freedom, has demanded "freedom to choose the subject, the style, unfettered by the straitjacket of established definitions of and boundaries between documentary or fiction, freedom to say, loudly and clearly, what ninety years of oppression had not allowed us to say" (70). Whereas Sembène, like and unlike the neorealists, dissolved generic boundaries from the side of fiction, Teno, Achkar, and Haroun have created a new language for African documentary. Teno's *Africa, I Will Fleece You* (1992) contains three intertwined narrative strands: an exposé of the continuing (and unnecessary) dependence on French books that has inhibited the growth of a Cameroonian publishing industry, a brief history of postcolonial Cameroon and a critique of the repression of journalists who

question the current government, and the director's memories of reading as a child, shown in the form of fictional reenactments in black and
white. Achkar's *Allah Tantou* (1991) slips back and forth between personal and national historical narrative, recounting the history of postcolonial Guinea through the story of his father, Marof Achkar, who served
as the ambassador and representative of newly independent Guinea to
the United Nations until his imprisonment by Sékou Touré's government.

Haroun chose to play himself in his *Bye Bye Africa* (1999), the first
feature film from Chad, which he says "constantly goes back and forth
between fiction and reality" (in Barlet 22). The film has been difficult for
reviewers to classify and has been variously called documentary, documentary fiction, fictional documentary, and docudrama. Haroun narrates
the story of his return to Chad after ten years in France after the death of
his mother, a trip taken with video camera in hand; it is a story that becomes one of the situation of the cinema in Africa. Surprisingly, Haroun
describes this reflexive, postmodern film as (neo)realist—"To film is an
act of love . . . reality is stronger when one watches with love. I believe
that neorealism is not dead in Africa: it is the genre which best recounts
my story, my people, and my history" (in Barlet 23)—implicitly referring to Rossellini's definition of neorealism as "following a human being,
with love." After Rocha's antagonism toward neorealism as a colonizing
influence, after Sembène's tentative acknowledgment of shared political
goals and filmmaking methods if not comparable styles, Haroun reclaims
neorealism as an influence and as potentially useful for an African cinematic project. He does so by using the vaguest of all of the definitions
of the movement offered by the neorealist filmmakers, leaving the term
as open as possible to any kind of realism he might wish to explore as he
places himself within a global history of cinema. We must follow Robert
Nelson's suggestion and speak of "appropriation" rather than "influence"
to acknowledge African filmmakers' transformation of a neorealist inheritance.

Like Italian neorealism and the New Latin American Cinema, African realism has been based on a series of refusals. Filmmakers have
rejected colonial images of Africa in the name of an authentic national
reality, renounced the simple and unquestioning documentary realism
that had been used to define them, and cast off dominant foreign cinematic languages to create their own realist style. In a comparable postcolonial situation to that of Latin America but with independence a much
more recent event, African filmmakers have until recently distanced

themselves from any possible European influence at the same time as European filmmakers and critics have been all too willing to assert an influence that would deny the difference of the much younger cinema. Twenty years ago, Roy Armes pointed to a "still-unwritten history of world cinema in which Western and non-Western modes of expression are entwined" (*Third World* 310). To begin to write this still unwritten history, we must investigate the place of African cinema in the context of world film history, the ways in which other national and international cinematic movements have influenced African filmmakers, and, most important, the ways in which they have taken these influences in new and particularly African directions. This is an indispensable task since, as Kaboré reminds us, "cinema is of vital importance to Africans because it can portray the world as Africans experience it. By creating their own cinematic images, Africans can confront and transform their reality" (in M. Martin 165).

Notes

1. Peter Bondanella has taken critics and film historians to task for focusing only on the realism and social commentary within neorealist films at the expense of the artifice acknowledged by filmmakers (*Italian Cinema* 34, 95).
2. Several critics claim that "neorealism" was first used in a cinematic context in 1942 to describe *Obsession*, either by critic Antonio Pietrangeli (Bawden 498) or by film editor Mario Serandrei in a letter to Visconti himself (Monticelli in Hill and Gibson 72).
3. See, for example, Diawara, "Popular Culture and Oral Traditions in African Film," *African Experiences of Cinema*, ed. Bakari and Cham 209–18.
4. For a detailed analysis of Sembène's use of reflexive techniques in *Black Girl*, see Landy, "Politics."

Chapter 10

Cinematic Neorealism:
Hong Kong Cinema and Fruit Chan's *1997 Trilogy*

NATALIA SUI-HUNG CHAN

The wave of the neorealism began in 1945 when Roberto Rossellini's *Rome, Open City* appeared. Neorealist cinema has been a hot topic continuously discussed by various scholars and adapted by different filmmakers from the 1940s to the present. . . . The national cinema that emerged after WWII, especially in Asia (Japan, India and Iran) and Latin America (Brazil, Cuba, Chile and Argentina) was, in fact, directly or indirectly, more or less influenced by Italian neorealist film.

Lam, "Yidaili Xinxieshizhuyi Dianying Zaipingjia" 93, my translation

In his article "Reevaluation of Italian Neorealist Films," written in Chinese in 1983, the Hong Kong film scholar Lam Lin-tong traces the tremendous influence of Italian neorealism on third-world cinema from a historical point of view. He argues that political unrest, economic disaster resulting from wars,[1] the intervention of Western imperialism, the demand for decolonization, and the independence movements of the third world formed the backdrop of the wide acceptance and social reception of neorealist cinema during the cold war. As an art form of resistance, neorealist cinema represents social solidarity, personal struggle, national survival, and the quest for freedom and democracy of ordinary Italians in the wake of Fascism during the 1940s. Third-world people who lived under political suppression and social inequality can be seen to have shared the experiences of these Italians. The political awareness of the reality of everyday life, the way of seeing others with compassion, and the moral principles of the struggle for survival portrayed in neorealist films not only stimulated third-world audiences to rethink their own situation but also helped them reshape their own modes of resistance. In

addition, the techniques employed by neorealists, such as location shooting rather than studio sets, using nonprofessional actors rather than film
stars, natural lighting, and documentary footage, provided a cheaper and
more practical way of production for third-world filmmakers who had
to work under poor material conditions (Lam, "Yidaili Xinxieshizhuyi
Dianying Zaipingjia" 93–95). Italian neorealist cinema, in other words,
presents itself as a political tool for third-world audiences to fight against
social problems of unemployment, famine, and racial and class conflicts.
It also functions as a cinematic form and aesthetic with which the filmmakers expressed their desire for human equality, political stability, and
social prosperity.

My essay begins with Lam's configuration of the great impact of
Italian neorealism on third-world cinema for two reasons. First, in working on Hong Kong cinema, I find it necessary to import neorealism
from its European film tradition into the context of the third world or,
even more significantly, into a Hong Kong film scholar's critical concerns. What Lam's argument provides is a strategy of intervention to
compare Hong Kong cinema with Italian neorealist films of the 1940s
on the one hand and, on the other, a way to sketch a wider horizon
of global filmmaking to contextualize my subject of research. Second,
Lam's historical analysis maps out the association between neorealist
cinema and third-world filmmaking in terms of their political and aesthetic concerns. These concerns, that is, the political agenda and its realistic form of expression, serve as a point of departure for my critical
study of Hong Kong cinema. In this chapter I examine how cinematic
neorealism represented in Hong Kong filmmaking responds to the social crisis of the 1997 "Hand-over." Here, neorealism is not strictly confined to the revolution of film production in 1940s Italy in its narrow
sense. It is understood rather as the way in which social and political
issues are articulated in film and in the mise-en-scène techniques associated with neorealist cinema. My comparative study of Italian neorealist
film and Hong Kong cinema does not intend to generalize or simplify
generic as well as cultural differences; the study is instead a cross-refer-
ence of my own discursive body of film studies: the work of the director
Fruit Chan, an independent filmmaker who has become well known
in recent years at international film festivals because of his unique film
style and social concerns. Chan produced his masterpiece, *Hong Kong
1997 Trilogy*, in the late 1990s. Working with a tight budget and under
poor material conditions, and adapting the cinematic devices of location
shooting, nonprofessional acting, historical realism, and documentary
effects, *1997 Trilogy* is highly appreciated as the record of the period of

the fatal transformation of the colony. Hong Kong began its transformation at midnight on June 30, 1997, when the old flag of the Crown Colony of Hong Kong was lowered at the official Hand-over ceremony. It ended 153 years (1844–1997) of British rule over the city and turned the colony into a new "Special Administrative Region" of China. The returning of a capitalist city to Communist China, however, has created political insecurity and social anxiety among the people of Hong Kong. Chan's *1997 Trilogy*, in these terms, acts like historical footage of the colony. In its cinematic practice of neorealism, it reports the sociopolitical transformation of Hong Kong before and beyond the Hand-over.

I begin my discussion with a brief documentation of the historical development of neorealist practice in Hong Kong cinema since 1950, when a group of leftist filmmakers fled to Hong Kong from Shanghai to set up the filmic model for later generations. It is worth noting that the Hong Kong New Wave Cinema that emerged in the late 1970s presents a new kind of cinematic neorealism, one initiated by Allen Fong and inherited by Fruit Chan in the 1990s. Inspired by both the local tradition of filmmaking of the 1950s and the Western influence of European cinema, Fong distinguishes his film style among the other New Wave directors by his documentary visual effects. Fruit Chan later promoted such visual impacts of cinematic neorealism in his *1997 Trilogy*. In the second part of my discussion, I give a comparative study of Chan's *1997 Trilogy* with such Italian neorealist films as *Shoeshine* (1946), *Bicycle Thief* (1948), *Umberto D* (1952), *The Children Are Watching Us* (1942), and *Rome, Open City* (1945) in terms of their cinematic representation. My goals are to open a critical terrain of neorealism in relation to Hong Kong cinema and to broaden the perspective of both neorealism and Hong Kong filmmaking on a global scale.

Hong Kong Cinema and Neorealism

The historical development of Hong Kong cinema in relation to neorealism can be traced back to the 1950s and the 1960s, when realistic films made up the majority of films produced.[2] It is significant that there is no historical evidence that Italian neorealism directly influenced the filmmaking of that period. Instead, Hong Kong filmmakers of the 1950s—especially those who came from mainland China after 1949—inherited the leftist tradition of film production from 1930s Shanghai. According to Lam Lin-tong's critical research on Western influence on Hong Kong cinema in the postwar period, the first Italian neorealist film screened in Hong Kong in 1948 was Vittorio De Sica's *Shoeshine*. Later, in 1952 and

1953, local audiences were introduced to Rossellini's *Rome, Open City,* Giuseppe De Santis's *Bitter Rice* (1949), and De Sica's *Miracle in Milan* (1951). Although these films were well received by moviegoers and film critics, Italian neorealism did not leave as great of an impression on local postwar directors as did left-wing realist cinema in Shanghai in the 1930s and 1940s (Lam "Yidaili Xinxieshizhuyi Dianying Zaipingjia," 156). However, the realistic film of Hong Kong in the 1950s and 1960s shared some characteristics with Italian neorealist cinema. Using film as a social caricature and a political reference of the time, they both shared a strong critical response to and social consciousness of what happened in everyday life. For example, a group of film workers including directors, scriptwriters, and actors launched a campaign called "Clean-up Cinema" in the early 1950s. They set up Union Film Enterprises Limited (Zhong Lian Film Company) in 1952 and dedicated themselves to promoting a certain standard of film production. Their goal was to fight mainstream and commercial pornographic and violent movies. The group called for consolidation of film workers, self-sacrifice, and a sense of community and social responsibility in filmmaking. Their representative works like *Family* (*Jia;* 1953), *Parents' Hearts* (*Fumu xin;* 1955), and *In the Face of Demolition* (*Weilou chunxiao;* 1953) heavily emphasized family ethics, human dignity, and social unity of the working class under poor living conditions in the postwar era. These films, which later became classics of Cantonese cinema,[3] were shot in realistic settings but with a melodramatic style and professional actors. As a small independent film company, Union Film had successfully produced many notable works under such constraints as limited markets, capital shortages, and limited production time. The company not only refused the market-oriented strategy of appealing to popular taste, but also pioneered a new cinematic model in which film was treated as a vehicle to teach moral and social values (Yu 44). For example, the melodrama *In the Face of Demolition* directed by Lee Tit tells the story of the struggle for survival of the working class during economic recession and unemployment. These characters include a dance hostess, an unemployed teacher who later becomes a rent collector, an unskilled laborer who dies in an accident at the end of the movie, a poor girl who is raped by her brother-in-law, a taxi driver, and their family members. They are all tenants of a communal apartment where they share love and death, joy and sorrow. They help each other and have an optimistic view of the future, although they have to experience everyday problems and the fatal disaster of a typhoon. *In the Face of Demolition* realistically portrays the human faith and social life of Hong

Kong in the 1950s. It established the canon of the genre at that time and became a Cantonese cinema classic that formed the grammar of a nostalgic trend used by Hong Kong filmmakers in the 1990s.[4] However, unlike most Italian neorealist films, Hong Kong cinema of the 1950s and 1960s did not use a documentary style. Most of the films were shot in studios and used well-known professional actors and actresses. It was not until the late 1970s when Hong Kong New Wave Cinema emerged under the influence of European cinema that a new kind of neorealist practice materialized.

Hong Kong's New Wave Cinema began when a group of young filmmakers, including Tsui Hark, Ann Hui, Allen Fong, and Patrick Tam, began their careers in the local film industry. Most had studied film and video production in the West and had completed their production training at local television stations. Their Western training enabled them to initiate advanced techniques of production and to bring to Hong Kong cinema a new and youthful vision about the life, culture, and history of their city. As Law Kar points out in his "Overview of Hong Kong's New Wave Cinema," the term "New Wave" in its local historical context refers to applications of innovative techniques, modernization of film language, new urban sensibility, and visual styles by the young directors who returned from their overseas studies (47). As a project of modernity, Hong Kong New Wave Cinema altered the visual landscape of Hong Kong cinema by transforming old and traditional styles of production.[5] For example, Hark's martial arts films like *Butterfly Murders* (*Die bian;* 1979) and *Zu: Warriors from the Magic Mountain* (*Xin shushan jianxia;* 1983) are groundbreaking works of Hong Kong cinema in terms of their new cinematic representation. The former adapts the plot development from Western science fiction and detective stories, while the latter uses computer special effects from Hollywood cinema. Hui's masterpiece, *The Secret* (*Feng jie;* 1979), is a story of murder mixed with various generic elements of comedy, romance, kung fu, horror, and detective films. Her *Boat People* (*Touben nuhai;* 1982), on the other hand, is a political allegory of the 1997 Hand-over.[6] Among these New Wave directors, Fong established his career by initiating a new kind of realistic and documentary style of filmmaking.

Born in 1947, Fong went to high school in Hong Kong and studied film production at the University of Southern California. He joined the production team of the Radio Television of Hong Kong (RTHK) in the late 1970s and produced such outstanding realist works as *Wild Child* (1977) and *The Song of Yuen Chau-chai* (1977). As a pioneer of the New

211

Wave and a realist, he directed his first feature film, *Father and Son* (*Foo ji ching*), in 1981. His other representative works include *Ah Ying* (*Banbian ren;* 1982), *Just Like Weather* (*Meiguo xin,* 1986), *Dancing Bull* (*Wu niu;* 1990), and *A Little Life Opera* (*Yisheng yitaixi;* 1997). He received the award for best director at the Hong Kong Golden Film Festival for his brilliant documentary dramas *Father and Son* and *Ah Ying* in 1982 and 1983, respectively (Teo 264–65). *Father and Son* depicts the conflict between the young and the old generations in Hong Kong in the 1950s and 1960s. The film tells the story of the struggle of a child who devotes himself to becoming a filmmaker but is opposed by his old-fashioned and patriarchal father. The father believes that the career of a film director does not promise a lucrative and bright future for his son. He therefore imposes his own values on his son and compels him to give up his desire. He even asks his elder daughter to marry a rich man who can financially support his son to study abroad because it is the only way for his son to increase his social status and get a good job after graduation. Shot in actual locations, like the public housing estates, streets, and factories of 1950s Hong Kong, the film portrays the social life of working-class families. It highlights its sense of realism by using natural lighting and nonprofessional actors. Stylized in everyday life episodes and documentary effects, it presents the director's respect and sympathy for poor people. Law Kar comments that *Father and Son* was imbued with a spirit of Italian neorealism, which was unusual for Hong Kong films of the 1970s ("An Overview of Hong Kong's New Wave Cinema" 48) when compared with other New Wave directors and mainstream Hong Kong cinema in the 1980s. In other words, Fong established his own style among other New Wave directors in terms of a new kind of cinematic neorealism.

Comedy and action cinema dominated mainstream Hong Kong filmmaking from the 1980s to the 1990s. Bruce Lee, Jackie Chan, John Woo, Chow Yun-fat, and Jet Li became famous locally and internationally because of their unique and outstanding performances in the action genre. Stephen Chiau, on the other hand, has been successful in the last two decades in the local box office with his "cinema of nonsense." This is a new type of urban comedy characterized by illogical plot development, unconventional acting, and language games in the dialogue. The second generation of the Hong Kong New Wave—Stanley Kwan, Wong Kar-wai, and Fruit Chan—joined the local film industry in the late 1980s.[7] Kwan's queer sexual films, Wong's urban cinema of human solitude, and Chan's realist genre about the colonial history of the city have established them as representatives of the new cinema. As an independent filmmaker outside the mainstream, Chan distinguished himself with his strong sense of social responsibility in his documentary drama.

Fruit Chan was born in Guangzhou in 1959 and raised in Hong Kong. Working as an assistant director, he entered the film industry in the early 1980s. He produced his first feature, *Finale in Blood* (*Danao guangchanglong*), in 1991. However, he established himself as a successful independent filmmaker in the late 1990s when he produced his *Hong Kong 1997 Trilogy*, a set of three related works that portray the sociopolitical situation of the colony before and after the Hand-over. The trilogy includes *Made in Hong Kong* (*Xianggang zhizao*, 1997), *The Longest Summer* (*Qunian yanhua tebieduo*, 1998), and *Little Cheung* (*Xilu xiang*, 1999). The making of *Made in Hong Kong* is a legend in the Hong Kong film industry. It was shot with leftover film stocks and starred nonprofessional actors. Produced under extremely difficult conditions and a box-office failure in the local market, *Made in Hong Kong* won various awards around the world. It was awarded the best screenplay at the Gijon International Youth Film Festival in Spain and was the best film at the International Film Critics Association in Korea and at the Nantes Film Festival in France. Chan himself received the award for best director at both the Taipei Golden Horse Film Festival in Taiwan and the Golden Film Festival in Hong Kong. With the success of *Made in Hong Kong*, Chan finished *The Longest Summer* and *Little Cheung* with a tight budget and labor shortage. These two films earned him numerous film awards at both local and international film festivals, but this did not improve Chan's working conditions. He still had to struggle under the pressure of low production costs and failure at the box office.[8] Chan's story, which is somewhat similar to that of the Italian neorealist directors, points to the unhealthy development and unfavorable working conditions of Hong Kong filmmaking. Although Chan's films have not been profitable, they are highly appreciated by film critics. It is true that *1997 Trilogy* does not appeal to popular audiences or the commercial market; however, it is a historical record of the colony during a crucial time.

Fruit Chan and Italian Neorealism:
Made in Hong Kong and *The Longest Summer*

Echoing De Sica's social theme of juvenile criminals in *Shoeshine*, Fruit Chan's *Made in Hong Kong* shares the same tragic sense of social cruelty inflicted on youth. *Shoeshine*, as Peter Bondanella describes, is an ironic

Made in Hong Kong (Xianggang zhizao) (Fruit Chan, 1997)

commentary on the social disintegration of postwar Italy. The director dramatizes the tragedy of childish innocence corrupted by the adult world and explores its tragic impact on the youthful friendship of the two protagonists, Giuseppe (Rinaldo Smordoni) and Pasquale (Franco Interlenghi) (Bondanella, *Italian Cinema* 53). The two shoeshine boys come from poor families and are good friends. They trust each other and earn their own living on the streets together. However, they become criminals later when they get involved in a black market scheme. Living in a prison camp under unjust circumstances, their friendship is gradually destroyed. Giuseppe dies in an escape attempt at the end of the movie while Pasquale is arrested and blamed for the incident.

Sharing the same melancholic tone with *Shoeshine*, *Made in Hong Kong* narrates the dead-end experience of three teenagers who live in social alienation under the political pressure of the 1997 Hand-over. The three protagonists, Moon (Sam Lee), Sylvester (Wenbers Li), and Ah Ping (Neiky Yim), all come from broken families. Moon is a young gangster who lives with his mother in public housing while his father keeps a mistress in a private apartment and does not take care of his family. Sylvester was abandoned by his parents at birth because he was born mentally handicapped. He earns a living as a street beggar. Ah Ping is an orphan who suffers from a fatal kidney disease and is waiting for a transplant. Documented in episodic style, the film depicts how the

214

three protagonists share their love and friendship, struggling through life and death in a harsh world. At the end of the movie, Sylvester is accidentally killed. Ah Ping dies of her fatal disease. Moon shoots himself by the side of Ping's gravestone after avenging Sylvester's death by killing the leader of the threesome. Ignored and corrupted by the adult world, Moon, Sylvester, and Ah Ping never enjoy parental affection or family life and support. Instead, they have to overcome all kinds of daily difficulties and solve their problems themselves. For example, Moon resorts to criminal acts after his mother leaves home. Ah Ping is sexually harassed by gangsters when her father runs away from home because he is in debt. Sylvester is rejected by his neighbors and is frequently beaten by hooligans. The film places Moon's voice-over at the center of the narration. His point of view makes value judgments on Hong Kong society at the dawn of the 1997 Hand-over; Hong Kong is a dark, dead-end city. Moon delivers a long voice-over before committing suicide,

> My father kept a mistress outside, and it's a reinvention of life for him. My mom left me. It's also a reinvention of her life. The government promo says, "There's no reinvention in one's life." It's all bullshit! That's why I hate adults. They always tell lies. They're all hypocrites! I was scared and helpless from the moment that my mom ran away from home. But now, I know exactly what to do . . . I wonder how many people would understand what Ping, Sylvester, Susan and me actually think? No one! But there's one thing that I'm sure—we are all very happy now because we don't have to face an uncertain world in the future! (my translation)

Made in Hong Kong portrays a parentless society, which symbolizes the political chaos of the colony in facing its uncertain future. The broken families of Moon, Sylvester, and Ping reflect reality. It is a corrupted and immoral world without law and order. Parents and the city government do not play their proper role and shoulder their responsibilities. The three adolescents are victims of social tragedy and are abused and exploited by the adult world. Ending their lives is one possible way to withdraw from the alienated world they were born in. Shot in actual locations, the public housing on celluloid is the background of the story on the one hand and the social setting of the movie on the other. The dark corridors, social space of the open area, playground, street markets, public toilets, crowded households, and tiny apartments of public housing signify both the social plane of the documentary drama and the personal experience of the director. Fruit Chan proclaimed in an interview in 1998 that his goal in producing *Made in Hong Kong* was to portray a gloomy future through the eyes of a few kids growing up in public housing. As an immigrant from mainland China in the late 1950s, Chan spent over ten years of his childhood in public housing. He seems to realize that public housing represents the dark corner of personal life as well as a microcosm of Hong Kong society. The history of public housing represents the development of Hong Kong (So). The life of the three protagonists embodies the director's own social experience; moreover, their tragic end presents his pessimistic view of the future. Hong Kong is a noisy city crowded with social problems without any hope.

Unlike *Made in Hong Kong, The Longest Summer* chronicles the process of the Hand-over from March 31, 1997, to July 7, 1998. It is filmed in a documentary style because most of the footage is shot at the actual location where the ceremonies were held and the fireworks were displayed. In an interview titled "Middle-aged and Jobless in 1997," Chan explains that he picked up his camera and started to shoot the ceremony of the Hand-over and its preparation at the beginning of 1997, although he did not have any concrete idea about the story then. The script did not come to him until he was inspired by the arrival of the People's Liberation Army on the morning of July 1. The scene of arrival was so fascinating and wonderful that he could not help asking himself, "Does Hong Kong own its army?" (Fong 53). In fact, Hong Kong as a colony did not have its own army, only the Chinese soldiers in the British military. Chan then decided to make a film about the identity crisis of these Chinese soldiers on the edge of time (Fong 53).

The Longest Summer tells the story of a group of retired Chinese soldiers, all of whom are middle-aged and have little practical training and no war experience. They become jobless when the Hong Kong Military Service Corps officially disbanded three months before the transfer of the territory's sovereignty back to China. This marked the end of an era during which Chinese soldiers served the British Army in Hong Kong for 140 years, and also left a group of unemployed soldiers stranded because the British government had no intention of giving them British citizenship after the Hand-over. Faced with unemployment, pressure from their families, and the struggle for survival, these soldiers risk their lives to rob a British bank. Because they have no experience with weapons, their plan fails and they are killed by another band of robbers. On the night of the Hand-over, the Chinese and British officials hold their ceremony at the Convention Center in Waichai, and display their fireworks afterward. At the same moment, the soldiers are killed by gangsters. With his mise-en-scène editing, Chan technically juxtaposes the scene of murder with the newsreel footage of the Hand-over ceremony and the fireworks. This creates a certain kind of political irony in which the director presents his critical attitude toward the future of the colony.

Similar to Rossellini's *Rome, Open City, The Longest Summer* depicts the political crisis of a city. Like postwar Rome, Hong Kong was in sociopolitical turmoil during the post-transitional period after the June Fourth Event in Beijing in 1989. The people of Hong Kong lost their confidence in the Chinese Communist Party (CCP) when the Chinese government crushed the democratic movement of the students at Tiananmen Square. They worried about the political future of the city. They did not believe that Hong Kong could keep its own political system unchanged and maintain its stability and prosperity after the Hand-over. As a result, many in the wealthy and professional classes left. Those who did not have the capital to emigrate to other countries had to live under political pressure in a chaotic time. British colonizers and Chinese officials had several political debates and conflicts during the post-transitional period. When the British intended to maintain their interests in Southeast Asia after 1997, the Chinese government tried to limit the British sphere of influence and to have more political power and privileges. However, the desires of the six million people of the colony were ignored by both colonizer and mother country. They did not have a seat or the right to voice their views in these political debates and negotiations. Political suppression and social depression, therefore, clouded the city. *The Longest Summer* casts the Chinese soldiers of the British Army to portray the people who failed to adapt to the Hand-over. These soldiers served the British Army on Chinese land for two decades. They are neither Chinese nor British. They are lost and helpless, afraid to face the uncertain future. The Hand-over does not promise them a secure and bright prospect; they become unemployed when dismissed by the British Army and disregarded by the Chinese government. In its mournful tone, *The Longest Summer* is an elegy of Hong Kong during its crucial transformation.

Rossellini's *Rome, Open City* captures the tragic life and act of resistance of the Italian people during German occupation. The protagonists, Don Pietro (Aldo Fabrizi), Pina (Anna Magnani), and Manfredi (Marcello Pagliero), are revolutionary martyrs. They seek freedom and democracy, and they suffer and sacrifice for their country. The director depicts how they endure their miserable lives in the struggle for peace. He shows his high respect for these figures by narrating their stories with a lyrical tone and realistic setting. For example, in the scene in which the Nazi soldier shoots Pina to death, the background music evokes a sense of solemnity. Pina's death is shocking, innocent, but dignified. The heavy beat of the music elicits a sense of anguish and sorrow. Pina is both the victim and the tragic hero of the political turmoil of postwar Italy. The death scene of the priest, Don Pietro, is another example. Don Pietro says before his persecution, "It's not difficult to die well, the difficult thing is to live well." He displays great courage and honor in his holy sacrifice. When he is shot, a crowd of children stands behind the iron bar to pay homage to the priest by whistling a song. This whistling has a double meaning. It is the secret code Don Pietro uses in the middle of the story to communicate with his political partners under the watchful eye of the Nazis. It also signifies a certain kind of courage of the children in overcoming their fear in a frightening and dangerous situation. The whistling of the song, in this respect, symbolizes the eternity of Don Pietro's human spirit and honor. His political consciousness and social awareness will pass on to the next generation. In other words, the children will try to achieve Don Pietro's unfulfilled wish and continue to struggle for peace and democracy. However, unlike Don Pietro and Pina, the Chinese soldiers in *The Longest Summer* are neither heroes nor martyrs but tragic figures. They are cast out from society when the British Army dismisses them. They are ordinary and selfish. They do not have any noble thoughts or ideals to improve their society. Instead, their only goal is to profit as much as possible within a short period of time. The director, in his black humor, presents their failure and death in an absurd way rather than in appreciation. For example, the male protagonist, Ga Yin (Tony Ho), is out of control when he discovers that gangsters killed his younger brother and partners at the end of the movie. He goes crazy, and violently opens fire and shoots the children at the teahouse. The juxtaposition of the bloody killing scene and the fireworks of the Hand-over ceremony portray the dead end of the city. The 1997 Hand-over does not open a new historical page for the colony but indicates the city's doom.

History and Narration: *Little Cheung*

Chan produced *Little Cheung*, the final episode of his *Hong Kong 1997 Trilogy*, in 1999. *Little Cheung* tells the story of working-class life in Yaumatei, an old district in the Kowloon side of the city that is saturated with crime and prostitution. The protagonist, little Cheung (Yiu Yu-ming), is a nine-year-old boy from a broken family. His father is patriarchal, and he runs a little restaurant at Yaumatei. Little Cheung's mother is a housewife who spends all her time gambling in the casino and does not take care of her family. Cheung's father expelled his eldest son from home when Cheung was only two years old. Cheung lives with his grandmother and a Filipino domestic helper named Armi. One day, Cheung runs across a girl, Ah Fan (Mak Wai-fan), in a dark alley. She is an undocumented immigrant from mainland China. The two become friends, and they make money by delivering meals to people's homes. However, Ah Fan is repatriated to her homeland at the end of the movie when the police discover that she is an undocumented immigrant. Almost at the same moment, Cheung's grandmother dies and Armi is fired. Cheung finds himself alone. This ends not only Cheung's exciting childhood and adventures but also the colonial time of the city. Echoing the theme and the sociopolitical setting of the two previous episodes, *Made in Hong Kong* and *The Longest Summer, Little Cheung* is set on the eve of the Hand-over, a crucial moment when the city's people have to face dramatic change. What Chan depicts in *Little Cheung* is how the ordinary people of the colony cope with their daily difficulties in anticipation of the 1997 Hand-over.

Like De Sica'a *Umberto D* and *The Children Are Watching Us, Little Cheung* focuses on the perspectives of the elderly and children. *Umberto D* presents the solitude of the elderly in modern society. It narrates the details of daily life of an old man, Umberto (Carlo Battisti), who is retired. The loneliness and difficulties of life become a spectacle through the viewpoint of the old man. His companionship with his pet dog and the domestic helper (Maria Pia Casilio) illustrates a certain kind of warmth among the poor. However, as an old-age pensioner, Umberto faces daily struggles, including homelessness when his landlady expels him from the apartment. His unsuccessful attempt at suicide at the end of the movie shows the alienation and cruelty of a society in which the elderly are abandoned and ignored. In a more critical tone, De Sica's *The Children Are Watching Us* narrates the story of how a little boy is destroyed by the adult world. An innocent child in a happy family at the beginning of the film, the protagonist is gradually ruined by his mother's adultery. After his father's suicide, he is sent to an orphanage. When his mother comes to visit him, he does not forgive her for what she has done to him and his father. He no longer trusts anyone, and retreats into his own solitude, anger, and sorrow. The film's title sounds like a warning;

Little Cheung
(*Xilu xiang*)
(Fruit Chan,
1999)

the innocent eyes of the child make a value judgment on the adult world. The film portrays the social and moral degradation of a world in which children are victimized.

As for Chan's *Little Cheung*, the story is also narrated from the perspectives of the elderly and children; the political transformation of the colony is seen through the eyes of the grandmother, little Cheung, and Ah Fan. In fact, the film's narration is divided into three parts: the oral history narrated by the grandmother and the voice-overs of little Cheung and Ah Fan. The grandmother's oral history of her life and the culture of the city is fragmented, disorderly, ambiguous, and nostalgic, and it is difficult to restore the history of the colony through her narration. Despite its documentary style and location shooting, *Little Cheung* nostalgically depicts the colony on the eve of the Hand-over: a retrospection on the past from the point of view of the present. The film is also a yearning for the "good old days" when the sovereignty of the city is about to be transferred to the Chinese Communist Party.

The social setting of the film is not only the background of the story and the characters but also the spatial representation of the political issue of the Hand-over. Yaumatei is an old town center where the working class used to live and work, beyond the reach of the modernization program and the urban planning of the local government. It retains the same street scenes and styles of Hong Kong of the 1960s and 1970s. Yaumatei is saturated with old shops, old ways of life, and traditional modes of thinking and values. In this sense, the grandmother's oral history works like the background narration of the nostalgic space of

Yaumatei. The fragmentary narration of the grandmother as well as the nostalgic sense of the place comprise the historicity of the colony. For example, when the grandmother murmurs about her youthful life, the camera moves from her wrinkled face to the old style of the interior of the household or to the street scenes outside. The director symbolically juxtaposes the narration and the social setting of the place with his mise-en-scène editing to create a sense of dislocation. The nostalgic mood of the character dislocates the linear development and narration of history. In addition, the dramatic change and the political turmoil of the colony dislocate the livelihood of ordinary people.

If the oral history of the grandmother represents the historicity of the city, then the voice-overs by little Cheung and Ah Fan signify the youthful view toward the future. The social scene of the Hand-over is seen from the child's perspective. Little Cheung narrates the first part of the film. His voice-over depicts the backgrounds of different characters. For example, in order to support her family in her hometown, Armi comes to Hong Kong from the Philippines and works as a domestic helper in Cheung's household. She collapses when she later discovers that her husband has kept a mistress back in the Philippines. David and Kenny are brothers who grew up in Yaumatei. They have a falling out when they have to share their family property. Ah Fan and her younger sister are undocumented immigrants from mainland China. They live with their parents in a small house in a dark alley. Because she is an illegal immigrant, Ah Fan cannot go to school. Instead, she washes dishes for a restaurant in Yaumatei. She always has to hide from the watchful eyes of the police. Cheung's narration is both a description of the details of everyday life of these common people in Yaumatei and a microcosm of Hong Kong society before and beyond the Hand-over. Ah Fan is classified as an illegal immigrant child although her father is a resident of Hong Kong. As an outsider of the community, she encounters discrimination in her neighborhood in Yaumatei. Little Cheung is the only person who accepts her and befriends her. This is because Cheung, as a child, does not share the social bias of the adult world. He does not think that Ah Fan's illegal status is an obstacle to social development and progress. In return, Ah Fan is his best friend in the district, the only one who can understand his joy and sorrow. Thus, Ah Fan's repatriation in the final scene of the movie is an unhappy ending to little Cheung's childhood.

The second half of the story is narrated by Ah Fan's voice-over. Her narrative point of view is that of an outsider describing the sociopolitical change of the colony. In her lyrical tone, she describes the final outcome of family conflicts and of the characters. For example, the grandmother dies and Armi is dismissed. Kenny decides to give up his property rights and goes back to the United States with his wife. David suffers from kidney problems though he successfully gets all the family property. These common people live their ordinary lives while the city experiences the undercurrent of political resentment in its acceptance of the Hand-over. The shift of narrative viewpoint from little Cheung to Ah Fan is significant in two aspects. First, in terms of its cinematic structure, it is necessary to give an alternative point of view when the plot development gets to the turning point in the middle of the film. Second, the shift of the viewpoint indicates the political change of the colony. Little Cheung's voice-over represents a kind of local voice in the context of everyday life politics. Ah Fan's narration, on the other hand, represents a new perspective from mainland China. It signifies the ongoing process of the transformation of the colony. Hong Kong has become a special administrative region, Hong Kong, China, after the Hand-over. The Hand-over, in its political sense, ends 153 years of British colonization and grants the city a new historical stage of development. At the same time, however, it begins a new era full of political uncertainty, social insecurity, legal crisis, and economic problems. Ah Fan's voice-over, that is, the perspective of an illegal immigrant from mainland China, represents a kind of paradoxical position. If her citizenship is unrecognized by both the Hong Kong government and Chinese authorities, then her narration about the story of the colony becomes a political irony. This is because her desire to become a legal immigrant as well as a member of the local community is finally rejected after a long process of negotiation. "Hong Kong Is My Home," the slogan issued by the Hong Kong government to promote a sense of belonging to the local community, becomes a political lie betraying the promise.

Concluding Remarks: Fruit Chan's Film Style

Neorealism is the greatest possible curiosity about individuals: a need, appropriate to modern man, to speak of things as they are, to be aware of reality, in an absolutely concrete manner, conforming to that typically contemporary interest in statistical and scientific results; a sincere need, as well, to see men with humility, as they are, without resorting to stratagems in order to invent the extraordinary; to be aware of being able to arrive at the extraordinary through inquiry itself; a reality, whatever it is, in order to attain an understanding of things.
Rossellini in Overbey 89

In his article titled "A Few Words about Neorealism," written in 1953, Rossellini defines Italian neorealism as a way of seeing men with humility and of speaking about things as they are. Neorealism, for Rossellini, is not only the artistic form of representation but also the philosophical truth of the world he lived in. As a way of presenting reality concretely, the subject of neorealist films is the world and its people and not the ornamental elements of the story or the narrative. What directors have to face and deal with in their works are the actual problems in society and the contemporary stories of common people. As Peter Bondanella points out, neorealism was not a "movement" in the strictest sense of the term, and any discussion of neorealism must be broad enough to encompass a wide diversity of cinematic style, themes, and attitudes (*Italian Cinema* 34–35). My study situates Hong Kong cinema in the context of neorealist practice and global filmmaking in terms of a number of aesthetic and philosophical components, including the mise-en-scène techniques of location shooting, nonprofessional acting, children's narrative viewpoint, documentary footage, and the director's homage to historical actuality, political commitment, and everyday reality. The realistic genre of Hong Kong cinema has established its own local tradition since the 1950s. Allen Fong and Fruit Chan enhanced its development in the 1970s and the 1990s, respectively. Chan's *1997 Trilogy*, however, in terms of its cinematic effects, is the best example of neorealist practice in Hong Kong filmmaking.

Nonprofessional acting and children's narrative viewpoint are two distinguishing film techniques in Chan's *1997 Trilogy*. By using nonprofessional actors, the director minimizes the production budget and creates a documentary cinematic style. Using children's narrative viewpoint enables the director to turn a critical eye on crucial aspects of social reality. As André Bazin emphasizes in his critique of Italian neorealist filmmaking, nonprofessionals are naturally suitable because they fit the characters physically or because there is some parallel between the roles and their lives. The natural acting of the characters, therefore, benefits the film by providing an element of authenticity (24). The audience can easily identify with the characters and the plot of the film when actors play their everyday selves on the screen. Almost all the characters of *1997 Trilogy* are played by nonprofessional actors. For example, Sam Lee, the protagonist of *Made in Hong Kong* as well as *The Longest Summer*, was originally an electrician. He is skinny, and he looks like a gangster. He always speeds on his skateboard on the basketball court. Chan picked him because of his playfulness and youth. Neiky Yim, the female character of *Made in Hong Kong*, comes from a single-parent family. She was a high school student with a great interest in fashion design when Chan cast her. Another example is the grandmother in *Little Cheung*. She is an ordinary elderly woman Chan found in Yaumatei. When shooting the scene of the grandmother's murmuring about her life, Chan simply set up the camera and lighting and asked the old lady to say something about herself. The director edited the footage and the voice-over in postproduction. Chan explained that the elderly are always unbelievably moving when they talk about the past.[9]

As mentioned before, children's narrative viewpoint within a neorealist genre enables the director to turn a critical eye on social discontent. Through the children's innocent perspective, the tragic effects of events and the irony of the film are displayed. The child acts not only as the victim of the tragedy but also as the witness of social reality. As Bazin points out, in the neorealist genre the children's perspective reveals the hidden message of the film and provides an ethical dimension and moral standpoint (53). By using nonprofessional actors and children's perspectives, Chan's *1997 Trilogy* successfully imprints its cinematic style of neorealism and, simultaneously, its sociopolitical concern about the 1997 Hand-over.

Notes

1. Lam points out that the outbreak of wars in the struggles for decolonization and national independence in Asia, Africa, and Latin America in the postwar period ruined the economic and social development of these third-world countries. There were also the problems of inflation, starvation, official corruption, and regional as well as religious disputes ("Yidaili Xinxieshizhuyi Dianying Zaipingjia" 94).

2. The 1950s and the 1960s were the high point of the Hong Kong film industry. More than 2,800 Cantonese films were made in these decades. In addition to realist films, other popular genres included opera films, youth movies, and martial arts films. In order to focus the scope of my research, I discuss here only the production of realist films. For a historical analysis of the other genres at that time, see Teo.

3. Hong Kong's dialect is Cantonese, but it is not the national language, which is Mandarin (Putonghua). Almost all films produced are in Cantonese, although some Mandarin films did exist in the 1960s. These Cantonese films were always dubbed into Mandarin before being sold to overseas markets.

4. The adaptation of the realist film of the 1950s and 1960s was a com-

mon practice of nostalgia cinema in the 1990s. For example, Peter Chan's *He Ain't Heavy, He's My Father* (1993) reproduces the characters, the social setting, and the moral message of *In the Face of Demolition*. For further discussion, see N. Chan.

5. Law Kar's "Overview of Hong Kong's New Wave Cinema" is a thorough historical investigation of the emergence of Hong Kong New Wave Cinema in terms of its social background, world politics, local cultural history, and the system of communication. For further discussion on the different film styles of the New Wave directors, see his *Hong Kong New Wave*.

6. In fact, the 1997 issue was not introduced by or suddenly discussed between Britain and China in the early 1980s. They had started their long and secret negotiations in the 1940s. When the issue was suddenly reported by the media in the late 1970s, most of the people of Hong Kong were anxious about their future because they believed that the agreement was settled only in terms of the self-interest of the two powers. The public response to the 1997 Hand-over was negative and pessimistic. When Hui shot *The Boat People* in 1982, there were a lot of hot debates concerning the future of the colony in both local and international newspapers, public and government sectors. For further discussion on the allegorical structure of the film, see Law Kar's Chinese article, "Xianggang Dianying di Haiwai Jingyan."

7. Kwan was Hui's assistant in the 1980s, and Chan was trained as a veteran assistant director for almost ten years before he produced his first feature in the 1990s. Wong worked with another New Wave director, Patrick Tam, for a long time, and Tam later became the editor of Wong's two films, *As Tears Go By* (1987) and *Day of Being Wild* (1990).

8. The production cost of *Made in Hong Kong* was around US$65,000, and its box-office returns were under US$125,000. The income of *The Longest Summer,* however, couldn't cover its production costs. It lost about US$250,000.

9. For the casting of nonprofessional actors in *1997 Trilogy* and the practical reasons for doing so, see Fong; Ye; and So.

Chapter 11

Re-creating the Witness:
Elephant, Postmodernism, and the Neorealist Inheritance

Thomas Stubblefield

> While the cinema used to make one situation produce another situation, and an-
> other, and another, again and again, and each scene was thought out and immedi-
> ately related to the next . . . today, when we have thought out a scene, we feel that we
> need to "remain" in it, because the single scene itself can contain so many echoes and
> reverberations, can even contain all the situations we may need. . . . Now it has been
> perceived that reality is hugely rich, that to be able to look at it directly is enough.
> Zavattini, "Some Ideas" 64

Cesare Zavattini's comments reflect a common observation of Italian
neorealism, namely its movement away from agency as a means to further plot development toward a pure cataloging of the visual milieu. It
is this general mistrust of causality that lies behind its episodic structures in which seemingly important events are denied appropriate setup.
For example, the killing of the farm family in *Paisà* (1946) is indicated
only by the cut from the guerillas waiting for a plane to a child crying
next to his dead parents. Alternately, events might be left open-ended, as
in the end of Roberto Rossellini's *Germany, Year Zero* (1947), in which
Edmund, the film's protagonist, spends the conclusion of the film simply
observing the seemingly random events of his surroundings. As a result of this breakdown of causality, rather than mastering narrative space
through agency, this new protagonist is given the task of recording the
world with his or her gaze, or as Zavattini states, simply "look[ing] at
[reality] directly" ("Some Ideas").

According to Gilles Deleuze, this transition can be understood as
representative of a changed relationship between the individual and

226

Elephant (Gus Van Sant, 2003)

space caused by the destruction of World War II. Specifically, as the aftermath of the war saw the proliferation of "situations in which we no longer know how to react to" and "spaces which we no longer know how to describe," traditional forms of cinematic realism in turn began to reveal their inadequacy, leading to a cinema in which causality and linearity were somehow no longer possible (Deleuze, *Cinema 1* xi). Out of this dissatisfaction with what Deleuze calls the movement-image came what he theorizes as the neorealist "pure optical image" and, more broadly, the regime of the time-image.

While perhaps coming to full fruition in later works,[1] the birth of this "cinema of the seer" is dramatized in Rossellini's *Rome, Open City* (1945), in particular in the film's recurring narrative device of the witness (Deleuze, *Cinema 2* 4). Through this device, the neorealist tendency toward pure optical images is endowed with a reciprocity. Thus, the act of seeing functions as both a means of perceiving and being perceived, allowing the Italian Resistance to circumvent agency in their struggle with the German occupiers. The device of the witness and its resulting "pure optical situation" not only acts as a rebuttal to the dehumanizing surveillance of the German bureaucracy but also provides an invaluable affirmation to a culture struggling to sustain its existence.

Elephant (2003), a film by Gus Van Sant on the Columbine shootings,[2] foregrounds the gaze in a similar fashion, and in general bears the distinct influence of Italian postwar cinema. In fact, in interviews following the film's release, Van Sant was rather candid about the influence of neorealism, along with other prominent mid-century European movements, on his work, particularly in the period that has followed *Finding Forester* (2000) and *Good Will Hunting* (1997).[3] In *Elephant* this appears most overtly in the film's use of nonprofessional actors, a certain faithfulness to a found location (a closed high school in Van Sant's hometown of Portland, Oregon), elliptical narrative, and a general interest in the everyday as a gateway to broader social, ethical, and philosophical questions. However, in light of the film's subject matter, perhaps the most significant element of this pastiche of neorealism is the resurrection of the witness, as if the penetrative power of the gaze might somehow reveal cause or culpability in an otherwise incomprehensible situation.

As the film's extended steadicam sequences follow meandering students through the high school hallways, traditional narrative development is overshadowed by the presence of these pure optical situations. *Elephant*'s protagonists, a handful of students who remain as nondescript as the spaces they inhabit, concern themselves solely with the optical recording of their surroundings, engaging only minimally in action or reaction to that which they observe. As a result, the narrative quite literally goes nowhere as these overlapping steadicam sequences come to form an extended loop.

From this temporal structure, a similar duality of the gaze emerges. Specifically, through the points of intersection within the loop, we encounter a series of mirror- or "crystal" images that would seem to offer the kind of reciprocity seen in *Rome, Open City*. However, the promise of this pastiche is complicated by a postmodern conception of time, in particular its tendency to experience the present as past. In light of this "consumptive" conception of time, a fully developed reciprocity and in a larger sense a coherent picture of the present as distinct from the past prove impossible. The result is that the film offers little in the way of an investigation or affirmation of the suffering surrounding the Columbine tragedy and instead functions as a kind of mourning for the loss of its own present. To fully appreciate the implications of the relationship *Elephant* has to Italian cinema, it is first necessary to look at the model of the pure optical image that neorealism provides.

A Diagrammatic Reality

Within the narrative of *Rome, Open City* a dialectic relationship emerges between the Italian Resistance and the occupying German forces in regard to their mode of perception of both the reality of war-torn Rome and one another. While in the case of the Italians, this relationship is the product of word of mouth and face-to-face contact, for the German occupiers, perception of reality is mediated by the bureaucracy's perpetual influx of data. In this manner, as surveillance supplants firsthand observation, maps, photographs, and documents come to figure prominently in the German construction of reality, to the extent that the act of perceiving is replaced by the collection of information. This process is relayed succinctly in the scene that introduces Major Bergmann and the German headquarters.

Before we enter the headquarters, we see a group of soldiers raiding Manfredi's apartment, presumably with the intention of capturing him. However, rather than looking through closets, underneath beds, or in other inhabitable spaces, the soldiers instead search desk drawers and stacks of papers. After coming up empty, the men then proceed to the terrace where they soon realize the search is hopeless. The film cuts from a shot of the soldiers surveying the rooftops to a slow zoom out of a map of Rome around which Major Bergmann and the police commissioner stand inside the German headquarters. The transition replicates the spatial collapse of the city into a map in almost literal terms, as if in looking at the representation of the city the officials are able to perceive the action we have just seen. This collapse points to a central dynamic at work within the German bureaucracy, namely, the extension of the reach of surveillance to that of omnipresence and the subsequent vacuum of information that such a state creates.

While remaining within the confines of the headquarters, the Major passes seamlessly through a series of discontinuous spaces. He negotiates between the spaces of a traditional office, interrogation rooms that house heinous instruments of torture, a network of prison cells, and a smoking parlor complete with a bar, card playing, and a piano, all without ever being more than a few steps from his chair. This near disembodied presence leaves the viewer unable to locate the Major precisely within the city while at the same time acutely aware of the centrality of his location, giving the impression of perpetual, unspecified presence. In Foucauldian fashion, this omnipresence serves as the foundation of "automatic power," whereby the subject internalizes the rule with or without the actual presence of the enforcer. In such a relationship, obedience is contingent upon the perception of perpetual presence, a presence that is manifest in the film's continued representation of the Germans as somehow existing outside the normal continuum of fluid space.[4]

Information behaves in a like fashion, as the second corollary of this collapse is the creation of a self-sustaining vacuum that ensures a stream of documents directed toward the bureaucrat's desk. Indeed, when we revisit the headquarters, the first image we see is that of the Major thumbing through a stack of underground newspapers, a scene indicative of a number of similar scenes that together establish a perpetual stream of information. This uninterrupted "flow" of newspapers, photographs, diagrams, and other papers is inextricably linked to the aforementioned illusion of a fluid presence throughout the city. As the Major explains, "Every night I *stroll* through Rome without leaving this room."

Despite its apparent efficiency, this mastery of space brings about a certain distortion regarding the Major's relationship to reality. After a soldier informs Bergmann that Manfredi has escaped the raid, the Major removes a photograph of the perpetrator from his desk. The commissioner asks, "How did you hook the man?" to which the Major replies, "We met here at this desk." The conversation proceeds as if the two men somehow believe that possessing the record or the image of a man is synonymous with possessing the man himself. We soon realize that with this influx of information comes a confusion of the "real" with its representation, a process of "simulation" which, as Jean Baudrillard posits, more than any other factor, defines contemporary life.[5] Therefore, in constructing rather than reflecting reality, the photographic image becomes anthropomorphic as the two men use the pronoun "him" to refer to the inanimate image. The paper trail has usurped the man.

In Deleuzian terms, this degeneration into simulation can be understood as an attempt to maintain a sensory-motor link to a reality whose temporal and spatial unities have been radically disjointed. As the sensory-motor schema proves ineffective in mastering reality, an inordinate emphasis is conferred upon the materiality of the image, leading to the simulations that fuel the Germans' hypertrophied structures of bureaucracy. In discussing Luchino Visconti's work after *Obsession* (1943), Deleuze notes a similar phenomenon, stating that "objects and settings take on an autonomous material reality which gives them an importance in themselves" (*Cinema 2* 4). However, he goes on to state that a vital component, if not defining characteristic, of the pure optical image is the protagonist's endowment of this material reality with his or her gaze. By disregarding firsthand observation, the German system of information gathering takes the material surface, embodied by the paper trail, as an end in itself. In this fashion, despite its insistence on efficiency and accuracy, the bureaucracy exists as a form of non-seeing and what seemed as a thoroughly modern enterprise is yet another illusion of progress. Baudrillard suggests that since simulation is always played out against nostalgia for the symbolic order of language, it resurrects myths of origin and authenticity in the process. It is this mythology that fuels the Germans' blind allegiance to simulation as notions of truth and representation are all but taken for granted, allowing the Italians to exploit such a system by way of the counterfeit. From fake books to forged identification cards to endless fictions that parody the notion of origins, the Italians turn the simulation back against the German forces, sending a whole host of false images into the vacuum. Indeed, it is the Germans' nostalgia for a symbolic order that allows Don Pietro to take advantage of his standing in society to engineer elaborate conceits of falsification from performing last rites on a healthy man to transporting money to opposition groups after curfew by way of "books without words," the penultimate anti-document.

Points of Resistance: Within and without the Document

The streets of Rome represents a middle ground between the German and Italian constructions of reality and therefore the site where their conflict takes place. While it is here that we see the telltale signs of the genre of realism (the hunger of the people, the black market exchanges, and the casual conversations of German soldiers), the film's rendering of this space seems to contrast starkly with expectations of such a genre. To understand the implications of this juxtaposition, it is necessary to call upon Deleuze's concept of the "any-space-whatever."[6]

With the dissolution of the sensory-motor schema, space no longer presumes a predetermined action or movement and therefore becomes indefinite, ambiguous, and even contradictory. It is in the streets of *Rome, Open City* that we find such spaces. For example, after Manfredi arrives at Francesco's apartment, Pina sends her son out to bring back Don Pietro. As the two walk back to the apartment, the film cuts from a long to medium shot by way of a curious slow wipe. The receding frame remains on-screen as the two begin their conversation, implying a double presence of the two actors, one that enters the left-hand side of the screen, the other hidden by the passing train. Similarly, as the edge of the wipe moves against the train's direction of travel in the exiting image, the train comes to occupy an impossible space, traveling through the city streets while simultaneously standing still.

Although usually associated with a period that preceded "the crystalline regime" of the time-image, the wipe in this context illustrates a nonchronological conception of time, representing a momentary departure from the film's empirically driven model of past-present-future. This brief fissure of the frame allows a folding back of time, whereupon the present moment coexists with its past.[7] In these momentary lapses of chronological time, the subject is placed in a position that enables him or her to exchange gazes with the past and future, that is, to see and be seen across time, and in this regard it can be said that the structure of time foreshadows and perhaps even catalyzes what will become a crucial element of the Resistance.

Reciprocity of Vision and the Trial of the Gaze

From the old women who remain on the lookout for the Germans to the eavesdropping children, the gaze is employed by the Italians throughout the film to reclaim the city of Rome. The act of beholding manifests in a number of different contexts, giving rise to a repetition of images of onlookers gazing through keyholes, skylights, and windows. Behind this penchant for looking lies an understanding that the Germans lack, namely "the necessity of investing objects with the gaze" (Deleuze, *Cinema 2* 4). In the dissimilarity between the two parties we see a shift from the action-image of prewar realism to the arrival of the pure optical image, the "cinema of the seer and no longer of the agent" (2). This arrival is brought about by the witness, an individual who prevails by foregoing action in favor of recording the reality before him or her.

In contrast to the simulations that circulate within the German bureaucracy, the gaze is characterized as a means of gaining access to the "real,"[8] a quality that is repeatedly associated with the all-seeing nature of God. For example, when Pina claims not to have started the raid on the bakery, the priest catches her lie, reminding her that he "sees everything." During the interrogation scene Don Pietro explains that he cannot reveal what he has seen because his secrets are guarded by "someone above you and me." Earlier, during her makeshift confession, Pina reveals her desperation regarding the suffering she has observed by asking Don Pietro, "Doesn't God see us?" Far from blasphemous, the question in this context reveals her belief in the transformative power of God's sight. It is as if in being seen by this perfect seer, one's reality is altered. By the time we reach the conclusion of the film, the notion of the witness as a reiteration of God's relationship to man has been firmly established, allowing the film's protagonists to circumvent the usual codes of heroism and prevail through nonaction, as onlookers.

However, the Italians come to articulate this relationship beyond the theological, eventually arriving at a Bergsonian assessment of perception, whereby there exists a continuum between the external world and internal mental world, leaving no distinction between being and being perceived. While Bishop Berkeley states, "To be is to be perceived" (*esse est percipi*),[9] the relationship that arises within *Rome, Open City* might be articulated as "to perceive and subsequently be perceived is to be." This takes form in a reciprocity of vision by which the act of seeing becomes in turn a way of being seen. In writing on Samuel Beckett's *Film*, Deleuze explains, "[H]is [the character's] perceptions become things that in turn perceive him: not only animals, mirrors, *a lithograph of the good Lord*, photos, but even utensils (as Eisenstein said after Dickens: the kettle is looking at me . . .) . . . I do not perceive them without their perceiving me" ("The Greatest Irish Film [Beckett's *Film*]," 24–25).

While in Beckett's view this double perception becomes a terrifying proposition, comprising the antagonist from which Buster Keaton attempts to flee throughout the film, for the Italians in *Rome, Open City* it allows a reclamation of space that in turn affirms existence, both national and personal. In contrast to the panopticism of the Germans, which constitutes an attempt to see without being seen, the gaze here operates as a means to both see and be seen, an affirmation that proves vital in light of the German occupation during which the Italians' cultural and political autonomy remains precarious to say the least.

This reciprocity of vision also informs the interaction among the Italians, so that face-to-face contact comes to form an almost tangible reminder of this duality of sight. In contrast to the succession of documents discussed earlier in regard to the Germans, we see the repetition of organic chains of perceivers: from the boys who pass secret messages among each other to the reciprocal eavesdropping but, most importantly, in the final scene when the priest is executed.

At the conclusion of the film, we find Don Pietro awaiting his death in an open field on the outskirts of Rome. As he is strapped into the chair, he suddenly hears the whistling of the group of boys beyond the fence, and his demeanor is transformed. The vindictive outburst we witnessed in the previous scene in which Don Pietro shakes his fist at the Germans exclaiming, "God's curse on you!" is replaced by a certain heroic tranquillity as the whistles serve as a subtle reminder of this reciprocal exchange.

Elephant and the Ghosts of Postwar Cinema

This idea of the witness and its promise of reciprocity is appropriated, nearly sixty years later, by the film *Elephant*. While all directors are subject to influence, Van Sant's work has a tendency to take this one step further with full-blown pastiche, perhaps most pronounced in his 1998 shot-for-shot remake of Hitchcock's *Psycho* (1960). Although not an exclusively postmodern device, pastiche nonetheless marks a significant point of departure from modernism in that it reflects a skepticism toward the new that is usually associated with the institutionalization of the avant-garde as well as a simple exhaustion of artistic forms. In light of the seeming impossibility of the new, past forms, as if by default, begin to resurface, providing what Frederic Jameson refers to as a "stylistic mask" for the contemporary ("Postmodernism" 114). In these terms, Italian neorealism is the "stylistic mask" through which *Elephant* speaks. Beyond the similarities mentioned above, this pastiche centers on an appropriation of the pure optical and sound image discussed in relation to *Rome, Open City*.

In an article titled "The Art Cinema as a Mode of Film Practice," David Bordwell states, "If the classical protagonist struggles, the drifting protagonist traces an itinerary, an encyclopedic survey of the film's world" ("The Art Cinema" 716).[10] Bordwell inadvertently establishes two fundamental characteristics that unite the pure optical image of *Elephant* and that of neorealism: a loose narrative form that no longer relies on movement and its associations of cause and effect for its defining logic and a protagonist who, rather than extending the sensory-motor schema through action, simply takes visual inventory of the film's world.

The structure of *Elephant* arrives at the direct image of time in slightly uncharacteristic fashion. With a series of prolonged steadicam sequences providing the basis of the narrative form, the film takes up where Orson Welles's deep focus photography or Yasujiro Ozu's extended takes left off. The subordination of time to movement is reversed by shifting the role of montage from an external force, such as the cut that governs the interrelations between images, to an internalized, intraframe relation between the various components of the mise-en-scène. However, the film's "external montage" is also a vital component of this shift. The chronological overlap of these sequences allows the film to repeat or recycle its events and thereby moves away from the logic of the sensory-motor schema toward intervals of discontinuity governed by pure time. As dramatized in *Rome, Open City*, the overarching consequence of this image of time is the foregrounding of the pure act of seeing.

Within this arrangement, it could be said that rather than reacting, the protagonist is acted upon, but only indirectly, as the performer
repeatedly eludes direct psychological or physical involvement in the
action he or she observes. In *Elephant,* this disconnect is rendered visually in the film's recurring composition in which the expression or reaction of the character is inaccessible because we see only the performers'
backs. However, the stoicism that characterizes the actors' performances
throughout the film informs us that regardless of the composition, such
a display is not to be found. This lack of expression is conferred upon
the identity of the characters themselves, who are barely distinguishable
from one another save for the strong primary color they wear (John =
yellow, Nathan = red, and so on).

In summary, the students of *Elephant* personify the "actor-medium"
of postwar cinema in that they are psychologically and physically separated from the action they observe and therefore similarly discourage the
kind of sensory-motor identification that the audience maintained with
the performer in the organic regime. By relinquishing agency, the students in turn break the chain of stimulus and response, choosing instead
to simply record with their gaze. Thus, the characters are seen "strolling,
rambling or wandering aimlessly," a condition Deleuze cites as defining
the pure optical and sound situation of neorealism (*Cinema 1* 120–21).

Despite this seemingly aimless wandering, a discernible narrative
structure emerges from the film's organization of time. This structure
works upon a series of overlapping sequences, which, with repeated
points of intersection, such as John posing for a photograph in the hallway or the circle of girls who ogle Nathan as he passes, comes to form an
extended loop whereby the action is repeated from multiple viewpoints.
We will first consider this loop in terms of its interaction of past and
present, a relationship I will refer to as "consumptive time," and then as
a revamping of the concept of "reciprocal vision" discussed in relation to
Rome, Open City.

The Loop as Consumptive Time

While Deleuze is openly hostile to the Lacanian foundation of contemporary cultural theory, I would like to briefly employ it here as a
means to illustrate a prominent conception of time in postmodernism, a
conception that will be reassessed in the course of our analysis. Lacan's
linguistic model of schizophrenia proposes that it is through the temporality of the sentence, specifically the interrelations of signifiers among
each other and to the whole, that we are in turn able to understand our

lived experience in cohesion. Thus, the failure to grasp language brings about a breakdown of the experience of time, whereby each moment is disconnected from any discernible whole. This chronological collapse grants an exaggerated significance to the moment, leaving the subject in a "perpetual present," which, according to Jameson, is not unlike that of the postmodern experience. In some sense, it is this lack of temporal integrity that grants the device of pastiche its apparent seamlessness so that the internal spectator of neorealism can metonymically substitute for the twenty-first-century protagonist without necessarily being anachronistic.

While a similar conception of time is being intimated by the structure of the loop in *Elephant,* this prospect takes an obsessive turn, and in this regard the phrasing of Jameson's concept may prove misleading for our purposes. As we will see, such a state of atemporality works not upon an expansion but a consumption of the here and now, which could more accurately be termed a "past present" (111–25).

Drawing on the work of Henri Bergson, Deleuze characterizes the past not as that which exists in our memory but rather as an entity in itself, composed of layers, levels, or pockets into which we enter through the act of remembering (*Cinema 2* 99). With this conception of the past, a possibility of redundancy exists whereby a single event can exist in more than one level, allowing time to expand beyond the "empirical succession of time: past-present-future" (xii). This process works upon a "forking of time" where once an occurrence takes place, time detaches itself from it and unfolds itself "instead of things unfolding within it" (Deleuze, *Difference and Repetition* 88).

Therefore, with the direct presentation of time comes paradox. Deleuze states, "[S]ince the past is constituted not after the present that it was but at the same time, time has to split itself in two at each moment as present and past"; in a sense, the present coexists with the past it will be (*Cinema 2* 81). In reconsidering Jameson's "perpetual present" in relation to *Elephant,* we can say the postmodern perception of such a process gives exaggerated importance to the present, but a particular component of that present, namely, the present-becoming-past. This unfolding of time then takes on a violent nature, becoming a consumptive force as the present is allocated to the past at the precise moment it comes to exist as present.

This consumptive quality of time is embodied in the film's picturesque opening and concluding shots. Here we see a menacingly accelerated sky where the present, once realized, is transported offscreen and consumed by layers of a nonchronological past, or as Deleuze refers to it, "the past in general."[11] In comparing the progression of sound in the film's introduction to that of its concluding scene, we find further evidence of this process. In the opening sequence, sound operates as a perfect "son-sign" as it reflects an undisturbed present. We hear only the casual ambiance of a playing field, despite the disturbed chronology implied by the image. However, in the concluding shot, we see the same accelerated sky accompanied by a rather incongruous mixture of Beethoven and synth music as if, through some violence performed upon the film, the two have become contemporary to one another. As one reviewer described the general feeling of the film, "It's as if something that had been built up with care and delicacy were swept away in a sudden unfeeling outburst" (O'Brien 39).

In this light, the structure of the loop reflects a condition of textuality comparable to the simulations constructed by the German bureaucracy in *Rome, Open City* in that, in both cases, images, words, and so forth serve to complicate the perception of the actual. As Jameson notes, in the realm of language, the inability to access the signified through a signifier leads to a certain obsessiveness in regard to the materiality of the signifier, as "when children repeat a word over and over again until its sense is lost and it becomes an incomprehensible incantation" ("Post-modernism" 120). Likewise, *Elephant* equates this disassociation with a certain peculiarity of time for which the loop is ideally suited. Specifically, through consumptive time, the loop slowly empties the frame by replacing the event with a recollection of the event, leaving only the husk of the image behind.

The ensuing emptiness of the frame in shots such as the vacant gymnasium, where we watch Michelle traverse its entirety with only the hum of the lights and ephemeral music, or the open practice fields return us again to the "any-space-whatever." In this context, these spaces "reap the consequences of a remarkable event" as if functioning as repositories of grief (Deleuze, *Cinema 2* 7). In his review of the film, Geoffrey O'Brien suggests a similar sentiment, stating that *Elephant* transforms the American high school into a "holy site." In a sense, the film functions as a form of ceremonial mourning for its own lost present, a presence that might have somehow allowed the tragedy to be averted or at least provide answers as to why it occurred in the first place.

Instead, the events of Columbine, despite their contemporariness, are allocated to the same Deleuzian continuum of undifferentiated past as the World War II references they evoke. When the two boys arrive at

Elephant (Gus
Van Sant, 2003)

the school, dressed in full combat gear and camouflage (a detail which,
in the context of a high school, would seem to contradict its original
purpose of allowing one to blend in), it is as if they had just stepped out
of the World War II documentary that they were watching only moments earlier and are both anachronistic and current. The same could be
said for much of the milieu of the film as we see break-dancers from the
1980s and punk rockers à la the late 1970s Sex Pistols coexisting alongside Shakespeare quotes and Beethoven sonatas. This curious mixture
alludes to the peculiar status of the present as coexisting with its own
past.

The Loop as Mirror and Reciprocity of Vision

In light of Deleuze's conception of time, perception and memory enter
into a unique relationship whereby every description or actuality gives
rise to a corresponding virtual image drawn from past memories. Deleuze refers to this process as one of becoming rather than being as each
time a virtual image is called up by an actual image, the object depicted
is reformed and created anew. This "double movement of liberation and
capture" (*Cinema 2* 68) of the image's two components constantly recy-
cles the image, so that description and its virtual counterpart repeatedly
replace the object.

In "subjective sequences" such as recollections and dreams, this fundamental circuit of the image is made visible, resulting in what Deleuze refers to as the "crystal image." The primary and most immediate means of bringing about such an image in the cinema is the mirror, which in its most pronounced instances, such as the palace of mirrors scene in the *Lady from Shanghai* (1947), allows for the complete indecipherability of the real and virtual (Deleuze, *Cinema 2* 68–70).

The points of intersection in *Elephant* in turn function as instances of this crystalline time, as a mirror of sorts. With the film's expanded duration this quality is perhaps not as immediately identifiable as that of an actual mirror, but if we remove these moments and place them side by side we see, in effect, a series of mirror images. This particular character of the loop, where the seer is subsequently seen by a seer who is subsequently seen by a seer and so on, continues what I referred to in the last section as neorealism's reciprocity of vision. However, while in *Rome, Open City* the realization of this dual quality of the gaze gives confirmation of the existence of both national and personal identities, in *Elephant* such instances are invariably comical and banal, making light of what might pose as truth.

It is here that we see most acutely the fundamental incompatibility of the time-image with notions of true and false. As dramatized in *Rome, Open City*, the organic regime implies a world based on causality, truth, totality, empiricism, and linearity; however, such associations bear little weight in light of pure time where the notion of truth is thrown into crisis by what Deleuze refers to as the "powers of the false." The word choice here may be a bit misleading, as the "powers of the false" does not represent untruth or a pluralism of truths or even a historicized and relative truth. Recalling that perception is characterized as a becoming rather than a being, an "objective illusion of indecipherability," it follows that within such a context the opposition of true and false simply no longer holds. As D. N. Rodowick explains, "Where the movement-image ideally conceives the relation between image and thought in the forms of identity and totality—an ever-expanding ontology—the time-image imagines the same relation as nonidentity: thought as deterritorialized and nomadic becoming, a creative act" (17). Within this understanding, the image therefore does not attest to a reality so much as it measures the power of thought of a given age.

We can now see that the power of falsification that the time-image in *Rome, Open City* granted the Italians relied on the presence of a fledgling or failed sensory-motor link, that is, the crisis of the action-image represented by the Germans. Since the counterfeit has no power to deceive outside the action-image, the completion of the regime of the optical image means the abandonment of notions of true and false. The witness then can only record the search for "truth" or causation as by necessity fruitless. Just as the on-screen "actor-medium" reflected the incomprehensibility of World War II, so does this new relationship attempt to replicate the film's central conceit: the impossibility of a totalizing explanation of the tragedy at Columbine.

However, such a conclusion would assume a perfect, ahistorical appropriation. What distinguishes *Elephant* from being a verbatim rehashing is of course the context into which it places such an image. The film's pastiche of the pure optical image does not simply replicate neorealism's attempts to represent an unfathomable reality with disconnected spaces governed by pure time; instead it forces a collision of postmodern time with such an image so that as the event of Columbine is no longer localizable in time, it leaves a hole of sorts, a palimpsest or memory of itself in which all that is discernible is the incessant and insatiable passing of time.

Notes

1. I am thinking here specifically of *Germany, Year Zero* (1947), *Stromboli* (1950), *Europe 51* (1952), and *Voyage in Italy* (1953), which, according to Deleuze, rather than representing a break with neorealism, as is usually alleged of the latter three, collectively comprise a perfection of the movement. See Deleuze, *Cinema 2*.
2. On April 20, 1999, Eric Harris and Dylan Klebold entered their high school in Littleton, Colorado, with automatic weapons and began firing. After killing twelve students and a teacher, the boys committed suicide in what was called the worst school shooting in U.S. history.
3. See Taubin.
4. Although discontinuous in nature, these spaces nonetheless represent movement-images in that they are governed by a logic based on the Major's movements and in this regard embody a subordination of time to movement.
5. My discussion of Baudrillard refers to, among others, *Simulacra and Simulation*.
6. Through the interval of the organic regime, the narrative space of a film comes to be defined by a cause-and-effect logic, the vehicle of which is the bodily action of the performer. However, the crisis of the action-image turns the interval toward the "irrational," so that

the construction of filmic space is no longer governed by movement but time. The result is empty, disconnected spaces that reflect the incomprehensibility of the postwar landscape. Deleuze often describes these "any-space-whatevers" as the embodiment of an impossible simultaneity, occupying both terms in binary opposition, such as the "deserted but inhabited" location (*Cinema 2* 8–9).

7. One way to understand the implications of this departure is through the genre of the time travel film. In discussing Alain Resnais' *Je t'aime Je t'aime* (1968), Rodowick refers to a phenomenon called the "the two body problem," which poses that, as a rule, the genre prohibits the encounter of past and present self. Underlying this convention is the notion of a "single consciousness" that exists independent of time and in turn an objective realm of the past, which protagonists can enter into while remaining conscious of their dislocation, i.e., without reverting to the consciousness they experienced at the time (115–18). In this context, the wipe represents a radical confrontation to such an understanding by positing a fluidity of consciousness that drives a nonchronological conception of time. As we will see, this conception of time comes to full fruition in *Elephant*.

8. I use the word "real" in quotes because it should be stated that as the time-image's conception of thought is one of becoming rather than being, it is in direct contradiction with the idea of an objective "truth" or a fixed "reality." This is dealt with in further detail later in the essay.

9. In particular, see Berkeley, *A Treatise* pt. 1, treatise 3.

10. In this piece Bordwell enumerates the defining characteristics of the art film and in the process traces a schema of development between the genre and classical cinema that bears an uncanny similarity to that of Deleuze ("The Art Cinema" 716–24).

11. See Deleuze, *Bergsonism* 51–72.

Chapter 12

Neorealism and Contemporary European Immigration

Laura E. Ruberto

In the second half of the twentieth century, Europe—geopolitically speaking, at least—saw its national boundaries become porous. The development of the European Union formally inaugurated in certain regards the continent's relatively new status as a destination for immigrants as opposed to a departure point for emigrants. The cultural ramifications of Europe's change are many, not the least of which are a number of films from the late twentieth century that represent in varying ways the contemporary history of immigration to Europe. Neorealism has come to have its own particular relationship to some of these films. Looking generally at what I call European "immigration films" from the 1990s, and more specifically at Gianni Amelio's *Lamerica* (1994, Italy/Albania) and Luc and Jean-Pierre Dardenne's *La promesse* (1996, Belgium), we see how the style of postwar Italian neorealism has been adapted and molded to late twentieth-century immigration concerns to create a cinematic expression that reflects the distinctiveness of a more culturally varied Europe.

Both films have influences that go well beyond Italian neorealism; however, they likewise take advantage of certain stylistic and technical choices that evoke the form and sensibility of post–World War II neorealist films. For example, the use at different times of improvisational scripts, nonprofessional actors, on-location shooting, and diegetic sound cinematically mimics neorealist films. Moreover, the gender roles in the films, in particular the development of characters whose relationship can be described as a male-male bond, so common in the postwar Italian examples, further link them to neorealism. Perhaps most notably, an over-

242

all sensibility evoked in the films—in great part due to their thematic emphasis on the plight of the downtrodden—marks a final association with neorealism, a loose genre that emphasized depictions of the everyday lives of the working class. Such immigration films, when seen through the lens of Italian postwar neorealist films, point to the ways in which film can "stir up emotions and indignation" in viewers, as Cesare Zavattini, often called the theorist of neorealism, once said in regard to Italian cinema (in Overbey 67–68).

The last decade of the twentieth century offers us myriad films produced within both Eastern and Western Europe that direct attention to the global movement of people. More specifically, these films address immigration to Western Europe, in particular immigration from Eastern Europe and Africa (although immigrants arrive to Europe from all parts of the globe). In so doing, the films comment on the role reversal Europe has undergone over the past one hundred years or so—from Old World to a new New World. By calling attention to this shift in status, such films recognize Western Europe's cultural presence within the process of globalization.

Statistics concerning the number and nation of origin of immigrants to Europe are nearly impossible to stabilize, mainly because of the large volume of clandestine movement and the now open borders between European Union countries. Generalizations about European migration and contemporary culture are also difficult to establish because the receiving countries have such diverse histories when it comes to issues of colonialism, imperialism, and emigration—all of which create different kinds of pressures regarding what might push or pull people to adopt any one particular country. We know that the case, for instance, of Algerians in France is one informed by a history of colonialism, war, and civil strife, while that of Algerians in Italy has a less directly contestatory, though perhaps no less complex, history. Similarly, although Europe as a whole has a long history of emigration of its own people, each country has a unique relationship to emigration. Mediterranean countries, such as Italy and Greece, central and eastern countries, such as the Czech Republic or Poland, and northern countries, such as Ireland, have had the highest rates of emigration. In the case of Italy, for instance, it was not until the mid-1970s that the number of people immigrating to Italy outnumbered the number of Italians who emigrated.

The 1990s European immigration films differ considerably in their style and sensibility—from the dramatic *La haine* (Mathieu Kassovitz, France, 1995) to the satirical *We Free Kings* (Sergio Citti, Italy, 1996).[1]

Suggesting a thematic connection, or even a loose genre, however, allows us to understand better how the cultural productions of a developing political state, that is, the European Union (affected greatly by the fall of communism, the continued global power of the United States, and its own growth as a federation of nations), reflect that state's apprehensions, problems, and potential. In other words, by connecting films around the theme of immigration, we can better imagine such cinematic cultural productions as a reflection of Europe's new role as it takes shape at the beginning of the twenty-first century.

In addition to theorizing these films as linked by immigration within a context of globalization, they are further linked through their insistence on a neorealist style, that is, a filmic mode of expression that makes use of certain traits of Italian neorealist films of the post–World War II era, while at the same time applying those traits, in whatever way is most useful, to the contemporary moment. By exploring contemporary European cinema in relation to Italian neorealism we might more productively uncover the relationship between cultural expressions and globalization, a point raised in other essays in this volume. Implicit in my intervention is a conception of neorealism that stretches well beyond the period of 1945–52.[2] A simple definition of neorealism does not suggest itself readily, especially since films designated as such were never part of an organized artistic movement but seen more as a style of filmmaking that developed in post–World War II Italy in reaction to the aesthetics and politics of Hollywood imports and the strict dogma of Fascism. Films marked as neorealist often share certain stylistic traits as well as a political agenda invested in exploring (and on occasion offering solutions to) social problems of the contemporary moment. In fact, Italian neorealist films—from Roberto Rossellini's *Rome, Open City* (1945) to Alberto Lattuada's lesser-known *Il mulino del Po* (*The Mill on the River Po;* 1948)—in essence do not always share much in the way of style. This apparent contradiction within films called neorealist has been discussed in depth by many (Millicent Marcus, Peter Bondanella, and Gian Piero Brunetta, to name three). While certain technical characteristics remain somewhat consistent throughout many neorealist films (nonprofessional actors, on-location shooting, diegetic sound, and a reflection of the contemporary moment), the more reliable marker perhaps is a mood or tone produced through such films. It is this mood, however resilient to definition, that has repeatedly helped critics decide which films to locate within the boundaries of the neorealist tradition. If we accept such a claim, even many Italian films produced well after 1952 can be seen as neorealist in nature. Films such as Pier Paolo Pasolini's *Mamma Roma* (1962), Gillo Pontecorvo's *The Battle of Algiers* (1965), Vittorio De Sica's *Two Women* (*La ciociara;* 1960), or Silvio Siano's *La donnaccia* (1963), all made by Italian directors in the 1960s, share with the earlier neorealist films an atmosphere of gritty realism created by, among other elements, on-location shooting and improvised, simple scripts. This emphasis on a neorealist sensibility, or, more simple still, a neorealist style, has the ability to link diverse films through their power to "stir up emotions and indignation" in viewers.[3] Correspondingly, films produced well beyond Italy and well after 1952 can be understood under the rubric of neorealism. Films that explicitly call attention to an association with neorealism include Eddie Romero's *Manila: Open City* (1986, the Philippines) and Lisandro Duque Naranjo's *Miracle in Rome* (1988, Colombia), and films with a less direct correlation include Jafar Panahi's *The White Balloon* (1995, Iran) and Satyajit Ray's *Pather Panchali* (1955, India).[4]

Examining contemporary European films in the light of neorealism allows us then to consider how they use a neorealist style to communicate ideas about the status of the immigrant in late twentieth-century European culture. This stylistic choice entails an inevitable number of limitations but at the same time affords its maker a clear mode of expression. Through their insistence on a neorealist sensibility such films create narratives sympathetic to the plight of immigrants and seem invested in improving race relations in Europe. Through the use of a neorealist style, they have the potential to recapture the progressive effects of that loose "genre."

The two films under discussion here— *Lamerica* and *La promesse*— consider migration to Western Europe through the perspective mainly of Western Europeans (in both cases, young, single men). Amelio's 1994 film was inspired by a factual story, whereas the Dardennes' 1996 film is straight fiction that comes across as plausible. Each director's treatment of contemporary migration illustrates aspects of Europe's continual struggle to balance its changed role as a New World. In *Lamerica*, neorealist elements are brought into contact with 1960s-era aesthetics. This highly stylized choice creates a visually striking and socially conscious narrative. In *La promesse*, neorealism and a more straightforward observational documentary style merge to create a film with a clear political message of tolerance and diversity. Amelio has explicitly discussed the influence of neorealist classics on his work; the Dardennes' neorealist style instead seems to have come indirectly via their documentary background.

Amelio's representation of immigrants, while bordering on senti-
mentality, attempts to move beyond a simple binary of immigrants and
non-immigrants (i.e., Western vs. non-Western, modern vs. traditional).
Amelio's insistence on a kind of contemporary neorealism—through
certain production and stylistic choices, the plot, and the overall atmosphere of the film—produces a representation of immigration that
encourages (presumably Western) audiences to evaluate more seriously
their role in the so-called immigration problem in contemporary Europe. The Dardennes' film similarly communicates a feeling of action.
The perspective of *La promesse*, in great part that of a young Belgian boy
(Igor), suggests a Western-identified viewer. Igor's criminal lifestyle is
by no means intended to reflect the common viewer's perspective. However, the film does implicate its viewers in the native Belgians' anti-im-
migrant prejudices to turn our sympathies wholeheartedly toward the
immigrants' troubles.

In addition, both films make use of the charged all-male relationships so common in postwar neorealist films. Neorealist films tended to
centralize relationships between men or boys—this arrangement emphasized the role of men and masculinity in postwar Italy with little
regard for women and femininity.[5] Despite the fact that both films have
a male-male bond that creates an association with the neorealist style,
La promesse modifies this relationship by the end of the narrative. This
retooled gendered relationship allows the film to function as a new reflection of a tolerant, diverse, contemporary Europe.

Gender and Neorealism

As I have argued, Italian neorealism includes a little talked about tendency to rely on what can be called a male-male bond, usually with at
least one young boy involved and always at the expense of positive representations of female characters.[6] This relationship is especially apparent in
works by Rossellini, De Sica, and Luchino Visconti—the three directors
Peter Bondanella calls the "masters of neorealism" (*Italian Cinema* 31).
In the two films under discussion, similar relationships exist. In *Lamerica*
we see a male-male relationship develop around Gino and Spiro/Mi-
chele, one that moves from a *Bicycle Thief*-like relationship in which the
son takes care of the father to a conventional father-son relationship in
which the older man shows the younger one the way, figuratively speaking. *La promesse* begins with an equally central father-son pair (Roger
and Igor), but by the end breaks with the male-male paradigm by por-

Bicycle Thief (Vittorio De Sica, 1948)

traying a burgeoning, platonic relationship between the young Belgian, Igor, and the immigrant woman from Burkina Faso, Assista.[7] By showing the promise of a cross-cultural friendship in the shape of a platonic male-female relationship, *La promesse* suggests the possibility of a future Europe open to difference, in the realm of both culture and gender.

Although many classic neorealist films include female characters, they are more often than not relegated to a marginal role of mother, girlfriend, prostitute, or evil seductress. When a female character manages to be both a realistic representation of a woman and central to the plot, such as Pina in Rossellini's *Rome, Open City*, the character is rarely allowed to live to see the closing credits. Antonio Vitti alludes to this tendency in neorealism when he discusses Giuseppe De Santis's 1953 *Un marito per Anna Zaccheo* (*A Husband for Anna Zaccheo*) (a film generally unavailable and unknown to critics, and one that overtly questions the social limitations placed on Italian women): "Women were present in Italian neorealist films, and even in the comedies, in specific roles: as wives and mothers; as the remorseful victims of sexual temptation; or as persecuted temptresses and martyrs sacrificed in the name of family

247

honor. Anna Zaccheo's character confirms De Santis's concern with the female social role, a theme he had already addressed in *Riso amaro, Non c'è pace fra gli ulivi,* and *Roma, Ore 11"* (*Giuseppe de Santis* 74). In place of the kind of female characters for which De Santis is well known, most Italian neorealist films emphasize male roles, especially within a male-male relationship.

A number of neorealist films focus their attention on relationships between two men—more often than not in a father-son relationship. A quick review gives us Francesco and Marcello in *Rome, Open City,* Giuseppe and Pasquale in De Sica's *Shoeshine* (1946), and Bruno and Antonio in De Sica's *Bicycle Thief* (1948). Rossellini's *Germany, Year Zero* (1947) has a contorted version of the male-male bond, between Edmund and his former schoolteacher, Herr Enning, who has pedophilic tendencies—here the relationship causes only tragedy. Rossellini's *Paisà* (1946) at first seems to go against the model, since the characters in the six separate vignettes form a collective protagonist. It begins with a strong, independent Sicilian woman, Carmella, but she follows in the footsteps of *Rome, Open City's* Pina and is killed by soldiers. The second vignette fits the male-male bond paradigm with Joe from Jersey, an African American G.I. who forms a disturbing and touching relationship with a Neapolitan boy, Pasquale. The only remaining female characters in the film are both victims of the war. Francesca is forced into prostitution and thus loses her chance for love and happiness, while Harriet, the U.S. partisan nurse, also loses her chance at love when she survives German gunfire only to find that her partisan lover, Lupo, has been shot to death. Visconti's *The Earth Trembles,* oft-cited as the most neorealist of neorealist films, differs from the preceding films in that the entire Valastros family is in many ways the protagonist of the film, and there is no clear male-male bond.[8] However, Visconti foregrounds one character, Antonio, and his relationship with his brothers and sisters. In De Sica's *Umberto D* (1952), considered by many the last neorealist film, the narrative focuses on the retired Umberto and his tragic, solitary life. Although the film counterposes Umberto's situation with that of his landlady and the domestic servant, Maria, the emphasis remains on the old man.[9] Even if he shares some of Maria's problems, he seems to find real friendship only in his dog, Flick. Indeed, "the old man and his dog" can be seen as a version of the male-male bond, and, in fact, it has been compared to the visual image of an earlier De Sica pair, Antonio and Bruno from *Bicycle Thief* (see Bondanella, *Italian Cinema* 64).

Thus the trend in Italian neorealist films to emphasize a relationship between men, often in a kind of parent-child relationship, underscores a

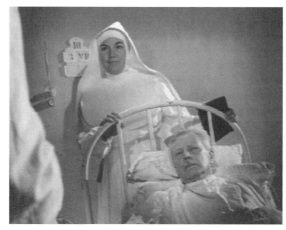

Umberto D
(Vittorio De Sica,
1952)

public role for men as producers of their society—men, boys, and masculinity generally become that on which a country depends for rebuilding itself after war. Likewise, women, girls, and femininity generally remain secondary actors in the building of that same society.

Lamerica

Though not unproblematic in its representation of immigrants (in this case Albanians), *Lamerica* approaches the theme of migration and Europe dialectically. The film takes place in 1991 in Albania, though in many ways it is more about Italy than Albania. It begins with a reminder from the past: newsreel footage of Mussolini's 1939 invasion of Albania and the Fascist dictator's plans to colonize the country. Thus, from the very beginning, Amelio historicizes and contextualizes the east. After World War II, Albania became part of the Soviet bloc until the government overthrow in 1991. With the borders open, Albanians began leaving in droves: in 1991, 40,000 Albanians went to Italy. In August of that year, within a single forty-eight-hour period, 20,000 refugees reached Italian waters, most without identification papers. In that two-day period Italian authorities turned away a large ship with Albanian refugees literally hanging from it. The front-page newspaper photos of the ship shocked people around the world, and soon a photo of the ship made its way into a Benneton advertisement. Amelio was inspired by this series of events.[10]

The film documents Albanians leaving at the same time as foreign investors are arriving to take advantage of the new capitalist system. It is an extremely stylized narrative, and yet its theme remains a charged reflection on contemporary Italy, migration, and the role of history in understanding the plight of contemporary immigrants. In particular, Amelio refers to two historical events to contextualize the narrative: Mussolini's 1939 invasion of Albania is paralleled with Italian capitalists' 1991 invasion of post-communist Albania, and Albanians' desire to immigrate to Italy is paralleled with (mainly southern) Italians' wish to immigrate to the Americas throughout the first half of the twentieth century. Amelio, who taught film production for years before turning to directing, has been repeatedly connected to what is sometimes called "a neo-neorealism" within Italian cinema. Vitti, among other film scholars, notes this "current" within contemporary Italian cinema: "La corrente più impegnata del nuovo cinema italiano è stata definita neo-neorealista" ([T]he most engaged current in the newest Italian cinema has been defined as neo-neorealist); he places Amelio at the top of the list of directors producing such works ("Albanitaliamerica" 259).[11] Amelio's brand of neorealism, however, is a combination of two different moments in Italian cinema history. He has openly discussed the two major influences on his work: Michelangelo Antonioni and De Sica. The De Sica influence is what gives Amelio's film a neorealist feel, one similar to *Bicycle Thief* or *Umberto D.* Antonioni, meanwhile, remembered for such films as *Red Desert* (1964) or *Zabriskie Point* (1970) inspires some of Amelio's aesthetic choices, such as his use of environment as a reflection of the state of a character's mind, or his use of cinemascope.[12] Together these two styles create a cinema that diverges from each original style and yet uses those styles for a determined purpose. Neither style is merely resurfacing on the cinematic landscape but being refashioned for a particular purpose.

The film's story revolves around a well-choreographed mistaken identity plot, in which a young Italian businessman, Gino, in Albania loses his Italian passport and must travel with Albanians on a ship and attempt to reenter Italy, effectively as an Albanian without identification papers. Gino and a colleague had gone to Albania to set up a shell company through which to launder money. They name a man who has been in a gulag for fifty years as their puppet CEO. As fate would have it, the man, Spiro, is actually Italian (named Michele)—he went to Albania with Mussolini's army, was imprisoned, and never returned to Italy. Gino and Spiro eventually journey back to Italy together. Through Gino's relationship with Spiro and his time in Albania he symbolically (and quite literally at times) recovers a history of Italian immigration and Italy's involvement abroad that contemporary Italians have forgotten. Gino comes to represent the generation that stayed behind—a generation that does not have a personal memory of or personal connection to Italy's past emigration.

Throughout much of the film Spiro is confused. His memory has stopped at age twenty, and he thinks he is preparing to immigrate to America, not back to Italy. His confusion is represented in the film's title—*Lamerica*, misspelled without an apostrophe after the *L* to exemplify Italy's past emigrants' illiteracy and Italy's new immigrants' conception of Italy as their America. Gino and Spiro develop a neorealist-style father-son relationship, and women are nearly absent from the narrative. (Although Spiro repeatedly talks about his wife, Rosa, back in Sicily, she remains offscreen as a forty-year-old memory.) The two main characters, Spiro and Gino, each take turns in the role of father and son—one picking up slack for the other at his neediest moment.

The film's reliance on nonprofessional actors (Spiro and the secondary characters are nonprofessional actors, either Albanian or Italian), reflection on contemporary life, and insistence on a kind of real-time effect also illustrate a link with neorealism. Furthermore, Vitti argues that the film is neorealistic in its images that are "totalmente diverso da quelle hollywoodiane" (totally different than those from Hollywood) ("Albanitaliamerica" 250). The on-location shooting, a slow-moving camera that pans across the ravished countryside and cities, and the many scenes in which editing choices encourage us to be patient and experience the moment in quasi-real time all point to an anti-Hollywood approach to filmmaking. To attain a more stylized expression, Amelio turns to another Italian director, Antonioni. Perhaps the best place to observe his debt to Antonioni is in the sequences outside the capital, Tirana. His expansive shots of desert-like landscapes and of people standing against barren, muted colors evoke similar shots from a film like Antonioni's *Red Desert*. Amelio takes Antonioni's photographic-like stills (long shots and close-ups against desolate backdrops) and adds certain thematic and technical qualities of neorealism.

The point at which Gino loses his Suzuki jeep is in essence the beginning of his transition from Italian to Albanian—his transition into an immigrant. At this point Gino's personal story comes through to us as a self-reflective "everyman's" story (another incidental link to De Sica's films and neorealism generally). Throughout the film Amelio uses consumer products and props to emphasize Gino's transition to pure humanity—a humanity that reflects a kind of old-fashioned liberal humanism. His expensive foreign car is stripped and his tires stolen, literally stripping him of his Italian bourgeois identity.[13]

Like the Albanians around him, Gino is forced to ride a crowded bus and later hitch a ride on the back of a truck. At first he continues to claim his difference by repeatedly affirming his Italian national identity. Eventually, he loses other props—his sunglasses, his stylish Italian clothing, and his clean-shaven face. By the next morning he is sleeping in a makeshift hostel, happy for the piece of stale bread and milk Spiro obtained for him. His transition to immigrant is complete when the police refuse to return his passport to him: "But in Albania, we are all, all without papers," the police chief tells him. This comment solidifies Gino's transition. And, when a few scenes later he is on a boat with Spiro and other Albanians hoping to make it to Italy, Gino has indisputably changed.

On the boat to Italy, Amelio comments plainly on the relationship between Albanians and Italians. The film verges on being too heavy-handed here (a critique sometimes brought against neorealist films as well). The closing shots of the multitudes are a final link to De Sica's meditations on working-class lives, reminiscent of, for instance, the pans of linen, bicycles, and other personal goods at the pawnshop in an early sequence of *Bicycle Thief*.[14] Throughout the film, and particularly in the final scene, Amelio's use of close-ups creates a kind of study of the immigrants' faces, a move that could lead one to accuse him of exoticizing the immigrants. This representation potentially exploits the characters, and yet the film's purpose seems more honorable, we might say, to the extent that political sympathy is the goal. Further, returning to Vitti's idea that Amelio's use of cinemascope helps avoid a cinematic colonization is yet another way to read these closing shots. Seeing the film as working within a kind of language of neorealism—rearticulated with a contemporary, Antonioni-esque accent—demonstrates one way contemporary immigration films use neorealism to express their own cultural ideas. The neorealist call to emotional action of which Zavattini spoke echoes plainly in Amelio's film, and viewers are urged to feel implicated in the story of globalization unfolding on the screen.

La promesse

If *Lamerica* evokes a documentary style only to challenge it by a kind of extra-stylized realism, Luc and Jean-Pierre Dardenne's *La promesse* embraces the documentary wholesale. Made in 1996 by two seasoned

Belgian documentarians, the film could easily be called an example of a fictionalized observational documentary. In line with an observational documentary, the film follows a kind of cinema verité style: it covers everyday occurrences that follow a logical chronology and has no flashbacks or historical images. Further, the use of handheld cameras, close-ups, and unobtrusive, diegetic music (popular European and world music beats), and the lack of any voice-over narration suggests other connections to both observational documentaries and cinema verité. These technical choices offer the film an immediacy of feeling, that is, a present-tense feel for the events, and are surprisingly similar to elements found in classic neorealist films. Moreover, cinema verité itself (through its emphasis on documenting an "unmediated" realism) shares much in common with neorealism, creating another association between *La promesse* and neorealism.[15] Thus, once again we see neorealism being put to use strategically in relation to the theme of late twentieth-century immigration and the working poor.

The film's simple plot involves Roger and his teenage son, Igor, father and son landlords, who set up a slum apartment for immigrants in an industrial area near Liege, Belgium. The dilapidated apartment building houses immigrants from Korea, Romania, Ghana, Turkey, and Burkina Faso. Roger and Igor also supply the immigrants with false papers, hire them to do construction work under poor conditions, and frequently turn in undocumented workers to officials (to keep the police off their backs).

Similar to *Lamerica,* the film is in effect more about Western Europeans than immigrants. Like Gino in Amelio's immigration film, Igor has a kind of consciousness-raising experience, in this case through his relationship with immigrants. The style of the film encourages viewers to identify somewhat with Igor's transition and to recognize their own prejudices within his extreme ones. Igor is pulled on the one hand by his desire to please his father and on the other by his own growing sense of the importance of human dignity. That Igor is a conflicted youth is clear from the beginning. One moment he steals from an elderly woman, the next he plays with his go-cart innocently with neighborhood friends. By the end Igor realizes that his sympathies should lie with people in need, not his greedy father.

Igor is his father's helper and accomplice. Early in the film, Hamidou, an immigrant from Burkina Faso, falls from a scaffolding at a construction site where he is working illegally for Roger. When Igor finds him, Hamidou, sensing his own death, makes Igor promise to take care of his wife, Assista, and their infant son. Igor agrees, comforts Hamidou, and attempts to bring him to the hospital. Roger, however, interferes and insists that he and Igor, in effect, bury Hamidou alive in concrete and garbage, refuse to tell either the authorities or Assista about Hamidou's death, and continue their illicit business practices. By burying him alive in the construction debris, the characters create a symbol of immigrants' status in Belgium: the immigrant in Belgium is a permanent part of the structure and foundation of contemporary Europe, one that can be ignored or hurt but will nonetheless leave his or her imprint.

Igor's conscience gets the best of him and he begins to find ways to help Assista and her child. Simultaneously, Roger, who is increasingly revealed as a pedophilic father figure rather than a loving one, becomes more arrogant and spiteful. The differences between the two characters neatly set up Igor's struggle to find his own voice, his own way of living in contemporary Belgium. The film begins with what appears to be a typical neorealist father-son relationship, one that quickly spirals toward a perverse version of that bond. Roger abuses Igor, beating him when Igor gives Assista money, for example. At other times, a calmer Roger almost coddles and overprotects Igor, acts bordering on pedophilia, or at least unhealthy behavior. For instance, a shower scene in which Roger helps Igor wash mud off his legs and feet—shot with a handheld camera and lots of close-ups of unclothed flesh—has a soft-porn effect. At another moment Roger gives Igor a crude tattoo that matches his own. This painful rite of passage comes across as both a touching moment between father and son and an unsettling one, as we understand this scarring as Roger's way to maintain control of his son; he needs Igor to remain faithful to him and his business. Indeed, Roger and Igor's male-male bond most closely resembles the neorealist pair of Edmund and Herr Enning in Rossellini's *Germany, Year Zero:* both begin innocently enough but quickly come across to viewers as based too much on an unbalanced power dynamic and unbridled desires, and both end with disturbing consequences.

If Gino's consciousness-raising occurs in great part through the gradual disappearance of material goods, Igor's occurs as he increasingly realizes that his father lacks human decency and has no respect for human life. The turning point for Igor comes when he learns that Roger framed Assista in order to sell her into prostitution. When Igor helps Assista run away, the male-male, father-son union is irreparably broken. While Assista is rightfully slow to trust Igor, eventually a new gendered paradigm forms. By the end a contemporary version of the male-male relationship has developed, but it is a cross-cultural and cross-gendered one. This new relationship is reminiscent of past neorealist bonds, but it is retooled for a contemporary purpose, thus showing the malleability of neorealism's style.

In the closing scene, Igor tells Assista that Hamidou is dead. The scene highlights the film's use of a neorealist style in several ways. The only sounds are the buzz of the fluorescent lights in the train station's underground walkway and muffled sounds from above. The tunneled walkway is empty except for Igor and Assista. The camera pulls back, not imposing on the pair, but panning back and forth between the two of them (keeping them visually, and thus emotionally, separated, though they stand only a few inches apart from one another). Assista silently walks offscreen, leaving Igor momentarily alone, until he runs after her. The camera stays on their backs as they walk toward the station's exit, away from the camera. They are alone but have each other. Words are unnecessary here. Their future is unknown both to us and to them, but a new alliance has been formed. The film ends solemnly by placing hope in this new alliance, a scene visually similar to the end of De Sica's *Bicycle Thief* in which Antonio and Bruno hold hands and move silently through the crowded streets. Like Antonio and Bruno, Igor and Assista's future is unknown, but their recently formed friendship is not. Through neorealist characteristics, the Dardenne brothers produce an image of a diverse European landscape, where a somber but genuine hope for unity can thrive.

A Few Concluding Remarks

Immigration films such as *Lamerica* and *La promesse* illustrate how a broader understanding of neorealism, now outside the confines of its original historical and cultural locations, can be further linked to socially conscious cinematic art. Neorealism here adjusts to meet previously unseen challenges. Its style is not only serviceable for a specific time and space but can transcend its original design. Furthermore, the films show us how the theme of contemporary immigration to Europe can be portrayed critically so that viewers may be encouraged to question their own perspective. Creating a link between 1940s-era and 1990s-era socially engaged films enhances our ability to recognize both groups' emphasis on promoting social change through art.

Before his untimely death in 1940 Walter Benjamin wrote an essay titled "Discussions on Collectivity in Art Generally," in which he reflects on the relatively new art form of cinema. He understands the movies as having a revolutionary potential in that they can be seen as an art form specifically made for the people. In particular, he is fascinated by Sergei Eisenstein's 1925 *The Battleship Potemkin*, which he recognizes as a film that creates a realistic and moving picture of the power of a group of people in light of state control and violence. While I will not presently make a case for a link between Eisenstein's films and neorealism (although I think such a comparison could rather easily be drawn), Benjamin's words nicely echo the sentiments of both Italian neorealist cinema and the two films I have analyzed here. Cinema, he asserts, is the only cultural location where "today's man can observe his immediate world and surroundings, the locales where he lives . . . [and can do so] in a way that makes his life intelligible, meaningful" ("Discussioni" 196). It is this meaningfulness that is likewise expressed in the classic Italian neorealist films and reprised in many of the 1990s European immigration films. Neorealism then can be seen to thrive, evolving as it is used, all the while retaining some of its original form.

Notes

1. In addition to the films just mentioned, we could add Bernardo Bertolucci's *Besieged* (1998), Carlo Mazzacurati's *Vesna va veloce* (1996), Merzak Allouache's *Salut Cousin!* (1996), Yuksel Yavus's *April Children* (1998), Thomas Arslan's *Dealer* (1999), Christophe Ruggia's *Le Gone du Chaaba* (1998), Krzystof Kieslowski's triad *Red* (1994), *White* (1993), and *Blue* (1994), Milcho Manchevski's *Before the Rain* (1994), and Xavier Koller's *Journey of Hope* (1990). Outside Europe, but also from the 1990s, we might think of such films as David Riker's *La ciudad* (1998) and Walter Salles's *Central Station* (1998) as similarly fitting the theme of immigration within the context of globalization.

2. Neorealism is conventionally marked as originating with Rossellini's *Rome, Open City* in 1945 and coming to an end with De Sica's *Umberto D* in 1952.

3. It should be noted that neorealism has often been criticized for clarifying social problems but not offering explicit ideas for fixing them. For example, Fernando Solanas and Octavio Getino, Argentine filmmakers and theorists known for Tercer Cine (the Third Cinema movement), see such limitations in Italian neorealist films. One could argue, though, that action from viewers can occur only if the film moves them or, to bring up the specter of Zavattini yet again, if a film stirs them up (see Armes, *Third World Filmmaking*, for the connection

256

between Solanas and Getino and neorealism). See also Overbey (10) for a discussion of neorealism's failure to create action in viewers. Editors' note: see the introduction of this volume for further discussion of Third Cinema and neorealism.

4. Editors' note: *Miracle in Rome* and *Pather Panchali* are discussed at length elsewhere in this volume.

5. Such a structure reinforces the idea that after World War II women were unimportant to the society that many of them had helped liberate from Fascism, an idea that has been addressed in depth by feminist thinkers and artists since liberation. For example, the Milan Women's Bookstore Collective concludes,

> One sees that numerous women have often participated alongside men in the great human quests for freedom, and have taken liberties for themselves which, however, they did not know how to keep after the quest, as far as the men were concerned, had ended. We think of the women who took part in the Italian Resistance or in the struggle for Algerian Liberation, as if defying the Nazis and Fascists or the torturers of the OAS were an easier thing to do than questioning the family hierarchy or changing the process of holding a political meeting. (140)

6. This discussion of gender and neorealism appears in a slightly different form in Ruberto, where the focus is on Giuseppe De Santis's 1949 film *Riso amaro* (*Bitter Rice*). See Haskell for a discussion of the male buddy film as a cinematic trend.

7. One of Amelio's other neorealist-inspired films, *Il ladro di bambini* (*Stolen Children;* 1992) recalls neorealism in its thematics, not to mention its title, and, similar to *La promesse,* manages to expand the male-male bond (in this case between Antonio and Luciano) to include a young woman (Rosetta).

8. See Bondanella, *Italian Cinema* or Brunetta for discussions of *The Earth Trembles* as a benchmark neorealist film.

9. Editors' note: see Wilson's essay in this volume for further considerations of *Umberto D.*

10. See Amelio on the making of the film for more information.

11. Unless otherwise noted, all translations are my own.

12. Vitti, rather idiosyncratically, suggests that Amelio's use of cinemascope removes the films from a documentary-like work and places it squarely within an artistic cinematic style. In so doing, the film calls attention to its own filmic qualities, moving away from a possibility of a kind of cultural imperialism on Amelio's part: "La scelta del cinemascope, invece di un'immagine naturalista, per dare al film una

dimenzione epica mostra le sue apprensioni e la sua onestà artistica. Il regista non voleva nascondere il fatto che stavano girando un film e non un documentario sui profughi albanesi" (The choice of cinemascope to give the film an epic dimension, instead of using a more naturalistic cinematic view, shows his [Amelio's] apprehensions and his artistic honesty. The director did not want to hide the fact that he was filming a movie and not a documentary on Albanian refugees) ("Albanitaliamerica" 260).

13. One should note the obvious irony in having Gino drive a jeep with a Bari license plate; Bari is the port city of entrance for most Albanian immigrants.

14. The reference to contemporary working-class identities in *Lamerica* is easily compared to a visually similar conclusion in another contemporary European film, the French film *Dream Life of Angels* (Erick Zonca, 1998). The film ends with a series of close-ups of factory workers, none of whom appear to be immigrants—an odd erasure of France's colonial past and present immigrant community. Such absence of cultural diversity in a contemporary film about the European underclasses seems particularly stark in relation to films such as *Lamerica* or *La promesse*.

15. See Thompson and Bordwell (531–34) for a brief discussion of the relationship between cinema verité and neorealism.

Chapter 13

'O Cuorp' 'e Napule:
Naples and the Cinematographic Body of Culture

Pasquale Verdicchio

A favorite stop on the itinerary of Grand Tourists, the city of Napoli
(Naples) was hailed as "one of the fayrest citees of the worlde" by William Thomas in 1549, in the first English book on Italy. The vagaries
and vicissitudes of vogue and taste were eventually to turn in Naples'
disfavor. Charles Dickens, who visited the city in 1845, seems not to
have retained a single pleasant recollection of it. The author observes
in his Italian travelogue, *American Notes and Pictures from Italy* (1846),
that "lovers and hunters of the picturesque [should] not keep too studi-
ously out of view the miserable depravity, degradation, and wretchedness
with which this gay Neapolitan life is inseparably associated," and further points to the "filth and the universal degradation" of the city by the
sea (413). John Ruskin, in his eagerness to praise the northern art and
architecture that he preferred, did not hesitate to make public his con-
tempt for Naples ("certainly the most disgusting place in Europe") and
its inhabitants known ("the most loathsome nest of human caterpillars
I was ever forced to stay in") (in Chaney 145). These sentiments affected
a degradation of the city's reputation that remained almost unchanged
until recent times. The qualities that had once made Naples a respected
if curious city became the very reasons by which it was eventually deni-
grated (Chaney 144–47). Film is a medium in which the south has been
particularly present within specific discursive parameters. In the following pages I will engage the reemergence of Naples as a sensuous and
active cinematic city. In its self-directed and regionally situated position,
which is inextricably tied to space (geographical, social, and cultural)
and the opportunity for expression, Neapolitan cinema undeniably also

functions nationally. It is in fact in film, the subject of this piece, that the strongest tension and engagement of issues has been established and pronounced, a contrast to the more homologous and apathetic national film products. The cinematographic horizon includes many more names than I can deal with here; I will discuss in a limited fashion the work of the Neapolitan filmmakers Pappi Corsicato, Antonio Capuano, and Mario Martone, all three extraordinary examples of an engaged, socially based cultural revolution. Their social engagement parallels that of the old neorealists' assumption of social responsibility through film. The poverty of resources with which this new generation had to contend and the political ends of their films also can be traced to that earlier group. Corsicato, Capuano, and Martone constitute what I like to refer to as the children of neorealism. That is to say, their visual vocabulary and social vision have been formed in part by and through neorealist film, in addition to which their very lives and the places they inhabit were in the past the subjects of neorealist representation.

Naples and "Porosity"

Among others, Walter Benjamin and Asja Lacis seemed to appreciate aspects of the city that made it a place of contradictions. In their essay "Naples," now collected in *Napoli*, they chose to describe the elusive character of the place by way of the term "porous." Though porous may indeed define the nature of the stone used in some Neapolitan architecture, the authors also intimate that the city's porosity "results not only from the indolence of the southern artisan but also above all from the passion for improvisation, which demands that space and opportunity be at any price preserved" (34, 39). Benjamin's description develops around the adaptability of the Neapolitan population and its less than "civilized" existence. In general terms, Benjamin does little to go beyond the usual descriptions and commonplaces about Naples and in fact repeats the well-known association of Naples with Africa and the Orient in a collective dismissal of all those places as primitive or uncivilized.

Though my concern here is not a critique of Benjamin's essay, I should nevertheless like to point out that the philosopher's reputation has led to the qualifier "porous" being accepted uncritically. The term has in fact acquired currency within the city itself, so much so that a recent anthology of essays on Naples, an appraisal of the city at the end of the twentieth century, appeared under the title *La città porosa* (1992). Acting in the spirit of this appropriation and restoration, I would like to extract from Benjamin's essay a sense for "porous" that can be positively developed from his observation of the population's aptitude for improvisation, and his observation that "[t]o do and to build are embroiled with each other in courtyards, arches, stairways. Everywhere is preserved a space that could potentially become a theatre of new and unforeseen constellations. Certainty and codification are everywhere avoided" (34). It is within this scope that representations of Naples in contemporary film have reached back and found fertile ground for an investigation into the influence that the preservation of cultural space has had in creating opportunities to offset the impositions of a malfunctioning nation.

In the bowels of the historical center of Naples, marking a small piazza that in contradiction of its size is known as the Largo Corpo di Napoli, is a not-so-monumental statue of the river god Nile. This sculpture depicts the Nile comfortably reclining on one arm, a cornucopia in hand and surrounded by little *putti* as personifications of the Nile's tributaries. Unearthed in the 1400s and restored in 1657, this statue known as '*o cuorp' 'e Napule* (the body of Naples) remains as an artifact of Alexandrine influence in the city, and a direct referent to this locale's renown as one of the city's "locations of power." This status is related to Naples' Egypto-Greco-Roman heritage, its pre- and extra-Christian cultures, and the associated ritualistic baggage. The Largo Corpo di Napoli sits within an area in proximity of which once ran the *vicus Alexandrinus,* where the temple to Isis was situated. As such, it is closely related to the Isiaic mysteries, the most important and secret in Naples' "esoteric" history, and to an aspect of Naples that lends this city its fascinating and contrasting character. 'O cuorp' 'e Napule stands as a sociocultural and historical metaphor that expresses the self-conscious physicality of the locale that partially delineates the subject matter of this essay.

Italian nationhood emerged concurrently with modernism within a geographical space that was both socially and economically unprepared to welcome either condition. At the cultural level, the requirements of nationhood were instrumental in the attempt to reduce heterogeneity through the imposition of a standardized national educational and linguistic system, if not in the out-and-out disregard for cultural variants. Subsequently, Fascism, with its own concerns for modernization and national homogeneity, also attempted to subsume non-official elements of Italian culture. So-called dialects were discouraged, and cultural and linguistic standardization was programmed. If one overlays this scenario with the destabilizing experience of emigration, it becomes obvious that the survival of cultural diversity in Naples and the south has always been precarious.

Although these issues have always been central to the concerns of southern intellectuals (Franco Piperno, Mario Alcaro, and Vito Teti, to name but a few), they have found little space within the national discourse. Most references to the south have been negative assumptions that it could only represent a problem to be somehow resolved. I will discuss the prevalence and role of neorealism as an engaged moment in this matter shortly.

Overall, it could be said that southern Italian cultures have tended to reflect upon their past. It would be too simple to misconstrue this as a nostalgic turn. Rather, it might be considered as an attempt to fix upon the only apparently stable point available in an environment in which progress and change have always been dictated from outside. Until recently, Naples and the south have only known governments and administrations that represented external interests, dominion, and influence.

In the early 1990s the Italian political scene changed drastically. The Christian Democratic Party (DC) that had managed the government for forty-five long years since the end of World War II collapsed and disappeared under the weight of scandal and corruption. The Italian Communist Party (PCI) reconstituted itself after the fall of the Berlin Wall and remained nameless for a period. The neo-Fascists underwent a facelift and reemerged with a polished image as Alleanza Nazionale. And the north saw the rise and strengthening of the separatist Northern Leagues under Umberto Bossi. This party's call for autonomy and independence based much of its rhetoric on racist principles from the early part of the nineteenth century. The whole set was complemented by the meteoric foundation and rise of the Forza Italia Party. Its leader, the multimillionaire media mogul Silvio Berlusconi, fashioned an American-style persona of charismatic deception that led him to two electoral victories. Forza Italia, apparently noncommittal in its name, is in fact a statement of laissez-faire liberalism that quickly attracted the survivors from the DC. This bolstered its ranks and, in alliance with the Northern League and Alleanza Nazionale, permitted its victories.

In the south, increased efforts in the struggle against organized crime and a general reassessment of the 1970s and 1980s resulted in a recalibration of the status of the south from an internal optic. This has been of extreme importance throughout the region and has constituted, in Naples as elsewhere, nothing short of a cultural revolution. This new trend must be contrasted with all that has been historically written, said, and shown of and about the south. Since the period of the Grand Tour the southern portion of the Italian peninsula has represented for the European psyche and imagination a fascinating and dangerous dark side of itself. The "invention of Southerness"[1] as a negative connotative qualifier should today be reconsidered with an attempt to narrate the south differently. In my view, this emergent discourse tends to engage a line of thought that, following in the footsteps of Antonio Gramsci, Ernesto De Martino, and others, is akin to postcolonial strategies.[2] The new southerness speaks from a horizon of differentiation that declares and claims status among legitimate cultures and societies. Mario Alcaro has shown quite clearly that the south's differently evolved social systems tend toward what he has termed a "società del dono" (a gift society) whose principles are in complete harmony with the ideals of democracy and cooperation.

Neapolitan culture, in contrast to the fabricated ethnic nationalism of today's Northern Leagues, proposes the unavoidability of history, that is, the meeting and merging of cultural, racial, and ethnic influences and a reciprocal contamination that translates into a vibrant and active cultural scene. On the other hand, the calls for a return to an idealized golden age of "northern culture," propagandized in the pages of the newspaper *La Padania* and the magazine *Il sole delle Alpi,* organs of the Northern League, cannot but seem static and silly in their declarations and Fascistic in their insistence.

Goffredo Fofi has written that, among other things, "today the south is in need of artists and intellectuals able to break with old logics and models" (8). Indeed, even as Fofi issued his call a good number of individuals had already begun to fulfill it.

Naples in the Cinema

Naples stands among the first European cities in the field of cinema, both as a subject and in the production of film. Especially in the early days of the medium, Naples was a boomtown for small and large production companies. The critic Franco Venturini addresses the influence of the "regional tradition" in Italian cinema on the origins of neorealism; in that context he writes,

> Between approximately 1909 and 1915, Italian productions [were] inspired by regional narrative, very often of a popular nature; such production was particularly abundant in Naples (it is quite proper to speak of a Neapolitan cinema) where people nourished themselves with a certain realist literature, from

Bracco to Serao. Today, unfortunately, that production is almost entirely lost. Almost the only things remaining are the titles remembered by critics like Paolella. Nevertheless, a few works were rescued, among which are numbered the most significant in a movement which unquestionably produced works of a high artistic level of achievement. Among them we must remember *Sperduti nel buio* (1914), *Cavalleria rusticana* (1915), *Assunta Spina* (1915), and *Teresa Raquin* (1915). (in Overbey 170)

More recently, Giuliana Bruno has uncovered the intimate link among Neapolitan cinema, life, and culture, and the particular characters of this cinematographic environment in her book *Streetwalking on a Ruined Map: Cultural Theory and the City Films of Elvira Notari* (1993). Notari's work, though long forgotten, emerges anew in Bruno's analysis as an "excellent example of film-making with a unique handling of social themes ... [and Notari emerges] as a director of exceptional talent, confirming the originality of the Neapolitan school" (12).[3]

Within the Neapolitan film school, which was important in establishing a realistic mode of representation, Notari's productions stood in contrast to the "super spectacles." Epic works such as Giovanni Pastrone's *Cabiria* (1914) had been quite popular and were incorporated into the cinematographic language of Fascism. Notari's films gave exposure to "values of local, regional, and popular culture and ... dialect" (14). Her custom of filming on the city streets, documenting everyday life as a form of entertainment and curiosity, also established a fairly important collective and more popular notion of the history of Neapolitan peoples and their culture (21). Remaining true to the goal of her work, that is, to provide information and entertainment to viewers, Notari's approach (on-location shooting, use of nonactors, temporal placement), in conjunction with the social issues it addressed, goes a long way in suggesting her work as a precursor to what would become known as neorealism.

Perhaps one of the most important aspects of Notari's cinematic ventures is the exportation of her films to the emigrated Italian population in the United States. The popularity of these works was such that it led to the establishment of sister production studios in New York. Notari's activities, in as much as they functioned and were grounded in a specific culture, history, and economics of production, reproposed with diverging emphasis the link between geography and history that informed national policies and defined the birth and development of the Italian nation.

In recognition of Naples' contribution to the cinema, the Museum of Modern Art in New York installed the exhibition "Napoletana: Images of a City" (November 12, 1993–January 1994). In conjunction with this exhibition a catalogue was produced that contains essays by Giuliana Bruno, Adriano Aprà, Goffredo Fofi, and Patrizia Pistagnesi, among others. What emerges from these pages is a comprehensive appreciation and view of a full-fledged cinematic tradition. The Neapolitan presence in cinema ranges from the earliest days of the medium, through recognized high points such as neorealism, to contemporary innovations driven by the search for expressive alternatives.

The exhibition made it quite clear that Naples has always been a city receptive to filmic practice and representation. After Rome, Naples is the city most often represented in Italian cinema. Nevertheless, the question remains as to whether Neapolitan cinema is a "regional" cinema or a version of Italian national cinema. Aprà's interpretation of the question begins with the proposal that linguistically there is no such thing as a Neapolitan cinema (95). In his opinion all cinema except *La terra trema* (1948) and *L'albero degli zoccoli* (1978) are in Italian or Italianized dialect, thereby eliminating one of the predominant keys to "regional" identity and definition: language. This could well be argued, since the influence of language standardization is not unidirectional but is manifested in varying degrees according to social and economic class, education, and environment.

For Aprà "all discussions about Neapolitan cinema depend on the scenic presence of the city or the region . . . they also depend on the presence of particularly 'Neapolitan' actors" (95). This definition is only partially valid. I believe a distinction must be made between films that use the city as a setting to fulfill a representational need and films made by Neapolitans as part of a localized "regional" discourse. The representation of the needs, preoccupations, developments, and social and political structures, though having a specific relationship to the rest of the nation, are also regionally driven. By the end of his article Aprà seems to in fact adjust his critique and, in offering the names of new Neapolitan filmmakers, proposes the presence of a "Neapolitan new wave which could teach even Italian cinema as a whole a thing or two" (143). Even while the authors of these essays recognize the presence of a "Neapolitan" cinema in the past, there is a lingering question regarding the existence of a "new" Neapolitan cinema and what its distinguishing characteristics might be. Among non-Neapolitans, Roberto Rossellini has probably had the most intense encounter with the city of Naples; a number of his films were set and produced there. Beginning with *Paisà* (1946) and with *Il miracolo* episode of *L'amore* (1948), to *La macchina ammazzacat-tivi* (1948–52) and the intense qualities of *Viaggio in Italia* (*Voyage to Italy;* 1953–54), Rossellini encountered Naples over and over through the lens. *Voyage* stands as a particularly significant contribution to the portrayal of the city and its perceived effects as a film that "consciously moved beyond neorealism and started exploring new avenues for the investigation and representation of Reality" (Gieri 158). More precisely, Manuela Gieri categorizes this as a "melodramatic imagination," in other words, an active interplay of relationships between people and their diverse environments and situations (85).

While the south was for a long time represented as a foil of sorts for the self-appointedly European north, most of the films that dealt with the region were made by non-southern directors. Luchino Visconti, the Taviani brothers, Rossellini, and others often used the south as a synecdochal red flag in the post–World War II years. Southern Italian regions, cities, and peoples became an important element of neorealist filmmaking and an ideological trope by which the nation was to measure its progress.

The reasons for filming in the south were often ideological or moral and served to emphasize both differences and similarities (they suffer similarly but are different from us). It may also have been a way to indirectly introduce a critique of Italian society by displacing it to a region that had historically been associated with certain societal and cultural faults ever since Unification. Beyond the postwar process of national reconstruction, neorealist films set in the south addressed unresolved issues central to the national question and the disparate realities that lingered therein. Among the cultural aspects that the films covered was of course language. The presentation of a linguistically diverse national landscape indicated the distance that still needed to be traveled to achieve a truly national culture and linguistic environment.[4]

Rossellini's own statements regarding neorealism give us insights into the necessities dictated by that period's often conflicted history and go partway to explain the perceived contradictions that a film like *Rome, Open City* (1945) might illustrate. Rossellini says, "There is no pre-conceived thesis . . . it refuses recipes and formulas. . . . There are those who still think of neo-realism as something external, as going out into the open air, as a contemplation of misery and suffering. For me, it is nothing other than the artistic form of truth" (in Overbey 89). He goes on to explain that "the subject of neo-realist film is the world; not story or narrative. . . . Neo-realism was born unconsciously as dialectical film, after which it acquired a heart-felt consciousness of the social, human problems during the war and the post-war period" (in Overbey 90). The narrative that precedes the film, projected over silhouetted scenes of the Eternal City, outlines what amounts to both a credo and a plan of action. Many of the named aspects of filmmaking in that very particular context later were integrated by others into what became known as neorealism.

> While the Nazis held Rome in their firm grip after the summer of 1943 a group of Italian filmmakers were planning underground a motion-picture record of the terrors inflicted on their compatriots in the declared open city. Working behind barred doors in cellars and attics in ravines and hills outside Rome they prepared their scenario. The day the Allied Armies marched in the producers and actors went ahead using equipment, much of which had been stolen from the Germans at the cost of Italian lives. Without studio lights, with electricity often unobtainable, and restricted to old scraps of film they completed *Open City,* the 1st post-war Italian picture. Except for a handful of principals the cast consists of ordinary Roman citizens picked off the streets and the scenes were filmed at the exact location of the particular incidents. (Opening credits, *Rome, Open City*)

Rossellini lays out a cinematographic plan that is an act of resistance, acted out by "ordinary Roman citizens," "filmed at the exact location of the particular incidents." The filmmaker and his crew make sure that the "real" story is told, even at the risk of their own lives. Rossellini thus liberates filmmaking as the peninsula has been liberated. And although the conditions in which film has to be born and thrive are difficult, much like for everything else in the country, it is the plain labor of common and courageous people that makes its survival possible.

In a 1954 interview with the journal *Cahiers du Cinéma,* Rossellini states that "life has changed, the war is over, the cities have been reconstructed. What we needed was a cinema of the Reconstruction" (in Hillier 209). *Voyage to Italy,* even as a post-neorealist film, stands as one of Rossellini's most important since it recognizes postwar reconstruction as inclusive of a more personal reconstitution of Rossellini's own attitude toward the function of cinema. That is when Rossellini and

others aimed their cameras on the landscape of interpersonal relationships, seeking answers to the personal meditations that had ensued during the euphoric period of liberation and reconstitution. By joining the
"partisan" rhetoric of *Rome, Open City* and the evolved cinematographic
philosophy of *Voyage to Italy*, we might begin to approximate the approaches of contemporary Neapolitan filmmakers.

Voyage to Italy is about a visit by an English couple (Alexander and
Katherine Joyce, played by George Sanders and Ingrid Bergman) to
Naples. The couple is on the verge of divorce, and they are visibly irri-
table and uncomfortable in each other's company. They are in Naples to
dispose of some inherited real estate. Immediately, their English sensibilities are confronted with the inexplicable influence of the Neapolitan
environment and social space in which they must function during this
trying period. Naples stands in as a place indicative of a more basic (not
to say primitive) emotional and sensual existence that will eventually aid
them in their reconciliation.

Through the restorative supernatural powers of the city of Naples
and its primitive culture, the couple finds their way to reconciliation.
Reading after reading of the film has credited the regenerative powers
of the city, but this does nothing more than extend the commonplace
exoticism of Naples and its inhabitants and avoids more complex questions that may need justification. The reconciliation is forced as much by
the protagonists' extraneousness and marginality from the local culture
as it is by the effect of the Neapolitan environment. The assumption that
the title suggests may be that Naples could constitute a viable stand-in
for Italy, but it is a romanticized notion of Naples that is appealing. The
actual situation of Naples and the south remains a hard pill to swallow
for most Italians, for whom to this day the region remains what it was to
the eighteenth-century French: "paradise inhabited by devils" (Croce).

Though there may be something to quibble about regarding at least
in part the role of Naples and Neapolitans in *Voyage*, what is important
in this film is the use of the city as a present and active background for
the situation of the story. Naples becomes an integral part of the dynamics of the film, but in a way that skirts danger. The city becomes the force
by which the future of the superimposed relationship hangs. The tension
between the city's reputation, its history, and the human needs it appears
to meet may turn out to be what has made *Voyage* one of the most influential films among some of the Neapolitan filmmakers now achieving
visibility and recognition.

I have taken the time to briefly discuss Rossellini and *Voyage* merely to point to the place that the south and cities like Naples have occupied in Italian cinema in general. Their function has been limited to acting as instruments for any number of programs or agendas, whether political, national, or personal, that do/did not directly include the interests of either the region or its inhabitants.[5]

Whether it is "the gateway to the Orient," "the end of Europe," or "the beginning of Africa," Naples is a city that many claim to know and few have truly walked or even visited. Yet the customs, behaviors, and reputation of Neapolitans as that of southerners in general is something that many are more than willing to describe and denounce. From the travelers on the Grand Tour to ethnologists and anthropologists intrigued by the presence of a population deemed "inferior" within the boundaries of a civilized Europe, Naples stands as a litmus test for the limits of the so-called civilized world.

The activities of contemporary cultural workers in Naples provide varying views into the strata of Neapolitan reality that are as layered and hardened as the lava flows of Vesuvius. But the ancient volcano is dormant and the analogy functions for the city itself. Piperno has written,

> If the Southern crisis is due to a collective amnesia and not economics, it is necessary now to make this loss known. The loss must be diminished and reversed with a period of recuperation rather than removal. The work of re-evocation becomes the condition for the re-establishment of the Southern Public spirit. By remembering the multiplicity of disappeared identities, to recall the tongues that lie dormant in the collective memory, by putting into action premodern knowledge and technologies, this is the way in which (however improbable it may appear) to open up toward the future to new civil liberties that the setting of the modern age has made possible despite itself. (26)[6]

Black marketers running deals on motor scooters, black market cigarette saleswomen calling home on their cellular phones, African baristas squeezing espresso from shiny machines, used needles scattered on sidewalks and impaling tree trunks, hypermodern business towers, and single-room family dwellings without either running water or toilet facilities. All these and more extreme contrasts exist in this ex-capital of the Kingdom of the Two Sicilies. Corsicato, Capuano, and Martone are representative of a new generation that acknowledges the existence of these disparate worlds within the urban sprawl of Naples. However, their first impulse is not guided by the need to tear down what has come before them and replace it. They do not shy away from the basic questions that have plagued this city with consistency. As such, readings of their works are useful in training ourselves to identify possible modes of survival and resistance. Their search challenges the general belief that the problems of this city are merely the expected outcome in a region inhabited by an inept population.

In the pages that follow I will address the questions raised above through a reading of the film *I Vesuviani* (1997) and other individual films by Corsicato, Capuano, and Martone. These three filmmakers are but a small sampling in cinema and other arts of efforts that have generated a noticeably strong revival of a regional project in Naples (and more generally in the south) during the last few years. Of course, high on the list among these issues remains the question of identity. With the continued successes of the Northern League and their associated parties, Forza Italia and Alleanza Nazionale, these films are as much an answer and challenge to the racist rhetoric of these entities as they are to the indigenous southern power structures (the Mafia, camorra, and *'ndrangheta* among them) that participate in the degradation of the culture for their own gain.

I Vesuviani

I Vesuviani is a collective effort by five very different directors. Pappi Corsicato, Antonietta De Lillo, Antonio Capuano, Stefano Incerti, and Mario Martone are all directors who had made critically acclaimed films before this anthological piece. Nevertheless, *I Vesuviani* stands as an introduction to the cinematographic and cultural renaissance that has now been very active in Naples for a decade. Although the directors differ greatly from one another in approach, technique, background, and trajectory, they are all related by location. The five films in the anthology are Corsicato's *La stirpe di Iana*, De Lillo's *Maruzzella*, Capuano's *Sofialoren*, Incerti's *Il diavolo nella bottiglia*, and Martone's *La salita*.

All of these films mix elements of realism, fantasy, and political allegory in a rather obvious way and are explicit about their cinematographic influences; hence the critical response was rather tepid. First and foremost, the resilience of cultures like the Neapolitan has been said to be a result of their openness to external and contaminating influences.

This trait is foregrounded in the anthology by each director, thereby continuing along a tradition of adaptive cultural survival and inventiveness. In an interview Capuano addressed this cinema's position on the Italian scene.

> A while back I was in Belgrade as part of a group whose films had been selected to represent Italian cinema. Surprise, surprise, the three films were all Neapolitan . . . *Vito and the Others, Death of a Neapolitan Mathematician* and *Libera* are three authentic innovative and original cinematographic signs. These are not cute films with well-wrought and smooth scripts. These are three strong cinematographic signs. (32)

The strength that Capuano speaks of is the strength of cultural survival. It is akin to Piperno's proposition of a recognition and reconstitution of the general characteristics that have lain dormant beneath the influence of a falsifying political and social order. And it is a strength that corresponds to neorealism's up-front creative and inventive strategies that courageously put up on the screen that which had previously been invisible.

Pappi Corsicato's *La stirpe di Iana* is a story of feminine empowerment that is obviously a fantasy. Five motorcycle-riding women, all bearing the names of masculine detergents (Atlas, Ajax, Dixan, Tide, and Fallo), scour the countryside in search of a young woman who has been kidnapped and threatened with marriage. The women encounter a variety of evil-looking, no-good men who challenge their efforts. These evildoers are easily overcome by the five super heroines' martial arts skills. The women fly, spin, kick, punch, and clean up the region. And they do so with a smile, knowing that they've made the world safer. This film is a delightful mix of spaghetti western, kung fu movie, and motorcycle gang mini-epic, including all of those genres' excesses and limitations.

But what is lurking beneath all this kicking and punching, hugging and crying? *La stirpe di Iana* is a representational slight at the supremacy of men in matters of strength and power, especially significant in this region where masculinity is almost synonymous with camorra. But this is also a nod at the more secret "mysteries" of Naples, the esoteric cults that look back to Isis. And so these women, with the support of a woman priestess who is both a Don Corleone type and spiritual guide and advisor, stand up to the power and abuse of male camorristi. These women and their "stirpe" are an indication of the existence of an alternative mode of being and living that is based on a shared belief in each woman's inherent value. Each woman has specific powers that she uses in concert with the others as a means of survival. To protect that bond no holds are barred. The spirit of collaboration and respect is accessible and available to those who are able to see beyond the conditioning that has brought them to live in, and accept, an exploitative system.

Maruzzella, by Antonietta De Lillo, depends on the presence of Enzo Moscato for its energies. Again, it seems that there is a challenge being thrown out that pits male and female attitudes against each other in a power struggle. In this story Moscato plays the film's namesake, Maruzzella. S/he lives in a porno film theater. What would anyone be doing living in a theater, one might ask incredulously. But a lack of housing and the structural problems that plague existing *dimorae* in the city of Naples have stretched Neapolitan adaptability and inventiveness in this sense as well. Maruzzella is someone who has adapted to the situation extremely well, carving out a space in the theater somewhere between host/ess and entertainer. As the men who frequent the cinema watch the films, and as the sounds of sexual exploration and pleasure fill the air, Maruzzella strolls the dark theater singing Neapolitan love songs. However, her real talent is in the domestic space that she has created within the confines of the theater. This space is her home, but she shares that domesticity with the men by concocting a whole array of culinary specialties.

As her he/she persona defies gender, her domestic activities also contrast tradition—not by the act of cooking, which in fact is considered a transgender activity in the Neapolitan context, but by cooking against the rules. She cooks whatever the men like, regardless of the specialized niche the dishes might occupy. For example, *pastiera* is a cake made for Easter and *casatiello* is Christmas bread. Maruzzella cooks them anytime only because the men like them even in between the prescribed holidays. But, most famous among her dishes is the one that carries her name. *Linguine alla Maruzzella,* or linguine with sea snails. Maruzzella prepares this dish with secret ingredients that she is unwilling to identify but that we are given to understand, by the theater manager, may contain an aphrodisiac spice.

Maruzzella provides theater patrons with an alternative domestic space. There they are free to enjoy the contours of femininity without women. It is a place in which gendered borders are less explicit and less binding. And all is well, until a woman enters the space. One evening Elvira enters the picture (theater), which initiates a series of events that will upset the balance of this "other" world. Perhaps sensing a competitor, Maruzzella appears to be a little perturbed by Elvira's presence ("What does she want?"). Following this scene, we see a large rat move across Maruzzella's kitchen floor. After the rodent has crawled out of our sight, we hear a loud whacking sound, telling us that Maruzzella has acted on her violent thoughts. It is important that in Neapolitan a rat is called *zoccola,* which is also a derogatory term for a woman.

One day, Maruzzella notices Elvira crying. S/he approaches her, and the two begin to see each other in Maruzzella's kitchen. There they discuss men, love, and food. Eventually they fall in love and by the end of the film they marry. An absurd plot and ending, or yet another illustration of adaptability? Can certain individuals who, having found mutual support, work with each other through differences and preconceived positions? In general, some of the criticisms leveled at De Lillo's film have to do with the unlikely attraction between Maruzzella and Elvira and their eventual marriage. This could be read as a sort of cop-out, a giving-in to middle-of-the-road traditional morals that would want to see Maruzzella's transgressive sexuality resolved. But does an institution like marriage really resolve the tension as if it were some sort of magic ritual? In my opinion, the marriage must be seen through another optic, one of adaptation and mutual aid for the two individuals in De Lillo's story. Maruzzella is the more adventurous, the more courageous partner. As s/he has done for so many, she comes to the rescue of Elvira and provides her with an insight into the function and workings of domesticity. The contradictions inherent in the film are there precisely to generate a tension against conservative traditionalist conditioning. It should not be a contradiction that the man is the more domestic individual in the couple. It should not be a contradiction that Maruzzella is able to function in more than one gender-associated sphere. And the marriage itself should not be a contradictory end in a relationship that brings together two compatible individuals. In the end, we may take these propositions as an allegorical reading of Naples, a way in which a supposedly dysfunctional city finds a way to survive by espousing and putting into action some of its most basic contradictions. But, we may also stop and consider that the marriage might be representative of a more human and revolutionary philosophy of life in which survival is part and parcel of the equation in which adaptation and inventiveness are components.

Antonio Capuano's contribution to the collection is *Sofialoren.* It is the story of Telemaco, a fisherman who lives in the old *rione* (section) *Terra* in the city of Pozzuoli. Although the city has been abandoned for over a decade due to seismic activity, Telemaco chose to remain in the area despite the danger. It remains unclear as to whether he remained as a result of his mental state or due to the lack of housing elsewhere. One day Telemaco catches an octopus. The octapod turns out to be a female and, as we eventually discover, a magical one at that. One night a young man tries to steal the octopus. Telemaco prevents the theft and they become friends. The boy lives in the outside world and not in this abandoned, magical environment that is the rione Terra. He is surprised that the fisherman does not have a television or any other modern contrivance.

Unperturbed, either by the attempted theft or by his apparent isolation and rudimentary lifestyle, Telemaco begins to tell a story. It is the story of Ulysses with a twist. Telemaco locates the story in the immediate vicinity of Pozzuoli and the *rione Mare*. These are, after all, some of the shores that Ulysses touched during his mythic voyage. Telemaco appropriates the story and inserts himself into the historic text. He assumes the inheritance of that Mediterranean identity and claims the shores on which he lives (coincidentally named Terra, or Earth) as his own. He is the Odyssean heir and the descendant of a race of sailors and fishermen. He is the emperor of the "Earth" as it has been bequeathed to him, abandoned and uninhabited.

The young man listens to the story without much reaction and then simply leaves. Telemaco then turns to talk to the octopus and decides to name her. The two names that he prefers, he tells her, are Pamela and Sofia Loren:[7] "She was from around here ... she lived around here!" he says, in a reference to Sophia Loren's local origins. It so happens that at night, after being baptized, the cephalopod transforms into a woman who shares the fisherman's bed. At this point Capuano inverts the Odysseus story. The next day a strange black man arrives at Telemaco's door. The man is searching for his long-lost sister who has been transformed into some sort of a fish. The odd thing about the black man is that he is in fact not black but a man painted black. Given the area's well-known history of Moorish influence, this appearance presents an interesting conundrum. Here is a white man, who is historically black, in blackface.[8] His presence posits a historical layering that is manifest in the contemporary context. It claims recognition of a hybridity and demands restitution of the land and culture of which it has been deprived. The information that the black man offers about his sister is rather vague. His language is a mixture of Portuguese and Africanized cadence. Oddly enough, in its conglomeration, it is rather similar to the dialect of the city of Pozzuoli

274

in which the episode takes place. What is this man searching for? His sister or a way in which to appropriate the magical octopus/woman? The aura of deception and intrigue is equally spread among all the characters in the film. Telemaco, the young man, and the black visitor are all unbelievable and appear to be less than what one might call psychologically stable. Is the deception a game or is it a mere result of the dull-witted banter between the individuals?

An altercation between Telemaco and the black prince takes them away from the apartment. The boy stays back with the octopus. When Telemaco returns he goes to sleep beside what he believes to be the octopus transformed into woman. In the morning, however, he wakes up beside the boy, who tells him of a beautiful dream about an African princess. Telemaco again goes after the black prince, this time to invite him up to see his sister. Upon their return to the apartment they find that the boy has cooked the octopus. Initially shocked at the thought, Telemaco and the black prince soon grab pieces of the octopus and begin to hungrily eat it.

This rather odd episode fuses a number of elements in its search for what might constitute a (re)creation myth of sorts. Pozzuoli has a long history steeped in mythology. This aspect has been misplaced and buried for a long time, and recently attempts have been made to reestablish ties with antiquity. With *Sofialoren* Capuano appears to be emphasizing the need to reclaim that history and overcome more superficial cultural connotations that have reduced the contemporary city to uninhabited rubble. *Sofialoren* is in the end the cannibalized body of culture. Loren, the actress, has become the sole cultural referent for a city rich in history and culture. Her body, an inflated and poor stand-in for the body of Putolean culture, is reintegrated by the actions of the protagonists, leaving open the possibility for a resettlement of the rione Terra.

Stefano Incerti's episode, *Il diavolo nella bottiglia*, recounts the Dr. Faustus tale through a homeless man and his attempt to escape his life. This is possibly the least interesting episode of the anthology. The various attempts by those who acquire the bottle to work outside existing economies of exchange leaves them, in the end, with empty hands and not even the adventure as a positive value. It may, however, be worth thinking of it in allegorical terms as a critique of what may be happening to Naples itself. Though Mayor Bassolino helped revive the city during his tenure, he made what many believe to be merely cosmetic changes. The idea that Naples may have sold its soul to the devil to achieve a superficial reprieve from its condition is not a far-fetched one in the minds of many inhabitants of the city. In fact, many of the city's basic problems persist and Bassolino recognized this. It did not seem, however, to be his plan to abandon progress on the surface with disregard for a further and more integral development of the city. Incerti's short may be seen as a warning not to take surface changes too literally and to look further than what is presented for a resolution.

And finally, Mario Martone's *La salita* closes *I Vesuviani* with the most direct reference to Naples and Mayor Bassolino. The set for this film is none other than Mount Vesuvius, the beautiful and threatening presence that looms over the city of Naples. The picturesque Vesuvius that dominates the Gulf of Naples dominates Neapolitan history and the Neapolitan psyche. Nothing that happens in the city escapes the gaze of the god Vesuvius. Martone's film depicts a generic mayor (there is no escaping the reference to Bassolino, however) who slowly hikes up the volcano in his overcoat and mayoral sash. As he climbs the mountain he meditates on his role as mayor and the path of the left in Italian politics. The mayor struggles with his conscience about the choices he has made for his city and for himself. On his ponderous stroll he happens upon characters who haunt his tenure as mayor (such as the unemployed and child laborers) and, with an old comrade, he discusses questions regarding the left's dwindling integrity.

The instrumentalization of Vesuvius as a stand-in for the city of Naples and the arduous challenge that it presents for Bassolino are almost too obvious to analyze. But the web of references does not stop there. They take a wider route around Italian politics and culture by including another important referent in the visual frame. As the mayor climbs up Vesuvius he acquires the company of a large speaking crow. A direct and obvious reference to Pier Paolo Pasolini's bird in *Uccellacci uccellini* (1966), this crow similarly challenges the traveler by presenting him with the many contradictions that have emerged in leftist politics over the decades. The difference between this crow and Pasolini's is that Martone offers an opening in which dialogue overtakes monologue, where community tends beyond and above the words of the ideologue. The crow in *Uccellacci uccellini* was the ideologue that had to be ingested and digested in order to be integrated and passed so as to extract from it the essential nutrients. Here, in *La salita*, while not proposing to resolve the issues and contradictions at hand, Martone insinuates the possibility of a dialogue between the left in power and the left in the streets. This is what Bassolino partially achieved during his administration and what Martone's film suggests.

I Vesuviani, then, is a collection of short films that play up Naples' esoteric dimension. All the directors stake their films' effectiveness in subterranean elements of Neapolitan culture. By contrasting these less realistic cultural aspects with preconceived ideas of Naples and Neapolitans the directors offer an opening toward alternative cultural realities. I would now like to briefly discuss three films by Capuano, Corsicato, and Martone that expand on the ground they cover in their Vesuviani contributions. As in *I Vesuviani,* all three full-length films are rooted in the existential realities of Naples in such an intimate way that they often appear surreal. In fact, it may even be necessary to coin a new term in reference to Neapolitan film of this period. The term should reflect the influences of postwar neorealism and the complex present conditions, something akin to magical realism but tending more toward what we might call magical neorealism.

Naples, Closed City: Antonio Capuano's *Vito e gli altri*

Capuano's *Vito e gli altri* is a film about the deeds and misdeeds of a group of Neapolitan children. The main character is Vito, whose life is only a stand-in for the lives of innumerable children under the influence of consumerism and who are prey to the illusions of capitalism. The film reflects the ragged and uncertain movements of Vito and his friends as they negotiate their lives. The narrative structure of *Vito e gli altri* reflects the disjunction of the subjects within their existential and social spaces. The children depicted in this film are constantly reminded of their vulnerability and marginality. They are extraneous not only to conventional institutions such as the family or school but also to elements that possibly most accurately define their existence. For example, television is presented as an overwhelming social presence in the lives of the children. They mimic television characters and events and stake their lives on the promises that it makes, even in the knowledge that the distance between their lives and the depictions of idealized childhood steeped in consumerism is insurmountable. Yet, that is the normative representation toward which the children are most drawn. Capuano often places a television monitor in strategic positions within his frames and assigns it a function either as removed commentator or surveilling eye.

Vito is indeed filmed in and around Naples, but Capuano and the other directors I am concerned with here do not put the city on display in the way that Rossellini does in *Voyage,* for example. As Neapolitans they gloss the city almost by shifting their gaze away from the more emphatic elements of its presence. They depend much less on the "touristic" attraction of Naples (folkloric quaintness, monuments, landmarks, and so forth) and more on its internal workings, its historiographical mechanisms. Capuano effectively comments on this by including, among the opening credits, a funding acknowledgment to the ministry of tourism. The irony of this credit is soon made apparent by the film.

Right from the outset, the film takes its place in Italian cinematographic history alongside Rossellini's *Rome, Open City* and the more contemporary *Ciao, Professore* (*Io, speriamo che me la cavo;* 1990) by Lina Wertmüller.[9] Nearly fifty years after *Rome, Open City* we seem to have come full circle and are required by the sociopolitical and economic climate to ponder the same question: What about the future? Sadly, the answer today seems to be much more pessimistic than that of the immediate post–World War II period.

The closing scenes of *Rome, Open City* are familiar to us. The children, who are participants in the struggle for freedom and democracy, witness the execution of Don Pietro at the hands of the Nazis and Fascists. As they turn to leave, their small, close-knit band is cast against the city of Rome. Their movement toward Rome and the foregrounding of St. Peter's, while the city's church bells ring out, is designed to offer hope for the future, an energizing proposal for a new Italy. Almost fifty years later, Capuano quite effectively answers that scene with his own.

Vito ends with a similar shot in which the camera pans from the Bay of Naples across the faces of the children who stand looking across at it. The bay itself functions as an objective correlative to the children. The bay that is reproduced in endless paintings and postcards as a symbol of beauty and culture is shown in this film in all its decadent splendor in the setting sun. The smog and industrial pollution now give the landscape its color. As the camera pans along the faces of the children, this is what they see, this is what they live, this is their environment and undoing. In contrast to the children of *Rome, Open City,* these children are motionless. They stand with nowhere to go and helplessly face the overwhelming scenery of their city: a devastated, failed industrialized littoral that emphasizes not only economic underdevelopment but also environmental disaster. The only way that this fatalistic future can be viewed is through the deceptively colorful sunset of a polluted atmosphere.

Vito is a film that reaches into the pit of the city's problems. Capuano situates his story among those whose situation is the most extreme and will be the most hopeless: children. The environment in which they live continues to suffer chronic unemployment and its associated legacies. Pressured by consumerist trends to make something (or many things) out of nothing, these children's lives turn to nothing. The blame for all the problems that have created such a situation is not passed on to any particular person or institution. It is a generalized blame leveled at all individuals and institutions, suggesting that it begins at a communal and familial level and spreads beyond, to other human relationships. It sheds a harsh light on the institutions that, like schools and the family, betray their own mandates. Instead of nurturing and providing for children, these institutions turn out to be the places of irreparable abuse. The omnipresent television set is high on the list of culprits bombarding, as it does, with its messages from morning through the night. Aside from representing the ever-present influence and suggestion of consumerism, television also provides a narrative soundtrack or commentary to the events that take place in its presence. Culturally it also sets up a juxtaposition of standardized Italian culture and language with the Neapolitan reality. Ettore Scola uses the radio, in his film *Una giornata particolare (A Special Day;* 1977), to represent the dictates of Mussolini and Fascism. Their disembodied voices are loud and strong in their emanations as the film's protagonists attempt to lead their lives away from Fascist ideology. Capuano uses the disembodied voice of ideology, as represented by television, to give the new fascism of consumerism presence in *Vito e gli altri.*

Vito e gli altri depicts an almost absolute absence of positive role models among the adult population; their presence is almost exclusively destructive, abusive, and negative. Compared to Wertmüller's *Io, speriamo che me la cavo,* it is rugged, rough, raw, and ultrarealistic. The environments are real and gut-wrenching. And, whereas *Io, speriamo* still grasps at hope and a resolution of the problems of the regions, *Vito* would seem to be a film strongly rooted in an absence of hope that is not fatalism but a more realistic declaration of the lack of opportunities resulting from an unbalanced national politics.

Capuano makes *Vito e gli altri* with knowledge of the history of failed suggestions for the rescue of the city and its future. Capuano appears to offer his own film not as an answer but as a compassionate question. In the end, the only way to get a clear view of the basic problems is to reach down beyond official stories and histories and attempt to determine a point of departure. Capuano achieves this in part through a disruption of conventional narratives and by undermining expectation vis-à-vis traditional institutions such as the family. The narrative

PASQUALE VERDICCHIO

structure of *Vito e gli altri* presents a history through misdirection. The first direction in which we cast our gaze, in many ways the most superficial and easiest, is wrong. Vito and the others are the result and heirs of a failed system that upholds unattainable material standards that are meant to supplant human relationships. By turning our eyes and expectations around 180 degrees Capuano trains us to see the fissures within the societal structures that we take for granted as stable and secure.

Libera Means Free, a Film by Pappi Corsicato (1991–93)

The city of Naples is the subtly present protagonist of the story rather than its grand protagonist. Except for the very localized "slices" of the city, we see little of it. Most of its presence is meant as a means of contrast for the characters. The film is organized in episodes with rough story lines. Each episode is named after a woman protagonist: Aurora, Carmela, and Libera. "Aurora," the first episode, has as part of its locale the fairly recent *centro commerciale*. This area is a development designed by a Japanese team of architects. It stands as both a monument to architectural design and innovation and as a perturbing and ridiculous joke rising high in the Neapolitan sky.

Within the space of the first episode Corsicato makes clear his tendency to either see or cast everything in a generic or normalized mode. If there is anything that we might call the main scope of the film, this is it. Great efforts are made in downplaying differences and leveling out the landscape. Gender, class, sexuality, and all other social or cultural differences are played for what they are. This points to Naples' own cultural character, in which such differences are not the cause of societal distress. The language especially points this out: it is not Neapolitan but an almost neutralized Italian. What this most certainly refers to is the effect of the neutralizing influence of standardized language/culture through the filter of consumerism.

"Aurora" means dawn, and possibly she represents the dawn of a new class. Distant from the tight, crowded, dark alleys of the center of the city, distant from the ancient and potentially stifling walls and narrow sunless streets of downtown, Aurora lives high up in one of the new development's towers. She is a woman steeped in the most contemporary furnishings and gadgets. Her wealthy husband is nowhere to be seen. She is alone, lonely, and depressed. Aurora cannot seem to escape the old. And, while she embodies a new class, she is also the dawning of a new consciousness, one that comes to realize the limits of superficial

280

materialism and seeks refuge in the bowels of the old city. Even the music she listens to in her ultramodern apartment is not music associated
with the new world but with the streets below. As she walks through her
modern condo, a mummified arm falls from the ceiling. Her reaction
is to simply kick it aside. We as viewers, however, must ask whether it
is an ancient remnant or something else. It may after all be a piece of a
body encased in the concrete structure, in other words a victim of the
camorra. If the latter it offers an indication of the corruption in which
developments such as the one in which Aurora lives are embroiled. In
either case, the old city persists in the very structures that also form the
new. Eventually it is the music of the streets, the same tune that Aurora
listens to up in her tower, that pulls Aurora back to the old city. The tune
that infiltrates the new architecture and engulfs it unrelentingly comes
from the streets below, sung by a former boyfriend who calls her to her
old life.

As with the other current films that deal with Naples, the bodies of
the city (and the body of the city) emerge in a variety of representations.
Corsicato's film brings into play the corporeal aspects of Neapolitan culture by establishing a tight relationship between the body, culture, difference, and marginality. He gets to the heart of the national discourse
on difference that marks north-south relations in one episode. He taps
into local mythology through the emphasis on racial and gender differences in one another, and he associates those with mysterious and
ancient sources of cultural energy. While these remain "mysteries" or
pure curiosity in an ultramodern world, they are received without question in the old city. There they fall into a symbolic order that is familiar
even in its mystery. In "Aurora" we are given the sensual body of a homosexual priest, a black baby belonging to Aurora's sister, and Aurora's own
displaced body, "facts" that are unquestioned and remained unanswered.
The statement of these "facts" makes up in part Corsicato's leveling cinematography.

The second episode, "Carmela," is about a young subproletarian
man who returns home after a stint in prison. In a matter of days he is
brought face-to-face with aspects of his life that he cannot escape. He
slowly uncovers his homosexuality with a young man in the neighborhood, he struggles with his drug addiction, he discovers a family secret,
and, because of his prison background, he is accused of being a thief. This
series of events that face the young Sebastiano as soon as he is released
from prison marks the direction of his life, for again Corsicato confronts
us with a series of statements and then leaves us to deal with them. In

"Carmela" Sebastiano hardly has the time to deal with any of the issues. The accusation of theft is taken at face value, and he is taken away by the police.

Corsicato's strategy in this episode is that of giving his viewers a companion in the person of Sebastiano. It is not Carmela who is the character to concentrate on here but her son. Sebastiano is open about his sexuality, his past, and his present; Carmela is not. And it is her secret that Sebastiano is informed of and then has to take away with him to prison again without the possibility of dialogue. The secret is that while Sebastiano believed his father abandoned the family when he was little, it was his mother who left. Aurora reveals this to Sebastiano and informs him that she is, in fact, his father. Corsicato signals the artificiality of the relationship that Aurora has carried on over the years by using an element similar to that used in "Aurora." He has an arm and then a leg fall and hit Carmela as she is walking out of her apartment. The arm is that of a mannequin, an artificial body. Sebastiano is the one to return the leg to the seamstress who dropped it. She makes advances that Sebastiano ignores, and thereby enters into a realm of jealousies and reprisals that will land him in trouble.

But what is important in "Carmela" is the movement and destination of bodies. Sebastiano, the young, sincere, visible homosexual southern body is contrasted with the hidden body of a false mother. This contrast is heightened by Corsicato's personification of the accusatory body as a woman named Italia. She is a woman about to be married. She values honesty and virtue. She is the real thief who falsely accuses Sebastiano. As a way of pointing a finger at the corrupt north-south relationship of the nation, Corsicato ends the episode by having Italia fall down a long flight of stairs (therefore south) in her wedding dress just after Sebastiano has been arrested. So as to further underline the corruption, as Italia falls she is "deflowered" by one of her high-heeled shoes.

In the last episode, "Libera," Corsicato again uses the name to signify the condition of the woman. Libera means free, and Libera runs a newsstand with her husband. He has been feigning illness for months, while Libera works all day. She inadvertently discovers that her husband is in fact meeting prostitutes at home during the day and decides to take action. With the help of a prostitute who frequents the newsstand, Libera sets up a number of appointments for her husband which she secretly videotapes. Given the lively interest in pornographic tapes at the newsstand, she turns her dilemma into a lucrative business. Though less allegorical on the more general north-south issues, this episode emphasizes the self-empowerment that is possible through collaboration such as that between Libera and the prostitute. The two women repossess the female body, previously used for labor and sexual pleasure by the husband, and reconstitute the order such that he is the one being used for their benefit.

"Libera" becomes Corsicato's signature film in a cinematographic environment in which these bodily representations are usually sensationalized and further mystified on the screen. Corsicato in effect "liberates" the bodies from those forms of representation and offers new ground rules for their presence. He projects them on the screen much as he has witnessed them in the social fiber of the ambiguous and multivalent space that is the city of Naples.

L'amore molesto, a Film by Mario Martone

Martone's films define the Neapolitan urban space wholly independently from the dictates of a media-imposed language. A working background in theater has possibly influenced Martone's conception of space; this is reflected not only in his choices of location but also in the placement of characters within the frame of his shots. Martone's work is strongly anti-television, which, by extension, because of what television programming has come to represent especially in its history in Italy, means it is also against linguistic standardization.

The background story line of *L'amore molesto* (1994) involves a Neapolitan woman, Delia, who lives in Bologna. She awaits her mother's arrival from Naples for her birthday. The mother never appears and is found dead. Delia goes back to Naples to find out what happened and is forced to confront the city, its culture, and her own unresolved history. The film is set up as a series of flashbacks that are painful reminders of a dread that must be faced in order to unravel the present. Delia resists the visions brought to her by the flashbacks. She cannot bring herself to believe them and tries to repair herself in the thought that, since they are memories, they may be flawed and are not to be completely believed.

Similarly, Delia's conflicted relationship with Naples has been erased from her mind. She has overcome her pain by forgetting it. Now her mother's death has forced her back into a tentative and anxious relationship with her city. She does her best to speak only Italian, but her cultural memory is so strong that she automatically lapses into Neapolitan. Throughout the film there are instances of blending, melding, and becoming that overwhelm Delia and lead her back into communing with her mother, family, and city. Only a review of her relationship with her mother, Amalia, will shed some light on her identity. By the end of the film the transformation is complete and the identification with the city is deep. Delia dresses in her mother's clothes and takes her mother's name.

Much of Delia's self-investigation is related to the men in her mother's life. The men Delia encounters are threatening, violent, and vulgar, but rather than being repelled by them Delia abandons herself to them. She gives in to the forced advances of a man called Antonio, who is mysteriously linked to her mother. Her father is a questionable character who initially evinces some empathy when he breaks down at the realization of not having achieved his promise as an artist. Yet all that we might come to feel for him is quickly undone when he turns violently against Delia. The reason for the breakdown of the relationship between Delia and her father is based on the mother's supposed infidelity and the daughter's role as the bringer of bad tidings, and it remains conflicted and dysfunctional.

Delia's relationship to Naples is, to put it lightly, ambivalent. She seems to have escaped its grasp and retains an aversion to it and its people. Martone's shooting of the film conveys the revolving and crowding ambient without ever actually emphasizing through obvious visual manipulation. If there is an oppressive character assigned to the city of Naples it is through a portrayal of the effects of a culture of poverty that has broken through the false floor of safe familial relationships and landed in close proximity to madness. The encircling strange effects of consumerism, politics, and their concomitant rhetoric in multicolored posters and products push the limits of reality, which is itself somewhere between a dream state and a state of unbelieving. Martone casts the stereotypically sunny city in dark shades of blue, red, brown, and black.

In the end, it is not the crowded populace that is at fault for the collapse of the city. Delia walks through the streets in her mother's bright red dress. While she earlier wore the same dress in an uncomfortable manner, now she is quite relaxed. Her body carries an air of comfort at having conquered the truth and the fear that circumscribed it. But, as is often the case with what we perceive as "truth," there are layers of perception and interpretation that tend to shift the initial impression with time. Delia's truth turns out to be a false truth that has conditioned her and her mother's lives as they have been lived. The truth that Delia finds and believes to be a key to her past is a lie that encloses another truth. The initial truth that Delia discovers and confirms comes from her own childhood memory of her mother's extramarital affair. Her truth was held as reliable even while it was denied because it came from a child. However, by the end of the film that first truth leads to an unraveling of layers that make of it a truth designed to deny another. For it is in the layers of denied truths, in the folds of memory, that the truth of Delia's own abuse as a child was hidden and her mother's supposed infidelity orchestrated to relieve Delia of her pain.

The relationship of Delia the daughter to Amalia the mother is rendered even more intriguing by the convoluted logic of denial. Amalia is almost quintessentially Neapolitan. Delia, who perceives her mother's infidelity and her father's instability as the result of some Neapolitan cultural virus, wants to escape that destiny. The mother's negative traits are the result of her own daughter's repressed memories and the family's apprehension about revealing the actual events. Throughout the film we see Delia crossing into Amalia's territory and reputation (if even only through dress) as she lets herself be manipulated by the men she encounters. Finally, Delia's need and effort to protect her mother's memory lead to an unsuspected revelation, one that discredits history as it has evolved and reveals it as the lie concocted to protect Delia. That revelation is available to Delia only through her mother's eyes. It is only by that process of becoming her mother, becoming Neapolitan, dressing in the costume of her rejection, and immersing her body in the body of the place she has abandoned that Delia can approximate her own history. The allegorical connections that could be pointed out to emphasize the need for a reassessment and a reconstitution of Neapolitan culture and the evolution of the city under the pressure of a constructed reality of national unity are many. I will conclude by pointing out that Martone is representative of an intellectual generation that crosses media, fields of expertise, and modes of expression in the reconsideration of Neapolitan life.

The directors I have briefly touched on in the preceding pages, and much of Neapolitan contemporary culture, are involved not in unearthing the culture of the past but in retelling a history and reformulating an identity. Naples today is a city in need of assessing and struggling with what and how it has become. Its cultural identity and its position are neither predictable nor unambiguous. Naples is an exciting and active city whose citizens appear to have reclaimed their own creative spirits and engaged their city as a living territory upon which to live and re-create their lives one day at a time. In this, Martone, Capuano, Corsicato, and the other intellectuals at work today in Naples and the south put into practice Fofi's principle that "art's indirect action is fundamental in every process of cultural transformation, and so much more so there where the disaster is above all cultural and rooted in a society's subjects thereby undermining and deviating its best tensions and hopes" (9).[10]

Notes

1. See Russo on the issue of "Southerness." She proposes that the south as a "different" social and cultural reality has been made evident through the work of writers such as Leonardo Sciascia, Carlo Levi, and Elio Vittorini, and photographers including Enzo Sellerio, Mario Giacomelli, Ferdinando Scianna, Marialba Russo, and Mimmo Jodice. Theirs is an attempt to go beyond the usual accepted values assigned to the Italian south; they do so through personal experience and political action.

2. Gramsci, founder of the PCI, extended his Marxism within a consideration of Italy's north-south problematics to include culture as a major component in the structuring of identity and politics. He addresses a revolutionary proposal by which an alliance of northern workers and southern peasants might bring about a national proletarian coalition to run the country and unify the country more than cosmetically, as had been done in 1871. While Gramsci thought the answer lay in a way "to orient industrial production to useful work that will promote peace between the city and the countryside, between North and South" (*The Southern Question* 17), he also recognized that the complicating factor was the racist views regarding the south that had been disseminated by reformist Socialists. In fact, the alliance never came to pass and the north-south dichotomy continues to condition Italian national politics and society.

3. Bruno analyzes the history and cinematographic production of this pioneer of cinema and proposes that Notari's and other Neapolitans' techniques could possibly be taken as precursors to neorealist cinematographic techniques that arose in post–World War II Italy. Notari's use of nonprofessional actors and on-location shooting (shooting in the streets and neighborhoods of Naples) were techniques that were initially necessitated by financial constraints. It soon became clear that such approaches lent a realistic dimension to the final product and brought it closer to the experiences of the audience. As such, even when finances became less problematic the simpler technical approaches remained. Neorealism's concern was also with creating an intimate portrayal of events with which audiences could identify;

their incorporation of technical standards similar to Notari's brought their films to life on-screen and in the experience of those who viewed them.

4. An indication of the existence of such a linguistically diverse environment can be found in two of neorealism's most renowned films, Rossellini's *Paisà* and Visconti's *La terra trema*. Language is a problem for those who speak some Italian in understanding dialect. In *Paisà* it could possibly have meant the life of the young Sicilian woman who is shot by the American soldiers because of a communication problem. Similarly, in the Naples episode, the young Neapolitan street urchin and the black American serviceman have linguistic problems and communicate through similar social status. In *La terra trema*, Visconti uses Sicilian dialect as a way to illustrate the distance that remains to be crossed on the Italian cultural landscape before a truly unified country can be established. This is not a call for standardization but a call to those who would obliterate linguistic difference to appreciate its cultural legacy and richness. More recently, there was a short-lived scandal at the Venice Film Festival when Martone's *L'amore molesto* was released in 1994. The film, shot mostly with Neapolitan dialogue, was presented with Italian subtitles. Martone seems to have supported the inclusion of subtitles, but others were offended by it. I would agree with Martone that it is best to maintain the integrity of the film and make it communicable by including subtitles as a way to resist perhaps the tendencies of producers and distributors to dub away the original language.

5. An exception among an older generation of filmmakers who situated their films in the south is Francesco Rosi, who is, unlike Visconti, Rossellini, and the Taviani brothers, a southerner. Two of his films that are particularly compelling and influential are *Le mani sulla città* (1963) and *Salvatore Giuliano* (1962).

6. In *La repubblica delle città*, Antonio Bassolino, then mayor of Naples, laid out a program by which cities like Naples could begin to take their destiny into their own hands. Of course this had to somehow inspire the alienated population, who had experienced abuse from all of its governments and administrations. Bassolino's plan was to put the city's cultural resources in the hands of those who had inherited them: the inhabitants. Making each neighborhood responsible for such resources in their vicinity would begin a process of reestablishing pride and a belonging that might eventually manifest itself in other initiatives.

Noi abbiamo rovesciato questo schema, cercando di fare del patrimonio culturale della città—quello storico, quello classico, ma anche quello moderno, contemporaneo, attuale—la principale risorsa di Napoli. Si è cercato in altri termini di rompere lo schema "imitativo" dello sviluppo. . . . Bisognava (e bisogna) selezionare tra le opere lasciateci in eredità quelle utile alla collettività, che necessariamente dovevano essere completate, . . . stiamo cercando anche di allargare il sentimento dell'identità cittadina a tanta gente che fino a questo momento non se ne sentiva coinvolta. (14, 21, 54)

We have reversed this pattern trying to make the cultural heritage of the city—the historical and classical one and the modern, contemporary and current one—the main resource of Naples. In other words, we have tried to get away from the "imitative" pattern of development. . . . It was (and is) necessary to select among the works left to us the ones that are useful to the community, which must be completed, . . . we are also trying to increase the sense of civic identity among many people who, up to now, did not feel to be a part of.

7. Perhaps this refers to Pamela Anderson and Sophia Loren. Loren was born and grew up in Pozzuoli. Anderson would be a reference to contemporary myths of beauty and femininity that match that which instituted Loren as the only cultural referent for Pozzuoli, overriding its rich cultural past.

8. A similar turnaround deceptive strategy occurs in Spike Lee's film *Bamboozled* (2000), in which two black actors react to their producer's racism by proposing they do a blackface act. Contrary to their intentions, the act becomes a success. This black over black, the doubling of identity that neither hides nor reveals, is an interesting strategy for establishing historical presence and denying stereotype while apparently foregrounding it.

9. Wertmüller's film is about the mistaken assignment of a northern teacher to a southern city near Naples. While he is appalled by the mistake and horrified by the prospect of having to work in such an environment of which he holds only preconceived ideas, the teacher comes to understand the plight of the children caught in the apparently hopeless situation. The film ends with the hint that there is some hope for a better world. However, the northern teacher imported this hope. None is to be had at the hands of any adult southerners. And so, while the film is probably meant to empathize with the situation in the south, it cannot do much more than lay the usual blame at the feet of those who live there. It would seem that even for an enlightened

intellectual like Wertmüller the southern question is too problematic and steeped in a spirit of national resentment and disgust, and that the only hope that can be imagined is one that is brought from the north.

10. L'azione indiretta dell'arte è fondamentale in ogni processo di trasformazione culturale, tanto più lo è là dove il disastro è innanzitutto culturale e si è radicato nei soggetti di una società illudendone e deviandone le speranze e tensioni migliori.

Chapter 14

In Memoriam: The Neorealist Legacy in the Contemporary Sicilian Anti-Mafia Film

MILLICENT MARCUS

It is no mere coincidence that two of the best films to emerge from the 2000–2001 season are historically based accounts of the lives and premature deaths of little-known anti-Mafia crusaders, and that the neorealist provenance of these works has been critically acknowledged. I am referring to Marco Tullio Giordana's *I cento passi* (2000), "a neorealist film beyond neorealism, hovering between reality, revolt, and dream" (in Quilici 5), and Pasquale Scimeca's *Placido Rizzotto* (2000), hailed as a latter-day example of "the best neorealism, that of Rossellini and of the authors who remained close to the facts, without embroidering on them."[1] Though these statements show how elastic the attribution of a neorealist source can be, authorizing in the one case an unadorned, factually rigorous reportage, and on the other, a flight into utopian and even oneiric transfigurations of the historical record, such recourse to neorealism reveals the debt that Italian engagé filmmaking since 1945 owes to the Rossellinian-Desichian-Viscontian postwar precedent.

I cento passi and *Placido Rizzotto*, however, in celebrating the exemplary lives and deaths of young social reformers, join ranks with Alessandro Di Robilant's 1994 film *Il giudice ragazzino* to form a mini-genre within the realm of *cinema politico*. In addition to the generalized indebtedness to neorealist paradigms, this mini-genre brings to the surface a tendency within neorealism that has hitherto escaped critical notice: its powerful memorialist impulse. Made as a tribute to the Roman resistance, *Roma, città aperta* (1945) eulogizes the populist heroics of Pina, Manfredi, and Don Pietro, while three of the six episodes of *Paisà* (1946) commemorate characters whose martyrdom would otherwise have gone

290

Germany, Year Zero (Roberto Rossellini, 1947)

unrecorded: that of Carmela (Sicilian episode), of the anonymous partisan who dies in Harriet's arms (Florentine episode), and of Cigolani, Dale, and their co-combatants (Po River episode). It could well be argued that the makeshift sign used to mark the grave of the executed partisan retrieved from the waters of the Po reveals, retroactively, the identity of Roberto Rossellini's first neorealist films as epitaphs, literally understood as writings on tombs. In so doing, these films fit into a venerable literary tradition crowned by Ugo Foscolo's *Dei sepolchri* (1807) where heroic history, properly memorialized, becomes the springboard for activist intervention in the present ("A egregie cose il forte animo accendono / L'urne de' forti, o Pindemonte"; ll. 151–52s).[2] Though such a literary inspiration would have been anathema to the apostles of cinematic purity à la Zavattini, the Foscolian memorialist tradition well accords with neorealism's aspirations to politically committed art. In Foscolo's verses, cemeteries are read as signifiers of a heroic engagement with life, forging continuity with a humanist past and inspiring a future of political activism much like the link that the neorealists sought to establish between the ideals of the Resistance and the postwar rebirth of a nation. In support of the notion of the contemporary uses of history, Antonio Gramsci observed that any interpretation of the past is really "current politics *in nuce*" (*Il Risorgimento* 114), while Friedrich Nietzsche argued for the construction of a monumental history to incite a will to action in the present.[3]

True to the memorialist impulse of neorealism, *Il giudice ragazzino,*
Placido Rizzotto, and *I cento passi* present themselves as epitaphic, as
cinematic tomb inscriptions designed to transmit the legacy of moral
engagement and social justice for which their protagonists died. In fact,
all three films end with written texts on-screen, the postscripts of their
respective narrations.

Il giudice Rosario Livatino è stato assassinato la mattina del
21 settembre 1990 lungo la superstrada Canecattì-Agrigento. I
mandanti sono tuttora sconosciuti. (*Il giudice ragazzino*)

Di Placido Rizzotto oggi non rimane neanche una tomba sulla
quale si possa versare una lacrima e i suoi miseri resti giacciono
dentro un sacco nei sotterranei della corte d'appello dei tribu-
nali di Palermo. (*Placido Rizzotto*).

Peppino Impastato è stato ucciso 9 maggio 1978. Nel 1997 la
Procura di Palermo ha chiesto il rinvio a giudizio di Gaetano
Badalamenti come mandante dell'omicidio. (*I cento passi*)[4]

In the case of Placido Rizzotto, Scimeca's film serves not only as epitaph
but as the very grave that history denied him, whereas the memorialist
function of *I cento passi* is made explicit in the last line of dialogue, when
Felicia Impastato exalts in the spectacle of the angry protest march on
the day of her son's funeral: "Non se lo sono dimenticato" (149).[5] With
this comment, the victim's mother endows Giordana's entire film with
the double function of epitaph and call to arms or, as Chiara Modonesi
puts it, "the moment has arrived to recount how every social, cultural
conquest arises from the initiative and courage of a minority, if not from
one sole individual. Not in order to engage in facile rhetoric, but, on the
contrary, to indicate the path of a model to imitate" (18).

In this trilogy of films about young, little-known martyrs in the
anti-Mafia cause, *Il giudice ragazzino* plays a pivotal role, marking the
transition from the cinema politico genre of the 1970s and 1980s to
the more poetic, nuanced, anthropological approach of the late 1990s.
Francesco Rosi, one of the founders of cinema politico (*Le mani sulla
città* [1963], *Il caso Maffei* [1972], *Lucky Luciano* [1974], *Cadaveri-eccellenti* [1976]), had already anticipated this shift with the lyricism of his
films of the "land"—*Cristo si è fermato ad Eboli* (1979) and *Tre fratelli*
(1981)—as had the Taviani brothers, whose more overtly ideological

mode gave way to the intense poetry of their Sicilian masterpiece, *Kaos* (1984). *Il giudice ragazzino* occupies a turning point in such a progression, displaying the trademarks of cinema politico while looking ahead to the epitaphic impulse that will emerge in the films of Scimeca and Giordana.

Set in the town of Canicattì (province of Agrigento) in the late 1980s, the film tells the story of the final years of Rosario Livatino, a young magistrate of impeccable virtue and intense investigative zeal who runs afoul of the Mafia and refuses to surrender to their tactics of intimidation. The only son of possessive and elderly parents, Rosario falls in love with Angela Guarnera, a beautiful and sympathetic lawyer, but the romance reaches an impasse. Rosario is too bound to his parents to contemplate living apart from them and Angela refuses the invitation to move into the Livatino household. Alone and driven more than ever by his professional mission, Rosario lives to see his mentor, Saetta, and his carabiniere coworker, Guazzelli, gunned down before he himself is assassinated on September 21, 1990.

True to its cinema politico heritage, *Il giudice ragazzino* presents itself as a *cine-inchiesta* whose action focuses on crime detection and procedures of judiciary investigation. In technical terms, the film is characterized by intrusive editing, ostentatious camera movements, and a tense musical score, all of which contribute to a fast-paced narration that rushes to its foregone conclusion. The film's generic self-consciousness surfaces, in slightly displaced form, through the cinephilia of the main character, whose only respite from work is the occasional video he allows himself to view after hours. In one such scene, as he watches the televised broadcast of *Ulysses*, Rosario explains the mechanisms behind cinematic illusionism to his mystified and gullible mother. Rosario's own taste runs to westerns (*Stagecoach* [1939] is featured prominently in his video collection), especially the films of Sergio Leone (*C'era una volta il west* [1968], *Il buono, il brutto e il cattivo* [1966], *C'era una volta in America* [1984]). By citing canonical and parodic forms of the western, Di Robilant announces his own film's simultaneous adherence to, and rewriting of, the genre from which it derives.

Of greatest importance to the development of the contemporary anti-Mafia film is the link between physiognomy and moral typology established in *Il giudice ragazzino*. Di Robilant insists on such a link in the framing action of his film in which the logic of the title is revealed. In the introductory sequence and in fragments scattered throughout the rest of the narration, Rosario delivers a speech at a luncheon held in his honor by the town worthies of Canecattì. While he proceeds to define his ideal of judgeship as a position of absolute integrity, the camera pans the faces of the audience members who listen with thinly veiled displeasure at this perceived threat to a corrupt and entrenched establishment. Though we do not know the identities of these listeners at the start of the film, when the framing situation recurs at various subsequent points, we learn who scowls behind their sunglasses and understand the motives for their profound unease. The unfolding narrative reveals those listeners to be either the very Mafia leaders against whom Rosario will unleash the power of his office, or the judge's cowardly colleagues, who are unwilling to stand up and be counted. In the film's final return to the framing situation, as Rosario completes his speech and is left alone at the podium after the crowd has ominously withdrawn from him, we realize the intensity of the threat that the protagonist's idealistic pronouncements pose to his immediate audience. Rosario's subsequent assassination is but the necessary consequence of the film's framing "logic"—the irreconcilable clash between the speaker and his listeners, between the claims of justice and those of a vice-ridden and complacent status quo. The cinematic language of that clash is a language of physiognomy, and it is here that the film's title reaches its fullest resonance. As the camera cuts between Rosario's clean, youthful face and those of his listeners, hidden behind sunglasses and/or the aging fleshiness of the chronically overfed, Di Robilant gives visual meaning to the moral terms that underlie his critique. The youthfulness of *Il giudice ragazzino* is indeed moral. He is the secular version of the New Man celebrated by St. Paul, whose theology equated oldness with spiritual decrepitude and newness with redemption through divine grace. The "oldness" of Rosario's listeners is likewise moral—it is the symptom of a putrefying body politic mired in corruption and sloth.

The narrative framework of *Placido Rizzotto* instead is anthropologically inflected. Scimeca announces his film's populist focus by introducing it with the figure of the folk narrator, or *cantastorie,* who conveys the saga of the slain anti-Mafia crusader as a kind of oral history, illustrated by a posterboard divided into panels depicting critical episodes in the protagonist's personal and public experience painted in a naïve, even primitive figurative style. Though the framing narrator is Placido's father, Carmelo Rizzotto, the film succeeds in incorporating the perspectives of a number of other key players in the drama so that the point of view becomes truly choral, reflecting the wide-ranging research conducted through interviews and archives that went into the preparation of *Placido Rizzotto.*

The film begins with a harrowing scene of World War II violence in Brescia, as partisans are being casually executed by Nazi soldiers. Placido Rizzotto, running to the aid of his comrades, arrives too late to save them but is able to gun down their executioners. This traumatic experience marks Placido for life and determines his commitment to social justice. Upon his return to his native Corleone he becomes a labor organizer dedicated to protecting the rights of the fieldworkers against their exploitation by local bosses. His activism culminates in leading the peasants in a campaign to occupy fields left uncultivated by the wealthy landowners of Corleone. Though warned of Mafia recriminations, Placido continues his political activities until the evening of March 10, 1948, when he is assassinated. On that same night, Lia, Placido's fiancée, is raped by boss Luciano Liggio with the knowledge and complicity of the girl's mother. One of the key witnesses to the assassination, a poor shepherd boy, is killed by a corrupt doctor who will himself be silenced by a Mafia hit after fleeing to Australia. An investigation follows, led with great determination by Captain Carlo Alberto Dalla Chiesa, who will come to national prominence for his prowess in fighting terrorism and will die by the hand of the Mafia, as will Placido's successor, Pio La Torre.

If the circumference of the film is marked by the *cantastorie* tradition, then at its center may be said to reside another popular folk model for Scimeca's didactic intent. I speak of the Passion play, enacted in Sicilian dialect by the local residents in the Cineteatro Martorana of Corleone. Though Scimeca does not gloss over the awkwardness and naivete of their performance, he nonetheless endows it with great dignity by conveying the powerful interactive bond that allowed the audience to identify with the characters onstage. Placido Rizzotto's own christological affinities are announced in the crucifix that presides over Corleone from the hillside where the protagonist, arms flung open, first greets his city upon returning from the war. Throughout the film, Placido will ascend to this vantage point to contemplate his mission and to remind us of his sacrificial destiny.

Just as *Placido Rizzotto* is framed by the naïve illustrations on the posterboard that accompanies the *cantastorie*'s narration, *I cento passi* privileges the pictorial arts through the figure of Stefano Venuti, painter and committed Communist, who will serve as Peppino Impastato's mentor from the age of ten until the latter's untimely and violent death twenty years later. As a portraitist, Stefano has a keen eye for faces: "Hai una bella faccia, pulita, occhi intelligenti," he says to the boy Peppino

as he delivers his Communist stump speech to an audience of two in
the main piazza of Cinisi (31).[6] The other member of the audience is
Peppino's uncle, Cesare Manzella, local Mafia boss and soon-to-be victim of Gaetano (Tano) Badalamenti in their struggle for control of the
organized crime scene in Cinisi. When Peppino commissions Stefano to
paint the portrait of his slain uncle, the episode presents, *en abyme*, Giordana's own art of portraiture. Ending with a reference to the Soviet poet
Vladimir Majakovsky, whose portrait Stefano has painted and whose
saga Peppino is curious to hear, this encounter contains, in miniature, the
ideal for engagé art to which the film as a whole aspires. "È una lunga
storia," Stefano warns, casting a look on Peppino that conveys the moral
weight of the testimony he is about to give. The child answers, "Rac-
contala," with the gravity that accompanies the sealing of a solemn pact
(39).[7] Giordana chooses to represent on-screen neither the story of Majakovsky nor Stefano's telling of it, opting instead to leap ahead some ten
years to show Peppino as a Communist militant engaging in a campaign
to occupy farmlands expropriated by the government for the expansion
of the local airport. The cut from the scene of childhood storytelling to
adult activism implies a causal relationship between the two events so
that the tale of Majakovsky becomes the catalyst, the exemplum that
replicates itself in the life of the listener. The unrepresented Majakovsky
account thus creates a vacuum into which the film viewer is irresistibly
drawn. Through ellipsis, we too are invested in the interpretive process
by which exemplary art can intervene to change the course of human
life. As receivers of the paradigmatic story of Peppino Impastato, we,
in turn, form the next link in the chain of artistically inspired social action.

Through his influence over the young man, Stefano replaces Peppino's biological father, Luigi, who is beholden to Mafia patronage for his
livelihood and is locked into violent conflict with his son. After a particularly savage family confrontation, Peppino takes his younger brother
Giovanni on a walk from their house to that of Tano Badalamenti, separated by the one hundred steps of the film's title, and rails against the
corruption and injustice of Mafia rule. In his anti-Mafia crusade, Peppino founds an independent radio station, Radio Aut, which uses the
airwaves to give voice to his countercultural campaign. It is now 1978,
Aldo Moro has been kidnapped by the Red Brigade, and the populace
of Cinisi holds the entire left responsible for the crime. Despite this,
Peppino decides to run for office and chooses the Democrazia Proletaria
ticket over that of the Communist Party, which he considers by now

ineffectual. Just before the election, Peppino is kidnapped and beaten by Tano's henchmen, who bind him to the railroad track and detonate a large quantity of explosives that had been bound around his waist. Though Peppino's tragedy is overshadowed by the discovery of Aldo Moro's slain body on May 9, 1978, the funeral procession of the young anti-Mafia martyr turns into a political protest of powerful and massive proportions.

Whereas *Il giudice ragazzino* plays off of earlier cinematic models and *Placido Rizzotto* avails itself of indigenous Sicilian folk culture in its struggle for generic self-definition, *I cento passi* invokes a vast array of media and art forms in what amounts to a veritable compendium of possible precedents for the contemporary filmmaker in search of a new language of engagement. To this end, Giordana's film devotes considerable attention to the rise of the Italian *radio libera* movement of the 1970s. The station established by Peppino and his friends, Radio Aut, was one example of a widespread impulse in Italy to use the airwaves to spread an alternative, countercultural voice. Umberto Eco estimates that there were over one thousand such independent stations in Italy by 1978,[8] and they included Radio Alice of Bologna, Onda Rossa of Rome, and the fictitious Radiofreccia of Reggio Emilia, subject of Luciano Ligabue's nostalgic 1998 film of that same title. Having been banned from performing political theater in the streets of Cinisi, and having been ousted from the pages of the radical newspaper *Idea Socialista,* Peppino resorted to the airwaves to exercise the free speech denied him in other public forums. "Quando non ci danno il permesso di fare un comizio, quando ci chiudono il circolo, quando ci sequestrano il materiale," Peppino explains to Barbablù, his equipment supplier, "l'aria non ce la possono sequestrare" (69).[9]

Of utmost importance is the fact that Peppino's revolutionary project is strictly regional in scope. He has no pretensions about reaching an audience beyond the limited confines of Cinisi. When Barbablù boasts, "Oggi basta un registratore e un'antennina per farci la radio. Ce ne saranno mille in tutta Italia," Peppino responds succinctly, "A me basta che ci sentono a Cinisi" (69).[10] In choosing to occupy the radio station to shake his own supporters out of their complacency, Peppino defines their political mission as follows: "Noi non siamo a Parigi, non siamo a Berkeley. Non siamo a Goa, a Woodstock o sull'Isola di Wight. Siamo a Cinisi, Sicilia. Dove non aspettano altro che il nostro disimpegno, il rientro nella vita privata . . . per questo ho voluto occupare simbolicamente la Radio: per richiamare la vostra attenzione" (107).[11]

In the many scenes involving the installation and operation of the broadcast studio, the film bears witness to the rise of a utopian community of young male idealists orbiting around a charismatic leader who embodies a transcendent social idea. Here, as elsewhere, Pasolini comes to mind, with his celebration of the subproletarian community of *Accattone* (1961), or the more constructive, culturally prestigious one of Jesus' disciples in *The Gospel According to Matthew* (1964), or of Giotto's workshop in the *The Decameron* (1971).[12]

Though anticinematic in its confinement to the small recording studio, the style of the scenes shot during radio broadcasting is of great visual interest, for it establishes an iconography of communicative power and revolutionary zeal. Sporting the elaborate headset of the radio announcer, hunching over the microphone, and delivering impromptu speeches of varying degrees of intensity, these "talking heads" become visual icons of a counterculture that has found its voice and revels in the freedom to use it. These are ecstatic images of the media outreach that even a limited technology can support, and as such they provide a model for an antispectacular yet cogent cinematic ideal. The energy and excitement that radiate from these scenes, however, are tinged with the knowledge of their transience, and the music—so redolent of 1970s tastes—lends an air of nostalgia to their evocation, which marks this period as irrevocably past.

The austerity of means that underwrites Radio Aut's success does not, however, translate into an anti-aesthetic stance on the part of Peppino (or, by extrapolation, Giordana). Instead, he exhibits a longing for beauty that reaches the level of doctrine. "E allora forse più che la politica, la lotta di classe, la coscienza e tutte 'ste fesserie . . . bisognerebbe ricordare alla gente cos'è la bellezza. Insegnargli a riconoscerla. A difenderla," says Peppino to Salvo after admiring the panorama from a mountain high above Cinisi. "È importante la bellezza," he continues. "Da quella scende giù tutto il resto" (63).[13] In classical terms, Peppino is advocating a concept of beauty that cannot be divorced from goodness or truth, and which, when recognized, will hasten the soul's journey to enlightenment. In practice it means the quest for a pedagogy that will reach a mass public through the appeal of the beautiful or, in less exalted terms, the pleasurable and the entertaining. As a public communicator, Peppino's task is to invent "a language that connects, in a poetically spectacular dimension, politics with aesthetics. . . . Impastato understands that it is politics, the facts, and the understanding of them that is the center on which to frame a communication that unites politics and poetry, radio and theater, low and high, direct and mediated messages, farce and morality" (Quilici). In his ability to reach mass audiences with his politically progressive message, Peppino becomes the organic intellectual heralded by Gramsci, able to penetrate the humus of popular culture to bring about its political awakening.

As the occulted example of Majakovsky suggests, literature provides a powerful model for the conversionary art to which Giordana's film aspires. At the very outset of *I cento passi*, poetry forms the basis of the film's quest for an alternative, nonmainstream identity. When the young Peppino recites Leopardi's "L'infinito" at the luncheon in honor of his cousin Anthony who has traveled from New York to Cinisi to find a bride, the boy's introductory words, in English, are fraught with meaning for the cinematic text to follow: "Dear Anthony and dear Cosima, my family offers you this poem to remember our language and our land" (20). For Anthony, who emigrated as a child and whose Italian is therefore halting, dialectal, and forced, the recitation of the Leopardian verses represents the opposite of the path the immigrant has chosen—that of Mafioso stardom in the underworld of New York.

For Peppino, the association with literary culture instead will inspire and fuel his dissident stance. It will lead him to Pasolini, whose "Supplica a mia madre" will be recited by mother and son as a duet in a scene rife with Oedipal tension. "È difficile dire con parole di figlio," Peppino recites,

> ciò a cui nel cuore ben poco assomiglio
> Tu sei la sola al mondo che sa, del mio cuore
> ciò che è stato sempre, prima d'ogni altro amore.

At this point, Peppino hands the volume to his mother, Felicia, who continues,

> Per questo devo dirti ciò ch'è orrendo conoscere:
> è dentro la tua grazia che nasce la mia angoscia.
> Sei insostituibile. Per questo è dannata
> alla solitudine la vita che mi hai data.
> E non voglio esser solo. Ho un'infinita fame
> d'amore, dell'amore di corpi senza anima.
> Perché l'anima è in te, sei tu, ma tu
> sei mia madre e il tuo amore è la mia schiavitù.[14]

Though Pasolini's poem continues for another eight lines, Felicia stops her recitation here, turns to her son with a stricken look, and holds that expression as the scene slowly fades to black.

Giordana's decision to write and direct this scene as a dialogue—to have Peppino and his mother share the reading of a single-voiced poem—is rich with dramatic implications. It means that not only does Pasolini's verse serve as a vehicle for expressing Peppino's Oedipal attachment but also that his mother is given an active, culturally engaged role in the process. She need not remain the passive object of filial adoration but can acknowledge, by vocalizing these verses, her part in this reciprocally binding and enslaving rapport. The poetic performance becomes an intervention, a way for Peppino to suture into the text of his own life the epiphanic power of Pasolini's art.

The activist function of literature is nowhere more evident than in Peppino's wickedly parodic rewriting of Dante's *Inferno*, which he reads over the airwaves of Radio Aut. Though irreverent to the point of transgression, this scene invites comparison with the film's opening sequence, where ten-year-old Peppino had recited the lines from Leopardi's "L'infinito" as a gift to the bride and groom, soon to depart for America. Both scenes depend, for their dramatic effect, on the inner audience's knowledge of the literary canon, and both scenes include extensive intercuts to the faces of the listeners, who recognize the sanctity of the textual sources. In both cases, Peppino is bolstered by the authority that knowledge of Italian literature confers upon him. In the film's earlier scene, it is he who has the privilege of bestowing upon the newlyweds Anthony and Cosima the cultural heritage for which the Leopardi poem stands, by antonomasia. And it is through Peppino's Dantesque parody, in the later scene, that Italian high culture will pronounce its condemnation of Mafia rule.

As in the earlier sequence, here too the camera cuts to reaction shots of Peppino's listening audience, increased exponentially by the medium of radio. Those awestruck by the ten-year-old's recitation of Leopardi are now fragmented into a number of varying response groups, from the men gathering to listen collectively in cafés and barbershops, to the solitary Felicia receiving the broadcast at home, to the amused carabiniere commander tuning in on his car radio, to Stefano Venuti gloating at party headquarters, and finally to Tano, who listens in stone-faced silence as the performance reaches its crescendo.

In the series of poetry readings that have punctuated the film, Peppino assumes a progressively more active and creative role. He begins as a passive vessel, merely parroting the Leopardian lyrics in a monotone indifferent to the text's gradations of meaning, but by mid-film he has advanced to the level of stage director who turns Pasolini's love poem to his mother into an anguished duet. This progression from passive recitation to active coauthorship culminates in the long and brilliant radio broadcast of Peppino's spoof on *Inferno,* titled *La cretina commedia.* Here, Peppino reinvents Dante's journey to the underworld in terms relevant to his contemporary anti-Mafia crusade, so that the City of Dis becomes Mafiopoli, the heretics in the 6th circle become the town worthies of Cinisi, and the sinners of Malebolge become the local Mafia bosses.

Peppino's use of Dante belongs to a broadened category of parody whereby the original text functions not as the target of ridicule but as its delivery system. This means that the dignity and authority of the medieval poem serves to indict the contemporary world for its failure to live up to its magisterial cultural heritage. Peppino's parody reveals him to be a profoundly engaged reader of the *Commedia,* attuned to the prophetic fury and the satiric bite of Dante's own social critique. In his creation of the Dante-inspired Mafiopoli, peopled with caricatures of Cinisi's ruling elite, Peppino is recapitulating the medieval poet's own transposition of local power politics onto an infernal landscape. In so doing, Peppino brings Dante's formidable moral and ideological apparatus—this gigantic judgment machine which is the *Commedia*—to bear on his indictment of Mafia rule. It would be no exaggeration to say that in making Dante his "ally" in this campaign, Peppino is stocking his arsenal with all the weapons of literary high culture in his war against the powers that be.

In composing his Dantesque parody, Peppino is attentive to the generic specificities of *il poema sacro* as well as to its social critique. Using the terza rima form, Peppino is led by the pressure of the end rhymes to construct neologisms worthy of Dante's own linguistic inventiveness.

> Cosi' arrivammo al centro di Mafiopoli
> la turrita città piena di gente
> che fa per profession l'ingannapopoli. (18)[15]

Beyond the imitation of such formal devices, Peppino appropriates Dante's most powerful mechanism for the poetic rendering of divine justice—the exercise of *contrapasso.* When Bertran de Born holds up his own severed head and announces to Dante that "Cosi' s'osserva in me lo contrapasso" (*Inf.* 28, 142),[16] he reveals the way in which infernal punishment involves the literalization of metaphors—the sowers of discord dismember the body politic, the lustful are levitated and buffeted by the storms of passion, the violent are submerged in boiling blood, and so forth. Accordingly, Dantesque contrapasso is the guiding principle of the punishments meted out in Mafiopoli. When Peppino describes "color che nella bocca / puzzano per i cul che han leccato,"[17] the well-known metaphor for sycophancy is made literal by means of its spectacularly unappetizing aftertaste (89).

Wordplay, such an important element in the medieval poet's realist view of language,[18] figures strategically in Peppino's portrait of the town officer, condemned to hell for relocating the local soccer field against the popular will. "Qui son dannato a soffrire di tifo," laments Peppino's vice mayor. "Tentai di spostare lo campo sportivo e tutti ora mi dicono che schifo" (90).[19] The pun on *tifo*, meaning both "typhus" and "team loyalty," provides its own built-in contrapasso, according to which sports fanaticism is equated with the literal illness afflicting the hell-dwelling official.

As Peppino's recitation of the Dante parody proceeds, the tight structure of his *terzine* begins to unravel, and disciplined satire gives way to a talking jag verging on hysteria. This textual model inspires Peppino to engage in his own courageous and provocative act of *poesis*, to channel his righteous indignation into composing an imaginative dystopia whose bitterness, like that of Dante, is a measure of the utopian disappointment it hides. Dantesque, too, is Peppino's outsider's status, or rather, his position as *internal* exile, whose alienated, oppositional role banishes him from the realm of normal familial relations, from party politics, from romantic attachments, and finally from life itself. If Dante, in giving voice to his exilic state, had to find a new medium, the *vulgare illustre* to replace Latin as the vehicle of his culture's most serious philosophical and spiritual concerns, for Peppino that venue was, of course, the *radio libera*, unencumbered by an institutional past yet possessed of the oracular authority that Italians had traditionally accorded this medium of pure voice.[20]

Perhaps most important for Peppino's recourse to Dante is the *Commedia*'s status as a motivational text, bearing witness to the poet's conversion experience in the hope of igniting the reader's own ardor for redemption. Throughout the *Commedia*, Dante incorporates examples of literary texts that serve as incentives to act—damnably in the case of Paolo and Francesca, but blessedly in the cases of Statius and the many others who found spiritual inspiration in the pages of Virgil. In

I cento passi Peppino's references to Dante function for the listeners of Radio Aut as Stefano Venuti's story of Majakovsky had for Peppino himself—as an exemplum, an attempt to awaken the public to the need for revolutionary action.

It should come as no surprise that Giordana's survey of literary and media precedents for a new committed cinema would include Italian film history as an important point of reference. Nor should it come as a surprise that one of the foundational films of the cinema politico genre, Francesco Rosi's *Le mani sulla città*, should be anthologized in *I cento passi* at the moment in which Peppino issues his manifesto of engagé art. The occasion is the screening of Rosi's film for the local Cine-club, succeeded by a discussion Peppino introduces with the following comment: "Un film è sempre un'opera d'arte. Non riproduce mai la realtà così com'è ma attraverso un certo sguardo interpretativo, un certo taglio, la reinventa questa realtà, la trasfigura e la carica di senso."[21]

It is not hard to read into these lines Giordana's own mission in *I cento passi*—to reinvent and transfigure the story of Peppino Impastato and to infuse it with meaning for a contemporary social context notoriously deficient in the kind of revolutionary fervor that animated the 1970s liberation movements and that drove this young man to martyrdom. In so doing, Giordana, along with Scimeca in *Placido Rizzotto* and Di Robilant in *Il giudice ragazzino*, has created not a requiem for political activism but an epitaph, in the memorialist tradition enshrined in literature by Foscolo, and in film by the founders of neorealism. At the level of Italian film history, neorealism itself, as recalled in the contemporary anti-Mafia film, functions as epitaph in the Foscolian sense. Through what could be called "epitaphic appropriation," neorealism has been invoked as a sepulchral text—one that marks the death of a movement in film historical terms but enjoins future generations to continue its legacy of politically engaged art. On the cusp of the new millennium, Giordana, Scimeca, and Di Robilant have certainly proven themselves to be worthy heirs of that legacy.

Credits

Il giudice ragazzino (*The Boy Judge*), 1994
Directed by Alessandro Di Robilant
Screenplay by Alessandro Di Robilant, Andrea Purgatori, Ugo Pirro
Based on eponymous book by Nando Dalla Chiesa
Photography by David Scott

Music by Franco Piersanti
Edited by Cecilia Zanuso
Sets by Giancarlo Muselli
Costumes by Catia Dottori
Cast

Rosario Livatino	Giulio Scarpati
Rosario's Father	Leopoldo Trieste
Rosario's Mother	Regina Bianchi
Angela Guarnera	Sabrina Ferilli
Migliore	Renato Carpentieri
Guazzelli	Paolo De Vita
Saetta	Roberto Nobile

Placido Rizzotto, 2000
Directed by Pasquale Scimeca
Screenplay by Pasquale Scimeca
Photography by Pasquale Mari
Edited by Babak Karimi
Music by Agricantus
Sets by Luisa Taravella
Costumes by Grazia Colombini
Cast

Placido Rizzotto	Marcello Mazzarella
Luciano Liggio	Vincenzo Albanese
Carmelo Rizzotto	Carmelo Di Mazzarelli
Lia	Gioia Spaziani
Capt. Dalla Chiesa	Arturo Todaro
Pasquale Crescione	Biagio Barone
Giovanni Pasqua	Franco Catalano

I cento passi (*The One Hundred Steps*), 2000
Directed by Marco Tullio Giordana
Screenplay by Claudio Fava, Monica Zapelli, Marco Tullio Giordana
Photography by Roberto Forza
Edited by Roberto Missiroli
Sets by Franco Ceraolo
Costumes by Elisabetta
Cast

Peppino Impastato	Luigi Lo Cascio
Peppino as a boy	Lorenzo Randazzo
Luigi	Luigi Maria Burruano

Felicia	Lucia Sardo Montaldo
Giovanni	Paolo Briguglia
Tano Badalamenti	Toni Sperandeo
Andrea Tidona	Stefano Venuti
Salvo Vitale	Claudio Gioè
Cesare Manzella	Pippo Montalbano
Cousin Anthony	Ninni Bruschetta
Cosima	Paola Pace

Notes

1. This is Mino Argentieri's comment in an interview conducted with the director (see "Pasquale").
2. "the [funeral] urns of the strong ignite the strong spirits to [perform] exceptional deeds, oh Pindemonte."
3. See Nietzsche, "The Use and Abuse of History."
4.   Judge Rosario Livatino was assassinated on the morning of September 21, 1990, along the Canicattì-Agrigento highway. The principals are still unidentified.

    Of Placido Rizzotto today, there remains not even a tomb on which to shed a tear, and his miserable remains lie in a sack in the cellar of the Court of Appeals of Palermo.

    Peppino Impastato was killed on May 9, 1978. In 1997, the attorney general's office of Palermo ordered that Gaetano Badalamenti be sent to trial as the principal of the murder.

5. "They haven't forgotten him." This quote is from the screenplay by Giordana, Claudio Fava, and Monica Zapelli. All quotes from the film's dialogue are from this text; all English translations are my own.
6. "You have a handsome face, clean, intelligent eyes."
7. "It's a long story." "Tell it."
8. See Eco 167.
9. "When they don't give us permission to hold a rally, when they close our club, when they confiscate our material, [at least] they can't confiscate the airwaves."
10. "Today it's enough to have a tape recorder and a small antenna to set up a radio station. There must be a thousand in all Italy." "For me, it's enough that they hear us in Cinisi."
11. "We aren't in Paris, we aren't in Berkeley. We aren't in Goa, or Woodstock, or the Island of Wight. We're in Cinisi, Sicily. Where they don't expect anything other than our disengagement, our return to private

life . . . for this reason I wanted to symbolically occupy the radio station: to attract your attention."

12. For Giordana, writer and filmmaker of *Pasolini: Un delitto italiano* (1995), the importance of the Pasolinian model can never be overestimated.

13. "And so, maybe more than politics, the class struggle, consciousness, and all these crack-pot ideas . . . we should remind people about the meaning of beauty. Teach them to recognize it. To defend it." "Beauty is important. Everything else flows from it."

14. *Plea to My Mother:*

> It is difficult to say with the words of a son
> what in my heart I so little resemble.
> You are the only one in the world who knows,
> what has always been in my heart, before any other love.
> For this I must tell you, what is horrendous to know
> It is in your grace that my anguish is born.
> You are irreplaceable. For this
> the life that you gave me is damned to solitude.
> and I don't want to be alone. I have an infinite hunger
> for love, for love of bodies without a soul.
> For the soul is in you, it is you, but you
> are my mother and your love is my bondage." (80, 81)

15. "Thus we arrived at the center of Mafiopolis / the towered city full of people / whose profession is to deceive the populace."

16. "Thus you observe in me the counter-suffering" (439).

17. "those whose mouths stink for the ass-holes that they have licked."

18. The medieval realist theory of language, encapsulated in the phrase "nomina sunt consequentia rerum," held that the relationships between words and things were not arbitrary and culture-bound but absolute and ontologically determined. Linguistic realism argued that words were existentially linked to their referents so that puns were therefore expressions of the hidden interconnectedness of all creation.

19. "Here I am damned to suffer from typhus / I tried to move the recreation field / and now everyone tells me how disgusting [it is]."

20. It was the Italian reverence for oratorical skill that made the radio such a powerful vehicle of propaganda during Fascism (Tannenbaum 225–29).

21. "A film is always a work of art. It does not ever reproduce reality just as it is, but by means of a certain interpretive gaze, a certain slant, it reinvents that reality, transfigures it and charges it with meaning." Inexplicably, this important excerpt from the film's soundtrack does not appear in the published screenplay.

Selected Filmography

1-2-3 Corona. Dir. Hans Müller. 1948.
Accattone. Dir. Pier Paolo Pasolini. 1961.
The Accused (Obžalovaný). Dir. Ján Kadár, Elmar Klos. 1964.
Ace in the Hole. Dir. Billy Wilder. 1951.
Africa, I Will Fleece You. Dir. Jean-Marie Teno. 1992.
Ajantrik. Dir. Ritwik Ghatak. 1958.
L'albero degli zoccoli. Dir. Ermanno Olmi. 1978.
Allah Tantou. Dir. David Achkar. 1991.
Alphaville. Dir. Jean-Luc Godard. 1965.
L'amore. Dir. Roberto Rossellini. 1948.
L'amore molesto. Dir. Mario Martone. 1994.
And Someday We Will See Each Other Again (Und finden dereinst wir uns wieder). Dir. Hans Müller. 1947.
And the Heavens Above (Und über uns der Himmel). Dir. Josef V. Baky. 1947.
Anguished Land (Terra em transe). Dir. Glauber Rocha. 1967.
Another Sky. Dir. Gavin Lambert. 1954.
Antônio das Mortes (O dragão da malade contra o santo guerreiro). Dir. Glauber Rocha. 1969.
Aparajito. Dir. Satyajit Ray. 1956.
L'Avventura. Dir. Michelangelo Antonioni. 1960.
A Bagful of Fleas (Pytel blech). Dir. Věra Chytilová. 1962.
Barren Lives (Vidas secas). Dir. Nelson Pereira dos Santos. 1963.
The Battle of Algiers (La battaglia di Algeri). Dir. Gillo Pontecorvo. 1965.
The Battle of Chile (La batalla de Chile). Dir. Patricio Guzmán. 1975.
Battleship Potemkin. Dir. Sergei Eisenstein. 1925.
Bellissima. Dir. Luchino Visconti. 1951.
Bicycle Thief (Ladri di biciclette). Dir. Vittorio De Sica. 1948.
Billy Liar. Dir. John Schlesinger. 1953.
Birds of Passage (Zugvögel). Dir. Rolf Meyer. 1947.
Birds, Orphans and Fools (Vtáčkovia, siroty a blázni). Dir. Juraj Jakubisko. 1968.
The Birth of a Nation. Dir. D. W. Griffith. 1915.
Bitter Rice (Riso amaro). Dir. Giuseppe De Santis. 1949.
Black Girl. Dir. Ousmane Sembène. 1966.
Black God, White Devil (Deus e o diabo na terra do sol). Dir. Glauber Rocha. 1964.

Bless Their Little Hearts. Dir. Billy Woodberry. 1984.
Blood of the Condor (Yawar mallku). Dir. Jorge Sanjinés. 1969.
Borom Sarret. Dir. Ousmane Sembène. 1963.
Breathless (À bout de souffle). Dir. Jean-Luc Godard. 1960.
The Boys. Dir. Sydney Furie. 1962.
Brief Encounter. Dir. David Lean. 1945.
Bye Bye Africa. Dir. Mahamat Saleh Haroun. 1999.
Bye Bye Brazil. Dir. Carlos Diegues. 1979.
Cabiria. Dir. Giovanni Pastrone. 1914.
Cadaveri-eccellenti. Dir. Francesco Rosi. 1976.
Camp de Thiaroye. Dir. Ousmane Sembène. 1987.
Casablanca. Dir. Michael Curtiz. 1942.
Il caso Mattei. Dir. Francesco Rosi. 1972.
Ceddo. Dir. Ousmane Sembène. 1976.
I cento passi. Dir. Marco Tullio Giordana. 2000.
Central Station (Central do Brasil). Dir. Walter Salles. 1998.
A Child Is Waiting. Dir. John Cassavetes. 1963.
The Children Are Watching Us (I bambini ci guardano). Dir. Vittorio De Sica. 1942.
Children of the Earth (Dharti ke lal). Dir. K. A. Abbas. 1946.
Christ Stopped at Eboli (Cristo si è fermato ad Eboli). Dir. Francesco Rosi. 1979.
Citizen Kane. Dir. Orson Welles. 1941.
The Citizen (Nagarik). Dir. Ritwik Ghatak. 1953.
The City (La ciudad). Dir. David Riker. 1998.
City of God (Cidade de Deus). Dir. Fernando Meirelles, Kátia Lund. 2002.
Closely Watched Trains (Ostře sledované vlaky). Dir. Jiří Menzl. 1966.
The Connection. Dir. Shirley Clarke. 1962.
The Contractor (Thikadar). Dir. Tulsi Lahiri. 1940.
The Cool World. Dir. Shirley Clarke. 1963.
Courage for Every Day (Každý den odvahu). Dir. Ewald Schorm. 1964.
Cremator (Spalovač mrtvol). Dir. Juraj Herz. 1968.
Crime and Punishment USA. Dir. Sanders brothers. 1935.
Crucial Years (Kristove roky). Dir. Juraj Jakubisko. 1967.
Daisies. (Semikrásky). Dir. Věra Chytilová. 1966.
David and Lisa. Dir. Frank Perry. 1962.
Death Is Called Engelchen (Smrt' sa volá Engelchen). Dir. Ján Kadár, Elmar Klos. 1963.
The Decameron (Il Decameron). Dir. Pier Paolo Pasolini. 1971.
Deserters and Pilgrims (Zbehovia a pútnici). Dir. Juraj Jakubisko. 1968.
Distant Journey (Daleká). Dir. Alfred Radok. 1950.
The Earth Trembles (La terra trema). Dir. Luchino Visconti. 1948.
Elephant. Dir. Gus Van Sant. 2003.
Emitai. Dir. Ousmane Sembène. 1971.
The End of a Clairvoyant (Konec jasnovidce). Dir. Vladimír Svitáček. 1958.

The End of a Priest (*Farářův konec*). Dir. Ewald Schorm. 1968.

Enginemen. Dir. Michael Grigsby. 1959.

The Entertainer. Dir. Tony Richardson. 1960.

Europe '51 (*Europa '51*). Dir. Roberto Rossellini. 1952.

Every Day except Xmas. Dir. Lindsay Anderson. 1957.

The Exiles. Dir. Kent MacKenzie. 1961.

Farewell (*Šťastnou cestu*). Dir. Otakar Vávra. 1943.

Father and Son (*Foo ji ching*). Dir. Allen Fong. 1981.

Une femme est une femme. Dir. Jean-Luc Godard. 1961.

Film. Dir. Alan Schneider. 1965.

Finding Forester. Dir. Gus Van Sant. 2000.

Firemen's Ball (*Hoří má panenko*). Dir. Miloš Forman. 1967.

Foot Path. Dir. Zia Sarhadi. 1953.

Foreign Land (*Terra estrangeira*). Dir. Walter Salles, Daniela Thomas. 1995.

Fury. Dir. Fritz Lang. 1936.

Gabbeh. Dir. Mohsen Makhmalbaf. 1996.

Germany Year 90 Nine Zero (*Allemagne 90 neuf zero*). Dir. Jean-Luc Godard. 1991.

Germany, Year Zero (*Germania anno zero*). Dir. Roberto Rossellini. 1947.

Gilda. Dir. Charles Vidor. 1946.

Una giornata particolare. Dir. Ettore Scola. 1977.

Girl with Green Eyes (*Ragazza con gli occhi verdi*). Dir. Desmond Davis. 1964.

Il giudice ragazzino. Dir. Alessandro Di Robilant. 1994.

Gone with the Wind. Dir. Victor Fleming. 1939.

The Good, the Bad, and the Ugly (*Il buono, il brutto e il cattivo*). Dir. Sergio Leone. 1966.

Good Times, Wonderful Times. Dir. Lionel Rogosin. 1965.

Good Will Hunting. Dir. Gus Van Sant. 1997.

The Gospel According to Matthew (*Il Vangelo secondo Matteo*). Dir. Pier Paolo Pasolini. 1964.

Grapes of Wrath. Dir. John Ford. 1940.

Greed. Dir. Erich Von Stroheim. 1924.

The Greenwich Village Story. Dir. Jack O'Connell. 1963.

Guelwaar. Dir. Ousmane Sembène. 1992.

Guns of the Trees. Dir. Jonas Mekas. 1964.

Heart of Spain (*The Abraham Lincoln Brigade in the Spanish Civil War*). Dir. Herbert Kline, Charles Korvin. 1937.

Here Are Lions (*Zde jsou lvi*). Dir. Václav Krška. 1958.

Hong Kong 1997 Trilogy. Dir. Fruit Chan. 1997.

Hour of the Furnaces (*La hora de los hornos*). Dir. Fernando Solanas, Octavio Getino. 1967.

How Angels Are Born (*Como nascem os anjos*). Dir. Murillo Salles. 1996.

In Front of Us, There Is Life (*Vor uns liegt das Leben*). Dir. Gerhard Rittau. 1948.

In the Face of Demolition (*Weilou chunxiao*). Dir. Lee Tit. 1953.

India, Seen by Rossellini. Dir. Roberto Rossellini, 1957–58.
The Inheritance. Dir. Harold Mayer. 1964.
Io, speriamo che me la cavo. Dir. Lina Wertmüller. 1990.
Kaos. Dir. Taviani brothers. 1984.
Killer of Sheep. Dir. Charles Burnett. 1977.
A Kind of Loving. Dir. John Schlesinger. 1962.
The King of the Street Cleaners (Çöpçüler krali). Dir. Zeki Ökten. 1977.
King Solomon's Mines. Dir. Robert Stevenson. 1937.
The Kitchen. Dir. James Hill. 1961.
The Lady from Shanghai. Dir. Orson Welles. 1947.
Lamerica. Dir. Gianni Amelio. 1994.
The Language of the Faces. Dir. Sanders brothers. 1934.
The Last Days of Pompei (Gli ultimi giorni di Pompei). Dir. Mario Caserini, Eleuterio Rodolfi. 1913.
The Last Illusion (Der ruf). Dir. Josef von Baky. 1949.
The Legend of Marilyn Monroe. Dir. Terry Sanders. 1964.
Libera. Dir. Pappi Corsicato. 1993.
Little Cheung (Xilu xiang). Dir. Fruit Chan. 1999.
The Little Foxes. Dir. William Wilder. 1941.
The Little Fugitive. Dir. Ray Ashley, Morris Engel. 1953.
The Loneliness of the Long Distance Runner. Dir. Tony Richardson. 1962.
The Longest Summer (Qunian yanhua tebieduo). Dir. Fruit Chan. 1998.
Look Back in Anger. Dir. Tony Richardson. 1959.
Loves of a Blonde (Lásky jedné plavovlásky). Dir. Miloš Forman. 1965.
The L-shaped Room. Dir. Bryan Forbes. 1962.
Lucky Luciano. Dir. Francesco Rosi. 1974
Lunch Hour. Dir. James Hill. 1961.
La macchina ammazzacattivi. Dir. Roberto Rossellini. 1952.
Madam Satã. Dir. Karim Aïnouz. 2002.
Made in Hong Kong (Xianggang zhizao). Dir. Fruit Chan. 1997.
The Magnificent Ambersons. Dir. Orson Welles. 1942.
Mandabi. Dir. Ousmane Sembène. 1968.
Le mani sulla città. Dir. Francesco Rosi. 1963.
March to Aldermaston (shortened version of *Deadly Harvest*). Group documentary, including Chris Menges and Lindsay Anderson. 1958.
Marty. Dir. Delbert Mann. 1955.
The Matrix. Dir. Andy Wachowski and Larry Wachowski. 1999.
Memories of the Underdevelopment (Memorias del subdesarrollo). Dir. Tomás Gutiérrez Alea. 1968.
Miracle in Milan (Miracolo a Milano). Dir. Vittorio De Sica. 1951.
Miracle in Rome (Milagro en Roma). Dir. Lisandro Duque Naranjo. 1988.
Modern Times. Dir. Charles Chaplin. 1936.
Mother India. Dir. Mehboob Khan. 1957.
Motorcycle Diaries (Diarios de motocicleta). Dir. Walter Salles. 2004.

Moulin Rouge. Dir. Baz Luhrman. 2001.

The Murderers Are among Us (Die Mörder sind unter uns). Dir. Wolfgang Staudte. 1946.

My Voyage to Italy (Il mio viaggio in Italia). Dir. Martin Scorsese. 1991.

Needle in the Haystack. Dir. Alex Viany. 1953.

New World (Naya sansar). Dir. K. A. Abbas. 1941.

Night Tide. Dir. Curtis Harrington. 1961.

Nine Queens (Nueve reinas). Dir. Fabian Bielinsky. 2000.

Nothing but a Man. Dir. Michael Roemer. 1964.

O Cangaceiro (The Bandits). Dir. Lima Barreto. 1953.

O Dreamland. Dir. Lindsay Anderson. 1953.

Obsession (Ossessione). Dir. Luchino Visconti. 1943.

On the Ascent (Udayer pathey). Dir. Bimal Roy. 1944.

On the Bowery. Dir. Lionel Rogosin. 1957.

Once Upon a Time in America (C'era una volta in America). Dir. Sergio Leone. 1984.

Once Upon a Time in the West (C'era una volta il West). Dir. Sergio Leone. 1968.

The Organ. Dir. Štefan Uher. 1963.

Paisan (Paisà). Dir. Roberto Rossellini. 1946.

The Party and the Guests (O slavnosti a hostech). Dir. Jan Němec. 1966.

The Party in the Botanical Garden (Slávnost'v botanickej záhrade). Dir. Elo Havetta. 1969.

Pasolini: Un delitto italiano. Dir. Marco Tullio Giordana. 1995.

Paths in Twilight (Wege im zwielich). Dir. Gustav Frohlich. 1948.

Peter and Pavla (Černý Petr). Dir. Miloš Forman. 1963.

Pierrot le fou. Dir. Jean-Luc Godard. 1965.

Pixote (Pixote: A lei do mais fraco). Dir. Hector Babenco. 1981.

Placido Rizzotto. Dir. Pasquale Scimeca. 2000.

The Plow That Broke the Plains. Dir. Pare Lorentz. 1936.

The Poet (Kabi). Dir. Debaki Bose. 1949.

La promesse. Dir. Luc and Jean-Pierre Dardenne. 1996.

Psycho. Dir. Alfred Hitchcock. 1960.

Pull My Daisy. Dir. Robert Flank, Albert Leslie. 1959.

The Pumpkin Eater. Dir. Jack Clayton. 1964.

The Queen of Sheba. Dir. King Vidor. 1953.

The Quiet One. Dir. Sydney Meyers. 1948.

Rear Window. Dir. Alfred Hitchcock. 1954.

Refuge England. Dir. Robert Vas. 1959.

Return of the Prodigal Son (Návrat straceného syna). Dir. Ewald Schorm. 1966.

Rio, 40 Degrees (Rio, 40 graus). Dir. Nelson Pereira dos Santos. 1955.

Rodrigo D: No Future (Rodrigo D: No futuro). Dir. Víctor Gaviria. 1990.

Rome, Open City (Roma, città aperta). Dir. Roberto Rossellini. 1945.

The Rose Seller (La vendedora de rosas). Dir. Víctor Gaviria. 1998.

Rotation. Dir. Wolfgang Staudte. 1949.

Salt of the Earth. Dir. Herbert Biberman. 1954.
Salvatore Giuliano. Dir. Francesco Rosi. 1962.
Saturday Night and Sunday Morning. Dir. K. Reisz. 1960.
The Savage Eye. Dir. Ben Maddow, Sidney Meyers. 1960.
Scarface. Dir. Brian de Palma. 1983.
Shadows. Dir. John Cassavetes. 1959.
Shoeshine (Sciuscià). Dir. Vittorio De Sica. 1946.
The Shop on Main Street (Obchod na Korze). Dir. Ján Kadár, Elmar Klos. 1965.
Sierra Madre. Dir. John Huston. 1948.
The Singing Street. Dir. Norton Park Group. 1957.
Skylarks on a String (Skřivánci na niti). Dir. Jiří Menzl. 1970.
The Solution (Samadhan). Dir. Premendra Mitra. 1943.
Something Different (O něčem jiném). Dir. Věra Chytilová. 1963.
Somewhere in Berlin (Irgendwo in Berlin). Dir. Gerhard Lamprecht. 1946.
Song of the Road (Pather Panchali). Dir. Satyajit Ray. 1955.
Sparrows Can't Sing. Dir. Loan Littlewood. 1962.
Stagecoach. Dir. John Ford. 1939.
The Star Goes to South (Hvězda jede na jih). Dir. Oldřich Lipský. 1958.
Star Wars. Dir. George Lucas. 1977.
Stolen Children (Il ladro di bambini). Dir. Gianni Amelio. 1992.
Stories of the Revolution. Dir. Tomás Gutiérrez Alea. 1960.
Story of a Love Affair (Cronaca di un amore). Dir. Michelangelo Antonioni. 1950.
Strange Victory. Dir. Leo Hurwitz. 1948.
Strawberry and Chocolate (Fresa y chocolate). Dir. Tomás Gutiérrez Alea, Juan Carlos Tabío. 1994.
The Strike (Siréna). Dir. Karel Steklý. 1947.
Stromboli (Stromboli terra di Dio). Dir. Roberto Rossellini. 1950.
Sullivan's Travels. Dir. Preston Sturges. 1941.
Sunshine in a Net (Slnko v sieti). Dir. Štefan Uher. 1962.
The System. Dir. Michael Winner. 1964.
T.V.A. Dir. J. Hamid. 1940.
A Taste of Cherry (T'am e guilass). Dir. Abbas Kiarostami. 1997.
A Taste of Honey. Dir. Tony Richardson. 1961.
Term of Trial. Dir. Peter Glenville. 1962.
Terra em transe (Anguished Land). Dir. Glauber Rocha. 1967.
They Were Sisters. Dir. Arthur Crabtree. 1945.
This Sporting Life (Io sono un campione). Dir. Lindsay Anderson. 1963.
Three Wishes (Tři přání). Dir. Ján Kadár, Elmar Klos. 1958.
Throw Me a Dime (Tire dié). Dir. Fernando Birri. 1960.
A Time out of War. Dir. Denis Sanders. 1954.
Together. Dir. Lorenza Mazzetti. 1956.
Too Late Blues. Dir. John Cassavetes. 1961.
Tre fratelli. Dir. Francesco Rosi. 1981.

Two Women (*La ciociara*). Dir. Vittorio De Sica. 1960.
Uccellacci e uccellini. Dir. Pier Paolo Pasolini. 1966.
Umberto D. Dir. Vittorio De Sica. 1952.
Uprooted (*Chinnamul*). Dir. Nemai Ghosh. 1950.
The Usual Suspects. Dir. Bryan Singer. 1995.
Valparaiso My Love (*Valparaiso mi amor*). Dir. Aldo Francia. 1969.
I Vesuviani. Dir. Pappi Corsicato, Antoinetta De Lillo, Antonio Capuano, Stefano Incerti, Mario Martone. 1997.
Viaggio in Italia. Dir. Roberto Rossellini. 1953.
I vitelloni. Dir. Federico Fellini. 1953.
Vito e gli altri. Dir. Antonio Capuano. 1991.
Wakefield Express. Dir. Lindsay Anderson. 1952.
The Wayfarer (*Pathik*). Dir. Debaki Bose. 1953.
We Are the Lambeth Boys. Dir. Karel Reisz. 1958.
Whistle down the Wind. Dir. Bryan Forbes. 1961.
The White Balloon (*Badkonake sefid*). Dir. Jafar Panahi. 1995.
Who Killed Pixote? (*Quem matou Pixote?*) Dir. José Joffily. 1996.
The Woman (*Aurat*). Dir. Mehboob Khan. 1940.

Sample Syllabus

Italian Neorealism's Influence on Global Cinema

This class will explore the relationship between Italian neorealism and global cinema and literature. Italian neorealism is a loosely defined film genre that includes political and didactic films that address social issues in a style that tended to provide ideological and aesthetic alternatives to Hollywood. After its heyday in Italy (roughly 1945–52) it greatly influenced directors worldwide, including filmmakers in India, Iran, Colombia, Argentina, Brazil, Czechoslovakia, the former Soviet Union, the United States, and China. This class will begin with an exploration of neorealism in Italy through the study of specific films, the reading of film theory, and a study of neorealism's literary antecedent, Italian verismo. We will then move to various global film and literary examples. No prior experience with film analysis is necessary for this course.

Required Reading
Italian Neorealism and Global Cinema, Laura E. Ruberto and Kristi M. Wilson, eds.
Selected essays available on reserve*
Among Women Only, Cesare Pavese
Hour of the Star, Clarice Lispector
The House by the Medlar Tree, Giovanni Verga
Strange Pilgrims, Gabriel García Márquez

Topics and Reading Schedule

Week One
Introduction to Course: Film and Ideology
READ: Zavattini, "A Thesis on Neorealism"*

Week Two
SCREEN: *Bicycle Thief* (De Sica)
READ: De Sica, "Why *Ladri di biciclette*?"* (in Overbey's *Springtime in Italy*)

315

READ: Bondanella on neorealism (in *Italian Cinema*)
READ: Rossellini, "A Few Words about Neorealism"* (in Overbey's *Springtime in Italy*)

Week Three
Literary Roots of Neorealism—Verismo
SCREEN: *The Earth Trembles* (Visconti)
READ: Begin *The House by the Medlar Tree* (Giovanni Verga)

Week Four
Continue reading *The House by the Medlar Tree*
SCREEN: *Rome, Open City* (Rossellini)
READ: Alicata and De Santis, "Truth and Poetry: Verga and the Italian Cinema"*

Week Five
Introduction to Neorealism in a Global Context
SCREEN: *Pather Panchali* (S. Ray)
READ: Ray, "Introduction" and "Some Italian Films I Have Seen"*
READ: Ruberto and Wilson's "Introduction" (in *Italian Neorealism and Global Cinema*)
READ: Biswas, "In the Mirror of an Alternative Globalism: The Neorealist Encounter in India" (in *Italian Neorealism and Global Cinema*)

Week Six
Third Cinema and Neorealism
SCREEN: *Miracle in Rome* (optional screening: *Miracle in Milan*)
READ: Armes, "Culture and National Identity" and "Cinema and Capitalism"*
READ: Crowder-Taraborrelli, "A Stonecutter's Passion: Latin American Reality and Cinematic Faith" (in *Italian Neorealism and Global Cinema*)
READ: *Strange Pilgrims* (Gabriel García Márquez)

Week Seven
Neorealism in Latin America
SCREEN: *Rodrigo D* (optional screening: *Umberto D*)
READ: Wilson, "From Pensioner to Teenager: Everyday Violence in De Sica's *Umberto D* and Gaviria's *Rodrigo D: No Future*" (in *Italian Neorealism and Global Cinema*)

Week Eight
SCREEN: Examples from German rubble-films and clips of Rossellini's
Germany, Year Zero
READ: Fisher, "On the Ruins of Masculinity: The Figure of the Child in
Italian Neorealism and the German Rubble-Film" (in *Italian Neo-
realism and Global Cinema*)
READ: *Among Women Only* (Cesare Pavese)

Week Nine
Neorealism and Cinema Nõvo (Brazilian cinema)
SCREEN: *Hour of the Star* (Amaral)
READ: *Hour of the Star* (Clarice Lispector)
READ: Traverso, "Migrations of Cinema: Italian Neorealism and Brazilian
Cinema" (in *Italian Neorealism and Global Cinema*)

Week Ten
Hong Kong New Wave and Neorealism
SCREEN: *1997 Trilogy* (optional, all three) (Chan)
READ: Chan, "Cinematic Neorealism: Hong Kong Cinema and Fruit
Chan's *1997 Trilogy*" (in *Italian Neorealism and Global Cinema*)

Week Eleven
Sembène's Neorealism
SCREEN: *Black Girl* (Sembène)
READ: Gabara, "'A Poetics of Refusals': Neorealism from Italy to Africa"
(in *Italian Neorealism and Global Cinema*)

Week Twelve
Iranian Cinema in the 1990s
SCREEN: *The Circle* (optional, *The White Balloon*) (Panahi)
READ: Interviews with Panahi

Week Thirteen
Czech New Wave Cinema and Neorealism
SCREEN: Select Czech films
READ: Učník, "Aesthetics or Ethics? Italian Neorealism and the Czecho-
slovak New Wave Cinema" (in *Italian Neorealism and Global Cin-
ema*)

317

Week Fourteen
Italian Neorealism Revisited
SCREEN: *Placido Rizzotto* (Scimeca)
READ: Verdicchio, "'O Cuorp'e Napule: Naples and the Cinematographic
Body of Culture" (in *Italian Neorealism and Global Cinema*)
READ: Marcus, "In Memoriam: The Neorealist Legacy in the Contem-
porary Sicilian Anti-Mafia Film" (in *Italian Neorealism and Global
Cinema*)
READ: Ruberto, "Neorealism and Contemporary European Immigration"
(in *Italian Neorealism and Global Cinema*)

Works Cited

Adorno, Theodor. *The Culture Industry: Selected Essays on Mass Culture.* Routledge Classics. London: Routledge, 2002.

Akomfrah, John. "Cinema and Liberties: Divergence or Dichotomy." *Ecrans d'Afrique* 7 (1994): 12–15.

Alcaro, Mario. *Sull'identità meridionale: Forme di una cultura mediterranea.* Saggi: Storia, Filosofia e Scienze Sociali. Torino: Bollati Boringhieri, 1999.

Alighieri, Dante. *Inferno.* Ed. and trans. Robert M. Durling. New York: Oxford UP, 1996.

Amelio, Gianni. *Lamerica: Film e storia del film.* Ed. Piera Detassis. Turin: Einaudi, 1994.

Aprà, Adriano, ed. *Napoletana: Images of a City.* Trans. Jennifer Franhina. Incontri Internazionali d'Arte, New York. Rome: Fabbri Editore, 1993.

Armes, Roy. *Patterns of Realism.* New York: A. S. Barnes, 1971.

———. *Third World Filmmaking and the West.* Berkeley: U of California P, 1987.

Atkinson, Michael. "Sembène's Universal Language." *Village Voice* Apr. 2, 2001 <http://www.villagevoice.com/issues/0114/atkinson.php>.

Bakari, Imruh, and Mbye Cham, eds. *African Experiences of Cinema.* London: British Film Institute, 1996.

Bambara, Toni Cade. "Reading the Signs, Empowering the Eye: *Daughters of the Dust* and the Black Independent Cinema Movement." Diawara, *Black American Cinema* 118–44.

Bandyopadhyay, Manik. *Manik Bandyopadhyay Rachanasamagra.* Vol. 2. Calcutta: Paschimbanga Bangla Akademi, 1998.

Banerji, Samik. "The Early Years of Calcutta Cinema." *Calcutta: Living City.* Vol. 2. Ed. Sukanta Chaudhuri. Calcutta: Oxford UP, 1990.

Barlet, Olivier. "Une relation d'amour avec le spectateur: Entretien avec Mahamat Saleh Haroun." *Africultures* 45 (Feb. 2002): 22–24.

Bartošek, Luboš. *Náš Film: Kapitoly z Dějin (1896–1945).* Praha: Mladá Fronta, 1985.

Bassolino, Antonio. *La repubblica delle città.* Interventi/31. Roma: Donzelli Editore, 1996.

Baudrillard, Jean. *Simulacra and Simulation.* Trans. Sheila Faria Glaser. Ann Arbor: U of Michigan P, 1994.

Bawden, Liz-Anne, ed. *The Oxford Companion to Film.* New York: Oxford UP, 1976.

319

Bazin, André. *What Is Cinema?* Vol. 2. Berkeley: U of California P, 1971.

Beiermann-Ratjen, Hans. "Realste Realistik im Film." *Filmpress* 13 (Sept. 2, 1949): 9.

Benamou, Catherine. "Cuban Cinema: On the Threshold of Gender." *Redirecting the Gaze: Gender, Theory and Cinema in the Third World.* Ed. Diana Robin and Ira Jaffe. New York: State U of New York P, 1999. 67–98.

Benjamin, Walter, and Asja Lacis. "Discussioni sulla collettività nell'arte in generale." Trans. L. M. Rubino (from German). *Teorie del realismo.* Ed. Edoardo Bruno. Rome: Bulzoni, 1977. 195–99.

———. *Illuminations.* Trans. Harry Zohn. New York: Schocken Books, 1969.

———. "Napoli." *Napoli.* Ed. Enrico Donaggio. Le Gomene 15. Napoli: L'ancora del mediterraneo, 2000.

Bentes, Ivana. "*Deus e o diabo na terra do sol/Black God, White Devil.*" Elena and Días López 89–97.

Berkeley, George. *Three Dialogues between Hylas and Philonous.* Oxford: Oxford UP, 1998.

———. *A Treatise Concerning the Principles of Human Knowledge.* Ed. Jonathan Dancy. Oxford: Oxford UP, 1998.

Berthier, Nancy. "Memorias del subdesarrollo/Memories of Underdevelopment." Elena and Días López 99–107.

Biswas, Moinak. "Bengali Cinema: The Literary Liaison Revisited." *Journal of the Moving Image* 1 (1999): 1–13.

Blesa, Túa. *Quiñientos años de soledad: Actas del congreso "Gabriel García Márquez."* Zaragosa: Universidad de Zaragosa, D. L., 1997.

Bogle, Donald. *Toms, Coons, Mulattoes, Mammies and Bucks: An Interpretive History of Blacks in American Films.* New York: Continuum, 1995.

Bondanella, Peter E. *The Eternal City: Roman Images in the Modern World.* Chapel Hill: U of North Carolina P, 1987.

———. *The Films of Roberto Rossellini.* New York: Cambridge UP, 1993.

———. *Italian Cinema: From Neorealism to the Present.* 1983. New York: Continuum Press, 1991.

Bordwell, David. "The Art Cinema as a Mode of Film Practice." *Film Theory and Criticism: Introductory Readings.* 5th ed. Leo Braudy and Marshall Cohen. New York: Oxford UP, 1999.

———. *Narration in the Fiction Film.* London: Routledge, 1985.

Bordwell, David, and Kristin Thompson. *Film Art: An Introduction.* 5th ed. New York: McGraw-Hill, 1997.

Brandlmeier, Thomas. "Von Hitler zu Adenauer: Deutsche Trümmerfilme." *Zwischen Gestern und Morgen: Westdeutscher Nachkriegsfilme, 1946–62.* Frankfurt/Main: Deutsches Fimmuseum, 1989.

Branston, Gill, and Roy Stafford. *The Media Student's Book.* 3rd ed. New York: Routledge, 2003.

Brož, Jaroslav. *The Path of Fame of the Czechoslovak Film.* Prague: Československý Film Export, 1967.

Brunetta, Gian Piero. *Cent'anni di cinema italiano: Volume 2 dal 1945 ai giorni nostri.* Rome: Editori Laterza, 1995.

Brunette, Peter. *Roberto Rossellini.* 1987. Berkeley: U of California P, 1996.

———. "Rossellini and Cinematic Realism." *Cinema Journal* 25.1 (1985): 34–49.

———. "When Neo-Realism Collided with Reality." *New York Times* Feb. 17, 2002, late ed.: AR33.

Bruno, Giuliana. *Streetwalking on a Ruined Map: Cultural Theory and the City Films of Elvira Notari.* Princeton: Princeton UP, 1993.

Buck-Morss, Susan. *The Dialectics of Seeing: Walter Benjamin and the Arcades Project.* Cambridge, MA: MIT P, 1995.

Burton, Julianne, ed. *Cinema and Social Change in Latin America: Conversations with Filmmakers.* Austin: U of Texas P, 1986.

———, ed. *The Social Documentary in Latin America.* Pittsburgh: U of Pittsburgh P, 1990.

Canella, Mario. "Ideology and Aesthetic Hypotheses in the Criticism of Neo-realism." *Screen* 14.4 (1973–74): 5–60.

Capra, Frank. *The Name above the Title: Frank Capra, an Autobiography.* New York: Macmillan, 1971.

Capuano, Antonio. "Alla riscoperta della visualità a Napoli e dintorni: Incontro con Antonio Capuano." *Cinemasessanta* 43.3 (2002): 28–36.

Cattrysse, Patrick. "The Unbearable Lightness of Being: Film Adaptation Seen from a Different Perspective." *Literature/Film Quarterly* 25.3 (1997): 222–30.

Chakravarty, Sumita S. *National Identity in Indian Popular Cinema, 1947–1987.* Delhi: Oxford UP, 1998.

Cham, Mbye. "Ousmane Sembene and the Aesthetics of African Oral Traditions." *Africana Journal* 13 (1982): 24–40.

Chan, Natalia Sui-hung. "Rewriting History: Hong Kong Nostalgia Cinema and Its Social Practice." *The Cinema of Hong Kong: History, Arts, Identity.* Ed. Poshek Fu and David Desser. New York: Cambridge UP, 2000. 252–72.

Chanan, Michael. *The Cuban Image: Cinema and Cultural Politics in Cuba.* Bloomington: British Film Institute/Indiana UP, 1985.

Chaney, Edward. "The Grand Tour and Beyond: British and American Travelers in Southern Italy, 1545–1960." *Oxford, China and Italy: Writings in Honour of Sir Harold Acton on His Eightieth Birthday.* Ed. E. Chaney and Neil Ritichie. New York: Thames and Hudson, 1984.

Chen, Albert H. Y. "The Court of Final Appeal's Ruling in 'Illegal Migrant' Children Case: Congressional Supremacy and Judicial Review." *Hong Kong's Constitutional Debate: Conflict over Interpretation.* Ed. Johannes M. M. Chan and H. L. Fu. Hong Kong: Hong Kong UP, 2000. 73–96.

Ciel, Martin. "Súvislosti Slovenskej Filmovej Teórie: 1945–1971." *Slovenský Hraný Film: 1970–1990.* Ed. Václav Macek. Edícia Signans. Bratislava:

Slovenský Filmový Ústav-Národné Kinematografické Centrum, 1993. 11–25.

Clarke, David, ed. *The Cinematic City.* New York: Routledge, 2000.

Corliss, Richard. "The Kids Are Alright." *Time* 153.10 (1999): 85.

Croce, Benedetto. "Il paradiso abitato dai diavoli." *Uomini e cose della vecchia Italia.* Bari: Laterza, 1956.

Dalle Vacche, Angela. *The Body in the Mirror: Shapes of History in Italian Cinema.* Princeton: Princeton UP, 1992.

Daniel, František. "The Czech Difference." *Politics, Art and Commitment in the East European Cinema.* Ed. David W. Paul. London: Macmillan, 1983. 49–56.

Das Gupta, Chidananda. *The Cinema of Satyajit Ray.* Rev. and enl. ed. New Delhi: National Book Trust, 1994.

Deleuze, Gilles. *Bergsonism.* New York: Zone Books, 1988.

———. *Cinema 1: The Movement-Image.* Trans. Hugh Tomlinson and Barbara Habberjam. Minneapolis: U of Minnesota P, 1986.

———. *Cinema 2: The Time-Image.* Trans. Hugh Tomlinson and Robert Galeta. Minneapolis: U of Minnesota P, 1989.

———. *Difference and Repetition.* Trans. Paul Patton. New York: Columbia UP, 1994.

———. "From *Cinema 1* and *Cinema 2.*" *Film Theory and Criticism: Sixth Edition.* Ed. Leo Braudy and Marshall Cohen. New York: Oxford UP, 2004. 240–70.

———. "The Greatest Irish Film (Beckett's *Film*)." *Essays Critical and Clinical.* Trans. Daniel W. Smith and Michael A. Greco. Minneapolis: U of Minnesota P, 1997. 23–26.

De Martino, Ernesto. *Sud e magia.* Saggi. 2nd ed. Milano: Feltrinelli, 2002.

De Sica, Vittorio. "De Sica on De Sica." *Vittorio De Sica: Contemporary Perspectives.* Ed. Howard Curle and Stephen Snyder. Toronto: U of Toronto P, 2000. 22–49.

Diawara, Manthia. *African Cinema: Politics and Culture.* Bloomington: Indiana UP, 1992.

———, ed. *Black American Cinema.* New York: Routledge, 1993.

———. "Black American Cinema: The New Realism." *Black American Cinema.* Ed. Manthia Diawara. New York: Routledge, 1993. 3–25.

Dickens, Charles. *American Notes and Pictures from Italy.* 1846. The Oxford Illustrated Dickens. New York: Oxford UP, 1957.

Dimitrov, Georgi. *The United Front against Fascism: Speeches at the Seventh Congress of the Communist International, August 1935.* Sydney: Current Book Distributors, 1945.

Donaggio, Enrico, ed. *Adorno, Benjamin, Bloch, Kracauer, Löwith, Sohn-Rethel: Napoli.* Napoli: L'ancora del mediterraneo, 2000.

E. R. "Hans Albers in der Trümmerstadt." *Volksblatt* Dec. 11, 1947.

Eco, Umberto. *Apocalypse Postponed.* Ed. Robert Lumley. Bloomington: Indiana UP, 1994.

Edelstein, David. "All in the Family." *Village Voice* Dec. 18, 1984: 82–84.

Elena, Alberto, and Marina Días López, eds. *The Cinema of Latin America*. London: Wallflower Press, 2003.

Elsaesser, Thomas. *New German Cinema: A History*. New Brunswick, NJ: Rutgers, 1989.

Elsaesser, Thomas, with Adam Barker, eds. *Early Cinema, Space, Frame, Narrative*. London: British Film Institute, 1990.

"Entretien avec Med Hondo." *Positif* 119 (1970): 22–26.

Évora, J. A. *Tomás Gutiérrez Alea*. Madrid: Cátedra/Filmoteca Española, 1996.

Feder, Elena. "In the Shadow of Race: Forging Gender in Bolivian Film and Video." *Redirecting the Gaze: Gender, Theory, and the Cinema in the Third World*. Ed. Diana Robin and Ira Jaffe. New York: State U of New York P, 1999. 149–203.

Fehrenbach, Heide. *Cinema in Democratizing German: Reconstructing National Identity after Hitler*. Chapel Hill: U of North Carolina P, 1995.

Fernandez, Hector D. "Rodrigo D—No Futuro." *Film Quarterly* 48.2 (1994–95): 48–49.

Fiala, Miloš. "Rozlet a Brzda (Naše Kinematografie v Létech 1957–59)." *Film a Doba* 2 (1969): 62–68.

Fisher, Jaimey. "Deleuze in a Ruinous Context: German Rubble-Film and Italian Neorealism." *Iris, Special Issue: Gilles Deleuze, Philosopher of Cinema* 23 (Spring 1997): 53–74.

Fofi, Goffredo, ed. *Luna nuova: Scrittori dal sud*. Lecce: Argo p.s.c.r.l., 1997.

———. *Narrare il Sud: Percorsi di scrittura e di lettura*. Napoli: Liguori Editore, 1995.

Fong, Cochran. "Middle-aged and Jobless in 1997: Fruit Chan on *The Longest Summer*." *Hong Kong Panorama 98–99*. Ed. Stephen Teo. Hong Kong: Urban Council of Hong Kong, 1999. 53–54.

Forgacs, David, and Robert Lumlet, eds. *Italian Cultural Studies: An Introduction*. Oxford: Oxford UP, 1996.

Forgacs, David, Sarah Lutton, and Geoffrey Nowell-Smith, eds. *Roberto Rossellini: Magician of the Real*. London: British Film Institute, 2000.

Foscolo, Ugo. "Dei sepolchri." *Rime*. Ed. Marco Cerruti. Milan: Feltrinelli, 1992. 107–22.

"Four Film Makers from West Africa." *Framework* 11 (Autumn 1979): 16–21.

Furhammar, Leif, and Folke Isaksson. *Politics and Film*. Trans. Kersti French. New York: Praeger, 1971.

Gabriel, Teshome. "Third Cinema as Guardian of Popular Memory: Towards a Third Aesthetics." *Questions of Third Cinema*. Ed. Jim Pines and Paul Willemen. London: British Film Institute, 1989. 53–64.

Gadjigo, Samba, Ralph Faulkingham, Thomas Cassirer, and Reinhard Sander, eds. *Ousmane Sembène: Dialogues with Critics and Writers*. Amherst: U of Massachusetts P, 1993.

Gallagher, Tag. *The Adventures of Robert Rossellini: His Life and Films*. New York: De Capo, 1998.

García Márquez, Gabriel. *Notas de prensa: 1980–1984.* Madrid: Mondadori, 1991.

———. *La soledad de América Latina: Escritos sobre arte y literatura, 1948–1984.* La Habana: Editorial Arte y Literatura, 1990.

Ghatak, Ritwik. "Ekmatra Satyajit Ray." *Chitrabikshan* 18.1–2 (1984).

Gieri, Manuela. *Contemporary Italian Filmmaking: Strategies of Subversion: Pirandello, Fellini, Scola and the Directors of the New Generation.* Toronto: U of Toronto P, 1995.

Ginsborg, Paul. *A History of Contemporary Italy: Society and Politics, 1943–88.* London: Penguin, 1990.

Giordana, Marco Tulli, Claudio Fava, and Monica Zapelli. *I cento passi.* Milan: Feltrinelli, 2001.

Glaser, Hermann. *Kulturgeschichte der Bundesrepublik Deutschland, Zwischen Kapitulation und Währungsreform, 1945–48.* Munich: Carl Hanser, 1985.

Godard, Jean-Luc. *Alphaville: A Film by Jean-Luc Godard.* Trans. Peter Whitehead. Modern Film Scripts. New York: Simon and Schuster, 1968.

———. *Godard on Godard.* Trans. Tom Milne. New York: Da Capo, 1972.

Goffredo, Giuseppe. *Cadmos cerca Europa: Il sud fra il Mediterraneo e l'Europa.* Torino: Bollati Boringhieri, 2000.

Gomez, Santiago Andres. "Los pulmones limpios: La obra de Victor Gaviria." *Kinetoscopio* 26 (1994): 79–86.

Gramsci, Antonio. *An Antonio Gramsci Reader: Selected Writings: 1916–1935.* Ed. David Forgacs. New York: Schocken Books, 1988.

———. *I Quaderni: Letteratura e vita nazionale.* 1975. Rome: Riuniti, 1996.

———. *Il risorgimento.* Ed. Maria Corti. Turin: Einaudi, 1952.

———. *The Southern Question.* Trans. and intro. Pasquale Verdicchio. Chicago: Bordighera, 1995.

Guerrero, Edward. *Framing Blackness: The African American Image in Film.* Philadelphia: Temple UP, 1993.

———. "Negotiations of Ideology, Manhood, and Family in Billy Woodberry's *Bless Their Little Hearts.*" *Black American Literature Forum* 25.2 (1991): 315–22.

Hames, Peter. *The Czechoslovak New Wave.* Berkeley: U of California P, 1985.

Haskell, Molly. *From Reverence to Rape: The Treatment of Women in the Movies.* Chicago: U of Chicago P, 1987.

Hay, James. *Popular Film Culture in Fascist Italy: The Passing of the Rex.* Bloomington: Indiana UP, 1987.

Hayward, Susan. *Key Concepts in Cinema Studies.* 2nd ed. London: Routledge, 2000.

Higson, Andrew. "The Concept of National Cinema." *Screen* 30 (1989): 35–46.

Hill, John, and Pamela Church Gibson, eds. *World Cinema: Critical Approaches.* New York: Oxford UP, 2000.

Hillier, Jim, ed. *Cahiers du Cinéma: The 1950's: Neorealism, Hollywood, New Wave.* Cambridge, MA: Harvard UP, 1985.

Hinrichs, Bruce. "A Trip to the Movies: 100 Years of Film as Art." *The Humanist* 56.1 (1996): 7–13.

Iordanova, Dina. "Balkan Cinema in the 90s: An Overview." *Afterimage* 28.4 (2001): 23–26.

Jameson, Frederic. *The Geopolitical Aesthetic: Cinema and Space in the World System.* Bloomington: Indiana UP, 1995.

———. "Postmodernism and Consumer Society." *The Anti-Aesthetic: Essays on Postmodern Culture.* Ed. Hal Foster. Washington, DC: Bay Press, 1983.

Jenkins, Henry, ed. *The Children's Culture Reader.* New York: New York UP, 1998.

Johnson, Randal, and Robert Stam, eds. *Brazilian Cinema.* New York: Columbia UP, 1995.

Kaes, Anton. *From Hitler to Heimat: The Return of History as Film.* Cambridge, MA: Harvard UP, 1989.

Kantaris, Elia Geoffrey. "Allegorical Bodies and Visions in Colombian Urban Cinema." *E.I.A.L.* Oct. 14, 2002 <http://www.tau.ac.il/eial/IX_2/kantaris.html>.

Kapur, Geeta. "Sovereign Subject: Ray's Apu." *When Was Modernism: Essays on Contemporary Cultural Practice in India.* New Delhi: Tulika, 2000.

Kapur, Rajiv. Personal communication, Apr. 23, 1999 (rogercom@albnet.com.br). International Movie Database <http://us.imdb.com/title/tt0117418>.

King, John. *Magical Reels: A History of Cinema in Latin America.* London: Verso, 1990.

King, John, Ana M. Lopez, and Manuel Alvarado, eds. *Mediating Two Worlds: Cinematic Encounters in the Americas.* London: British Film Institute, 1993.

Klein, Richard. *Cigarettes Are Sublime.* Durham: Duke UP, 1993.

Klotman, Phyllis Rauch. *Screenplays of the Black American Experience.* Bloomington: Indiana UP.

Kopaněvová, Galina. "V Září, v Sorrentu." *Zborník Fóra Mladého Filmu '89.* Ed. Jan Jaroš, Martin Ciel, and Peter Dubecký. 1969. Edícia Fóra Mladého Filmu. Zväzok 4. Bratislava: Správa Účelových Zariadení MV SZM, SFÚ-SFT, 1989. 21–27.

Kosík, Karel. "Epilogue: Karel Kosík." Trans. Peter Kussi and Adolf Hoffmeister. *The Politics of Culture.* Ed. Antonín J. Liehm. New York: Grove Press, 1973.

Kracauer, Siegfried. "Basic Concepts." *Film Theory and Criticism: Sixth Edition.* Ed. Leo Braudy and Marshall Cohen. New York: Oxford UP, 2004. 143–54.

———. *Theory of Film: The Redemption of Physical Reality.* Princeton: Princeton UP, (1960) 1997.

Kreimeier, Klaus. "Die Ökonomie der Gefühle: Aspekte des westdeutschen Nachkriegsfilms." *Zwischen Gestern und Morgen: Westdeutscher Nachkriegsfilme, 1946–62.* Frankfurt/Main: Deutsches Fimmuseum, 1989.

Kučera, Jan. *Filmová Tvorba: Základní Otázky Filmové Estetiky. (Přednášky pro Večerní Školu Filmové Tvorby).* Praha: FAMU, 1959.

L. M. "Im Dschungel der zertrümmerten Stadt: Der neue DEFA-Film 'Irgendwo in Berlin' uraufgeführt." *Volksblatt* Dec. 20, 1946.

Lam Lin-tong. "Yidaili Xinxieshizhuyi Dianying Zaipingjia [Reevaluation of Italian Neorealist Films]." *Lam Lin-tong Lunwenji* [Collective Essays of Lam Lin-tong]. Hong Kong: Subculture Publishing, 1996. 93–111.

———. "Zhanhou Xianggangdianying Fazhandi Jitiaoxiansuo [The Historical Development of Hong Kong Cinema in Postwar Time]. *Zhongguo Dianying Meixue* [Aesthetics of Chinese Cinema]. Taipei: Yunchen Cultural Publishing, 1991. 155–81.

Landy, Marcia. *Fascism in Film: The Italian Commercial Cinema: 1931–1943.* Princeton: Princeton UP, 1983.

———. *Italian Film.* Cambridge: Cambridge UP, 2000.

———. "Politics and Style in *Black Girl.*" *Jump Cut* 27 (July 1982): 23–25.

Law Kar, ed. *Hong Kong New Wave: Twenty Years After.* Hong Kong: Urban Council of Hong Kong, 1999.

———. "An Overview of Hong Kong's New Wave Cinema." *At Full Speed: Hong Kong Cinema in a Borderless World.* Ed. Esther Yau. Minneapolis: U of Minnesota P, 2001. 31–52.

———. "Xianggang Dianying di Haiwai Jingyan" [The Overseas Experience of Hong Kong Cinema]. *Overseas Chinese Figures in Cinema.* Ed. Law Kar Hong Kong: Hong Kong Urban Council, 1992. 15–21.

Lawton, Ben. "Italian Neorealism: A Mirror Construction of Reality." *Film Criticism* 3.2 (1979): 8–23.

Lenning, Walter. "'Irgendwo in Berlin' Uraufführung des neuen DEFA-Films in der Staatsoper." *Berliner Zeitung* Dec. 20, 1946.

"A Letter from V. I. Pudovkin and N. Cherkassov." *Chinnamul, Nimai Ghosher prabandha baktrita sakkhatkar, ebong tar jiban o kaj samparke alochona.* Ed. S. Basu and S. Dasgupta. Calcutta: Cine Central and Monchasha, 2003.

Liehm, Antonín J. *Closely Watched Films: The Czechoslovak Experience.* White Plains, NY: International Arts and Sciences Press, 1974.

———. "Miloš Forman: The Style and the Man." *Politics, Art and Commitment in the East European Cinema.* Ed. David W. Paul. London: Macmillan, 1983. 211–24.

Liehm, Mira. *Passion and Defiance: Film in Italy from 1942 to the Present.* Berkeley: U of California P, 1984.

Liehm, Mira, and Antonín J. Liehm. *The Most Important Art: Eastern European Film after 1945.* Berkeley: U of California P, 1977.

Lizzani, Carlo. *Riso amaro: Un film diretto da Giuseppe De Santis.* Rome: Officina Edizioni, 1978.

Lopez, Ana M., John King, and Manuel Alvarado, eds. *Mediating Two Worlds: Cinematic Encounters in the Americas.* London: British Film Institute, 1993.

Lotman, Jurij. "The Illusion of Reality." *Semiotics of Cinema.* Michigan Slavic Contributions 5. Ann Arbor: U of Michigan P, 1976. 10–22.

Lukacs, Georg. "Narrate or Describe?" *Writer and Critic and Other Essays.* Trans. and ed. Arthur Kahn. London: Merlin Press, 1970.

MacCabe, Colin. "Realism and Cinema: Notes on Some Brechtian Theses." *Screen* 15:2 (1974): 7–27.

MacCann, Richard Dyer. *Film: A Montage of Theories.* New York: E. P. Dutton, 1966.

Macek, Václav. *Dušan Hanák.* Bratislava: Nadácia FOTOFO, Slovenský Filmový Ústav—NKC, Filmová a Televízna Fakulta VŠMU, 1996.

Macnab, Geoffrey. *J. Arthur Rank and the British Film Industry.* London: Routledge, 1993.

Marcus, Millicent. *Italian Film in the Light of Neorealism.* Princeton: Princeton UP, 1986.

Martin, Gerald. "On Magical and Social Realism in García Márquez." *Gabriel García Márquez: New Readings.* Ed. Bernard McGuirk and Richard Cardwell. Cambridge: Cambridge UP, 1987.

Martin, Michael T., ed. *New Latin American Cinema.* Detroit: Wayne State UP, 1997.

Mast, Gerald, Marshall Cohen, and Leon Braudy, eds. *Film Theory and Criticism.* New York: Oxford UP, 1992.

Milan Women's Bookstore Collective. *Sexual Difference: A Theory of Social-Symbolic Practice.* Bloomington: Indiana UP, 1990.

Modonesi, Chiara. "Cento passi verso la libertà." *Acting* 1 (Sept. 2002): 5–18.

Moeller, Robert. *Protecting Motherhood: Women and the Family in the Politics of Postwar West Germany.* Berkeley: U of California P, 1993.

Moretti, Franco. "Conjectures on World Literature." *New Left Review* ns 1 (Jan.–Feb.): 2000.

Mosse, George. *Nationalism and Sexuality: Middle-Class Morality and Sexual Norms in Modern Europe.* Madison: U of Wisconsin P, 1985.

Mouesca, Jacqueline. *Plano sequencia de la memoria de Chile: Veinticinco años de cine chileno (1960–1985).* Madrid: Ediciones del litoral, 1988.

Mukherjee, Meenakshi. *Realism and Reality: The Novel and Society in India.* Delhi: Oxford UP, 1994.

Mukhopadhyay, Mohinimohan. "Chhabir Nutanatwa." Rpt. in *Chitrasutra* Nov. 1996.

Myerson, Michael. *Memories of Underdevelopment: The Revolutionary Films in Cuba.* New York: Grossman, 1973.

Nagib, Lúcia, ed. *The New Brazilian Cinema.* London: I. B. Tauris, 2003.

Nandy, Ashis. *The Intimate Enemy: Loss and Recovery of Self under Colonialism.* New York: Oxford UP, 1983.

Nelson, Robert. "Appropriation." *Critical Terms for Art History.* Ed. Robert Nelson and Richard Shiff. Chicago: U of Chicago P, 1996. 116–28.

Nichols, Bill. *Representing Reality.* Bloomington: Indiana UP, 1991.

Nietzsche, Friedrich. *Beyond Good and Evil.* Trans. Walter Kaufmann. New York: Vintage Books, 1966.

———. "The Use and Abuse of History." *Thoughts Out of Season II.* Trans. Adrian Collins. Edinburgh: T. N. Foulis, 1915. 6–100.

Nochlin, Linda. *Realism.* London: Penguin, 1971.

Norton, Chris. "Black Independent Cinema and the Influence of Neo-realism: Futility, Struggle, and Hope in the Face of Reality." *Images Journal: A Journal of Film and Popular Culture* 5 (1997) <http://www.imagesjournal. com>.

Nowell-Smith, Geoffrey, ed. *The Oxford History of World Cinema.* Oxford: Oxford UP, 1996.

O'Brien, Geoffrey. "Stop Shooting." *Artforum* Oct. 2003, 39–42.

Overbey, David, ed. and trans. *Springtime in Italy: A Reader on Neorealism.* Hamden, CT: Archon Books, 1978.

Palencia-Roth, Michael. "Los peregrinajes de García Márquez o la covación religiosa de la literature." *Quinientos años de soledad: Actas del congreso "Gabriel García Márquez."* Coord. Rosa Pellicer and Alfredo Saldaña. Zaragosa: Tropelías, 1992.

Pasolini, Pier Paolo. *Pier Paolo Pasolini: Poems.* Ed. and trans. Norman Macafee. New York: Random House, 1982.

"Pasquale Scimeca e il mondo contadino del dopoguerra." *Cinemasessanta* 42 (March–April 2002): 6–7.

Paul, David W. "Introduction: Film Art and Social Commitment." *Politics, Art and Commitment in the East European Cinema.* Ed. David W. Paul. London: Macmillan, 1983. 1–22.

Petty, Sheila, ed. *A Call to Action: The Films of Ousmane Sembene.* Westport, CT: Greenwood Press, 1996.

Pfaff, Françoise. *The Cinema of Ousmane Sembène, a Pioneer of African Film.* Westport, CT: Greenwood Press, 1984.

Piech, Stefan M. "The Impact of the 1989 Velvet Revolution on the Former Czechoslovakian Film Industry." *Innovation* 10.1 (1997): 37–60.

Pines, Jim, and Paul Willemen, eds. *Questions of Third Cinema.* London: British Film Institute, 1989.

Piperno, Franco. *Elogio dello spirito pubblico meridionale.* Le esche 11. Collana genius loci e individuo sociale. Roma: Manifestolibri, 1997.

Plutarch, Lucius Mestrius. *Lives of Aristeides and Cato.* Trans. David Sansone. Warminster, Wiltshire: Aris and Phillips, 1989.

Pradhan, Sudhi. "Bharatiya Gananantya Sanstha Ebang Bharatiya Chalachitra." *Chitrakalpa* 29 (1982).

Prasad, Madhava. *Ideology of the Hindi Film: A Historical Construction.* Delhi: Oxford UP, 1998.

Procaccini, Alfonso. "Neorealism: Description/Prescription." *Yale Italian Studies* 2 (1978): 39–57.

Quilici, Gianni. "*I cento passi.*" *La linea dell'occhio* 39 (Spring 2001): 5.

R.S.F.S.R. *Problems of Soviet Literature: Reports and Speeches at the First Soviet Writers' Congress* [Vsesoiuznyi Sjezd Sovetskikh Pisatelei in 1934 Moscow]. London: Greenwood, 1979.

Rajadhyaksha, Ashish, and Paul Willemen. *Encyclopaedia of Indian Cinema.* London: British Film Institute and New Delhi: Oxford UP, 1994.

Ray, Satyajit. *My Years with Apu.* New Delhi: Penguin Books India, 1996.

———. *Our Films, Their Films.* Calcutta: Orient Longman, 1976.

Reich, Jacqueline, and Piero Garofalo, eds. *Re-viewing Fascism: Italian Cinema, 1922–1943.* Bloomington: Indiana UP, 2002.

Rentería Mantilla, Alfonso, ed. *García Márquez habla de García Márquez.* Bogotá: Rentería Editores LTDA, 1979.

Report of the Film Enquiry Committee. New Delhi: Ministry of Information and Broadcasting, Govt. of India Press, 1951.

Rhode, Eric. "Satyajit Ray: A Study." *Sight and Sound* 13.3 (1961): 132–36.

———. "Why Neorealism Failed." *Sight and Sound* 30.1 (1960): 26–32.

Robin, Diana, and Ira Jaffe, eds. *Redirecting the Gaze: Gender, Theory and Cinema in the Third World.* New York: State U of New York P, 1999.

Robinson, Davis. *From Peep Show to Palace: The Birth of American Film.* New York: Columbia UP, 1996.

Rodowick, D. N. *Gilles Deleuze's Time Machine.* Durham: Duke UP, 1997.

Romano, Ruggiero. *Paese Italia: Venti secoli di identità.* Saggi. Storia e scienze sociali. Roma: Donzelli Editore, 1994.

Romm, Mikhail. *Selected Works in 3 Volumes.* Vol. 1. Moscow: Iskustvo, 1980 (in Russian).

Rondeli, Levan. *Tradition and Screen.* Tbilisi: Ganatleba, 1978 (in Russian).

Rossellini, Roberto. "Due parole sul neo-realismo." *Retrospettive* 4 (Apr. 1953).

———. *My Method: Writings and Interviews.* New York: Marsilio, 1987.

Rouch, Jean. "Sandy et Bozambo: Entretien avec Jean Rouch sur Sembène Ousmane." *CinémAction* 34 (1985): 86–94.

Roud, Richard. *Jean-Luc Godard.* New York: Doubleday, 1968.

Ruberto, Laura E. *Producing Culture: Representations of Italian and Italian American Women at Work.* Diss. U of California–San Diego, 1999.

Russo, Antonella. "The Invention of Southerness: Photographic Travels and the Discovery of the Other Half of Italy." *Aperture, Immagini italiane* 132 (Summer 1993): 58–69.

Saldívar, Dasso. *García Márquez: El viaje a la semilla: La biografía.* Madrid: Santilla, S.S., 1997.

Schonberg, Michael, trans. *The Take One Film Book Series.* Toronto: Peter Martin Associates Ltd. in Association with *Take One Magazine,* 1971.

Sembene, Ousmane. "Sembène parle de ses films." *CinémAction* 34 (1985): 25–29.

"Séminaire sur 'Le rôle du Cinéaste africain dans l'éveil d'une conscience de civilisation noire.'" *Présence Africaine* 90 (1974): 3–203.

Shandley, Robert. *Rubble-Films: German Cinema in the Shadow of the Third Reich.* Philadelphia: Temple UP, 2001.

Shaviro, Steven. *The Cinematic Body*. Minneapolis: U of Minnesota P, 1993.

Shiel, Mark, and Tony Fitzmaurice, eds. *Cinema and the City: Film and Urban Societies in a Global Context*. New York: Blackwell, 2001.

Silverman, Kaja. *Male Subjectivity at the Margins*. New York: Routledge, 1993.

Sitney, P. Adams. *Vital Crises in Italian Cinema*. Austin: U of Texas P, 1995.

Škvorecký, Josef. *All the Bright Men and Women: A Personal History of the Czech Cinema*. Trans. Michael Schonberg. Toronto: Peter P. Martin Associates, 1971.

Smith, Dennis Mack. *Mussolini*. New York: Knopf, 1982.

Snead, James. *White Screens Black Images*. New York: Routledge, 1994.

So, Susanna. "Made in Hong Kong—Interview with Fruit Chan." *Hong Kong Panorama 97–98*. Ed. Stephen Teo. Hong Kong: Urban Council of Hong Kong, 1998. 56–57.

Sobchack, Vivian Carol. *The Address of the Eye: A Phenomenology of Film Experience*. Princeton: Princeton UP, 1992.

Sobolev, Romil. *How Cinema Became an Art*. Kiev: Mistetstvo, 1975 (in Russian).

Solanas, Fernando, and Octavio Getino. *Cine, Cultura y Descolonización*. Buenos Aires: Siglo XXI Argentino Editores, 1973.

———. *A diez años de hacia un Tercer Cine*. Mexico D.F.: Filmoteca UNAM, 1982.

Sorlin, Pierre. *Italian National Cinema: 1896–1996*. London: Routledge, 1996.

———. "Neorealism or the Complexity of Urban Relationship." *European Cinemas, European Societies, 1939–1990*. Studies in Film, Television and the Media. London: Routledge, 1991. 117–26.

Spackman, Barbara. *Fascist Virilities: Rhetoric, Ideology, and Social Fantasy in Italy*. Minneapolis: U of Minnesota P, 1996.

Speranza, Paolo, ed. Republication of 1966 issue of *Cinemasud: L'eredità del neorealismo*, 2002.

Stam, Robert. *Tropical Multiculturalism: Comparative History of Race in Brazilian Cinema and Culture*. Durham: Duke UP, 1997.

Studlar, Gaylan. *In the Realm of Pleasure*. Urbana: U of Illinois P, 1988.

Tannenbaum, Edward. *The Fascist Experience: Italian Society and Culture, 1922–1945*. New York: Basic Books, 1972.

Taubin, Amy. "Part of the Problem." *Film Comment* 39 (Sept.–Oct. 2003): 26–33.

Teno, Jean-Marie. "Freedom: The Power to Say No." Bakari and Cham, *African Experiences of Cinema* 70–71.

Teo, Stephen. *Hong Kong Cinema: The Extra Dimensions*. London: British Film Institute, 1997.

Teti, Vito. *La razza maledetta*. Roma: Manifestolibri, 1998.

Thompson, Kristin. *Breaking the Glass Armor: Neoformalist Film Analysis*. Princeton: Princeton UP, 1988.

Thompson, Kristin, and David Bordwell. *Film History: An Introduction*. New York: McGraw-Hill, 1994.

330

Trančík, Pavol. *Niektoré Estetické Problémy Filmu.* Bratislava: Slovenský Filmový Ústav, 1966.

Ukadike, N. Frank. *Black African Cinema.* Berkeley: U of California P, 1994.

———. "The Creation of an African Film Aesthetic/Language for Representing African Realities." Petty 105–17.

———. *Questioning African Cinema.* Minneapolis: U of Minnesota P, 2002.

Van Wert, William F. "Ideology in the Third World Cinema: A Study of Ousmane Sembene and Glauber Rocha." *Quarterly Review of Film Studies* 4.2 (1979): 207–26.

Vasudevan, Ravi. "The Politics of Cultural Address in a 'Transitional' Cinema: A Case Study of Indian Popular Cinema." *Reinventing Film Studies.* Ed. Christine Gledhill and Linda Williams. London: Arnold, 2001.

Velardi, Claudio, ed. *La città porosa: Conversazioni su Napoli: Massimo Cacciari, Antonio D'Amato, Gustaw Herling, Mario Martone, Francesca Venezia.* Soglie. Napoli: Edizioni Cronopio, 1992.

Verdicchio, Pasquale. *Bound by Distance: Rethinking Nationalism through the Italian Diaspora.* Cranbury, NJ: Fairleigh Dickinson UP, 1997.

Verdone, Mario. *Storia del cinema italiano.* Roma: Tascabili Economici Newton, 1995.

Vieyra, Paulin Soumanou. *Le cinéma Africain: Des origines à 1973.* Paris: Présence Africaine, 1975.

———. *Sembène Ousmane: Cinéaste.* Paris: Présence Africaine, 1972.

Vitti, Antonio. "Albanitaliamerica: Viaggio come sordo sogno in *Lamerica* di Gianni Amelio." *Italica* 73.2 (1996): 248–61.

———. *Giuseppe De Santis and Postwar Italian Cinema.* Toronto: U of Toronto P, 1996.

Vogel, Amos. "Limits of Neo-Realism." *Film Culture* 3 (June 1957): 17–20.

Wakelin, Michael J. *Arthur Rank: The Man behind the Gong.* Oxford: Lion Publishing, 1996.

Wali, Monona. "Life Drawings: Charles Burnett's Realism." *The Independent* 11.8 (1988): 16–22.

Wang, Chris. "The End of an Era: Little Cheung." *Cinedossier: The 37th Golden Horse Award–Winning Films.* Ed. Ya-mei Li. Taipei: Taipei Golden Horse Film Festival Executive Committee, 2001. 93–95.

Whyte, Alistair. *New Cinema in Eastern Europe.* London: Studio Vista Ltd., 1971.

Williams, Raymond. "A Lecture on Realism." *Screen* 18.1 (1977): 61–74.

———. "Realism, Naturalism and Their Alternatives." *Explorations in Film Theory: Selected Essays from Cine-tracts.* Ed. Ron Burnett. Bloomington: Indiana UP, 1991.

Wood, Robin. "Alphaville." *The Films of Jean-Luc Godard.* Ed. Ian Cameron. Studio Vista, 1967.

———. *The Apu Trilogy.* London: Studio Vista, 1972.

Wyke, Maria. *Projecting the Past: Ancient Rome, Cinema and History.* New York: Routledge, 1997.

Yau, Esther C. M. *At Full Speed: Hong Kong Cinema in a Borderless World.* Minneapolis: U of Minnesota P, 2001.

Ye, Nianchen. "Can't Pass Up a Good Story: From Little Cheung to Durian Durian." *Hong Kong Panorama 1999–2000.* Ed. Law Kar. Hong Kong: Urban Council of Hong Kong, 2000. 22–24.

Yu, Mo-wan. "A Study of Zhong Lian Film Company." *Cantonese Cinema Retrospective, 1960–69.* Ed. Shu Kei. Hong Kong: Hong Kong Urban Council, 1982. 41–45.

Žalman, Jan. *Films and Film-makers in Czechoslovakia.* Trans. George Theiner. Prague: Orbis, 1968.

———. "Umlčený Film: Kapitoly z Bojů o Lidskou Tvář Československého Filmu: Part 1." *Film a Doba* 36.3 (1990): 138–46.

———. "Umlčený Film: Kapitoly z Bojů o Lidskou Tvář Československého Filmu: Part 5." *Film a Doba* 36.7 (1990): 385–94.

Zavattini, Cesare. "Some Ideas on the Cinema." *Sight and Sound* 23 (October–December 1953): 64–65.

Žižek, Slavoj. *Looking Awry: An Introduction to Jacques Lacan through Popular Culture.* Cambridge, MA: MIT UP, 1992.

Contributors

DAVID ANSHEN is an assistant professor of English at the University of Texas Pan-American. He has published widely on topics related to postmodernism, Marxism, film, and issues of realism and representation in film and literature. His work has appeared in various journals, including *CineAction* (2000) and *Bridges* (2002). He is coediting an anthology on the work of William Faulkner in relation to capitalism.

MOINAK BISWAS is a reader in film studies at Jadavpur University, Calcutta. He writes on Indian cinema and culture in Bengali and English, and has contributed to various journals and anthologies. He edits the *Journal of the Moving Image*, a publication of Jadavpur University, and has recently edited *Apu and After: Revisiting Ray's Cinema* (Seagull Books, 2006).

TOMÁS F. CROWDER-TARABORRELLI teaches literature and humanities in the Introduction to the Humanities Program at Stanford University. He has received a 2007 Mellon Grant to complete a book on the travel letters of Domingo F. Sarmiento. He also writes about the Argentinian Dirty War and the process of mourning in documentary film. He has published in the *Journal of the West* (2005) and coedited *Bakhtin and the Nation* (Bucknell, 1999). His fiction has appeared in *EUDEBA* (1998) and *Prism* (1989–90).

NATALIA SUI-HUNG CHAN is an assistant professor in the Department of Cultural and Religious Studies at the Chinese University of Hong Kong and an editor of *Envisage: A Journal Book of Chinese Media Studies* in Taiwan. Her recent publications in Chinese include *Decadent City: Hong Kong Popular Culture* (Oxford, 1996), *City on the Edge of Time: Gender, Special Effects and the 1997 Politics of Hong Kong Cinema* (Oxford, 2002), and *Female Heteroglossia: Media and Cultural Readings* (Youth Literary Books, 2002). She is also the anchor of a radio program about the performing arts in Hong Kong.

JAIMEY FISHER is an assistant professor of German at the University of California–Davis; before teaching at Davis, he was assistant professor of German at Tulane University. He is the author of *Disciplining Germany: Youth, Reeducation, and Reconstruction after the Second World War*, which will appear in 2007 as part of the Kritik series of Wayne State University Press; he is also coeditor, with Peter Uwe Hohendahl, of *Critical Theory: Current State and Future Prospects* (Berghahn, 2001). He was a Federal Chancellor (Bundeskanzler) Fellow of Alexander-von-Humboldt-Foundation for an extended research period in Berlin.

RACHEL GABARA teaches Francophone African and European literature and film in the Department of Romance Languages at the University of Georgia. She is the author of *From Split to Screened Selves: French and Francophone Autobiography in the Third Person* (Stanford, 2006), and her articles have appeared in *New Literary History, French Cultural Studies,* and *Quarterly Review of Film and Video.* She is completing a second book, tentatively titled *Reclaiming Realism: From Colonial to Contemporary Documentary in West and Central Africa,* which traces the history of documentary cinema in sub-Saharan Africa.

MILLICENT MARCUS is a professor of Italian at Yale University. Her specializations include Italian cinema and medieval literature. She is the author of *An Allegory of Form: Literary Self-Consciousness in the "Decameron"* (Anma Libri, 1979), *Italian Film in the Light of Neorealism* (Princeton, 1986), winner of the Modern Language Association's Howard R. Marraro Prize, *Filmmaking by the Book: Italian Cinema and Literary Adaptation* (Johns Hopkins, 1993), winner of the American Association of Italian Studies' Presidential award, and *After Fellini: National Cinema in the Postmodern Age* (Johns Hopkins, 2002), winner of the Flaiano International Award for Italian Studies. She has also published numerous articles on Italian literature and film, and is now working on Holocaust memory in contemporary Italian literary and media culture.

ANTONIO NAPOLITANO is an Italian film scholar. His chapter has been republished here from the postwar film journal *Cinemasud.*

LAURA E. RUBERTO directs the Humanities Program at Berkeley City College in California, where she also teaches film studies, women's studies, and philosophy. Her *Gramsci, Migration, and the Representation of Women's Work in Italy and the U.S.* is forthcoming with Lexington Press/Rowman and Littlefield. She coedited *Bakhtin and the Nation* (Bucknell, 1999) and edited a special issue of the *Journal of the West* (2004). She is a 2006 recipient of a Fulbright Research Award to Italy.

THOMAS STUBBLEFIELD is a Ph.D. candidate in the Program in Visual Studies at the University of California–Irvine. Previously, he served as an adjunct professor in art history and film studies at Columbia College, Chicago, and at the University of Wisconsin–Parkside. His most recent publications include "Now and Again: Time, Perception and Cultural Memory in the Late Works of Gus Van Sant" in *Time and Memory in Narrative* (2007) and "Ritwik Ghatak and the Role of Sound in Representing Post-Partition Bengal" in *Postscript: A Journal of Film and the Humanities* (2006).

334

CONTRIBUTORS

ANTONIO TRAVERSO lectures in film history, theory, and production at Curtin University, Western Australia. He completed his doctorate at Murdoch University in 2003 with a dissertation on the philosophy of vision and has more recently published papers on minority cinemas, transcultural vision, and the visual representation of traumatic memory. A filmmaker himself, Traverso was born in Chile and has lived in Australia since 1987.

LUBICA UČNÍK worked as a television producer for Czechoslovak Television, Bratislava. She migrated to Australia in 1980 and completed a Ph.D. in philosophy at Murdoch University, Western Australia, where she is now a lecturer in philosophy. She is the author of *European Discourses on Rights: The Quest for Statehood in Europe: The Case of Slovakia* (Peter Lang, 2003).

PASQUALE VERDICCHIO is an associate professor of Italian and comparative literature at the University of California–San Diego. His books include *Bound by Distance: Rethinking Nationalism through the Italian Diaspora* (Fairleigh Dickinson, 1997), *Devils in Paradise: Writings on Post-Emigrant Culture* (Guernica, 1997), and a translation of Antonio Gramsci's *The Southern Question* (Guernica, 2006). He is also a widely published poet and photographer.

KRISTI M. WILSON teaches documentary film and writing in the Program of Writing and Rhetoric at Stanford University. She is the founder and director of the Stanford Film Lab. She has published work on film, literature, and philosophy in, among other places, *Signs* (2003), *Yearbook of Comparative and General Literature* (2000), *Screen* (1999), *Literature/Film Quarterly* (1999), and *Quaderni di Cinemasud* (2006).

Index